# CIO Leadership for Cities and Counties

## Emerging Trends and Practices

Dr. Alan R. Shark, *Executive Editor & Author*

PUBLIC TECHNOLOGY INSTITUTE • WASHINGTON, DC

Library of Congress Cataloging-Publication-Data
Shark, Alan
CIO Leadership for Cities & Counties: Emerging Trends and Practices
p. cm.
ISBN 1-4392-4078-7

Chief Information Officers. 2. Information technology-Management. 3. Leadership. I.Title

"The only thing changing faster than the technology that local government depends on to do its work is the job descriptions of those who run it. Modern CIOs aren't just technologists. They understand people, politics and policy, and know as much about managing bucks as managing bits. This is the user guide for tomorrow's government leaders."

—Mark Stencel, Executive Editor and Deputy Publisher,
*Governing* magazine and GOVERNING.com

"The most effective technology deployments, be they in government or business, help organizations transform business processes and improve service delivery to their customers. This helpful guidebook provides 30 chapters' worth of practical, enduring lessons about the challenges we face daily—and how best to tackle them. It should be an indispensible addition to the bookshelf of any public CIO."

— Paul J. Cosgrave, CIO, New York City

"The job of CIO in a city, county or State government is a lonely job. You are expected to be an expert on technology, policy, politics and public administration, but with little training or time to become educated on this broad set of disciplines. With this important new book, PTI brings much needed advice, support and companionship to the lonely government CIO!"

—Bill Schrier, Chief Technology Officer, City of Seattle

"As the role of the public sector CIO has increased in stature over the past decade, the materials to prepare that CIO have been sorely lacking. This book is the first comprehensive publication to successfully guide public CIOs through their various areas of responsibility, including policy, technology, and management issues. Every public sector IT professional who works as a CIO or aspires to the CIO seat should invest in this exceptional read!"

—Shannon Howle Tufts, PhD, Director, Center for Public Technology,
UNC School of Government, The University of North Carolina at
Chapel Hill

"This book is a must have reference for anyone who manages technology in the local government. A great combination of theory and practice, the contributors to this volume have fought the battles and won the wars that keep local government in the forefront of real-world technology change. Hundreds of years of combined experience in organizations large and small address the enduring issues, the current challenges and the future opportunies that technology brings to government operations that are closest to citizens. This is an important book at an important time."

—Michael Armstrong, CIO, City of Corpus Christi, Texas

"It is so exciting to have a book by and for leaders in the public sector technology space. These jobs can be lonely given that these roles are not exactly that of our peers within our organizations, nor are they exactly that of CIO's in private sector industry positions. It emphasizes the relevance of organizations like PTI that bring us together across the nation. This is a great tool for CIO's and their management teams to read together to discuss relevant issues!"

—MOLLY RAUZI, CIO, CITY AND COUNTY OF DENVER

"This collection of topics are foundational to the *leader*, who will guide an organization from IT alignment to true integration between the business and IT. Used effectively, this collaboration will prepare the current and future CIO for the evolution of IT being a natural part of the business."

—CHARLES T. THOMPSON, CGEIT, CIO, CITY OF PHOENIX

"Alan and an incredibly knowledgeable group of CIO practitioners have provided local government CIOs with a wealth of accumulated knowledge and real-world expertise. Through these chapters, these authors have truly demonstrated vast expertise, experience, and commitment to public service. I salute them all!"

—BERT J. JARREAU, CHIEF INFORMATION OFFICER, NATIONAL ASSOCIATION OF COUNTIES, WASHINGTON, DC

"The economic downturn is hurting all Local Governments across Europe, and CIOs share the opportunity to be key leaders. Helping them and leveraging technology to bring innovation to their constituents and boost the economy requires very special skills and capabilities. To succeed the CIO must be the bridge between technology and public policy. This book from Public Technology Institute shares experiences from across the Atlantic and is a precious source of examples and ideas to learn from."

—GIORGIO PRISTER, PRESIDENT, MAJOR CITIES OF EUROPE—IT USERS GROUP

# Contents

# Preface

A few years ago, I was serving as a guest instructor for the University of Florida Institute of Government's (FIG) certified chief information officer program. In reviewing the assigned readings, I was surprised to learn that all the reference books used throughout the course were written by and from the perspective of the private sector. In speaking with program director Ric Dugger, who confirmed they were unaware of any book written for and by city and county technology authorities, I vowed to take this on as a high-priority project. Now, some two years later, I am both pleased and proud to announce the first such attempt is now complete. In addition, plans are already under way for the second, revised edition.

This book contains information not found in any one place until now. This book is not about technology—it is about how technology should be managed. An experienced group of practitioners within local government and the corporate community have painstakingly taken time out of their busy schedules to share their knowledge and practical experience. For simplicity sake, we use the term "CIO" (chief information officer) to denote anyone who holds the responsibility for serving as the chief technology executive staff person regardless of title.

With billions of dollars being spent every year by cities and counties, the technology enterprise requires exceptional leadership skills as never before. Not only must we ensure that our technology infrastructure works, our technology infrastructure must be built, protected and maintained with an eye toward ever-changing advances in technology. Today's CIOs must not only embrace and comprehend enterprise technology in all its dimensions, he or she must also be a strong leader, motivator, strategic planner, diplomat and politician. They need to be well versed in the language and nuances spoken by those who are deep into technology as well as those who need things explained in a more basic, non-technical manner.

We live in a world that requires ongoing professional and educational development at all levels. Simply receiving a college degree or certificate is no longer a life-long credential as it once was. City and county managers have access to practical hands-on certification programs, as do lawyers and accountants. Each of those professions requires ongoing education requirements to remain certified as a means of demonstrating updated skills and knowledge. CIOs, given their burgeoning responsibilities, require no less and, we believe, much more.

This book's initial focus was aimed toward helping new and aspiring technology managers recognize and achieve a proven set of competencies. While the initial goal has not changed, the authors realized that this book also could serve as a useful guide to those who interface with the CIO as a means of better understanding the complexities that confront them. That might include city and county managers, mayors and other elected leaders who would like to have a better understanding of just how technology management is or can be applied to their respective jurisdictions.

From the start, those of us at the Public Technology Institute, the Florida State University's Institute for Government, the University of North Carolina's School of Government Center for Public Technology, and recently added Rutgers University School for Public Affairs and Administration have committed ourselves to work toward a common criteria for the creation of a national curriculum—leading to certification programs for CIOs throughout the nation. This book helps take us a step closer to reaching our collective dream.

# Acknowledgements

Many wonderful and talented people must be recognized for their direct and indirect involvement in this book. This, of course, begins with having the support and active engagement of more than 36 remarkable author/contributors. Without their hard work and dedication, this book would not be possible—for they represent its soul and content. I would like to thank our corporate friends at IBM, Microsoft, Motorola, EMA, Booz Allen Hamilton, Miller Van Eaton, Plante & Moran, RPost, and Cisco for their help and follow-through in reaching out and identifying great contributors. While not authors, I would like to recognize Erin Nisson from IBM and Arlene King from Motorola for their tireless and wonderful help.

Special thanks to Ric Dugger at the Florida Institute for Government for his wisdom and fellowship, and reaching out to me for help in the successful CIO certification program offered by the Institute, which is part of Florida State University. His friendship and my involvement with him and the institute led to the inception of this project. He is a true visionary and pioneer. Dr. Shannon Tufts, friend and colleague, also served as a great inspiration for all her work, too, as a visionary and pioneer in the creation of a CIO certification program at the University of North Carolina.

I would like to express my gratitude to PTI's board of directors who wholeheartedly supported this book from the very beginning. Dale Bowen, who has been invaluable to me as one of two PTI deputies, was always there to offer ideas, helped in identifying some of the authors and aided in some of the project's coordination activities. On the production side, I was very fortunate in recruiting the talented Lindsay Isaacs, who served as the project's copy editor. Lindsay's day job is serving as the managing editor for *American City & County* magazine and did all her magic afterhours—many long afterhours—and did a magnificent job in editing while always maintaining a positive attitude. I am also forever grateful to Sally Hoffmaster for her work as graphic designer for the cover and page layout of the entire manuscript. Given the complexities of working with 36 authors and contributors we intentionally left the end-of-chapter reference styles as they were submitted.

The birth of any book cannot be contained to a neat and tidy 9-5 workday. I am not sure with technology being what it is we will ever see that again. Instead, projects like this book eat into personal time often late at night and on weekends. So, I would be derelict if I did not recognize the strong and enthusiastic support of my wonderful partner-for-life and spouse, Nancy.

Finally, I would like to thank the 300 plus technology executives that I met and interviewed in one form or another during the past four years for sharing their knowledge and experience, and offering personal inspiration and encouragement.

# PART ONE:

# CIO Leadership
# & IT Governance

# 1. CIO Leadership for Cities and Counties: An Evolving Role

**DR. ALAN R. SHARK**

## A brief history of the rise of the CIO

Today, no private sector company would consider operating without a Chief Information Officer (CIO) or Chief Technology Officer (CTO)—yet many cities and counties continue to struggle to define what type of technology position best fits their needs and budget, as well as what type of governance structure works best. Local governments only recently began to consider such titles as CIO or CTO. Traditionally, those whose main responsibility was technology—be it for a department, division, agency or jurisdiction-wide—were called director of technology, director of office of information and technology, director MIS, if not CIO or CTO.

Typically, a CIO is responsible for an enterprise and all the business units of a particular unit or jurisdiction with an eye toward leading, managing and integrating all communication and information technology applications. The CTO position, by contrast, usually is considered a more technically oriented position and is more focused on technology solutions as opposed to navigating the political and administrative functions. In practice, it appears that the titles have been used interchangeably and carry little distinctive differences as compared to what is found in the private sector.

So, one may ask, do titles really matter? The answer is both yes and no. More important than a title is what are the duties, responsibilities and expectations of the senior technology staff person? How many staff does the person have managerial responsibility for? What size budget? What is the complexity of the business lines?

The rise in stature of the CIO and CTO within the city and county arena has grown or evolved, as some would say, along with the ever-increasing complexity for managing communication and information technology. Today, there are more than 3,000 counties and 36,000 cities and townships in the U.S. The CIO or CTO is becoming one of the most important "new" key positions in local government, and there is every indication that the position will continue to grow in stature and strategic importance. Exactly where they sit and their exact tittles will depend largely on the type and size of any given local entity.

## The new city and county CIO leader

After four years of traveling across the country and meeting and interviewing technology executives from well over 300 local government agencies and jurisdictions, I have observed overwhelming consistency in trends and common needs. The role of the head technology staff person, whom we shall refer to as the CIO, is growing in complexity and required skill sets. Many have expressed frustration that the jobs they were originally hired for has changed along with growing expectations. Some even went as far as to state they felt somewhat unprepared or lacked key staff support to help them carry out an increasing amount of demands—some more political then technical.

When asked about issues of governance, a surprising number of CIOs felt their formal reporting relationship was a serious obstacle in effectively carrying out their responsibilities. Many reported through a chief finance officer, deputy mayor, assistant city manager or other administrative officer. CIOs working in smaller jurisdictions usually reported directly to the city or county executive. For the smaller jurisdiction CIO, problems were more focused on lack of resources and having to work extraordinary hours with corresponding pressures.

The most important factor regarding governance came down to decision rights: Who makes the final IT decisions, for what department or agencies, and what is the agreed-upon process? That of all issues was the most critical from the CIO's point of view.

Those CIOs who were deemed the most successful by their peers noted that they reported to mayors and county executives who understood and embraced technology. They went on to add that they often were involved in jurisdiction-wide meetings, and everyone knew they had the complete support and respect of the CEO. Some were recruited into that positive leadership environment, while others were lucky and gifted to work their way into the inner circles of public management.

Cities and counties with exceptional leadership teams included Denver; New York; Seattle; Chicago; Houston; Austin, Texas; San Francisco; Phoenix; the District of Columbia; Los Angeles County; Harris County, Texas; Johnson County, Kansas; Fairfax County, Virginia; Montgomery County, Maryland; Arlington County, Virginia; and Miami-Dade, to name a few.

Perhaps most startling was the lack of discretionary funds for travel, training, key memberships, and consulting and research services. It seemed the larger the jurisdiction, the proportionately less funding there was—despite the millions spent on IT. Mid-size jurisdictions appeared to fare better when it came to discretionary funds.

Just about everyone interviewed seemed to agree (many quite strongly) that city and county CIOs need a greater sense of professional recognition as well as an on-going need for more continuous professional development. Certified city managers, assistant city managers, attorneys, and even certified MS or Cisco engineers seemed able to justify their professional development activities and requirements more often than CIOs.

Junior and aspiring CIOs expressed strong support for a CIO Certification program—something along the lines that the Public Technology Institute (PTI) has promised in the very near future. In fact, no less than three universities have embarked upon CIO certifications programs and have created a consortium to help coordinate learning opportunities for CIOs. The name is the *Consortium for State & Local Government Technology Leadership Development* and comprises Florida State University's Florida Institute of Government, University of North Carolina's School of Government Center for Public Technology, and Rutgers University School of Public Affairs and Administration. PTI has been designated as the administrative secretariat for the new consortium.

The need for certification went beyond recognition for the sake of recognition. CIOs honestly wanted to learn more about current trends and practices, new management systems and techniques, and who they could turn to for advice and help.

The two most common complaints that cut across all lines was (1) the lack of consistent support from among elected leaders—and they longed for champions; and (2) the fact that most felt they spent 75% to 95% of their time in crisis mode, responding to emergencies much like a firefighter, and too little time contemplating strategic planning, and planning for new solutions and applications.

Unlike CIOs, fire chiefs do much more than fight fires. They work on prevention, staff development and training, and keeping up on the latest in technology, too. CIOs are clearly at a proportionate fiscal disadvantage when it comes to responsibilities.

## Toward greater CIO certification and recognition

Having worked in varying degrees with each of the universities in the consortium, a common curriculum outline has emerged that covers just about every skill set required for today's CIO. The consortium members agreed that re-certification would be necessary and that it should occur about every three years. Candidates could earn credits by attending recognized continuing education programs in the field, as well as writing and speaking about solutions, applications, and other tactical or strategic experiences. If there was one major skill set to be demonstrated, everyone agreed it would be leadership in terms of needs, styles and effectiveness. What follows is what PTI and Rutgers University is contemplating as an on-line program for CIO Certification. Naturally, there will be some pre-qualification criteria that would include letters of recommendation, years in service in a leadership role, and a signed promise to abide by a voluntary code of ethics.

What follows is a draft outline, absent of the weighting of each criteria prepared by PTI of what one can expect by way of a course curriculum for CIO certification. Certainly "leadership" would be weighted at least 30% of the overall criteria. Whether the reader has any interest in such a certification, the outline serves as a reinforcing message as to the significant responsibilities in which today's CIO leaders must demonstrate proficiency.

### 1. Leadership

Leadership theory and practice tops everyone's list. For the purposes of certification, there are six key areas that will be examined. They are:

◆ Skills
◆ Styles
◆ Measurement
◆ Decision making
◆ Collaboration
◆ Managing expectations

### 2. IT governance

IT governance examines the structure of the jurisdiction's decision-making process in terms of how decisions are made, by whom, and where the IT function is placed within the jurisdiction's organization chart. What types of governance models are being used today? What are the strengths and weaknesses of each? Aside from reporting relationships, how is information best communicated? In addition:

- ◆ Styles
- ◆ Assessment
- ◆ Models
- ◆ Communication
- ◆ Public-private partnerships

## 3. Strategic planning

Here, strategic planning is analyzed for style, process, as well as available tools, methods and best practices. In addition:

- ◆ Plan and strategy development
- ◆ Process
- ◆ Needs analysis
- ◆ Identification and positive relations with key stakeholders/customers/elements
- ◆ Public-private partnerships

## 4. Citizen, public and external relations

CIOs increasingly are having to interact with citizens and their representative organizations. At times, there is a language barrier as to technical terms and jargon versus what the public really wants to know in a way they can best understand. Issues like 311 and citizen records (or relationship) management is increasingly being embraced as a tool to better engage citizens and provide greater transparency into government effectiveness. But, like any key public manager, communication skills are vital to the success of the public enterprise. And finally, managing expectations from among elected leaders, senior public officials and the public at large is a key metric for success or failure.

- ◆ 311
- ◆ CRM
- ◆ Web portal development and services
- ◆ Communication skills; written, oral, political
- ◆ Managing expectations

## 5. Network security and operations

With growing threats from computer viruses, spam, phishing schemes, and identity or records theft, the CIO is ultimately responsible. Where and how data is stored, and the back-up and restoration policies that govern data is of the upmost importance. Maintaining data centers and other technology equipment and software is also critical.

- ◆ Storage
- ◆ Data center(s)
- ◆ Security policies and oversight
- ◆ Equipment
- ◆ Software
- ◆ SaaS (Software as a Service)
- ◆ Cloud computing
- ◆ Managed (outsourced)

- ◆ Acquisitions
- ◆ Disposal (equipment)
- ◆ Policies

## 6. Contract management

CIOs must understand the local, state and federal laws governing contracts for equipment, services and among various agencies.

- ◆ SLAs (Service Level Agreements)
- ◆ Contracts
- ◆ MOUs (Memorandums of Understanding)
- ◆ Strategic partnerships
- ◆ Legal considerations and obligations

## 7. Human resource development

Technology may be considered just a tool, and even the best equipped need to rely on well-trained and motivated staff. In the past, CIOs didn't have to worry as much about HR as they must today. In a competitive environment, it is difficult to attract and retain great staff in public service when the private sector generally pays so much more.

- ◆ Training and development
- ◆ Recruitment
- ◆ Retention
- ◆ Motivation
- ◆ Evaluation

## 8. Innovation: Learning and nurturing

CIOs often are expected to heed the call to help develop a vision for innovation in a city or county environment. Here, best practices and case studies on what has worked and hasn't— and as importantly, why—are explored. New social web-based tools are being tested, and new ways to improve communications while better engaging citizens is essential.

- ◆ Creating the vision
- ◆ Creating opportunities
- ◆ Cultivating an innovation culture
- ◆ Web 2.0, 3.0
- ◆ Collaboration
- ◆ Green IT initiatives

## 9. Purchasing and acquisition

Many former CIOs have found themselves in trouble when it comes to purchasing and acquisition. Understanding contract law and the rules governing purchasing and acquisitions cannot be taken lightly. Those looking to ignore the rules or take short cuts in the name of expediency can find themselves indicted and could wind up in jail as well as other monetary penalties.

- ◆ Best practices
- ◆ Ethics

- ◆ Bidding dos and don'ts
- ◆ Cost benefit analysis
- ◆ Evaluation and review
- ◆ RFP, RFQs, RFIs, etc.
- ◆ Legal requirements and obligations

## 10. Knowledge and records management

State and federal laws require millions of documents, e-mails and even text messages as public records to be saved and stored for a specific period of time—this in addition to regular public records and documents. Today, with increasing turnover in employees at all levels, it has never been more essential to create and maintain sound records and knowledge management policies and programs. For example, what is the policy for capturing the data stored in someone's computer or telephone e-mail? How is institutional memory stored and indexed?

- ◆ Policies and procedures
- ◆ Identification of knowledge management markers
- ◆ E-discovery requirements

## 11. Enterprise Resource Planning (ERP)

Someone once remarked that ERP really stood for "early retirement program," usually reserved for the CIO in charge. ERP is actually an enterprise-wide information system designed to coordinate all the resources, information and activities needed to complete business processes

Many departments and agencies grew with their own data and communication systems. ERP is both a goal and process to develop common platforms and systems to reduce redundancy, while at the same time increasing efficiencies of scale, greater system integration, ease of use, ease in maintenance and, hopefully, reduced costs over time. The problem with ERP is not just in its inherent complexities, but the political buy-in from the internal customers who are often asked to do business in a slightly different manner. Judging by experience, change never comes without pain.

- ◆ Processes
- ◆ Policies
- ◆ Models
- ◆ Understanding the enterprise

## 12. Communication technologies

Broadband in all its forms is truly the information highway that carries voice, data and video. Many cities already have fiber networks, but everyone acknowledges there is more to be done for economic growth and national security. While fiber is by far the most robust of the "highway" types, there is still a compelling need for wireless access, too. There are many new and emerging wireless technologies that need to be evaluated and piloted. It is imperative that every CIO keep abreast of the latest technologies, trends and opportunities in this fast-changing area.

- ◆ System integration
- ◆ Applications
- ◆ Broadband (generic)

- ◆ Fiber
- ◆ Wireless
- ◆ Field support

## 13. Financial and performance management

Anecdotal information has been replaced with more sophisticated tools and requirements. There is a greater need than ever before to better cost-justify and monitor projects and programs—operating and capital budgets alike. Successful CIOs will need to continue to demonstrate how to develop argument-proof return on investment (ROI) reports. This is where some of the older "techies" find it difficult to adjust to the increasing demands for financial reporting and accountability. To complicate things, the newest efforts are to add greater citizen engagement and transparency (all positive and necessary), but which also take more time away from what some perceive as their core responsibilities.

- ◆ Budgeting and justifications
- ◆ ROI
- ◆ Capital budget
- ◆ Financing
- ◆ Forecasting
- ◆ Performance measurement techniques and tools
- ◆ Presentation skills

## 14. Energy and sustainability

Given all the attention to global warming, rising energy costs, pollution, and maintaining energy-grabbing computers and datacenters, there are many new technological breakthroughs that are occurring that are designed to increase efficiencies and reduce costs. Many see cities and counties taking the lead and setting an example. Most of the new energy solutions have a technology component that every CIO needs to be kept abreast on.

- ◆ Green IT polices
- ◆ Fleet management
- ◆ Smart buildings
- ◆ Smart lighting and monitoring
- ◆ Recycling and reuse
- ◆ Energy Star compliance
- ◆ Solar and wind energy
- ◆ Energy Star programs

## 15. Ethics and social equity

Perhaps the category that gets the least attention—but is no less important—is ethics and social equity. In many ways, ethics is a key ingredient of leadership but deserves to be highlighted in its own category to help illustrate the fact that ethics and ethical behavior reach every form of public management. It concerns itself with purchasing, contracting, decision-making, employee relations, and working with public managers and the public itself.

Social equity is related but different. While ethics usually involves a code of conduct, social equity is an area of concern regarding whether government in its programs and services is adequately taking into account the needs of the underserved. A subpart might be called "digital equity" or "bridging the digital divide," where technology could either serve as a bridge or a barrier for ethnic minorities, the elderly and perhaps those with physical handicaps. Here, the traditional public administration argument has centered on the two "e"s: Is it *efficient*, and is it *effective?* We simply add a third "e:" Is it *equitable?*

♦ Polices and practices
♦ Digital divide considerations
♦ Implementation and compliance

As one can see, rather than listing sample position descriptions of CIOs, listing required skill sets seemed to serve as a better example of the growing complexity they face. The demands have grown, as have budgets and expectations. And, there appears to be a new trend toward hiring either CIOs from the private sector or hiring technology executives with broader, perhaps less technical, skills, too. At least for the midsize city and county, the CIO must be a great leader and have the ability to address many divergent audiences. He or she needs to be a translator as well as an arbiter between the pure techies and the pure non-techies. There is no doubt that after listening to the hundreds of technology executives throughout the U.S., everyone expressed a deep commitment to their jurisdiction, and, despite some imposing challenges, they love what they do!

So far, this chapter has summarized the current state of the local government CIO. Many of the newer CIOs spoke of anticipating their next job. They mentioned that what is often overlooked is the need to know what to ask for that next CIO position. A number of new CIOs stated they wished they had asked better questions during the interview process. And, for those who believed they asked the right questions, or for those intending to apply for a CIO position, what follows stems from years of experience in the field and can simply be called the 20 questions you need to ask before you accept your next position.

## What every CIO needs to ask before accepting.....

It is not only important to ask these questions, it is equally important to wait for the answers. Many people get so excited that they fail to understand the answers to their questions or shrug them off as not being that important. But, once you have accepted a new position, it is usually too late to make any real changes to your understanding or employment contract. No matter how excited one may be, it is important to take the time and do the necessary due diligence.

## 20 must-ask questions and must-know answers

1. Whom do I report to?
2. What were the incumbent's strengths and weaknesses?
3. What do you see as the primary opportunity and challenge?
4. What are the jurisdiction's top five goals?
5. What is the capital budget?
6. Who decides the budget?
7. How involved is senior management?
8. How involved are elected leaders?
9. How will success be measured?

10. How competent is the current IT staff?

11. What are the five biggest problems IT staff have recently faced?

12. How is the IT function viewed within other departments, divisions and agencies?

13. How much latitude will I have in innovation?

14. How will IT interface with other agencies, divisions and departments?

15. What kind of discretionary budget will I have? For travel, memberships, training, subscriptions, PDA, data air card, research?

16. What resources will I have for my staff—personal development, training, memberships and subscriptions?

17. How is IT defined?

18. How is the overall strategic plan decided? What is the process? Who is in charge?

19. How much real political support can I expect from:
    a. The chief executive?
    b. Key elected leaders?
    c. The citizen community?

20. How do you want me to primarily report to you?
    a. Weekly briefings in person?
    b. Daily briefings?
    c. E-mails?
    d. Written reports?
    e. A combination of the above? In what order of preference?

## The future city and county CIO leader

The role of the new CIO leader is emerging, but as pointed out earlier, the skill sets will need to change, too. Not only is technology changing at an unprecedented and exponential rate, but so, too, is the U.S. population. It is estimated by the U.S. Census Bureau that there will be 60 million people more added to the U.S. population by the year 2030. Local governments provide numerous population-sensitive services that must be provided in increasing volumes with population growth (e.g., roads, education, garbage collection, policing, social services). Technology will have to play a key role in helping to provide better quality services in ways that also save time and taxpayers' money.

A survey of CIOs that PTI and Input conducted in the summer of 2008 yielded an impressive 15.5% response rate. Responses were from jurisdictions within 37 states. When asked about priorities, public safety/interoperability and e-government services far outpaced the rest of the field. That is probably due to the fact that police officers are the single largest employee outlay of city and county governments. Also, the large number of e-government related transactions and services lend themselves to delivered self-service. There was also a renewed effort to develop systems for greater citizen transparency and engagement, especially for financial and budget information.

We know from hundreds of interviews and surveys that the CIO position is receiving heightened attention, and the position itself continues to involve. The need for greater professional development leading up to actual CIO certification is sorely needed. And, given the make-up of the new city and county CIO leader, it would not be surprising to see greater turnover, as many CIOs have expressed the only way to advance financially is to move to another jurisdiction. The CIO leader of the future will have been exposed to technology at an earlier age and will be more impatient with the slow pace of change typically found in local government. But, at the same time, many will accept the pace as a welcome trade-off from the high-pressure, short-term goals often associated with the private sector. Quality of life issues will become more important to the next generation, and that will help balance impatience with the greater public good.

Technology solutions are no longer a luxury for local governments, as they must continually seek ways to satisfy their customer/citizens, just as private companies struggle with much the same. The CIOs whose collective commentary found its way into this chapter all strongly agree that they truly enjoy the challenges of working for the public good. And that's good for all of us.

---

## Discussion questions

1. What are the various pros and cons of specific reporting relationships?
2. Is the title for the current technology executive reflective of today's environment?
3. What are the five greatest technology-related challenges facing your jurisdiction?
4. Would having a CIO certification course help you to better realize your career goals?
5. What are the top three questions that stand out among the 20 questions, "What every CIO needs to ask before accepting..."
6. How will the newer generation CIO differ from his or her predecessors?
7. Is it a good or bad thing to hire new CIOs from the private sector? Why?
8. What kind of discretionary budget do you have for training, memberships, consulting, etc.?
9. What is your total IT budget, and what portion do you have responsibility for?

**Dr. Alan R. Shark** *currently serves as the Public Technology Institute's executive director/CEO. He also serves as Assistant Professor at Rutgers University's School of Public Affairs and Administration. As an author, lecturer and speaker on technology developments and applications for most of his distinguished career, Dr. Shark's experience both balances and embraces the business, government, education and technology sectors. His most recent book* Beyond e-Government & e-Democracy: A Global Perspective *is available from Amazon.com.*

*Dr. Shark has been elected as a Fellow of the National Academy of Public Administration (NAPA), as well as Fellow of the Radio Club of America (RCA), and Fellow of the American Society for Association Executives (ASAE). Dr. Shark holds a doctorate in Public Administration from the University of Southern California's Washington Public Policy Center.*

# 2. The New Frontier of Technology Leadership

**DR. DENA HURST AND RODERIC R. DUGGER III**

## Sharing experiences

Welcome, as you begin a journey in learning by working your way through this special book, a collection of thoughts from successful public service leaders and industry experts in the challenging arena of local government information technology leadership. This chapter will focus on the research and experiential information that has been gathered through personal experiences and study, coupled with efforts developing, implementing and managing the Florida-based Certified Public Technology Leadership (CPTL) certification programs for local government technology managers.

One of only two such programs, the CPTL programs evolved out of a need defined by the Florida Local Government Information Systems Association (FLGISA): the need to grow the leadership capacity of Florida's local government technology professionals so that they can more effectively serve as leaders in their organizations and be prepared to effectively contribute as a member of their city or county's executive leadership team. Local governments, like every other type of organization, increasingly rely on technology as a means to conduct business, and so the decisions they make around the types of technology used, the manner in which different technologies are used to extend effectiveness, enhance communications and empower leadership for better strategic planning and quality decision making, and the policies and procedures governing their use will become correspondingly more significant. And likewise, the roles of Chief Information Officers (CIOs), technology managers, and technology support staff will grow not only in scope, but also in purpose and importance.

FLGISA, fulfilling its mission to assist CIOs and technology managers in providing the best possible service in the most efficient way to their customers, the citizens of the state of Florida, turned to the Florida Institute of Government (Institute), a statewide institute housed at Florida State University. The Institute's mission, to enhance the capacity of public service and non-profit organizations to better to serve their communities, as well as the value it places on learning and leadership development, complements that of FLGISA. From the partnership grew two statewide certification programs—the Certified Public Technology Manager (CPTM) and the Certified Chief Information Officer (CCIO)—that further the professional development of technology professionals beyond technology-specific certification and education opportunities.

Based on the success of the programs, the CIO for the State of Florida has requested the Institute extend the program to include a version for state and regional technology leadership professionals. The core of the two certification programs will remain the same for both groups, and the state version will have sessions customized to focus on specific needs based on state business practices. What makes the program replicable is that it is based on a core curriculum that is broadly applicable to any public service technology leader or manager, with only minor refinements needed to customize specifics to a particular audience. The curriculum also includes space to allow the program team to incorporate new trends and emerging technologies as learning topics, which keeps the program dynamic and relevant.

## Florida's CPTL program overview

The educational focus of the two CPTL certification programs is leadership and business acumen, with the push to help local government technology managers and CIOs become essential members of their organizations' executive leadership teams. To engage participants in the learning and to ensure the highest possible transfer to practice, the programs are structured to provide both in-class and out-of-class work. Participants also are assigned peer mentors from program graduates. The mentors work with the participants for the duration of the program.

Both certification programs are offered annually and run for a full year. The participants meet face-to-face for quarterly 20-hour work sessions. Prior to each session, they complete a preparatory assignment; and following each session, they complete a concluding assignment. The assignments are not simply busy work. Each assignment is designed to help participants actively engage new knowledge and techniques as practice for agents of change. Participants also must complete a Capstone Project that demonstrates command and application of the concepts, tools and techniques the program provides. They present their projects to their classmates at the end of the year, prior to graduation, and the final project is shared with appropriate CPTL program graduates through a special but secure "model projects library."

Upon successful completion of each program, graduates are required to earn professional development units to maintain relevant knowledge and concept awareness and, thus, their certification. Because a major focus of the CPTL programs is on leadership development, a percentage of those professional development units must be leadership work or learning.

## Leadership and team work: The keys to success

Local government CIOs and IT leaders are expected to serve effectively in pressure-packed, challenging jobs with ever-changing responsibilities. What used to be a technical job is much more than that today. It requires business leaders that first and foremost build enabling partnerships with the leadership teams they serve.

Beyond that, the job also requires the oversight of a wide range of technology: specialty software products, common business software products, process analysis, custom software systems development and support, complex hardware environments, office productivity tools, various telecommunications services, plus a myriad of support services, training and more. The technology leadership role of today, and in the future, requires a broader approach and a larger view of the world than was expected a few years ago.

Florida is fortunate to have many qualified and well-rounded technology leaders in local government, and the same is true for cities and counties across the nation. However, there are still many cities and counties having trouble finding or developing such technology leaders.

As the CPTL program team views the evolving IT industry and the changing role of local government, the individual providing technology thought-leadership and the management of innovative solutions for a local government organization (large or small) needs to be:

- ◆ A **customer service-driven** individual who understands that **technology is a service business,** a service that impacts almost every aspect of the entire county or city;
- ◆ A "**people person**" **leader** and project management facilitator;
- ◆ An innovative thinker and **change-agent** for progress who takes the **enterprise view** of everything;
- ◆ A **strategic thinker,** ready to work with executive leaders to plan for the future;
- ◆ A team player interested in the **success of others**—operational units, internal service units and management—and willing to engage with each as a customer to help meet each area's needs in accordance with the city's or county's priorities;
- ◆ A business person able to coordinate and integrate various technology systems into solutions that work and are consistent with their government's overall goals using a **governance** approach that keeps the business leaders engaged in making informed enterprise decisions requiring IT priorities and purpose;
- ◆ A financial, HR, legal and procurement process-minded person who is able to facilitate **good business;** and
- ◆ A knowledgeable technology thinker, with a **proactive approach,** who is willing to take some calculated risks, is eager to stay abreast of the changing field, and who recognizes that they need to depend on others with special area knowledge to enable organizational success rather than being trapped by the "not invented here" mindset.

Simply stated, there is a shortage of people fully prepared for this dynamic role. Just as important to the IT arena long term is the need for lifting the information technology profession and setting the stage for tomorrow. As other professions have done, today's successful IT leaders need to invest in creating an institutionalized approach that brings higher credibility to the profession and shapes IT leadership for the future.

Florida confirmed that the list above, while extensive, is and will always be incomplete because of constant change. The role of IT leadership requires a lot of talent, and it also requires that the IT leader be engaged as part of the county or city leadership team. IT leaders need to set the tone by proactively seeking integrated enterprise solutions and mutual success rather than being seen as an IT "reaction force." Leadership and teamwork are the keys to success.

## The approach to leadership development

The CPTL programs begin the curriculum by defining the term "technology;" its meaning is relevant to CPTL's approach to public technology leadership work. Excerpting from the Oxford English dictionary, the word "technology" is defined as:

1. The branch of knowledge that deals with the creation and use of technical means and their interrelation with life, society, and the environment, drawing upon such subjects as industrial arts, engineering, applied science, and pure science.
2. The terminology of an art, science, etc.; technical nomenclature.
3. The sum of the ways in which social groups provide themselves with the material objects of their civilization.

It is derived from the Greek *tekhnē*, meaning art or craft, and *logía*, which means systematic. Though in modern discourse, "technology" has become synonymous with mechanization or computerization, it is important to keep in mind that, particularly for technology professionals serving the public sector, technology has as much to do with the interaction of individuals and society at large with its technological objects as it does with the objects themselves. Thus, the program emphasizes growing relationships among people—within the local government organization and within the community at large—and exploring creative ways technology can enhance those relationships.

To say that the ways in which people interact with one another—person to person, business to client, government to citizen—and carry out the business of the day are changing is trite, to say the least. Change always has been an ever-present force in the natural world, and change, particularly technological change (as understood from the above definition), has governed human affairs since the earliest civilizations.

However, the last century has been not only one of change, but also one marked by an exponential increase in the rate of change from previous eras and the apparent ease with which the impacts of change reach into nearly every aspect of people's daily lives. Technological developments, from the industrialization occurring at the turn of the twentieth century to the mechanical, scientific and medical advancements that grew out of the wars in the middle of the century, and the rise of personal computing and the Internet, have become a force pushing larger social changes.

Looking at the course of human history,[1] the rapidity of technological advances and the breadth of their influence mark the twentieth century, and thus far the twenty-first century, as unique. In past eras, there was consistently a time lag between the development of new theories and technology and the changes that must occur in a society to support them. That lag was due to two primary factors. One factor was the length of time it took to communicate ideas and the means available to disseminate them. Another factor was the rigidity of existing social and cultural structures, which often viewed new developments as threats to traditional ways and knowledge. Theoretical and technological changes persevered, eventually eroding those barriers and delivering people to the current state of instantaneous communication and globalization.

The rapid and expansive nature of technological changes today is driving changes in the structure of businesses of all sizes and, by necessity, the structure of government at all levels. As the role and functions of government are continually redefined, the products and services provided by governments will continue to shift, as will the demands placed on public leaders and employees by the people they serve. That pressure of change will be felt most keenly at the local level, where people have the greatest access to decision makers.

Successful public leadership will depend on the ability to adapt quickly to political and social changes, which also requires understanding and adapting to technological changes. As simple as that sounds, such a flexible approach runs counter to the models for success that have dominated organizational thinking until rather recently. Success in the past was based on a leader's ability to make tasks consistent and replicable, and to establish protocols and procedures that would ensure continued (and manageable) consistency. While that work of managers will continue to be important, strong organizational and community leaders can no longer rely on such a mechanical approach to yield results. As the work of government is changing and the structure of government is changing, the work of its leaders, by necessity, is changing—and the new work of leaders revolves around vision, alignment and engagement.

# The new frontier of technology leadership

A number of specific trends that directly impact the nature of leadership have been consistently cited in relevant literature,[2] and many of those trends are already noticeable. Foremost, organizations will be more open and, consequently, democratic. The flattening of organizations, the simplification of organizational hierarchies, the dismantling of bureaucracy already can be seen in many industries. Traditional organizational boundaries, both horizontal and vertical, will continue to weaken. Critical decisions will be made collectively, based on the engagement of and input from project teams or other groups of employees, not just by those at the top of the organization.

For any organization, governments included, the generations of employees entering the workforce during the next twenty years will tend to have little patience for bureaucracy and hierarchy, and the behaviors such structures foster, e.g., respect based solely on status, compliance with policies and procedures which may be viewed as arbitrary, slow promotion up a rigid chain of command, and so forth. That independent, individualist mindset is going to be felt in technology fields, as new employees will be the generation of bloggers and mashers who are used to interacting as much through YouTube or MySpace as in the non-virtual world.

The growing pains organizations will experience as the old ways slowly give way to the new approaches may cause confusion, discomfort, even fear that things are headed in the wrong direction. The transition from the military-industrial theories to new, holistic practices will not be easy. However, from the CPTL perspective, the results can be transformational.

The talent of individuals will come to be valued above status or position in the organization. Ideas will be solicited from all employees in accordance with their interests and capacities, rather than their professional duties or assigned roles. To make the system viable[3] and ensure that ideas put forth have a base of relevancy, employees will be most effective when led by a shared organizational vision and set of values, and when they understand the nature of the organization's work from an expansive and inclusive perspective.

Ideas for improving the organization will be shared within organizations, and organizations will encourage research, development and reinvestment at all levels. Creativity will not only be encouraged, it will be rewarded. Innovation will be as important to helping governments serve their communities as it will be to helping any other type of organization conduct its business.

As ideas arise from the collective wisdom of an organization, and as communication and collaboration grow across traditional boundaries, leaders may have less direct control over employee conversations and actions. The influence of leaders will no longer be just the result of seniority, status or title, but also will arise from their ability to engage others in a shared vision and keep them aligned toward fulfilling a shared purpose.

Responsibility and accountability will be more easily shared and governed. Flatter organizations, greater information sharing, and greater transparency in vision, purpose, values and workflow will enable organizations and their employees to better align work efforts. That said, there still will be many times when individual accountability and responsibility remain critical.

If it is accepted that such trends are beginning, then it is also evident that traditional management theories will need to evolve as the blended style will evolve. Command-and-control methods are designed to tightly manage structures, policies and deadlines. They focus on ensuring that employees complete certain tasks in specific ways according to a schedule. Employees and their managers are seldom given authority to shape their work, to openly discuss its relevance or its results. It is assumed that if each employee completes his or her tasks, then the larger body of work will be completed.

There are venues where that approach still is appropriate for organizational success; however, when employees aren't strictly limited in the scope of their work, when they begin to share ideas up, down and sideways, when they seek additional meaning in their work, leaders will find themselves challenged to do things differently. That is why the CPTL program team has chosen to develop a leadership development certification—because the work of leaders is changing, and adapting to the new work will require new ways of thinking.

## A theory of leadership

To better understand leadership, the CPTL program team went back to the root of the verb "lead," which is found in the Old English *lædan* meaning "to cause to go with one;" another form of *lædan is liðan,* which means "to travel." To lead, then, implies a journey of sorts, and in the context of the CPTL programs, leadership is viewed as moving from the current reality, the current ways of leading, the current world views to a shared future vision of leading dynamic, people-centric organizations.

To simplify the framework, the CPTL curriculum has reduced the leadership function of a leader to three critical responsibilities: to **design** systems that nurture the creative potential of others; **teach** the organizational vision, purpose and values to all stakeholders; and **steward** the organization toward fulfillment of its vision and purpose.[4] That means that leaders spend more of their time working "on the system"—keeping the work of the organization aligned with the organizational vision and keeping the personal vision of each employee aligned with the organizational vision—and less of their time working "in the system"—directly providing services or working on project tasks. That approach represents a shift to emphasizing organizational relevance, collaborative enterprise perspectives and results, rather than seeing individual tasks or projects as separate and distinct work efforts. Success is measured by the consequences of the results rather than by simple completion of a unit of work.

As one reads this section, keep in mind that an Information Technology leader will be providing a version of leadership in many directions—thus, many systems. Directions like the technology organization they personally lead; second is the relationships between themselves, as a service area, and the operational/administrative segments of the greater organization whose success they are to enable; and third is to those persons elected or appointed to lead the entire organization.

A leadership model currently in practice, and the one upon which the CPTL certification programs is based, was designed to teach organizations how to generate desired results by growing the capacities to adapt to change, innovate and cultivate the creative potential of its people through the power of learning. That model is the Learning Organization, a set of theories and tools popularized in the early 1990s by Peter Senge (most notably in *The Fifth Discipline and The Fifth Discipline Fieldbook*) and it has been continually refined through ongoing research and in-the-field practice, particularly in the area of Conversational Leadership. The model was selected because it is both timely for use in today's governmental organizations, and it integrates with innovation through change. It also has a solid base of theory and research, and has been successfully used in large organizations and small ones, government agencies, schools, private corporations and non-profit organizations.

The primary root of Senge's work is systems thinking: a set of theories and practices the teach leaders to see the whole of any system in all its complexity. In this work, a "system" is understood as a collection of individual elements that come together to fulfill some shared purpose. Systems exist everywhere. Though most people, if asked to point out a system, could easily cite environmental systems, telecommunications systems, or other systems with which they routinely interact, they often forget that families, teams, societies, political parties and organizations are all systems. Philosophical and scientific theories or organizational visions are systems. Even human bodies are systems.

The components of a system are held in place by the structures, the patterns of interrelationships among the key elements of the system. Structures include tangible (on paper anyway) hierarchies and operating procedures. They also include "hidden" processes, such as individual or group attitudes and beliefs, or the "unwritten" rules.

Seeing the whole is a discipline that takes concentrated effort. Generally, all that is asked of individuals is that they meet their own responsibilities. After all, it is common thinking that if each person completes his or her own tasks, then the whole takes care of itself. As a line of logic, that thinking is difficult to refute, as it seems to intuitively make sense. For instance, if residents of a neighborhood all keep their individual yards clean, then the neighborhood remains in good shape. If each person completes a portion of a project within deadline, then the whole project will be completed within deadline. But, to think in that way is actually to commit a logical error, for it assumes that characteristics of the part can be transferred automatically to the whole, and that, as is known from experience, is not always the case.

To be effective, "systems thinking" requires that leaders keep in mind a number of critical assumptions. First and foremost, they must recognize that systems thinking is a long-term approach and requires a long-range mindset.

It also requires an open mindset, as the plurality of voices in the system must be heard. Such openness sparks the creativity in groups, but it also can engender fear. The sharing of ideas can lead to people's core beliefs and assumptions, those that define who they think they are and the role they think they fill, being questioned. That can be very uncomfortable and lead to resistance to the systems work.

Also, because of the emphasis on interrelationships, a system that can be subdivided logically into components still must be viewed as a whole — or as the big picture. Everyone's work should contribute to the whole system, every project must relate to the overall organizational purpose and desired results, every employee must be invested in the success of all. No parts of the system are off-limits.

To work on the system, it is essential that the root causes—of both intended and unintended consequences—be identified. That requires an eye toward the whole system. An occurrence in one part of the system may trigger an effect not in that same part of the system but in a separate one.

And, finally, systems are dynamic; they are always in a state of ebb and flow, growth and diminishment. Change, therefore, is a constant and must be managed as such, but it also must be managed to the benefit of the system and its components. In the case of the environment, natural systems change to accommodate the continued survival of the species within it. An organization must similarly operate under guiding principles, the equivalent of natural laws, and, as it is an artificial construction, with some purpose mutually agreed upon by its members.

## Why CIOs should care about leadership

The days of the super leader are gone. Management theorists, like the new generation of natural scientists, have advanced in their thinking to acknowledge that cooperation, not competition, is what keeps systems alive and thriving. It is more beneficial to a system, an organization, to develop the interrelationships of all the members, rather than allow just a few to rise to superstar status. Recognize that the following comments are relevant to how a technology organization operates. However, the same concepts apply to how IT leadership works with the business management team and the executive leadership team of any county or city.

Like a shift from linear thinking to systems thinking, a shift from super leadership to the new leadership requires that leaders embrace a few critical assumptions. These observations are relevant to the senior technology manager's organization. However, it is important to recognize that these same assumptions need to be applied by the IT leadership to all customer organizations of the technology team serves.

First, the quality of interrelationships directly impacts the quality of results—the stronger the relationships, the stronger the results. That is easy to see in the context of families or friendships; the stronger the relationship to another, the more vested a person is in that individual's success and in the sustainability of the relationship. The same holds true for professional relationships, as well. The key for leaders is to understand how to create healthy *professional* relationships that embrace learning, personal responsibility, and accountability for results.

Second, virtually all of the patterns of events or behaviors that are noticed are the result of the system, NOT the people working in the system. That is a difficult concept to put into leadership practice, and it seems to invalidate any notion of personal accountability. That is not the case. That assumption arises from systems thinking theory. If leaders understand that individuals do not act in isolation, that their ideas, and, therefore, their actions are informed by the larger system, then leaders must see beyond the person to the elements of the system that are allowing success or failure.

Third, the vast majority of people in the system are doing the best they can *given what they know and the current reality as they see it.* Most of us do not intentionally set out to make a wrong decision or do bad work. Thus, it is helpful if leaders not over react to individual actions or decisions as good or bad, and accept that undesired results or consequences may require us to seek new information and revisit the "system"—and sometimes change prior decisions or actions. That is a powerful concept based on assuming each person is doing their best. Sometimes that will not be the case, and when a pattern of "less than desirable" performance from an individual is identified and appropriate adjustments not responded to—it may mean that they are in the wrong place.

And finally, an assumption that many of us have put into practice without fully understanding the wisdom behind it, the fundamental unit of change in a knowledge society is the team, NOT the individual. Well-functioning teams can accomplish exponentially more and better results than individuals acting alone.[5]

The capacities that have been demonstrated through the Institute's teaching and technical assistance work with leaders who follow a systems thinking-based approach include being able to:

♦ Steward the system, rather than control it;
♦ Clarify and align the actions of individual employees and teams rather than poke and probe in unfolding processes;
♦ Redirect their work time from trivial and ritual task-oriented actions to strategic leadership (from working *in* the system to working *on* the system);
♦ Foster creative freedom within explicit boundaries;
♦ Support learning (their own and that of their employees); and
♦ Guarantee accountability.

to bring about a better understanding of their employees, their communities, and their purpose and processes. It is now the leader's job to grow the relationships that will bring about change, to build collective understanding around purpose and desired future reality. And, that means fostering a system that embraces learning and change, and that has structures that allow thinking, reflecting and conversations to occur.

---

### Discussion questions

1. What specific pushes for technology-related services is your organization currently facing from the residents of your community?
2. What pushes for services are you or your department currently facing from your city or county leaders and colleagues?
3. Do you believe the leadership of the operational and administrative segments of your city or county government sees IT as an enabler of their success or as competition for limited resources? If you are not seen as an enabler, why is that the case? Design an action plan to solve that serious problem.
4. What trends do you see facing your department in the next five years?
5. How do you, as a leader, feel when you reflect on those trends?
6. How will the changes you see coming impact how you work—the work you do and the way in which you do it?
7. If you could tell your organization's leadership one thing about the trends you see, what would it be and why?
8. If you could tell the citizens of your community one thing about the trends you see, what would it be and why?
9. How do you think a technology leadership program can help your community? Your state?

**Dena Hurst**, *Ph.D., provides the educational support and development for the certified public technology leadership programs. She is a leadership consultant, and focuses her practice and research on growing the leadership capacity of individuals, teams and organizations. Her approach is based on Conversational Leadership, the use of adult learning and conversation theory, styles and techniques as a means of creating alignment and engagement around organizational and* *personal dreams. Dena completed her undergraduate work at Stetson University, majoring in Economics with a minor in Philosophy; she completed her graduate work in Philosophy at Florida State University, specializing in social and political thought.*

*Ric Dugger, CCIO, invested fourteen years providing Information Technology (IT) services in the private sector before moving into the public sector. His work experience includes industries such as financial, retail, health care, insurance, military, law enforcement, secondary education and university education and governmental IT. Currently, he serves as the CIO for the Florida Institute of Government (IOG), where he works to improve the IOG by leveraging technology. Examples of that effort are the Certification programs for public service Chief Information Officers (CCIO) and Public Technology Managers (CPTM). The programs were designed especially for Florida local government IT leadership in corporation with Florida's Local Government Information Systems Association. Florida's State agency CIO Council is interested in expanding the program to address a few needs unique to the state government.*

## REFERENCES

1    See David Park, *The Grand Contraption: The World as Myth, Number and Chance*, Princeton, NJ: Princeton University Press, 2005.

2   See such professional publications as *Harvard Business Review* and CIO spanning the past 18-24 months for ongoing discussions of trends in human resource development, change management, managing across generations, and ways technological advancements are influencing the workplace and workforce. See also Thomas Friedman, *The World is Flat*, NY: Farrar, Straus and Giroux, 2006, and Jared Diamond, *Collapse: How Some Societies Choose to Fail or Succeed*, NY: Viking, 2005.

3   See James Surowiecki, *The Wisdom of Crowds*, NY: Anchor, 2005, for an analysis on the successes of collaboration.

4    See Peter Senge, "The Learning Organization: The Promise and the Possibilities," *The Systems Thinker*, 7(9), pp. 1-12.

5    For more information on this topic, see Peter Senge's work on team learning and James Surowiecki's *The Wisdom of Crowds: Why the Many Are Smarter Than the Few and How Collective Wisdom Shapes Business, Economies, Societies and Nations*, Little Brown, 2004.

# 3. Chief Information Officers: Leading Through Challenges and Change

## DR. BRUCE W. DEARSTYNE

## Introduction

Chief Information Officers (CIOs) in cities, counties and other local governments face unprecedented challenges and opportunities, and rising and changing expectations. Government operates on *information*, particularly digital information, arguably its most important resource other than its "human resources"—people in the public workforce. Legislators need information to make laws and policies; mayors and other executives require it for decision making, management and program evaluation; government employees need it to carry out their responsibilities; citizens access it to check on government programs and interact with government; and citizens, auditors and others study it to assess government responsiveness and accountability.

Government information must be systematically and efficiently managed, just as other key resources are managed, in the interest of economical government and responsive public service. Moreover, government, like other institutions, is changing because of demographic, social, economic and other forces. Traditional ways of organizing and carrying out work are giving way to newer styles, attuned to imaginative use of information, particularly in a digital form. The following chart illustrates some of the changes:

| Traditional | Emerging |
|---|---|
| Government's mission and role are well defined | Government's mission and role are changing, constantly being redefined |
| Leadership is mostly directing, managing | Leadership is more about vision, mission, empowering and guiding |
| Change is relatively slow, linear, predictable, managed | Change is relatively rapid, organic, guided rather than managed |
| Change is a source of apprehension | Change is seen as natural, inevitable |
| Programs are relatively static | Programs are more adaptable, agile, fluid |
| Multi-levels, more hierarchy, more supervision | Fewer levels, less hierarchy, more empowerment |
| Decision making is mostly centralized | Decision making is more decentralized |
| Individual achievement is valued | Value of collaborative, team-based work is on the rise |
| Information and knowledge often hoarded | Information and knowledge more shared, distributed |

Information technology (IT) is an essential tool for creation, storage and access to information, and CIOs need to be virtuoso IT managers. But, CIOs are transitioning from the **information**

**technology** arena to the **strategic information management** arena, where highly developed leadership, management, negotiation and communication skills are essential. Dynamic CIOs are becoming architects for what might be called "information proficient" government, strategically putting information to work for the good of the government and the people it serves (see "Information-proficient government: Characteristics" at the end of this chapter).

There is considerable literature on IT and the management role of CIOs. This chapter discusses eight leadership strategies for success as a city or county CIO:

1. Develop a leadership mindset
2. Develop your personal competencies
3. Define your mission and role
4. Become adept at leading change
5. Explain, report, communicate, educate
6. Stay resilient and keep moving in hard times
7. Develop strategies for emerging issues, challenges, opportunities
8. Avoid critical mistakes

## 1. Develop a leadership mindset

CIOs manage essential services and programs, but the CIO's position also should be one of *leadership*. An alternative title such as "Director of Strategic Information Management" might help dramatize the importance and reach of the responsibilities. Leaders, in contrast with managers, are transformational, expansionist, change agents. They are dissatisfied with the status quo; realize that the expectations of their "customers," including mayors and county executives, are constantly changing; and move their programs from their present state toward a new (hopefully, better) state.

Leaders *model the way* by demonstrating their personal values and commitment to organizational priorities; *inspire a shared vision* by imagining exciting possibilities, appealing to shared aspirations, and enlisting others toward a common vision; *challenge the process* by identifying opportunities to change, grow and improve their programs; *enable others to act* through delegation, empowerment and fostering collaboration; and *encourage the heart* by recognizing excellence, celebrating victories and creating a sense of community.[1]

The CIO Executive Council, an affiliate of CIO magazine, has developed a set of recommended "executive competencies" which include:[2]

**Strategic orientation:** "....the ability to think long-term and beyond one's own area. It involves... business awareness, critical analysis and integration of information, and the ability to develop an action-oriented plan."

**Change leadership:** "...transforming and aligning an organization through its people to drive for improvement in new and challenging directions...energizing a whole organization to want to change in the same direction."

**Collaboration and influence:** "....working effectively with, and influencing those outside of, your functional area for positive impact on business performance."

**Results orientation:** "....being focused on improvement of business results."

## 2. Develop your personal competencies

CIOs who lead and manage dynamic programs need to develop or hone a set of personal traits — knowledge, skills and abilities that provide the basis for keeping their programs fresh and responsive. Those competencies include technological proficiency but also encompass leadership, business and personnel management, communications and other skills. One useful list of competencies for information professionals includes:[3]

♦ Seeks out challenges and capitalizes on new opportunities
♦ Sees the big picture
♦ Communicates effectively
♦ Presents ideas clearly; negotiates confidently and persuasively
♦ Creates partnerships and alliances
♦ Builds an environment of mutual respect and trust; respects and values diversity
♦ Employs a team approach; recognizes the balance of collaborating, leading and following
♦ Takes calculated risks; shows courage and tenacity when faced with opposition
♦ Plans, prioritizes and focuses on what is critical
♦ Demonstrates personal career planning
♦ Thinks creatively and innovatively; seeks new or "reinventing" opportunities
♦ Recognizes the value of professional networking and personal career planning
♦ Balances work, family and community obligations
♦ Remains flexible and positive in a time of continuing change

Another useful perspective explains personal competencies in terms of application of key personality traits:[4]

**Observation:** The capacity to stand back or above and take a bird's eye view of yourself, the people you interact with, and the setting and circumstances in which you are working.

**Self-restraint and emotional control:** The ability to stay cool, evaluate situations objectively, consider alternatives, avoid hasty decisions, and resist the temptation to say or do something that might have a negative effect.

**Focus:** The capacity to maintain attention on priority issues; avoid distractions, boredom, and fatigue; make appropriate decision; follow up; and give attention to an issue until it is resolved.

**Tolerance for stress and ambiguity:** Leaders must be able to thrive in stressful situations and to cope with uncertainty, change, shifting contexts, and other ambiguities.

**Organization:** The ability to "keep track of things," including projects, priorities, people and groups; to maintain systems and organize work; and organize information resources such as e-mail and information on the Web.

**Planning and prioritization:** The capacity to set priorities, work out a road map so that you and the program arrive at an established destination or goal, meet benchmarks along the way, and not get distracted or sidetracked

**Flexibility:** This is the balance to planning and prioritization. Effective leaders can revise plans in the face of obstacles, setbacks, new information, new opportunities and unanticipated threats.

## 3. Define your mission and role

Many elected officials and government executives still think of CIOs as essentially information technology service providers—the people who make computer and software systems operate. That is still an important responsibility. But, too often the CIO's work is considered to be "support" or "administrative" in a way that understates its importance. The role of CIO has expanded and become more strategically important and central to the operation of government. CIOs should to be entrepreneurial and improvisational, defining the rationale and mission of their programs. Accenture advises that "cultivating high performance through information management," including ensuring availability of information for decision making and aligning information management with enterprise priorities, should be a priority for all CIOs.[5]

The mission of CIO as an architect of institutional advancement and change management is emerging at the federal and state, as well as the city and county levels. "Transforming IT to support the mission," is the title of a recent survey of federal CIOs. "The purpose of IT is to support the organization's mission, calling for greater alignment between IT plans and operations, and the support IT must bring to mission programs and functions."[6]

"The state CIO has risen to and must be seen within state government as a *change leader* who leads and facilitates government organizational transformation efforts" in line with executive and legislative priorities, says a white paper from the National Association of State Chief Information Officers (NASCIO). CIOs encourage resilient, agile government through, for instance, facilitating the flow of information to the people who must have it for their work, and leveraging enterprise architecture as a management discipline and not just as a methodology for managing technology.[7]

In the 2008 "Public CIO Survey" conducted by *Public CIO* magazine, the top "IT management priorities" reflected the challenge to lead, manage relationships and services, and handle the "political" issues that are inevitable in government:[8]

- ◆ Align IT with business goals
- ◆ Cost controls
- ◆ IT governance
- ◆ Intergovernmental collaboration
- ◆ Funding
- ◆ Project management
- ◆ Workforce retention and recruitment
- ◆ Dealing with political/legislative challenges

CIOs should play at least these roles:

1. Lead strategic planning initiatives that define how information should be generated, assembled, stored, accessed, and used to obtain maximum benefit and economy for government
2. Consult and work with agency and department heads to define their strategic information management needs and lead, manage, or support their initiatives to develop systems and capacity to meet those needs
3. Develop initiatives to align information resources with governmental priorities
4. Strategically address government-wide information management issues, such as security, legal compliance and management of e-mail

5. Manage, or partner with agencies in the management of, IT and information management-related projects
6. Provide reliable, responsive information technology services
7. Keep information and IT programs fresh and responsive by monitoring and adapting innovative approaches

## 4. Become adept at leading change

City and county CIOs are in the *change* business because government employees' expectations, technology, public expectations and government priorities are always in a state of flux. Static programs are likely to be marginalized or scaled back; dynamic ones are much more likely to prosper. CIOs have to keep their programs vibrant, and they also should spearhead broader changes in government to make better use of information to improve efficiency and services. One helpful framework suggests that effective change is a multi-step process:[9]

♦ Establish a sense of urgency, show what is wrong with the status quo, demonstrate what will happen if no action is taken, highlight the positive consequences of action.

♦ Build a "guiding team" of managers and opinion leaders who will support change and get others to support it as well.

♦ Create a vision of how the program should change.

♦ Find multiple ways to communicate about the need to keep moving toward the new vision.

♦ Enable others to take action in a positive direction through team assignments, breaking down barriers, opening encouraging change initiatives and providing resources.

♦ Create short-term "wins," milestones that demonstrate the possibility of progress, encourage supporters and discourage opponents.

♦ Consolidate gains and keep the momentum going, including changing assignments and reporting relationships where appropriate.

♦ Anchor new approaches in the culture, e.g., through new ways of recruiting, mentoring and training, emphasis on competencies appropriate for the new style of work, new approaches to rewarding teamwork.

## 5. Explain, report, communicate, educate

CIOs sometimes become so involved with providing IT, developing information systems, assisting offices and other pressing work that they neglect to *communicate*. Busy legislators and executives don't have (or take) the time to fully understand information's strategic role in government; busy government employees want technology tools and information systems but don't fully understand the CIO's mission. All this means that the CIO must spend a good deal of time communicating, informing, reminding, encouraging, cautioning, and sometimes, cajoling. They should build networks within the government, which can also double as advocacy groups. A few suggestions:

♦ Establish an advisory committee with representatives from key executive offices (e.g., mayor, county executive); management offices (e.g., administration, budget); important "customers;" and outside experts and citizens. Use the committee to get advice but also to disseminate the CIO's perspectives back to the offices and groups its members represent.

♦ Develop, hone and, as appropriate, customize a few key themes, e.g., government runs on information; availability of information promotes employee productivity and contributes to morale; information is the basis for our interface with the public; good information management saves (rather than costs) money; information management dovetails with open, accountable government; it makes good business sense to invest in information systems even in hard times.

♦ Develop an informal network of peer managers throughout local government as a means of getting the word out, keeping people informed, getting input and feedback, and, as appropriate, garnering support for budgetary resources.

♦ Issue reports on the role and impact of the work of the CIO's office, projects, new IT selections, issues and problems upcoming in the future, and other topics that show the government's leaders and employees what the CIO is doing.

♦ Start a CIO's online newsletter or blog. Use it to convey personal perspectives, explain complicated issues, explain controversial decisions, outrun and get ahead of the rumor mill, etc.

♦ Maintain a user-friendly web site that conveys key messages; provides a basis for interaction; and, generally, serves as a good model for other agencies' web sites and for the local government's web site/portal.

♦ Prepare carefully for meetings and budget hearings with issues expressed in terms that other attendees can understand and appreciate (avoid being overly-technical).

♦ Ask to be invited to meetings where it will be useful for a CIO's perspective to be presented because the issues involve IT or information management (in the final analysis, most issues in local government involve one or the other or both).

♦ Carry out a debriefing or "after-action review" after every significant project or other initiative, disseminate the "learnings" and plow them back into the work.

## 6. Stay resilient and keep moving in hard times

Cities and counties are entering difficult fiscal times. An October 2008 NACo survey reported that 59% anticipated a shortfall for next year, and 73% anticipated cutting back services; 91%, budget cuts; 91%, employment freezes; and 64%, layoffs.[10] Nearly 80% of fiscal officers surveyed by NLC in mid 2008 predicted their cities would be less able to meet responsibilities in the following year. "The economic downturn will continue to translate into reduced city revenues, while demand for services and increases in costs will continue to put pressure on the spending side of the ledger."[11] Thirty-eight percent of city and county CIOs expect budget reductions next year, according to a 2008 PTI/INPUT survey.[12]

IT and information services should expect to do their share of economizing and belt-tightening. But, the work of the CIO supports the operation of just about all other local government offices. CIOs should work to ward off disproportionate cuts by demonstrating the value of information to government and making the business case for how they use their budgetary resources. They should call on their network within government for support.

Furthermore, bad times may be an opportunity in disguise. Better use of information resources can help bolster governments' operations and services; encouraging IT innovation may save money. Investing in information systems can be a way of streamlining operations and reducing costs.

CIOs should consider: achieving cost savings by moving IT services to outside contractors or vice versa; increasing cooperative information management initiatives with government offices; eliminating "silos" and consolidating IT systems; improving project management by ramping up the use of project management software; automating manual systems; switching from paper-based to electronic records systems; improving information access systems to help employees more efficiently find the information they need for their work (particularly useful if hiring freezes or layoffs are required and staff are called on to take up the slack); moving transactional capacity and services to the local government's portal; encouraging the disposition of obsolete records in line with legal requirements; developing initiatives to retain the knowledge of retiring employees, e.g., through recording their advice and insights about how to do things in electronic databases; and fostering better and more economical collaboration through the use of collaborative systems, discussed below.

## 7. Develop strategies for emerging issues, challenges, opportunities

Progressive CIOs look for opportunities to innovate (see sidebar "CIOs and innovation" at the end of this chapter for some examples). They look ahead to both challenges and opportunities, and develop strategies and tactics to turn them to the government's advantage, if possible. Organizations such as PTI play a critical role in offering educational opportunities, furnishing guidance, pointing to best practices and providing discussion forums. A few examples of emerging issues:

**Information as a distraction.** End-user studies show people are overwhelmed and distracted by a barrage of incoming information from e-mail, text messaging, web sites, and other sources. A typical worker in the U.S. receives some 200 e-mails per day. An AOL survey reported that 46% say they are "hooked on e-mail; 50% say they e-mail while driving; 15%, from church. Stress and diminished productivity result.[13] CIOs can assist through educational opportunities to demonstrate how to use—and not overuse—information tools, evaluate information and integrate information into work.

**Collaborative software information systems.** CIOs need to take the initiative to implement collaborative tools, technologies and systems developed to extend the utility of the Internet and take advantage of the growing popularity of online information exchange forums. There are many models, including such things as Wikipedia, the online encyclopedia maintained by users; MySpace, Facebook, YouTube, and Twitter for sharing of personal information; online collaborative initiatives such as InnoCentive and IBM's Innovation Jam; and collaborative work tools, such as wikis and blogs. Cities and counties are beginning to adopt them for information sharing; Denver Mayor John Hickenlooper, for instance, created his own YouTube channel. There is immense potential for fostering citizen interaction with government, and for dramatically increasing employee collaboration, e.g., through the use of wikis for projects.[14] The opportunities for engagement, collaboration, interaction and productivity are dramatic. But, so are the risks of rushing into a new area without adequate understanding and planning. CIOs can lead the way through education and selection of appropriate technologies.

**Cloud computing.** A fall 2008 *InformationWeek* survey defines "cloud computing" as "an environment where any type of IT resource may be provided as a service." The concept is still fluid and emerging; large companies such as Microsoft, IBM and Google are working to shape it (and provide the services), but dozens of start-ups also are taking the field; and there is considerable discussion over such issues as cost, application, and security. This may be the beginning of a revolutionary change to provision of IT services by external providers, with institutions, including local governments, buying capacity and services as required. It is too soon to know for sure,[15] but the

# Information-proficient government: Characteristics

Leaders of local governments and in particular the Chief Information Officer should aim for what might be called "information-proficient" government: making optimal, economical use of information to serve the public and carry out government's services. Information-proficient government has the following traits:

♦ There is a strategic plan for the management of information that ties it to government-wide priorities.

♦ Policies are in place that guide the creation, access, use and retention/disposition of information.

♦ Information proficiency is baked into the government through the deployment of knowledgeable IT, records and other information professionals in the government's agencies and offices, working in concert with the CIO.

♦ Elected officials and chief executives have the information they require to make strategic plans, align resources with priorities, assess outcomes, assess performance and keep government attuned to changing expectations and needs.

♦ Agency directors have the information they need to make program management decisions, deliver services and assess program performance.

♦ The public can access clear, well-organized, easily-understood information about the government's operations and services and their own neighborhoods.

♦ The official web site/portal makes it easy for the public to conduct online interactions with government.

♦ Information is managed according to legal guidelines and requirements, including retention and disposition of records according to state and local regulations.

♦ Provision is made for security, including restricting or blocking access to confidential or sensitive data, guarding information systems from unwarranted access, and preparing for manmade or natural disasters.

♦ The organizational culture thrives on information sharing; imaginative use of information fosters creativity; information hoarding and "stovepipes" are discouraged.

♦ The government adopts new information strategies, technology, tools and systems after careful investigation and customization.

CIO's role in exploring, guiding, encouraging or cautioning their governments will be crucial. If governments decide to move in this direction, CIOs may begin redefining themselves less as proprietors of services and more as managers of relationships with external providers.

**Web site/portal as transactional interface.** Many cities and counties are gradually transforming their websites from communication and information-sharing sources to online meeting places where citizens can interact with government legislators, express their views on pending legislation, learn more about what is going on in their neighborhoods, pay taxes and obtain permits, and otherwise interact with local government offices. Some of the collaborative applications noted above hold promise for accelerating the trend. The optimal CIO role here, besides ensuring that the technology is robust and responsive, is to identify best practices, suggest and install new applications, monitor implementation and use, and devise measures to evaluate how well the applications are working.

**Electronic records management.** In too many local governments, the work of the CIO and the work of the records management/archival offices are on separate, uncoordinated tracks. CIOs create IT and information systems, but records managers guide management of the records they produce, including retention and disposition, and state records management/archives offices issue regulations about creation and preservation of records and provide retention/disposition schedules. There are some possible administrative strategies here, including consolidating the two functions. But in most settings, the best approach is communication and cooperation to ensure that recordkeeping capacities are built into electronic information systems; records are distinguished from non-records; and provision is made for retention of, and access to, electronic records for as long as they are needed for administrative, fiscal, legal, research and other purposes.

**Legal preservation and access.** This issue is related to the management of electronic records and is likely to be complicated by each of the other developments in this section. Two examples of the growing complexity: "E-FOI"—electronic Freedom of Information—with new requirements to make electronic records, such as e-mail, more easily accessible; electronic discovery, a requirement to make relevant records or information available to one's opponent in litigation. How to set up e-mail systems with possible FOI requests in mind? How to manage "instant messaging" systems to capture information? Is the local government's web site/portal a "record," and, if so, how should it be managed? What about outside access to the information in wikis, collaborative platforms where the information content is continually in flux and issues of who-contributed-what-when may have legal significance? CIOs should partner with local government counsel and records management offices to develop policies, guidelines, education and technology to meet those issues. They also need to keep an eye on rulings of state FOI offices and court decisions on access, privacy and discovery.

## 8. Avoid critical mistakes

CIOs may find their work complicated by unclear expectations, indifferent bosses, inadequate budgets, critical "customers" and other unsettling factors. There is an old and not-so-funny joke that CIO actually stands for "career is over!" Inspired leadership and sound management will overcome most of the problems. There are at least 10 mistakes that should be avoided:

# CIOs and innovation

Chief Information Officers should develop innovative approaches to delivering their services, particularly to: (A) reduce costs; (B) improve responsiveness to the public's need for information and ability to transact business with government; (C) integrate information resources and make access easier; (D) advance specific legislative or executive initiatives; and (E) work with community groups and residents to improve city and county services.

1. Assuming that the CIO's position is mainly technical and that his or her colleagues in government will be satisfied and not want more if computer systems operate well.
2. Proceeding haphazardly without guidance from carefully developed plans, priorities and operating principles.
3. Not building a relationship with the city or county legislative body to ensure that they have a solid understanding of the role of IT and information in government, and why investing budgetary resources makes sound business sense.
4. Not building a relationship with the mayor, county executive or other government chief executive officer that demonstrates the role the CIO plays in ensuring that information is available for key decisions and policy development.
5. Not carrying out enough discussions with "customers" to build deep understanding of their needs, get their confidence and garner their support.
6. Starting a change initiative but stopping too soon before it is fully anchored in policy, procedures and culture.
7. Overemphasizing regulations, requirements and threats of negative consequences for non-compliance at the expense of education, collaboration, use of models and best practices for guidance, and emphasis on positive consequences of good information management.
8. Under-communicating, based on the assumption that everyone in government understands (or should understand) and supports what the CIO is trying to do.
9. Letting the tactical (getting things done day-to-day) trump the strategic (taking the longer view, refreshing the program's vision and mission, mulling what needs to be done and how to do it)
10. Not tending to "self renewal," e.g., sharpening personal skills and acquiring new ones, honing ability to set and balance priorities, and dealing with pressure and stress.

---

## Discussion questions

1. This chapter says that leaders are "transformational, expansionist, change agents." Can leaders with that orientation also be successful managers, that is, getting the work done day-to-day?
2. What are the three most important personal competencies that a CIO needs to lead a successful program, and why are they the most critical?

3. If a CEO has strong views of what a new CIO should do, but the CIO believes a different role is more appropriate, what steps should both the CEO and the CIO take to reach a consensus?
4. What are the best approaches for a CIO to lead change, particularly in a time of budgetary constraints?
5. What are the best strategies for making the case that the work of the CIO is essential to local government?
6. This chapter mentions 10 critical mistakes that CIOs may sometimes make. Which seems to be the most critical, and why?

**Dr. Bruce W. Dearstyne** *is a former professor at the College of Information Studies, University of Maryland, where he continues to teach graduate leadership, management and information management courses as an adjunct professor. Prior to joining the Maryland faculty in 1997, he was, for many years, a program director at the New York State Archives and Records Administration, and responsible for publications and services to cities, counties and other local governments. He is the author of approximately 100 articles and several books, most recently,* Managing Records and Information Programs: Principles, Practices, and Management Techniques *(2009).*

## REFERENCES

1 James M. Kouzes and Barry Z. Posner, *The Leadership Challenge* (4th ed., San Francisco: Jossey Bass, 2007).

2 CIO Executive Council, *About the Future-State CIO Program —Assessments.* https://www.cio-executivecouncil.com/public/futurestatecio

3 Special Libraries Association, "Personal Competencies," in *Competencies for Information Professionals* (2003). Http://www.sla.org/content/learn/comp2003/index.cfm

4 Chuck Martin, Peg Dawson, and Richard Guare, *Smarts: Are We Hardwired for Success?* (New York: AMACOM, 2007), 15-29.

5 Accenture, *"Cultivating High Performance Through Information Management,"* 2007. http://www.accenture.com/NR/rdonlyres/D4B8A20E-996E-4ABF-9395-A4CFD734C784/0/AIMsCIOBrochure.pdf

6 Information Technology Association of America, *Transforming IT to Support the Mission* (18th annual survey of Federal CIOs, February 2008), 13. Http://www.itaa.org/upload/news/docs/2008CIOSurveyFinal.pdf

7 NASCIO, *Transforming Government Through Change Management:* The Role of the State CIO. 2007. Http://www.nascio.org/publications/documents/NASCIO-Transforming%20Govt-Research%20Brief.pdf

8 "The 2008 Public CIO Survey," *Public CIO*, Feb. 6, 2008. http://www.govtech.com/gt/print_article.php?id=261394

9 Dan S. Cohen, *The Heart of Change Field Guide: Tools and Tactics for Leading Change in Your*

*Organization* (Boston: Harvard Business School Press, 2005).

10 National Association of Counties, *State of the County Economic Survey*, October 2008. Http://www.naco.org/Template.cfm?Section=Publications&template=/ContentManagement/ContentDisplay.cfm&ContentID=29007

11 National League of Cities, *City Fiscal Conditions in 2008*. National League of Cities *Research Brief* 2008-2. September 2008. http://66.218.181.91/ASSETS/A49C86122F0D4DBD812B 91DD5777F04D/CityFiscal_Brief_08-FINAL.pdf

12 *State of City and County IT: 2008 National Survey.* Http://www.pti.org/index.php/ptiee1/more/420

13 Basex, *Information Overload: We Have Met the Enemy and He is Us.* 2008, http://bsx.stores. yahoo.net/inovwehamete.html; AOL's Fourth Annual E-Mail Addiction Survey Results. 2008. Http://mobile.aol.com/gallery/email-survey

14 *Government 2.0: Building Communities with Web 2.0 and Social Networking.* Report by Government Technology's Digital Communities program. 2008. Http://www.govtech.com/dc/resource.php

15 Michael Biddick, *A Walk in the Clouds: Analytics Report.* September 2008. Http://www.cloudcomputing.informationweek.com

# 4. Transformation of the Local Government CTO/CIO

**DR. NORMAN JACKNIS**

## Abstract

The position of Chief Information Officer, which developed only relatively recently, already faces two divergent paths—one more tactical and the other more strategic. This section will focus on how the situation came to pass, focusing on the nature and skills of the people who are in the position, their relationship to the chief executive officer of the government, the expectations and actions of citizens, and the changing nature of technology. Then, the impact of future technology trends on the CIO will be explored.

## Some history

Like their counterparts in the private sector, even before there was a desire for centralized information technology (IT), the modern day internal government IT staff often started out as a part of the Finance department of local governments. Although some larger government IT staff undertook programming, their basic role was to help automate the accounting books and produce payroll checks.

While here and there in public safety or infrastructure agencies, some other local government agencies purchased technology, the largest investments usually were made on behalf of financial functions, and that activity was usually the first example of government use of information technology. In some governments, that legacy still makes it easier for financial systems to be approved than most others.

The new IT function often was labeled "management information services" (MIS), headed by a bureau director. Hidden away in a well-enclosed "data center," the function was, in fact, relatively invisible in the overall organization—except, of course, when there was a problem producing the payroll.

The creation of the relatively inexpensive, but usable, personal computer (PC) in the early 1980s led within a decade to its subsequent acquisition by various departments of government. That posed a threat to whatever central control the MIS group might have had. Sometimes, their reaction and desire for control went to extreme lengths. There were some government IT people who installed software on users' PCs that prevented users from even seeing Microsoft Windows on their screens when that operating system was made available in the early 1990s.

At the same time, as computing power was being distributed outside of the data center, there was an increasing demand for all kinds of software to help governments become more productive. Ultimately, both the executive and legislative leadership of local government realized that the more visible and important operations of IT were so diffused that the situation was almost chaotic.

Responding to the same situation at the federal level, the U.S. Congress in the mid-1990s enacted what is now called the Clinger-Cohen Act to create a job of Chief Information Officer in each federal agency/department.

The private sector, detecting the same problems and trends, also started to use the position of Chief Information Officer. That had special significance in corporations, where there had been a pattern of using Chief X Officer to indicate a position reporting to or close to that of the Chief Executive Officer. So, there were Chief Financial Officers, Chief Marketing Officers and now Chief Information Officers.

By the late 1990s, with massive budgets allocated to resolve problems of the millennia change in 2000 and with the initial awakening of the public sector to the possibilities of the Internet, the use of the title Chief Information Officer became widespread in local government.

## The two paths for the current CIO

But did anything really change?

For some IT managers in government, there was a more prestigious title (CIO versus MIS Manager), sometimes a department of their own (rather than being subordinate to Finance) and perhaps a little salary increase. Otherwise, they were, as in the past, focused mostly on financial systems and not present in discussions at executive levels of the government. Their focus remained on "keeping the trains running."

Even their role as technologists was constrained, because many of their governments had scant money for the development of home-grown systems and software development. Thus, the job of this kind of CIO also became more "vendor management" than systems development, with a necessary emphasis on assuring that their governments obtain the performance that the vendors promised. These CIOs deploy IT products and services, rather than create them.

For other CIOs, however, there was a substantive change in the role to accompany the change in title. The CIO was expected by government leaders to take on a more important and visible role. That was especially the case in the larger, more affluent suburban counties and the largest cities of the US.

Here is an example of the kind of advertisements that started to appear:

> "The [X government] is seeking a CIO with exceptional managerial, leadership and technical skills. The CIO must have an understanding of public sector policy and budget development and of the dynamics of working in a large political entity such as [X's] government. The ideal candidate will be a progressive visionary and a proven strategic thinker."

That job definition makes clear that success as such a CIO rests upon a three-legged stool:

- ♦ The CIO must be able to manage people and operations, providing a relatively flawless and consistent level of systems performance;
- ♦ The CIO must have technology expertise (relative to his/her peers in the government) and even a vision about the uses of technology; and
- ♦ The CIO must act as a member of the senior leadership of the government, and, as such, be a successful "politician" or, to use a less emotion-laden phrase, a successful "change agent."

The percentage of each day spent weighing on each of the three legs will vary depending upon the nature of the political environment, the size of the government, its traditions, etc., but none can be ignored. And, a successful CIO must have skills in each area, even if he/she has others on staff with greater skills in any one of the areas.

In the early days after the initial creation of the CIO position, there was a realization that some of the people in that position had mostly managerial skills and very limited technical skills. So, some governments added a second position of Chief Technology Officer (CTO) or used the CTO title instead of Chief Information Officer. The idea was that a CTO was more expert in technology, and the team of a CIO/CTO might cover all the skills needed to get the job done.

As a practical matter, not many governments created two such positions. The distinction between the two titles also has gotten quite muddied in recent years. For example, when Barack Obama called for the creation of a federal CTO position in the White House, he defined the job in such a way that it actually matches the classic description of a CIO. So, at this stage, there is not much point in trying to distinguish the two positions.

In the original Star Trek television series, there were two characters whose expertise in technology was an essential part of the job: Scotty and Spock. Scotty, down in the "engine room," made sure the ship would keep moving as fast as Captain Kirk requested. Spock was on the deck with the commander, providing strategic advice and direction. In a nutshell, those two characters exemplify the two kinds of roles that government CIOs can adopt.

Many of the more strategic CIOs also were given the power to enforce their vision, so that they would run all IT operations of their governments, be responsible for the creation and delivery of all new systems and have an absolute veto over any department's attempt to purchase IT products and services.

The differences are reflected as well in the amount of money that a government devotes to IT. Typically, the first, more tactical CIO has an ever-lower percentage of the budget to work with than the more expansive, strategic CIO. Note that it is all relative, because local government, in general, is not known for devoting more than 2-3 percent of its budget to IT, at most. Contrast that with Gartner's review of private sector investments, where "mainstream adopters" spent about 5% and "leading-edge" technology adopters spent about 11% of their revenue on IT.

Perhaps the difference in budget reflects the higher or lower importance assigned to IT by others in the government, but the difference in approaches by the two types of CIOs also plays a role. The more limited CIO seems stuck in justifying new investments by looking only at IT costs. That is often starting out from a losing position—that the investment does not impact the business of government. (For a CIO with the skills and ambition, getting stuck in such a situation is often the impetus for a job search in a more supportive workplace.)

The more strategic CIO tries to look at the total cost of government operations where the investment is targeted (not just IT) as a benchmark, and then compares a usually lower total cost (including labor, IT and other factors) after a new system is put in place. That is usually a more persuasive argument for the business of government.

In government, it also is easier to get money for services that citizens see directly, such as those on the Internet. To the degree that such "citizen-facing" services are more likely to be part of the ambitions of the more strategic-type of CIO, it makes it a bit easier to get more funds.

A similar pattern plays out in the way that CIOs manage their own staff. If IT is not considered strategic, but just a second line, support function, then a more directed style is evident and required. However, for the CIO who has to deliver new technology, it is necessary to maximize the creativity of the staff and, in that case, a more collaborative style is appropriate.

## The divergence is growing

In a form of the "rich getting richer," it is interesting to note that the bifurcation of the CIO role in government has continued to grow, rather than resolve itself into a common understanding of what the CIO should do.

Indeed, the first kind of operations-focused CIO has faded back into relative obscurity, after the basic work of automating departments and creating web sites was done. (In a few local governments, even the web work was divorced from the more general IT functions, and the CIO had no control over the public presence of the government.)

In contrast, many of the more strategic CIOs have expanded the interpretation of their title to include "chief innovation officer" and officer in charge of analysis of the performance and operations of the overall government. The CIO, in such cases, is often the eyes and ears of the chief executive. In the past, the budget department was expected to play that role. But, with IT staff seeing into the daily on-the-ground operations of every part of the government, that role is more naturally played by the strategic CIO and his/her staff.

In the last several years, there has been much discussed in both private and public sectors about the need for IT to be "aligned" with the business. But the way that the two types of CIOs achieve that reflects much on their different approaches to the job. For the more tactical CIO, alignment is reactive—looking more like running to catch up to the latest whim expressed by some powerful official elsewhere in the government. To the more strategic CIO, alignment can well mean taking the lead to help redesign the operations and policies of other departments so that they can achieve maximum results from their investment in technology.

With such new experience under their belts, the more strategic role of the CIO has opened up new career paths—from close, trusted advisor to the Mayor/County Executive-Administrator to official roles as deputy chief executive or chief administrator in the government. It is, perhaps, just a matter of time before one of the strategic CIOs is elected to the post of chief executive officer of their government. Certainly, technologists from the private sector, most notably New York City Mayor Bloomberg, made their technology backgrounds a significant part of their appeal to voters.

## From cocoon to butterfly?

It is important to understand where the early careers of CIOs help or hinder their ability to step up to the larger strategic role. After all, it requires a transformation much like the bursting of a butterfly from a cocoon.

The most common background for CIOs is business application programming, although many also have been consultants to large organizations and developed a strategic perspective through that experience. Some have come up from the infrastructure side of the IT business, with previous experience running the data network or data center.

Whether from a software or infrastructure background, early in their careers, CIOs lived in a world where imperfection was unacceptable. Zero bugs and zero downtime were the goals. (Many IT people, of course, did well on tests in school, so that was a natural predilection on their part.)

Unfortunately, when the CIO operates at a senior level, perfection is an elusive and often counter-productive goal. In many governments, the demand for IT services and products so far outstrips the available resources, that the job is a continuous juggling act. The issue for a CIO, as with any C-level executive, is to identify which balls—business projects—must be kept in the air and which ones may be dropped. If a CIO tries to keep all of the balls in the air with equal effort, he/she will fail and will likely find that the highest priority balls go down first – along with his/her career prospects.

Similarly, the typical early career of a CIO focuses on processes and procedures. As a senior executive, though, the CIO learns often that changing the culture of the organization has wider impact on how the staff behaves than trying to impose procedures that may widely be ignored anyway.

That is especially important in an era when the demand for innovation is increasing, and the CIO must change the traditionally conservative culture that exists among most non-managerial IT staff. In fact, it is often the dirty little secret of the IT world that the very people who ask others to change all the time—the IT folks—are most reluctant to change their own ways. They are stuck in their own cocoons.

## Relationship to the Chief Executive/Administrator

The discussion so far has focused on the outlook, temperament and skills needed by a CIO who wishes to pursue the higher level, strategic approach to the role. But all of that becomes irrelevant if he/she does not establish and maintain an appropriate relationship with the person who is in charge of the whole government and with other key players.

Some local governments have a council-manager form of government, in which a policy-making (essentially legislative) body hires a professional manager to run the government. That becomes a little tricky for the CIO because power tends to be somewhat diffused. There is no single source of executive power because the manager is not an elected official and serves at the pleasure of other elected officials. However, that kind of situation also enables the politically skilled CIO to build coalitions among the different players.

In other local governments, the chief executive is elected as a mayor, county executive or county judge. The chief elected executive, combining both political and administrative power, tends to have the stronger role, which makes the relationship between that one person and the CIO even more important for the CIO.

If the partnership between the most important executive and the CIO is strong, truly innovative and important IT work will get done in the government. If it is not strong, if the chief executive "doesn't get it." then there will be little long-term success for the CIO, no matter what his/her skills.

There are a series of simple questions that the CIO needs to pose, although understanding that answers may well be nuanced.

1. What is most important to the boss: re-election, a long-term legacy, just reducing taxes…? And, is there a way that the CIO can help the boss with what's most important?
2. What is the vision that the boss has for the government. and does that boss understand the ways that IT can help achieve that vision?
3. Does the Executive have the budget to realize the vision?
4. How much authority will the CIO have over the direction and spending on IT?
5. In what symbolic ways will the boss show that the CIO is part of the inner circle of power in the government? (For example, office proximity, title, inclusion in small meetings alone or with others already recognized for their high position, etc.)

If the CIO has the requisite political and organizational skills, he/she will be able to quickly determine if there is the possibility of success as the new kind of strategic, visionary CIO. If either of the partners—the chief executive and the CIO—fails to understand and support their partnership, then frustration and, ultimately, failure is likely. If the partnership is strong, then it is very likely that the residents of the city/county will benefit from transformational and very innovative uses of technology.

## The future

As in the past, developing trends in technology will shape the choices and roles of the CIO. Some trends already have emerged, even if they are not yet fully developed and deployed. There are two that are especially significant to the government CIO.

First, there are all of the variations on computing services that are "out there" somewhere on the network. That would include what is called "cloud computing," software-as-a-service, service-oriented architectures, web-based services and the like. Already there are offerings available for local government from such big companies as Google, Amazon and Salesforce.com.

There is also nothing to stop a CIO from offering similar services over the network to governments other than his own. In the name of shared services or criminal justice cooperation, some of that has occurred in the past within some metropolitan areas. With the global and ubiquitous nature of the Internet, there is no reason why a health inspection system developed in Pennsylvania could not be made available to a municipality in Australia as a web-based service.

For those CIOs with the resources and ambitions, that opens up a new range of possible activities. Such a CIO might, in effect, become the CEO of a business that provides the IT services to others —and perhaps finds a way to spread the cost of development and running the systems over more than just his/her own local government's budget. That takes the CIO's role into a fairly new direction that goes beyond the government that he/she is a part of.

Second, there is the increasingly active role of the user (i.e., the citizen) in taking advantage of technology made available both by the government and others. It is now fairly common for people who are not part of a government's IT staff to use mashup tools to combine data from the government with data from other sources (like Google Maps). In the aftermath of Hurricane Katrina, for example, citizens in New Orleans created a mashup website to track where and how far behind the city was in demolishing houses that became hazards in their neighborhood.

It is not just the mashup phenomenon, but a range of social networking software tools that citizens are beginning to use to organize themselves and apply pressure to local government. The website "Fix My Street" enables citizens to take pictures of potholes, post them on the Web and deliver that data as a complaint to the local government.

To an extent, those offer alternatives to the forms of software that government CIOs would create or purchase, because they are out of the control of the CIO. The fact that there is also a large inventory of open source—which means free—software for citizens to use only makes it easier and cheaper for people outside of the IT department to do what the IT department used to monopolize.

The strategic CIO has to be a politician. Currently, that means he/she has to build alliances and provide leadership within the walls of government. In a future world of extensive citizen creation of public-oriented technologies, the CIO will have to extend those political skills to include the general public, as well. Being a good internal politician has been a stretch for many local government CIOs. The new trend will force even more CIOs out of their comfort zones.

Traditionally, chief elected officials and other local political leaders have primarily depended upon paid civil service, non-profit agencies or paid outsourcing firms to deliver public services. In a future world of networked, collaborating citizens, those same leaders may be able to facilitate the creation of public goods and services without depending as much on those intermediate paid organizations. That kind of collaboratively created public service can only occur if the right technologies are in place and the government culture is supportive. Will the local government CIOs of the future be ready to do their part in the new world?

---

## Discussion questions

1. Should a person becoming a government CIO arrive from the private sector or public sector? Why is one background better than the other?
2. Should a newly elected Mayor, County Executive or Chief Administrator select someone from within the existing staff, or hire from the outside? What are the advantages and disadvantages of each?
3. How would you assess your strengths in each of the three legs (skills) of the CIO stool mentioned above?
4. As a CIO, on what basis would you decide what projects should be pursued? How would you prioritize them?
5. As a CIO, to what degree would you be willing to deploy applications that use readily available, inexpensive web tools but may not meet normal IT performance standards? What experiences and other factors have led to your views on this question?
6. In a few cases in the private sector, the CIO also is asked to take over marketing functions. Is something similar a good idea in the public sector?
7. In 10 years, what would you expect a local government CIO to be doing each day?

**Norman Jacknis,** *director, Cisco IBSG Public Sector (Cisco's strategic advisory unit/think tank), served more than 10 years as CIO and commissioner of Westchester County, N.Y., where he was responsible for all of the government's technology. He is Chairman of the Fairfield-Westchester Chapter of the Society for Information Management (a national association of CIOs and senior IT executives). Dr. Jacknis served as co-chair of the technology and architecture committee of the New York State CIO Council, participated in the Federal/State/Local Partnership for Intergovernmental Innovation and continues as the technology adviser to the County Executives of America. Prior to his public service, Dr. Jacknis had diverse experience as an executive in the software industry. He received his PhD, MA and BA from Princeton University.*

# 5. IT Governance

**JOHN K. BEAIRD AND LIZA LOWERY MASSEY**

## Introduction

While much has been said about the importance of information technology (IT) and business alignment, many IT shops struggle to achieve it. IT governance is the key. The increased interaction between IT and the business units (departments) that results from the process, coupled with leadership's determination of priorities, both ensure that IT understands and is focused on the organization's priorities and goals. IT no longer has to guess which initiatives are most important or react to the squeaky wheel.

Research supports that organizations with a strong IT governance program are more successful.[1] Despite that, public sector organizations still struggle with implementation. Organizations that lack a strong IT governance program are fairly easy to identify by symptoms that include the following.

- ◆ IT, on its own, decides which projects get done and what technologies are implemented
- ◆ There is a "disconnect" between IT and everyone else
- ◆ IT is overwhelmed
- ◆ IT projects are delayed or not as successful as they should be
- ◆ IT is not respected and/or lacks credibility
- ◆ The organization views IT as an evil but necessary function
- ◆ The IT budget is something to defend
- ◆ The business units take on an "I'll do it myself" mentality
- ◆ Multiple IT systems exist for similar needs

The results are consistent, too: low customer satisfaction, a lack of buy in and appreciation from the business units, and, most critically, a lack of alignment of IT with the organization's strategy and direction. The foundation of implementing a strong IT governance program is to better understand what it is and how it works.

Fundamentally, IT governance broadens participation in decision making related to the allocation, use and management of the organization's IT resources. In addition, it shifts responsibility for the organization's business strategy away from the Chief Information Officer (CIO) or IT Director and back to the organization's leadership team, where it belongs. Despite involvement of more people and a shift in responsibilities, CIOs and IT Directors actually gain control over their functions by giving back responsibility for the organization's strategic direction and gaining control of the technology strategy.

The purpose of establishing IT governance is to create a conscious, organized process for making decisions related to investments in and management of an organization's IT resources. The objectives are to maximize value of the investments, increase the success rate of IT projects, manage expectations and demand for IT services, and improve customer satisfaction. Most often, governance is established to address many IT-related issues including:

♦ Developing the organization's IT strategy;
♦ Determining priorities and resource allocation levels for investments in IT;
♦ Adopting standards, policies and guidelines; and
♦ Identifying common IT resources to share across the enterprise.

Once the organization develops the business strategy and needs, supporting IT initiatives can be identified, prioritized and funded. The result: IT can more easily focus its resources and attention on the approved set of deliverables versus trying to do everything for everyone.

## Benefits of IT governance

♦ Improves communication
♦ Encourages collaboration
♦ Increases buy in
♦ Ensures alignment of priorities
♦ Focuses IT resources
♦ Manages demand
♦ Sets expectations
♦ Improves oversight

## Benefits for the organization

What does the organization gain from IT governance? Those two golden terms: efficiency and effectiveness. When IT governance is implemented, the organization gains efficiency by maximizing the value of IT investments, increased success rates of IT projects and increased customer satisfaction by managing expectations and demand for IT services. In all times, effective use of public funds is critical. IT leaders are charged with the most sacred of trusts, the trust of public funds. Through IT governance, IT leaders ensure that public funds are put to the best possible use in support of the organization's strategy and direction.

Settling disputes and considering exceptions to the organization's standards and policies are important aspects of IT governance. In most organizations that do not have IT governance, disputes and exceptions turn into win-lose battles that are won by the department head who is the most powerful. That approach leads to inconsistencies, hard feelings and power struggles. Airing issues through the governance process leads to more fact-based decision making and shines the light on bad actors.

## Benefits for the CIO and IT department

What do the CIO and IT department gain from IT governance? When IT governance is implemented, the CIO and IT department gain effectiveness through alignment with the business unit's needs and priorities, focusing their efforts on IT projects and services that matter the most to the organization. Support for IT projects from the business units is a key factor for project success. Having IT governance in place ensures that support. IT governance also keeps IT from making decisions in a vacuum by involving the business units in IT-related decision making. Quite often, the CIO and IT department become traffic cops, telling one customer no and another yes, based on the resources and talent they have available at the time. That approach takes the responsibility for business decisions away from the business units. IT governance puts those decision back in the hands of the business.

Often, IT leaders complain that non-IT staff spend too much time worrying about the technology and not enough time trying to understand their own business processes and needs. The good news is that, implemented correctly, IT governance diverts departments from their obsession with specific technologies, especially if it is coupled with strategic planning. It takes time, but IT governance results in non-IT folks thinking more about their business processes and needs, as well as the needs of the entire organization, allowing IT to focus on the technologies required to address them.

## The language of IT governance

An important step in implementing IT governance is to understand its terminology and key concepts. Generally accepted definitions of common governance related terms follow.

**Business**—A term used to describe the organization's service delivery units, typically called departments. It is used to distinguish between IT and the other functions in the organization.

**IT governance**—Principles that determine how IT-related decisions are made and how conflicts are resolved within the organization's traditional hierarchy and across the organization's functional and political boundaries.[2]

**IT governance decision-making areas**—The five IT-related areas for which governance decisions are made.[3]

*Business applications needs*—Requirements for IT-related solutions that are based on the needs of the organization's business units, and solve a business problem or address a business need or gap.

*IT architecture*—An integrated set of technology choices that guide the organization in satisfying business needs. It consists of policies and rules that govern the use of IT and layout a migration path for new investments.

*IT infrastructure strategy*—A plan, typically created by IT, that is approved by the organization's leadership and serves as the foundation for IT capability (both technical and human). The goal of the strategy is to implement IT infrastructure that is shared throughout the organization and centrally coordinated.

*IT investment and priorities*—Decisions regarding how much and where to invest in IT including project approvals and justification techniques.

*IT principles*—Statements approved by the organization's leadership and distributed throughout the organization that define how IT is used in the organization.

**IT governance roles**—The IT governance decision-making bodies that align with the five areas of IT decision making. Multiple roles can be filled by a single governance body.[4]

*IT Council*—A governance body that identifies IT values and sets IT-related ground rules, such as IT principles.

*IT Investment Board*—A governance body that performs IT value analysis and determines priorities for resource allocation.

*IT Management*—Staff responsible for the organization's IT function.

*IT Project Office*—Trained staff who manage and report on IT project implementation.

*Office of Architecture & Standards*—A governance body that determines IT value standards, such as the acceptable level of IT project risk, appropriate IT-business alignment, etc.

**IT governance approaches**—The six possible approaches for obtaining input and making decisions related to IT. An organization can use one or more of the following approaches to address IT governance decision areas. It is not necessary to use the same approach for input and decision-making, nor is it necessary to use the same approach for more multiple decision areas.[5]

*Business monarchy*—An IT governance approach where the organization's business units make IT-related decisions.

*IT monarchy*—An IT governance approach where the organization's IT professionals make IT-related decisions.

*Federal system*—An IT governance approach where C-level executives—such as the CEO, CIO, CFO, COO or equivalents—along with the organization's leadership, such as department heads and IT management, jointly make IT-related decisions.

*IT duopoly*—An IT governance approach where IT management and the organization's business leaders, such as department heads, jointly make IT-related decisions.

*Feudal system*—An IT governance approach where individual business units or process leaders make their own IT-related decisions.

*Anarchy*—An IT governance approach where individuals or small groups make their own IT-related decisions without much oversight or direction from leadership or the IT department. Typically, this approach is not the result of a conscious choice by the organization's leadership but is due to a lack of governance.

**Stakeholders**—Individuals and groups of people who are directly impacted by actions taken. For IT governance or projects, stakeholders include the organization's leadership, employees, customers, IT staff, and even vendors and suppliers.

## Governance roles and decision-making bodies

Each IT governance body should include a manageable number of key representatives who are respected by their peers and committed to getting things done. Since the governance process requires a partnership between the organization's leadership team and IT, it depends upon a fairly high level of trust. If that trust is absent or low when IT governance is instituted, it will develop or increase as the IT governance process matures.

The five (5) decision making areas (Principles, Investments, Infrastructure Strategy, Architecture, and Business Application Needs) align closely with the five (5) recommended decision-making bodies or roles (IT Council, IT Investment Board, IT Management, Architecture and Standards Body, and Project Office) involved in governance. One to five actual governance bodies can be formed to address the decision-making areas, with one governance body handling more than one decision area, if desired. For instance, small to medium organizations may use the Leadership Team (i.e. chief executive and department heads) to address both IT principles and investment decisions. Because the goal is to integrate IT governance into the organization's standard operations without adding more committees, meetings or overhead, use of existing decision-making bodies and processes is highly desired.

The relationship between the governance roles (decision-making bodies) and decision-making areas is depicted in the following chart. Again, one governance body can address more than one decision-making area.

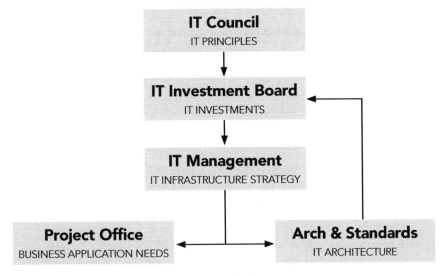

**Figure 5-1.**

The greatest area of interest often is determining IT investments or priorities, i.e. which IT-related projects make it to the top of the list and receive approval and funding to move forward. This decision area requires a participatory approach that ensures each department is represented equally. If the organization is small, the IT Investment Board may include the entire leadership team – the organization's chief executive, department heads and the CIO. In larger organizations, a representative type approach might be needed to keep the number of participants to around 11. Because this decision making body may have to resort to voting on priorities, an odd number works best to prevent ties. Once available resources are applied to the resulting list of priorities, IT has its acknowledged, approved and, most likely reduced, To Do List. Additionally, IT no longer has to say no to IT project requests. Instead, the requests are vetted through the governance process.

## Determining the best approach

Which decision-making approaches are best for an organization depends largely on the current hierarchy and culture of the organization. It is important not to get caught up in finding a single "best" approach for making each decision, as each area may be addressed most effectively by a slightly different approach. For instance, research finds that the predominate approach used by government for adopting IT principles is a federal approach for obtaining input, i.e. C-level executives working with the organization's leadership and IT management, and a duopoly for making decisions, i.e. IT management with the organization's business unit leaders. The following chart summarizes the predominant approaches used by government.[6]

| Decision Area | Input | Decision |
| --- | --- | --- |
| IT Principles | Federal | Duopoly |
| IT Architecture | Federal or Duopoly | IT Monarchy |
| Infrastructure Strategy | Federal | IT Monarchy |
| Infrastructure Strategy | Federal | Federal or Duopoly |
| IT Investment | Federal | Business Monarchy or Federal |

## Fitting in

So, how does IT governance fit into the overall organizational structure, and what are the reporting relationships? How does it relate to strategic planning, budgeting and operations? Most importantly, who makes the final decisions?

As stated, IT governance shifts responsibility for the organization's business strategy away from the CIO or IT Director and back into the realm of the organization's leadership team. Ownership by the organization's leadership is paramount to success and means that the leadership team is ultimately responsible for making IT governance decisions. To be transformational, IT governance must be seen as the organizational effort, not another IT initiative.

IT governance does not fundamentally change the decision-making process; The organization's leadership team continues to make decisions as appropriate or make recommendations to elected officials as is the case with budget adoption, legislative changes, etc. The governance process simply increases business leader's role in making technology-related decisions and ensures that the IT department's efforts are aligned with the organization's priorities and needs. The most significant change is that IT service levels and priorities are determined by the business, not the IT department.

If existing decision-making bodies are used for IT governance, the question of reporting relationships is mute. If new decision-making bodies are created, such as a technology investment board, then reporting relationships must be determined. No single approach works in all cases. The organization must determine the appropriate makeup of the decision making body and placement in the organization structure. Additionally, each decision-making body should have a chair, who is not from the IT unit.

IT governance plays a key role in each phase of the overall strategic business cycle, as depicted to the right. During planning and budgeting, IT governance determines how technology supports the organization's business strategy by defining IT service levels and determining IT priorities through investment decisions. During execution, IT governance is critical for oversight

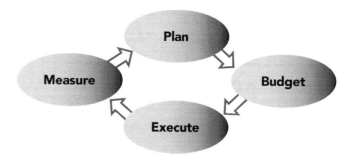

Figure 5-2.

of IT project implementation and management, adoption of IT standards and policies, as well as handling emerging initiatives and issues. Finally, IT governance plays a key role in the measurement phase by comparing results against adopted service levels and identifying areas for improvement that are then addressed in the planning phase.

## Getting started

When IT governance does not exist within an organization, selecting one decision-making area and identifying a specific goal, such as adopting IT principles or prioritizing IT initiatives for budget development purposes, is a great way to get started. Once that decision area is addressed and the governance body is working well, the organization can move to the next area, and so on, gaining confidence with each successful implementation. Organizations should expect to adjust or change their governance approaches as time passes and the organization's leadership and/or culture changes.

The process of establishing IT governance identifies decision-making bodies (roles) to address IT issues (decision-making areas) through the use of one of six decision-making styles (approaches) for input and making decisions. In order to determine the makeup of the governance bodies and appropriate approach for each area, an analysis of existing decision-making bodies and styles is conducted. Additionally, the IT strategic planning process is helpful in identifying governance requirements and approaches.

The recommended steps for establishing IT governance follow.

**1. Information gathering**—Identify individuals and groups who will be interviewed to provide background for and input into development of the proposed IT governance program. Interviews can be conducted individually or in groups, and are typically held with the organization's leadership, including department heads, key staff with insight into the organization's culture and decision-making processes—such as budgeting—and IT staff. Information gathering also can be done in conjunction with the IT strategic planning process.

**2. Analysis and design of proposed governance program**—Use the information obtained in the previous step to formulate a proposed IT governance program. Use best practice approaches, such as the one outlined in this chapter, as a framework for your recommendations. Keep in mind that an important goal is to use existing decision-making bodies and processes to the fullest extent possible, minimizing the addition of committees and processes.

**3. Review and revise proposed governance program**—Review the proposed IT governance program and related recommendations with the organization's leadership for consideration and feedback. Make adjustments if necessary based on their response.

**4. Gain approval and begin using IT governance model**—Once final adjustments are made to the IT governance program, it should be officially adopt by the organization's leadership so that it is not just seen as another IT program. Ensure that the program is clearly communicated to the organization at large and conduct the first IT governance meeting using the adopted model.

Due to the organization-wide nature of governance and the issues it addresses, some organizations find that it is necessary to seek the services of a third party to assist with development of the governance program and facilitate implementation. The bottom line is to ensure that IT governance is seen as an organizational initiative not just another fad forced upon the organization by IT.

## Governance in action

Turn the clock back several years, and the Las Vegas, Nevada, Metropolitan Police Department (Metro) was suffering from many of the symptoms outlined in the beginning of this chapter. Metro, one of the largest local law enforcement agencies in the United States, provides public safety services to one of the fastest growing areas in the country. With a population approaching 2 million and nearly 40 million visitors a year, technology plays a key role in enabling Metro to meet its ever-increasing service demands. Like most organizations, the issues around IT evolved naturally as a result of a growing dependence on constantly changing technologies, resource constraints and limitations, an increasing level of technology sophistication among end users, and an IT function that was overwhelmed and struggling to adapt to the changes and demands.

Desiring to improve the situation, Metro's leadership embarked upon an assessment that led to implementation of an IT governance program. When the assessment was conducted, the list of active IT projects numbered nearly 100. The good news was that Metro employees had many great ideas and, often, access to funding to implement them. The bad news was that the situation led to an overwhelming amount of demands coming at IT from all directions with no unified prioritization and no requirement to align the requests with the organization's strategy. As a result, the department saw little progress on its numerous IT projects, and both the end users and IT were frustrated.

By following the process outlined in this chapter, an IT governance program was established by using existing decision-making bodies and following decision-making processes that were well entrenched in the department. For Metro, the initial IT governance activities focused on adopting and communicating IT principles, reviewing and prioritizing IT initiatives, and reorganizing the IT function to better support the department's operations.

The results—a sanctioned, understandable organization-wide, decision-making process that ensures leadership makes management decisions and IT makes technology decisions. The list of nearly 100 active projects was trimmed to a little more than a dozen agreed-upon top priorities that became the IT function's focus. Additionally, the IT function's efforts were closely aligned with the organization's strategy. Most importantly, the level of frustration decreased significantly, and overall, everyone—end users, IT and the department's leadership—is pleased with the results. In a very short period of time, the IT governance process rebuilt credibility and greatly increased trust in IT.

## Conclusion

While implementing IT governance can cause concern about losing control, in reality IT actually gains control of its IT-related responsibilities and sheds those responsibilities that more appropriately belong to others. Additionally, IT can move from battling for control to working cooperatively through IT governance. Choosing to participate in IT governance is an important step in becoming a more responsive IT entity. IT governance is an inclusive process that breaks down the barriers between the business and IT, where the rewards strongly outweigh the efforts. The bottom line is that implementing IT governance is a win-win. The organization gains the business control it needs for success, and the IT leaders and IT department gain the credibility with the entire organization and freedom to successfully deliver the right IT services, which the business demands.

## Discussion questions

1. Describe how IT governance helps or would help achieve business and IT alignment in your organization. How would the improved alignment support the organization's overall strategy?

2. Consider the IT governance decision areas (IT Principles, IT Architecture, IT Infrastructure Strategy, Business Application Needs, and IT Investments and Priorities) and map them to existing decision-making bodies in your organization. Does your organization have a decision-making body for each decision-making area? Can an existing decision-making body manage more than one area?

3. As you consider existing or potential decision-making bodies for each governance decision making area, identify the type of IT governance approach—business monarchy, IT monarchy, federal system (C-level executives, business leaders & IT), IT duopoly (IT & business leaders), feudal system (business units or process leaders), and anarchy (each individual)—used for input and decision making.

4. Describe how IT governance supports (or does not support) the overall strategic business cycle (plan, budget, execute and measure) in your organization. How could it be improved?

5. Describe how IT governance helped or could help IT gain more control of responsibilities that are appropriate for IT and transfer to business leadership responsibilities that are more appropriately theirs.

6. If you want to implement or enhance IT governance in your organization, where would you begin? Who would you enlist to assist you?

**Liza Lowery Massey** *left public service in 2005 to establish The CIO Collaborative to provide CIO advisory and consulting services. She is also an adjunct professor in the College of Business for the Executive MBA program at the University of Nevada, Las Vegas, a Senior Fellow with the Center for Digital Government, and a Columnist for* Public CIO *Magazine. Previously, Ms. Lowery Massey served as the CIO for the City of Los Angeles and, prior to that, the City/County of San Francisco. During her public sector career, she was recognized in the Top 25 Doers, Dreamers & Drivers of IT in Government. Ms. Lowery Massey can be reached at liza@ciocollaborative.com. Visit www.ciocollaborative.com for more information about The CIO Collaborative.*

**John K. Beaird** *serves as President of The CIO Collaborative. Most previously, he was an IT Manager for Clark County, Nevada, and prior to that served as IT Director in Clark County, Nevada's District Attorney's Office. He has extensive, hands-on experience and a thorough understanding of public sector IT needs. Mr. Beaird has proven leadership skills in business-focused IT alignment in complex, diverse and often competing environments. His strong project management skills are proven by successes ranging from IT strategic planning consulting engagements to managing complex system conversions for thousands of users. Mr. Beaird can be reached at john@ ciocollaborative.com.*

# REFERENCES

1 Peter Weill, Director, Center for Information Systems Research (CISR) and Senior Research Scientist at MIT's Sloan School of Management and Jeanne W. Ross, Principal Research Scientist at CISR, *IT Governance: How Top Performers Manage IT Decision Rights for Superior Results,* Harvard Business School Press (June 2004).

2 ditto

3 ditto

4 Murphy, Tony, *Achieving Business Value from Technology,* John Wiley & Sons, Inc., 2002.

5 Peter Weill, Director, Center for Information Systems Research (CISR) and Senior Research Scientist at MIT's Sloan School of Management and Jeanne W. Ross, Principal Research Scientist at CISR, *IT Governance: How Top Performers Manage IT Decision Rights for Superior Results,* Harvard Business School Press (June 2004).

6 ditto

# 6. IT Consolidation: Tearing Down the Silos

**RICHARD MCKINNEY**

It has been my experience that if you bring a group of government CIOs, CTOs and IT directors together and ask them to talk about their respective organizations and the current challenges they face, it usually doesn't take very long for the word "silos" (sometimes "stovepipes" or "cylinders of excellence") to creep into the conversation. And, while the exact definition and meaning of silos may vary slightly from conversation to conversation and from jurisdiction to jurisdiction, the term certainly has come to symbolize for many people what is the current greatest challenge for IT in state and local government. And, it's one of those terms that we seem to always use in a negative sense. The decentralization of IT over the past 20 or so years has left its toll, and so we curse the silos and the stovepipes. But, what exactly does that tell us about where we have been, and perhaps more importantly, what does it tell us about where we need to go?

As the former CIO of the Metropolitan Government of Nashville and Davidson County, having served in that capacity from 1999-2005, I personally grappled with the difficult issues of IT decentralization and its consequences. When I accepted the position in late 1999, we had just received advance word from Governing Magazine that in its "Grading the Cities" report to be released in its February 2000 issue, it would be giving Nashville a grade of D+ in the area of information systems, the lowest grade given to any of the 37 major cities in the survey. And, not surprisingly, in its critique, it pointed directly at our decentralized approach to IT and the legacy mess that it had created. So, for the next six years, understanding and correcting the ills of decentralization was the principal focus of our efforts to turn the situation around. As I try to trace the origins of decentralization and the promise and potential of a new approach often referred to as IT consolidation, I will try to draw on those experiences to illustrate the challenges that are a part of this transformation.

## IT's evolution in state and local government

Let's begin by tracking the evolution of IT in state and local governments from its beginning to the present day. It's often helpful to understand where you have been and how you got to your present circumstances in order to chart a new course. And, while some may correctly argue that there are certainly some exceptions to what I'm about to outline, my experience over the years in talking with literally hundreds of my peers at all levels of government across this county leads me to strongly believe that this story of evolution varies only slightly from jurisdiction to jurisdiction, and that the exceptions are few and far between and are clearly outweighed by the similarities.

Information technology in state and local government began in the 1960s with early mainframe computers. Central IT shops often began as data processing divisions embedded in the finance or administrative departments, although many eventually became independent and separate departments. The computer shops typically began by providing very basic accounting and payroll services. Some of the systems were commercially developed off-the-shelf software, while many others were internally coded and developed software systems. But, whether an embedded division or a separate department and whether driven by commercial software or home-grown systems, the highly centralized IT shop was the sole source for computing power in the government. It required highly skilled, formally trained and specialized staff, and in most cases relied heavily upon the relatively expensive maintenance and support of the mainframe vendor. In many ways it was, as they say, "the only game in town." That was the heyday of centralized mainframe computing. But, as Shakespeare once wrote, "Therein lies the rub."

As the 60s rolled into the 70s, many of the departments of government began to resent what they perceived to be marginal to poor performance at a high cost, often made even worse by poor customer service. They grew tired of their perception that their businesses were being taken for granted. They believed that their unique line-of-business needs were not understood by the central shop and, therefore, were not being met. That combination of performance issues, rising costs, poor customer service, and what is often a complex and difficult-to-understand billing system, naturally led many departments to question both the cost and value of what they were receiving. The IT shop was seen strictly as a cost center, one that did not know the business, living in an ivory tower and speaking a funny language that no else understood. But, with essentially nowhere to go, their only option was to grow even more dissatisfied and to make that dissatisfaction widely known. That dissatisfaction with the only game in town sowed the seeds for the exodus that was about to take place.

Beginning in the late 70s and into the early 80s, new technologies became commercially available that began to change the balance of the equation. Smaller, departmental-sized computers (sometimes referred to as mid-range computers) hosting a new generation of commercial off-the-shelf, line-of-business applications led a number of departments and agencies to conclude that they would be much better off if they could buy, install and control their own separate IT environment. It was like the second coming. And, who could really blame them for thinking that local control might mean better service at a better price? Wouldn't most of us have seized such an opportunity given the same set of circumstances? I suspect some of you reading this are the very ones who thought it wise and made the decision to bolt. I certainly have to include myself.

And so, with the clear hope and promise of doing a better job of meeting their IT needs, departments began to procure, install and operate their own information systems. It is important to note here that those decisions were not driven by a desire to get in the "IT business" per se. They didn't wake up one day and decide to buy shiny metal objects, but rather they were driven by a desire to buy, build and manage the mission-critical business solutions unique to their departments. It was the promise and potential of the software and not the ownership of the hardware that was generating the buzz and the incentive. What went unnoticed is that as each department set off in a different direction, no two vendors' technologies were capable of working with one another, further isolating one department from another. And so, the silos and stovepipes began to rise across the state and local government landscape. The shift from a centralized to a decentralized IT world was in full swing.

As the 80s gained speed, another factor rapidly accelerated and then radically altered the shift: the emergence of the personal computer. At first, the PCs were stand-alone workstations, often bought and used simply for the computational power of the new and unique "spreadsheet" technology, and/or the ease of a new generation of word processing. Ironically, many of the central IT shops initially resisted the new technology, often deriding the PC as nothing more than a "toy."

They failed to recognize the transformative and empowering effect it was having on the workplace and on the workers themselves.

But the PC hardly remained a toy. What began as the simple stand-alone DOS-based command line computers of the mid-80s, steadily falling in price and at the same time doubling in processing power every several years in accordance with what became known as Moore's law, eventually evolved into the more powerful and complex networked graphical user interface workstations that began to emerge in the mid-90s.

Parallel with the steady hardware evolution, another factor contributed to the continued transformation. The software developers who had originally built the first generation of mission critical business applications on the mid-range platforms that initiated the process of decentralization increasingly moved their application development to the emerging industry standards of the graphical user interface—the Windows/Intel (Wintel) and Unix platforms. No longer tied to a specific hardware manufacturer as they were in the mid-range era, the next generation of applications found a broader marketplace. And so, the "dumb" terminals that once connected everyone to the first-generation departmental mid-range computers were steadily replaced by local area networks (LANs) of powerful PCs connected to increasingly sophisticated file, print and application servers.

By the mid to late 90s, the pendulum had swung almost entirely from one extreme to the other, from the initial centralized shop to the decentralized end of the continuum. So, let's stop for a moment and take a look across this decentralized landscape. The typical government found itself with an IT shop and staff in virtually every major department. Most departments had separate local area PC networks. And each had similar but disparate hardware, software, staff and services.

To give you an example: When I assumed the role of CIO in Nashville in late 1999, the city government had major IT installations in approximately 19 separate physical locations. It is hard to refer to those locations as data centers, as many of them hardly qualified as such, in some cases occupying nothing more than a broom closet. There were approximately 57 separate LANs with separate user domains and 11 email systems. Of the 240+ IT employees citywide, only 70 resided in the central shop. To put it simply, Nashville was reinventing the wheel in almost every department. And, early attempts to build a wide area network (WAN) by stitching together all of the LANs that had been built and configured independent of one another virtually guaranteed that the WAN performance would be very erratic and undependable.

So, in all of the governments (and in most businesses, lest we forget that this phenomenon is not unique to the public sector) that followed similar and parallel paths, it might be easy to be critical of the decisions that led to decentralization, hindsight always being 20/20. But that would be unfair. It would be an attempt to rewrite history and affix blame where none is deserved. Decentralization was not a mistake. It was the natural progression based on the evolution of the technologies themselves. And to be fair, some departments independently achieved their objectives and built reasonably capable and competent IT shops. That has to be acknowledged and applauded. But typically, most did not fare as well. Outside their core business competency, they struggled with IT infrastructure issues, vendor relations, systems development and maintenance, and all of the various underlying technical issues that IT independence requires.

The once-strict discipline of IT went out the window, as well. Backups, code documentation practices, etc., were spotty to non-existent. What they thought and hoped would be a clear path to better business solutions too often became a day-to-day struggle with the technical infrastructure itself. And. that struggle with the technical infrastructure too often kept them from being able to focus on those mission-critical business solutions. The business solutions that were to be the objective of the decentralization often became the victims instead. At the same time, the elected officials with enterprise responsibility could no longer see into all aspects of the government as the decision-making information was decentralized, as well.

What happened to the central IT departments during all of that? Often increasingly marginalized, the central shops continued to work with the few remaining departments that, for a number of different reasons, chose not to make that exit. They continued to depend upon the home-grown and increasingly antiquated applications residing on their legacy mainframe computers. Their budget and staff size steadily decreased. Worse, morale often plummeted as the central shops began to accept their diminished role. And, of course, performance suffered as a result.

In Nashville, the self-fulfilling downward spiral by the IS department had for years run parallel to the less-than-successful decentralization attempts by most of the other departments. Together, those two tracks brought us to the D+ grade from Governing Magazine. We had hit bottom. That was the bad news. But, the good news was that we had hit bottom. How is that possible? Think of it this way: When your organization is considered at the bottom, in virtual "last place," there is not much of a legacy to defend or protect. In a very ironic twist, that failure became our blue sky. Think of it as the "if you ain't got nothing, you got nothing to lose" opportunity. We seized that opportunity to change, and that became our mission and our focus.

Before we move on to discuss what came next, let's take note that this is obviously just one condensed version of how stovepipes took over the IT landscape of state and local government organization. Is it typical? Having discussed the subject of "stovepipes" many times with my peers from around the country, I know that no two stories are exactly the same. But, there are many common threads that run through all of them. The similarities far outnumber the differences. How we got where we are might vary from jurisdiction to jurisdiction, but the consequences of decentralized stovepipes are all too familiar to most of us. They are at the genesis of many of the problems we are grappling with today. Those consequences include:

- ◆ threats to network and data security due to competing and conflicting network hardware and software technologies and policies;
- ◆ missed cost-saving opportunities/economies of scale by procuring, hiring and maintaining disparate technologies and support staff;
- ◆ difficulty in sharing of data, either internally or externally, due to conflicting data standards and technologies;
- ◆ lack of governance, enterprise standards and policies, making future planning and budgeting difficult, if not impossible.

There are certainly others, but whatever the set of circumstances that led to the decentralization of IT in the governments we serve, today it is dealing with these consequences that should teach us and drive us to finding a better way to do business.

# Centralized or decentralized?

So let's ask ourselves this question: centralized or decentralized? We have established that centralization didn't work because a single, central IT shop could not manage and support the myriad of unique mission-critical business solutions needed by all of the different departments and agencies. We also have established that the decentralized model did not work for the reasons outlined above. So, where do we go from here, and what do we mean when we talk about IT consolidation?

It is widely known that in survey after survey of CIOs and CTOs over the past several years, IT consolidation is consistently the number one issue. And yet, the term "consolidation" is itself controversial to some, often interpreted by its skeptics and detractors as a thinly veiled desire to return to the "good old days."

But, is it true that consolidation is nothing more than advocating a simple return to centralization? Knowing what we know about the past, that would seem destined for failure both from a technical as well as a political perspective.

Or can consolidation be instead a whole new way of thinking about IT? What if we could stop the pendulum from swinging back and forth, and agree to find the appropriate balance point between centralization and decentralization instead? What if we could agree that some basic enterprise core infrastructure, business productivity and application services can be most effectively and efficiently delivered by a central service provider?

Take email as a simple and obvious example. Why would any government need or want more than a single email system? Beyond email, there is a whole range of other basic IT services that are not unique to each department and provide a ready cost-savings opportunity to consolidate into a shared enterprise service. If we could agree on that, then could we also agree that the management of departmental-specific services and applications would still be best handled by the departments themselves in a decentralized model? Because let's remember that what triggered decentralization in the first place was the department's need to control its mission-critical solutions and not a desire to get into the IT hardware business.

## The five essentials to successful IT consolidation

OK, problem solved. We have found the balance point between centralization and decentralization, and now the transformation can begin. Right? Well, it's not that easy. If it were, consolidation wouldn't have been the number one issue on everyone's list for as many years as it has been. There seems to be a host of issues and roadblocks with consolidation that have slowed its acceptance, adoption and deployment. The slow but steady shift from centralized to decentralized spanned a considerable number of years, and it is going to take a reasonable amount of time, effort and agreement to re-engineer the arrangement.

So, what are those issues and roadblocks, and what will it take to overcome them? In a general over-arching sense, probably the greatest impediment to change is the never-to-be underestimated power of the status quo. As has been noted, in the typical decentralized government there are any number of departments with their own IT shop. To put it plain and simple, that is someone's home turf. The departmental IT directors aren't going to just hand over their networks, infrastructure and basic services to the central IT shop, regardless of how good an opening argument the CIO makes. Nor should they. There are a number of important factors that have to be in place in order for this type of re-engineering to succeed.

## Strong executive support

Without a doubt, the first point—and the most essential ingredient in any attempt to reconsider the IT direction, policy and governance—is strong executive support. The mayor, the county executive or the governor must be directly involved. Without their involvement and without their political clout, it would be difficult, if not impossible, to generate the type of support needed. I have seen a number of successful IT consolidation projects over the past few years, but I do not know of a single one that did not have strong and unwavering executive support. It is first among equals. Whether we like to admit it or not, government has a very strong inclination toward the status quo, and that inclination has to be directly confronted and surmounted. A CIO alone cannot make that happen.

I quickly learned that when I first assumed the role of CIO in Nashville. In my initial conversations with the department IT directors about our decentralized legacy situation, I heard quite clearly from them that any proposal to consolidate basic IT services was going to be met with considerable skepticism. It didn't matter to them whether it was the right or responsible thing to do. Their primary concern was their ability to meet the needs of their department. Initially, they really did not believe that consolidating would help them in any way. They were of the opinion that the central IT shop would not be able to provide them with the same level and quality of service that they currently enjoyed by managing their own shop. They were quite content, and in some cases very determined, to remain decentralized.

So, I quickly learned that consolidation had to be first and foremost a business decision, and that decision had to be made by the executive decision makers, in that case the mayor and the finance director. So, I took my concerns and my ideas to them and convinced them that the overlap and duplication of hardware, software, staff and services had a considerable financial cost as well as a very real security threat, and that the financial and human resources we were leaving on the table with our duplication were the very resources we needed to invest to make improvements in our overall IT service delivery. Without their strong support, no argument would have been good enough to convince the various departments that change was in everyone's interest. The mayor and finance director agreed to drive consolidation through their relationships with the departmental directors and through the budget process.

## Reliable enterprise services

But, there is a catch-22, a flip-side to strong executive support. It's the old "careful what you ask for, you might just get it" maxim. One of the common side effects of decentralization was the deterioration of the central IT shops, both in terms of physical, as well as human resources. Often left with less and less to manage over the years, the central IT shops lost significant numbers of employees and talent, as well as the confidence and trust of the independent departments.

Again, in my experience in Nashville, the Information Technology Services Department (ITS) had become a shadow of its former self, and departmental morale was at an all-time low. When I first met with the ITS department, they were quite candid with me about their difficult situation.

They were under-funded, under-staffed, poorly trained and, as a result, were not held in high regard by the outlying departments. We first had to restore our ability to win the departments' trust and their business before we could have any meaningful conversation with them about our collective future. We had to quit thinking and talking about them as adversaries and start recognizing them as customers and partners. We had to demonstrate that we could once again be a reliable and cost-effective provider of enterprise services.

This is a key lesson for anyone tackling IT consolidation: Moving away from the decentralized mode is going to take hard work, time and patience. I have seen a number of IT consolidation projects that moved faster than the actual rebuilding of the central department's capabilities. That is a recipe for problems and sometimes failure. In Nashville, we decided to start rebuilding from the ground up—literally—with the network.

During the late 90s, there was one new enterprise assignment given to the ITS department, and that was building and maintaining a WAN. The WAN was to connect the various LANs that had been architected and built independent of one another by the various departments. Email, data sharing and access to the emerging Internet were the driving forces behind the need for a WAN.

The WAN was built using the dark fiber that Metro had negotiated with the CLECs (companies that set up shop to compete with BellSouth for local phone service) as part of their franchise agreements with the government. Two pairs of dark fiber wherever they went were reserved for the government's use. The major government buildings in the commercial part of town were immediately within reach of that fiber.

However, from day one, the WAN lacked an overall planned enterprise design. Instead, it was built more as an accommodation to the various LAN technologies and communication protocols arrived at independently and used locally by the departments. That lack of a central planned design created a network that was unacceptably unreliable and vulnerable to attack. And, because the responsibility for the WAN had been given to the central ITS department, its subsequent problems only reinforced the department's long-held reputation of poor service. So, that was our first priority.

We spent most of the first year largely focused on the WAN. Not only did that focus stabilize and eventually repair and rebuild the WAN, it began to repair the ITS department's reputation as well. Even more importantly, in doing so it provided us with an issue platform upon which to have a dialogue with the various departments about the network and enterprise services in general. That dialogue eventually led to a mutually beneficial approach to the network's control, operation and governance. We all came to understand that the logical network was every bit as important as the physical network, and that the logical network required us to talk to one another about standards, communication protocols and policies. We had to decide together how we wanted to build the network that would serve us all.

It became apparent and instructive to us that a basic service like the WAN needed to be provided and controlled as a centralized, enterprise service. And, the wave after wave of viruses and worms that we battled during that time period only further reinforced the point. We learned the hard way that the network could not have many masters. In today's world, any inconsistency in network design and/or its operation is the crack in the door through which viruses and worms seek to deliver their payload.

So, I tell this story to make a second point: Any consolidation effort has to be built upon the central shop's ability to deliver quality services. The departments of government cannot and should not be required or forced to relinquish authority over the provisioning of basic services without the assurance that the central shop can deliver a reliable enterprise service that meets or exceeds the requirements of the departments. For centralized hardware services to succeed, the delivery of that service has to be high quality and have high availability. The network has to work. The servers have to work. Service level agreements (SLAs) have to be carefully crafted to spell out in detail the performance expectations and measured targets. They have to clearly and carefully delineate the delegation of responsibilities between the central service provider and the customer. Ultimately, we will be judged not how we perform during good times but on how we respond in times of crisis to a particular situation and how we follow the terms of our SLAs.

We all know that there is no way to build a perfect network or perfect hardware platform. Even achieving 99.9% reliability means almost nine hours a year where you are "down." So, how we perform during a service interruption or a crisis, and how we define, execute, measure and report our performance through an SLA is everything to our customer and our relationship. Best practice is that the central IT shop is willing to enter into meaningful and enforceable SLAs much as they would if they were to outsource the delivery of the service to a contracted private sector partner. Any consolidation effort that does not begin with an honest search for a definable win-win will make an already difficult transition that much more problematic and contentious.

## Governance

A third essential follows right on the heels of the second, and that is a governance structure that brings everyone to the table and gives everyone a voice. Again, the consolidations that I have seen that looked more like forced death-camp marches result in the same type of animosity that existed during the waning days of centralization. If the goal of consolidation is to find the balance point between centralization and decentralization, and to stop the pendulum from swinging back and forth from one extreme to another, then that consolidation effort should be seen as beneficial to all concerned.

The best and probably only way that can be accomplished is to adopt a governance structure that both informs and builds consent. Now, understand that doesn't mean that everyone can or should agree with every decision. Lest we forget, those decisions ultimately and rightfully reside with the business decision makers. But, the execution of those decisions can and should have input from all of the parties involved and represent everyone's best efforts to achieve a win-win.

In search of a governance model that would build on our early success, we decided to embark on an enterprise IT strategic planning process. Early in our second year, we engaged a consulting firm, Gartner Consulting, to objectively guide us through the planning process. Our goal was to take stock of where we were and to collectively lay a blueprint for where we wanted to go.

First, a technical advisory team was assembled to work closely with Gartner through the initial assessment and inventory stage. The team was composed of technical IT representatives from numerous Metro departments, both large and small. The team also was chosen to clearly include and represent those departments that were initially cool to the idea of making any changes. It was our hope going in that their participation and collaboration would give the final product a better chance to be broadly accepted. Without their buy-in the plan wouldn't stand a chance of broad acceptance.

Second, we formed an executive review committee. The committee's purpose was to review and eventually approve the findings and recommendations of the technical review team. The committee was composed of business (not IT) representatives from the same wide range of departments that were chosen for the technical review team.

A funny thing happened as the technical team worked their way through the long and difficult process. Technology by technology, or "brick by brick" as Gartner referred to it, they surveyed each and every facet of IT—a total of 50+ technical "bricks," including databases, network protocols, operating systems, etc. Each brick was studied and inventoried. That first step came to the painful conclusion that our government, because there was no central authority and coordination over IT purchasing, owned nearly every technology on the market.

In addition to inventorying the current state, the technical team also was required to make firm recommendations, again "brick by brick," as to where Nashville as a whole needed to be two and five years out with each of the different technologies, what was to become a standard, and which technologies needed to be retired. To do that, the team had to step outside their customary role of thinking about IT strictly in terms of the needs of their respective departments. *That was the key breakthrough.* Sitting through a series of meetings with a roomful of their peers forced everyone to see and think about IT in terms outside of their local departmental responsibility, and to directly face the consequences and challenges Nashville had with so many disparate, competing and conflicting technologies with few or no standards. For us, that is where our standards-definition methodology began. Standards didn't have to be imposed. They could be born out of a fair and open discussion of issues by those affected by them.

Their final product reflected a remarkable shift in perspective. They reached a consensus that Metro Government had to begin to develop and enforce enterprise IT standards and policies. They recommended the formation of a series of communities of interest, forums that would bring inter-departmental teams together to tackle specific concerns like network security, imaging and any other IT issues and technologies that spanned multiple departments. They recommended a governance model that would lead to the creation of an Information Systems Council and the creation of a formal CIO position. Those recommendations were approved by the mayor and issued as an executive order.

The transformation in perspective that the technical team experienced has, over the years, proven to be even more valuable than the final strategic planning document itself. Working together and achieving consensus showed us all that there was a mutually acceptable way out of our shared dilemma. We could and should find the balance point between decentralization and centralization.

Over the next year, we began to implement the recommendations. The communities of interest began to meet and to work through their respective issues. New and emerging technology standards were set and accepted. The Information Systems Council began to meet, approve and issue IT policy, as well as further review IT needs and the aspirations of the various departments. We replaced the aging WAN's original ATM equipment with a more robust SONET backbone, setting the stage for tackling voice/data convergence. We created a revolving fund that allowed us to standardize and centralize the purchase of desktop PCs and software, with a stated goal of a three-year refresh period. The responsibility for purchasing, configuring, deploying and maintaining PCs shifted from the departments to central ITS. With departments now seeing new standardized PCs being delivered and reliably supported as an enterprise service, confidence in the ability of ITS to meet their needs continued to build. And, the cost of centralized hardware and software purchasing fell dramatically as we began to flex the muscle and leverage of our increased purchase bargaining power.

Our fourth year, 2003, ended with the Center for Digital Government ranking Nashville in sixth place in their annual Digital Cities Survey, a top 10 ranking that has been maintained ever since. We clearly had reversed our downward spiral and restored a measure of credibility to both our department and our government. We had a meaningful governance structure and strategic planning process in place.

## Planning

So now, with strong executive support, restored confidence in our ability to provide reliable enterprise services, governance and strategic planning setting our direction, we began the planning process for server consolidation. We all knew that the process of combining our physical assets and staffs was going to be a challenge, and it was a challenge that all of us recognized could not be done overnight. The breadth of decentralization meant that we were going to have to proceed in a methodical step-by-step basis. We decided that we would begin with some of the smaller agencies and departments, especially those who were admittedly struggling with their decentralized IT shop and needed (and now wanted) our assistance. Some might call that picking the low-hanging fruit, and that is a fair way to describe our approach. By starting with smaller departments, we allowed ourselves the opportunity to learn and discover all of the challenges and pitfalls that the consolidation of core infrastructure and human resources entails.

In each department, we began with a discovery process that allowed us to identify the servers and other hardware that would be moved to our central data center. We also inventoried each department's IT staff. Our goal was to identify those positions that were primarily assigned to their core infrastructure and those positions that were responsible for maintaining their applications and core business solutions. That was in keeping with our plan to leave decentralized the department's ability to support their mission-critical applications locally.

Smaller departments presented somewhat of a challenge in that there was considerable overlap between infrastructure and applications, with some employees wearing a number of hats when it came to support. We overcame that challenge by building a matrix that identified the percent of time each staff person devoted to a range of infrastructure and application activities, and then totaled those percentages to arrive at a fair estimation of composite FTEs for each activity. That allowed us to determine the number of positions that would be transferred with the physical infrastructure and the number that would be left in the department in application development and support.

The thorny issue that remained was to determine which specific employees would be transferred and which ones would remain. We worked hard to make that determination as fair as possible and then worked equally as hard to make the transition for the transferred employees as seamless as possible, acknowledging that while servers had no opinion about where they sit, employees do. We recognized that, at first, they would be unable to see what would happen to them after consolidation. It is those same employees who are going to make or break your consolidation.

So, as a team we met with each transferred employee to talk about their career future with the stated purpose of achieving a win-win. That proved to be of immense help in dispelling the employee's understandable trepidation. That aspect of consolidation and its impact on success cannot be overstated. While IT is, without a doubt, a technical endeavor, its ultimate success depends considerably more on the human angle than it does on the hardware and software. To miss that point is to invite failure. Good communication is absolutely critical.

By beginning with the consolidation of the smaller and less complex departments, we fine-tuned the process as we progressed and, thus, set the stage for the consolidation of the larger and more complex departments. They watched the process unfold and were increasingly reassured that consolidation would be successful and that their service needs would be met. Each departmental consolidation plan was fully documented and included a full service level agreement that spelled out enforceable performance measures that took into account the unique requirements that varied somewhat from department to department. The entire consolidation process took more than a year to complete.

To be fair, and in the interest of full disclosure, the one exception for server consolidation was the police department. For both policy and physical reasons, we decided to leave their hardware in their data center. The physical reason was very simple: They had a considerable amount of equipment in their well-maintained data center, and we simply would not have been able to accommodate their server footprint in our central data center. The policy reason was they made the argument that the security nature and needs of their business required them to remain segregated. While it is true that you could make a very strong counter-argument that those needs still could be accommodated in a single data center, we made the political and management decision to grant them that autonomy. That decision was made in the full light of our governance structure and process.

So, the fourth lesson learned is that there is no substitute for careful consolidation planning, review and execution. Unfortunately, there isn't a reproducible blueprint that could be handed from one jurisdiction to another. I have tried to use my Nashville experience, not as a plan to be imitated, but rather as an example of how one step connects and leads to another. It is an organic process that has to take into consideration the unique requirements and circumstances that every jurisdiction, large or small, faces. No two jurisdictions are the same, and no two consolidations can be the same. Their eventual success lies in the discovery and mediation of those differences, and in the ability for reasonable people to sit down and discuss what is in the best interests of the enterprise and how those interests can be met.

## Balance

So to the final point: Where is the balance point between enterprise and departmental needs and responsibilities? Do we draw the line above both the network and hardware layers but below the application layer? It would be nice if it was that simple, but it is not.

The application layer can and will run both centralized and decentralized applications. Determining whether or not an application should be centralized or decentralized, we first have to define the nature of the business process. Some business processes are generally consistent across the entire enterprise and obviously should be centralized. Take the enterprise applications that are provided as part of an ERP system—general ledger, A/R, A/P, payroll, asset management, etc.

Every department, for example, shouldn't do payroll in a separate application. Besides robbing the economy of scale of having just one application to own and maintain, it would further complicate overall enterprise analysis and reconciliation of critical business data. The enterprise has a responsibility to manage those types of applications centrally.

Some applications are a hybrid of enterprise and department, like GIS. While the enterprise will find it beneficial to maintain a central GIS application, each department should own and manage its unique layers. Having that standard allows local control and enterprise analysis at the same time.

Lastly then, there are other applications that address business processes that are unique to a single department. They obviously are managed best by the specialists who understand the underlying business processes that the software addresses. Again, thinking back to what spawned the exodus of the department from the centralized model, you will see an attempt to find a better business solution. Their pursuit and embrace of decentralized technologies was fueled by the promise of better business solutions. If we can free them from the responsibility of having to build and maintain IT infrastructure outside their core competency, we can give them the opportunity to refocus and concentrate on the business processes that should be served by that application layer. It is the design, control and management of the application layer that ultimately determines the quality of the business solutions to the government and to the departments.

In review, here is what I would offer as the five essentials to successful IT consolidation.

1. **Strong executive support**—Without the political will and clout to advance, no consolidation plan can gain the necessary traction and ultimately be successful. This prerequisite is first among equals.
2. **Reliable enterprise services**—Departments and agencies cannot and should not be expected to rely upon the enterprise delivery of services without the assurance that those services will be equal to, if not better than, the services they have historically provided themselves with the decentralized approach.
3. **Governance**—A transparent and collective means is needed to ensure that all voices are heard, and that the IT planning and decision making is a joint effort that includes all of those who rely upon their business needs being met by the centralized provisioning of services.
4. **Planning**—The careful documenting, architecting and execution of the transfer of the appropriate physical and human resources to the enterprise service provider should include a communication and marketing plan for the affected employees. Dropping them an email won't do; you need 1:1 and town hall-style meetings. Listening to those affected is central to good planning.
5. **Balance**—Find the workable balance point between enterprise and departmental needs. A successful consolidation clearly defines the difference between enterprise and departmental needs, and addresses those needs with a win-win service delivery.

So, is the IT consolidation model the answer? Can we centrally manage reliable, secure and cost-effective core infrastructure services and enterprise business applications, and at the same time provide departments with the hardware and software platforms they need to manage their decentralized, departmental-specific, mission-critical applications? And in doing so, can we finally stop the pendulum from swinging back and forth from one end of the continuum to the other by learning from our past successes and mistakes and incorporating the best of those experiences into a balanced service delivery model? That is the challenge that we accept when we say embrace our current situation, tackle the difficult technical and political questions of IT consolidation, and declare that it is time to "tear down the silos."

## Discussion questions

1. What, if any, are the obstacles to IT consolidation in your jurisdiction? Do you have a plan to tackle those obstacles? Where do your business decision makers stand on the issue?
2. Does your jurisdiction have a governance model that brings all of the IT interests together for meaningful enterprise technical and policy discussions?
3. Does your central IT shop have a reputation for quality service? If not, what can you do to rebuild that capacity?
4. Do you have the resources you need for careful consolidation planning? If not, how can you build that capacity?

**Richard McKinney** *is a Government Technology Advisor for Microsoft State and Local Government. Richard joined the State and Local Government team in November of 2005. Prior to that, Richard served as Chief Information Officer for the Metropolitan Government of Nashville and Davidson County, a consolidated city/county government. In that role Richard led the Department of Information Technology Services from a "last place" ranking in the 1999 Governing Magazine "Grading the Cities" survey to a top 10 finish in the Center for Digital Government annual "Digital Cities" survey in each of the past three years. Prior to working for Nashville city government, Richard was the Director of Information Services for the Tennessee General Assembly from 1995 to 1999. He served as Assistant Commissioner of Administration for the State of Tennessee Department of General Services from 1987 to 1995. Richard holds both a Masters Degree in Public Administration and a Bachelor of Science degree from Tennessee State University.*

# 7. Information Technology Governance

**ADAM J. RUJAN**

## Introduction

Information Technology managers are the people who deliver the steak after the vendors sell the sizzle. I have yet to meet a practitioner who will disagree with that description.

With the endpoint for technological advancement nowhere in sight, each new announcement from a major vendor offers new possibilities and new challenges. IT governance is the approach that an organization takes to managing its investment in technology, as well as managing the people and processes it affects.

Most cities and counties have commoditized the purchase of basic technology components. Buying things like PCs, printers and thumb drives tend to be routine purchasing transactions. In most jurisdictions, there are well established policies and procedures for executing those transactions. Those types of purchases fall well within the existing governance structures of most cities and counties.

When technology offers the opportunity to improve interactions with constituents, streamline enterprise-wide processes, or reduce the cost of a service defined by statute, the guidelines and rules are usually insufficient. Those types of technologies offer lots of sizzle, but their deployment is far more complex.

Implementing technologies of that sort may require policy changes or even new laws to be written. That elevates the technology investment to a strategic level, calls for more complex decision criteria and relies on the governance structure to formulate the appropriate decision.

Frequently, those types of technologies represent a significant expenditure. As with most technology, the price tends to decrease with broad adoption. Technologies offering the opportunity to transform old bureaucracies are becoming affordable to most communities. Once a challenge reserved for only the largest cities, technology governance challenges now are becoming commonplace. Web-based solutions, document management and data warehousing are a few examples of technologies in that category. As a practical matter, more cities and counties are searching for best IT governance practices to resolve technology implementation and management issues.

As an example, the CIO of a mid-sized city recently shared her experience installing a new Enterprise Resource Planning (ERP) system. It was their first fully integrated ERP, and the city was eager to realize as many productivity improvements as it could. Unfortunately, it spent more than two years locked in arguments between the departments over issues such as basic process changes, data ownership, and authorizations and security clearances. Those arguments became so contentious that the city manager created an entirely separate department to manage the ERP system and its related processes. The ERP department is not the finance department, nor is it the IT department; It is an entirely separate department reporting to the city manager.

The new department is authorized to referee the disagreements and has been in place now for several years. As a practical matter, the costly department could have been avoided through more appropriate governance structures. Had the existing governance structure anticipated the issues that were likely to be raised, and developed a process for resolving some of the inevitable conflicts, the city would have saved considerable time and cost.

IT governance is the key to integrating the people, processes, technology and information that are necessary to meet an organization's business goals. A definition of IT governance that I find to be comprehensive is the Australian Standard for Corporate Governance of Information and Communication Technology, 2005, which reads:

> *The system by which the current and future use of IT is directed and controlled. It involves evaluating and directing the plans for the use of IT to support the organization and monitoring this use to achieve plans. It includes the strategy and policies for using IT within an organization.*

The purpose of this chapter is to assist organization leaders, boards and council members to better understand how to govern their investments in IT for optimum value and improve their organization's business operations. Although not intended as a model for complete implementation of IT governance, the information in this chapter is written so that employees associated with local governments at all levels may better understand the importance and purpose of IT governance and how it works.

This perspective is particularly important given that one of the key strategies to ensure that IT governance works is to continually evaluate and monitor its operations at all levels in the process. Another principle upon which IT governance is based is ensuring that IT delivers value to the organization and manages its resources well. Within any organization, the senior management team provides policy and direction:

◆ IT management implements technology programs based on that direction;
◆ IT staff deliver the programs and provide feedback and service levels back to the management team.

It becomes obvious that formal communication among all levels is critical to the success of the IT governance model.

## Driving forces for stronger IT governance

### ROI considerations

A fundamentally sound explanation and argument for the premise that an effective IT governance must be in place for an enterprise to be efficient was demonstrated by authors Peter Weill and Jeanne W. Ross in their book *IT Governance: How Top Performers Manage IT Decision Rights for Superior Results* (2004, Harvard Business School Press). The authors maintain that the real reason IT often fails to deliver value is that organizations have no formal system in place for guiding and monitoring IT decisions. Their book argues that organizations need IT governance systems to ensure that IT investments are made in accordance with the goals of the organization. In fact, they assert that an appropriate IT governance structure is the leading determinant in whether the organization realizes the promised return on project investment.

It is not uncommon for the elected officials and upper level management of a local government to experience difficulties when determining the value on their IT investments. A local government usually can accurately identify how much has been spent on a project, such as a large ERP system, or even multiple document imaging systems used by disparate departments. They also will typically track the ongoing costs of investments, such as the ongoing data maintenance associated with a geographic information system (GIS).

Monitoring the costs associated with such systems is important. The costs can run hundreds of thousands of dollars for even a small city. Eventually someone will ask, "Did we get a good return on our investment?" The challenging part is almost always quantifying the return and, in many cases, even identifying the returns.

At issue is the evolving nature of many of today's technologies. Specifically, most of the costlier systems allow local governments to realize substantial gains in efficiency and effectiveness across one or more departments. Those types of costs are not readily tracked by standard fund accounting systems, the accounting method used by the public sector. Unless a local government specifically establishes an approach to tracking returns, it may never really know the returns that it has received from a technology.

That challenge also played out for my friend at the city with the ERP department. The city controller was the original project champion. He identified the need for improved reporting, functionality and the fact that the old accounting system was no longer being supported by the vendor. The controller convinced the manager and city council that replacing the system was necessary. When the controller and the IT director went shopping, they found a host of vendors and systems available on the market. Many of the systems offered workflow capabilities, document imaging modules and other impressive features that offered to save the users time and money. The city bought one of the impressive systems based on the fact that it fixed the controller's problems and offered the city streamlined business processes. After all the implementation challenges, the mayor asked, "Did we really get the promised return on our investment?"

The controller was focused on converting a large number of management reports for the elected officials and training his staff to use the new system. The CIO was fighting implementation fires. The DPW director was focused on designing the new cost accounting system to better track the costs of future road projects. The community development director spent her energy ensuring the new reports were capable of responding to the needs of her funding sources. Etc., etc., etc. All of those responsible and competent managers were tending to their areas of responsibility, so nobody is able to answer the mayor's question. Nobody identified in any comprehensive way all of the impacts of the new system, and nobody (including the new ERP department) established any comprehensive baseline or measures to track improvement. They tried after the fact to calculate a return on investment, but found it a frustrating and time consuming exercise. The mayor never got a complete answer.

In hindsight, the city did realize many of the vendor's promises and experienced some significant productivity gains. It may have even exceeded the hoped-for ROI but cannot prove it. The project champion, the controller, only had operational responsibility for one department. While that is typical, the returns are realized in many departments. The multi-departmental or enterprise nature of these technologies is what defies "standard" accounting.

IT governance is part of the solution. Appropriate IT governance models specify the ROI analysis that the organization will require. As such, the participating users can be engaged in identifying and tracking the costs and savings up front. That makes the task of calculating the ROI for any IT project a very possible and realistic analysis.

## Transformational nature of technologies

A second major driving force for stronger IT governance in an organization is the transformational nature of many new enterprise level technologies. Specifically, the ability of technologies—like workflows, wireless communication, imaging and handheld devices—to enable workplace transformation is well established. Those technologies and others have allowed some very significant changes to not only how work is performed but also to the nature of the work.

In a government setting, the kinds of services and, in some cases, how the services are provided may be prescribed in statute or in the organizations charter. In most cases, the rules were established long before the current technology. In some New England communities, for example, the rules may even extend back to the 1600s when some forms of local government were created. Those statutes, policies, procedures and promises were based on the technology of the day. It is not unusual, therefore, that current technologies require changes to the organization that extend well beyond the hardware and software.

Project sponsors are typically at a manager or department head level. Their level of authority is often limited to their organizational boundary, and possibly to only nominal changes to processes for which they are responsible. Any significant transformation, such as going "paperless" or streamlining a process that spans multiple departments, can easily require authorization from the highest levels of the organization. If the transformation requires a change to a statute, authorization may even extend to the voters.

A strong IT governance model will anticipate changes to process, policy and job duties within the confines of their organizational authority (i.e. up to the legal authority of the elected officials). The model forecasts such changes to ensure that a project can be successful. For example, a high functioning organization will identify the changes that are expected, and assemble a team with the competencies and authority to simultaneously address the people and process aspects of the technology project at hand. Evidence of failures include "shadow systems" (duplicate systems that are maintained because the user cannot rely upon the "main" system), and many significant implementation cost overruns where a new technology has been modified to duplicate the existing process.

## Alignment with management objectives

Strategic alignment is concerned with making investments in harmony with strategic objectives (content, strategy and goals) so that an organization has the capability to deliver business value. Strategic alignment also ensures that departments will more likely use IT resources to achieve their business objectives in an efficient and effective manner; closely aligning projects with the organization's common business goals.

One of the major purposes of effectively aligning IT governance with management objectives is to ensure that there is an effective allocation of limited resources between competing interests. To achieve that, a system or process is needed to better communicate the organization's business needs and strategies, costs, benefits and associated performance tradeoffs. That will provide direction to and enable the CIO and senior management to align decision-making with the organizational goals and optimize the IT investment decision.

Approaches to making major technology investment decisions are as varied as the local governments that make them. Some focus on limiting projects and use a "squeaky wheel" approach to investing. Others report they have used another county's or city's solution only to be disappointed that the solution didn't fit their problem. Some admit to feeling overwhelmed by the technology possibilities and delegate the IT governance challenge by letting department managers make independent decisions. It is not uncommon to hear department directors confess that they do not really understand how their own organization makes major technology investment decisions.

Project Portfolio Management (PPM) is a component of IT governance that addresses that challenge. Even mid-sized organizations will have multiple projects in progress and multiple lists of proposed future projects. In fact, it is very common to find medium-sized cities and counties maintaining multiple future project lists that contain hundreds of individual project requests.

The essence of PPM is identifying, tracking and measuring decision-making criteria. A continual assessment of IT projects generally results in a reshuffling of priorities and budgets. Because one of the primary purposes of PPM is to determine the optimal mix and sequencing of proposed projects, all levels of the organization participate in the assessment.

Another major goal of PPM is to ensure that an organization's portfolio of IT-enabled investments is aligned with the organization's strategic objectives. As a result, departments across the organization analyze the information and make recommendations so that projects do contribute value. Weill and Ross (224) report on companies that follow a specific strategy. They demonstrate that companies in the private sector with above-average procedural controls tend to have 20 percent higher profits than companies that follow the same strategy but had poor control.

The same principles apply to the public sector in that appropriate control and alignment of investment strategy will maximize the return to the local government. A comprehensive IT governance strategy has the possibility of not only providing greater control over IT demands, priorities and expenditures, it also can improve the level of engagement between IT and management objectives. The approach shows even more positive results as decisions, particularly at the senior level, are made in a known and consistent manner.

## Organizational considerations

IT can be deployed through a very centralized IT department. IT can be deployed through a highly decentralized model of IT professionals embedded in user departments. In most cases, the actual model is a combination of both approaches. The objective of IT governance in a hybrid model is to find the right balance for the particular organization.

The centralized approach tends to offer greater economies of scale, higher levels of standardization and consistency, and tighter enterprise security. Highly decentralized models tend to be more user-centric, responsive and optimize costs at a local level. The typical tradeoff is efficiency versus user satisfaction.

An appropriate IT governance model will create a forum to find that balance and determine the most advantageous deployment and support strategy. Further, the balance between efficiency and end-user satisfaction is based on the needs of the organization, which are not static. Organizational needs change based on economic conditions, priorities corresponding to election cycles, and even changes and evolution in technology.

To illustrate the need for balance, consider an average-sized county located in the Midwest. Its public safety operations were typical with respect to technology. Its shop included a significant number of IT staff, which managed many of the software applications, dispatch operations, and much of the hardware and related equipment. That level of decentralization was appropriate originally due to the unique nature and needs of the public safety community. Unique records systems, specific dispatch regulations and requirements, and a unique operating environment all contributed to the need for a specialized unit to optimize the technology applications delivered to the various public safety units. Not surprisingly, user satisfaction ratings ran high among the public safety professionals, who received technology that closely matched their requests through the highly decentralized IT deployment strategy.

At the urging of vendors and others in the law enforcement community, the agency financed and built an entirely duplicate infrastructure to serve as the communications backbone for the various public safety operations. The rationale for the duplicate infrastructure was for greater "security,"

| IT Organizational Model | Typical Strengths | Typical Weaknesses |
|---|---|---|
| **Centralized** | • Economies of scale<br>• Uniform standards<br>• Architectural control<br>• Asset protection<br>• High integrity<br>• Enterprise security | • Danger of isolation<br>• User frustration<br>• Communications costs |
| **Business Partner** | • Business unit led initiatives<br>• Leveraged development standards<br>• Central architectural control<br>• Sourcing and budget flexibility<br>• Development and sharing of best practices<br>• Distribution of competencies<br>• Business/Technology integration | • Management support of governance must be strong<br>• Enterprise architectural diffusion<br>• Challenge of matrix management<br>• Potential redundant costs<br>• Unproductive technical diversity |
| **Decentralized** | • Responsiveness<br>• Business awareness<br>• Local control of priorities<br>• Appropriateness of solutions<br>• Local cost control<br>• Rapid development<br>• High integrity | • Architectural diffusion<br>• Redundant cost and efforts<br>• Lack of long-term flexibility<br>• Enterprise learning<br>• Isolation of best practices<br>• System integration challenges<br>• Data consistency and sharing challenges<br>• Central IT frustration |

**Figure 7-1.** Organizational Model—Graphic 1

and as such, the agency was advised to build separate LANs, WANs and communication systems to avoid unauthorized access to confidential information. That perception of greater security may have been based in some fact at one point in time. An independent review of the infrastructure indicated that with the evolution of technology and advances in IT security protocols, the centrally managed network was actually more secure than those systems that are managed separately. The IT professionals embedded in the public safety department did not have a formal background in IT and were falling behind with respect to best IT security practices. Consequently, the county spends a significant amount of its IT budget annually to maintain, upgrade and install duplicate, public safety infrastructure, which is actually less secure.

The optimal approach, as many cities and counties are finding, is a balance between the two. A business partner-type of arrangement between centralized IT resources and the decentralized embedded resources appears to be the optimum configuration in many cases. Business partner models tend to maximize the use of available competencies within the organization, take advantage of best practices and technology standards, while optimizing the unique business needs of the user department. The disadvantages include some ongoing unavoidable redundancies and a more complex matrix management task. The need for strong IT governance becomes very apparent when trying to operate under that type of structure.

## A model for effective IT governance

The information presented in this chapter is not an exact template for other organizations to follow. Formulating the structure of IT governance and demonstrating its active role in the organization is both an art and a science. An effective approach to strengthening IT governance is to integrate it into the organization's existing management structures, existing approval paths and existing meeting structures. Approaching IT governance in that way greatly increases the likelihood of both adoption and ongoing use of the key structures and decision-making processes.

It is important to keep in mind that implementing good IT governance is almost impossible without an effective overall management structure. The framework, regardless of the organizational model, defines which decisions need to be made, who is involved in making them, how they are made and the process for ensuring the decisions are carried out appropriately. At its core, the IT governance model seeks to direct the IT investment, including defining ROI considerations, establish and monitor an effective deployment strategy, and establish policies for the use of IT in the organization.

The CIO office cannot be a surrogate for IT governance, but is pivotal in facilitating and implementing IT governance. In smaller organizations, the CIO office may be one-person, while larger organizations may share the space with several staff members. The CIO office participates in both policy development, acting as a key advisor to senior management, and deployment, with primary responsibility for enacting policy and delivering results.

A key component of strong IT governance is the active involvement of senior management. Large organizations may establish an IT steering committee. In many small- to mid-sized organizations, that includes inserting IT decision-making into the "cabinet," or senior management team, which frequently consists of department directors and the city/county manager, along with the CIO.

The key responsibility of the cabinet is to direct the IT investment decisions. It is the keeper of the ROI model and develops the criteria for project approval and funding. It also monitors and gives

| | IT Policies & Procedures | IT Standards | Annual Technology Planning |
|---|---|---|---|
| **City/County Manager (CMO)** | • Approve recommended IT policies and procedures<br>• Communicate IT procedures | • Approve recommended standards<br>• Communicate standards | |
| **Cabinet/ Management Team** | • Review and recommend IT procedures to CM | • Approve IT standards | • Review and update, as needed, the Strategic Technology Imperatives in terms of relevance and priority |
| **CIO Office** | • Recommend policies and procedures to the Cabinet for approval | • Recommend IT Standards to the Cabinet for approval<br>• Identify IT standards that need to be developed<br>• CIO to participate on Standards Committee | • Draft updates to the Strategic Plan |
| **Technology Standards Committee** | | • Develop and maintain IT standard deviation request process<br>• Develop and recommend City IT standards to the Cabinet for review<br>• Review and provide recommendations related to City IT Standards deviation requests<br>• Maintain the IT standards repository for the City | |
| **Ad-Hoc Committee (Line of Business)** | • Understand the relevance of developed IT policies and procedures to the technology standards function<br>• As needed, develop IT procedures in areas deemed necessary by the Cabinet | • Understand the relevance of developed IT standards as it applies to the subcommittee's charge<br>• Review deviation requests from City IT standards and recommend to the Cabinet | |
| **Department IT Liaison Staff** | • Understand the relevance of developed IT policies and procedures to their Line of Business (LOB) | • Understand the relevance of developed IT standards as it applies to their IT initiatives | • Review and update, as needed, technology goals applicable to the LOB |
| **Central IT Staff** | • As needed, develop IT procedures in areas deemed necessary by the Cabinet<br>• Identify areas where IT procedures need to be developed<br>• Participate in the development of IT procedures<br>• Implement recommended and approved IT procedures | • Assist with the development and communication of IT standards for those areas that are deemed as core to the City ITS function | • Provide input to Plan |
| **Department IT Staff** | • Review and provide feedback on draft IT policies and procedures<br>• Participate in the development of IT procedures that impact their area of operation<br>• Implement approved IT procedures as appropriate<br>• Adhere to and support the developed IT procedures | • Review and provide feedback on draft IT standards<br>• Adhere to and support the developed IT standards | • Provide input to Plan |

**Figure 7-2.** Organizational Model—Graphic 2

| Annual Technology Budgeting | Departmental and Line of Business Projects | Enterprise Projects |
|---|---|---|
| • Review and approve budgets and requests to the City Council | | • Authorize and support enterprise level projects |
| • Develop and maintain the ROI model<br>• Develop and maintain the project prioritization criteria and weightings<br>• Review, rank and prioritize adhoc committee, CIP and non-CIP project requests to the City Manager | | • Gives life to potential enterprise initiatives that may originate from multiple sources (City ITS, departments<br>• Initiate the Cabinet subcommittee to evaluate enterprise initiative feasibility<br>• Conduct periodic monitoring of enterprise projects |
| • Develop recommended IT budget | • Approval of all IT projects based on IT Strategic Plan and standards | • Approval of all IT projects based on IT Strategic Plan and standards |
| • Develop ROI and budget requests for enterprise projects | | • May provide project oversight to multi-departmental projects |
| • Review and rank departmental IT initiatives | • Often first line of support | • Often first line of support |
| • Work with departments in developing project ROIs<br>• Provide staff capacity input to the Cabinet | • Coordinate with department IT staff or perform directly | • Support enterprise projects |
| • Participate in development of project ROIs<br>• Identify IT initiatives for the upcoming fiscal year | • Coordinate with Central IT<br>• Implement department level projects where appropriate | • Coordinate with Central IT |

life to major enterprise-level projects. Additional responsibilities of the cabinet include approving IT standards, and reviewing and updating as needed, the strategic technology imperatives in terms of relevance and priority.

The roles and responsibilities of the city/county manager's office (CMO) tend to be focused on carrying out policies. Approving recommended IT policies and procedures and communicating those procedures throughout the organization are major responsibilities of the CMO. The CMO also approves recommended IT standards and reinforces that information throughout the organization. As part of the budget cycle, the CMO reviews and approves budgets and requests to the elected governing body for approval.

The well-managed CIO office usually participates on the cabinet and is responsible for recommending policies, plans and standards to the management team. CIO office responsibilities typically include drafting updates to the IT strategic plan, particularly for annual technology planning and developing the IT budget. Additional responsibilities regarding business and organizational projects include approving all IT projects based on the IT strategic plan and ROI criteria established by the cabinet.

A complete IT governance model also generally defines roles and responsibilities for all central IT as well as decentralized user department-embedded IT staff, and defines the critical linkages between the two. Those relationships are subject to change over time at the direction of the cabinet, corresponding to the needs of the organization. Additionally, the governance model may identify both standing and ad hoc committee structures.

For example, many organizations have a standing IT standards committee, comprised of representatives of central IT as well as user departments. The responsibilities of a technology standards committee may include:

- ◆ establishing technology usage standards,
- ◆ developing and recommending architectural standards to the cabinet for review,
- ◆ developing and maintaining the IT standard deviation request process,
- ◆ reviewing and providing recommendations related to the organization's IT standards deviation requests; and
- ◆ Maintaining the IT standards repository for the organization.

An example IT governance model for a mid-sized organization is included in the Organizational Model—Graphic 2. Again, the specifics can vary based on the size of the city/county and on the management structures used for general governance of the organization. The core principles and features of the model, however, appear to be reasonably scalable and applicable across a wide range of public sector organizations.

## Conclusion

Accelerated and pervasive technological change is likely to continue to be a dominant feature of the future environment for organizations. The ability of organizations like cities and counties to manage that change will be determined in part by their ability to manage their IT investments well. That, in turn, will be dependent on their ability to integrate best IT governance practices into their decision-making processes.

Clarifying the decision-making process and areas of accountability in an organization go a long way to reduce the risk of increased costs and poor performance. An IT investment represents a strategy to improve an organization's performance. The closer aligned the investment is to specific organization objectives and policies, the more likely there will be performance improvement. Successful organizations respond quickly to changing market conditions and improve their performance by taking careful risks. IT governance contributes greatly to that model by assessing risk and facilitating the people and process changes that surely will accompany the technological change.

## Discussion questions

1. Why is IT governance becoming an issue for many communities?
2. What are some characteristics of strong IT governance models?
3. What are some characteristics of weak IT governance models?
4. What is the goal/purpose of IT governance?
5. Why is measuring return on investment so elusive in some cases?
6. What is the role of Project Portfolio Management (PPM)?
7. Why is PPM an important concept?
8. What are some arguments for centralizing or decentralizing IT staff?
9. What is the role of the CIO in IT governance? Other senior managers?

**Adam J. Rujan,** *is a Partner with the Government Consulting practice of Plante & Moran, a large management consulting and accounting firm. He has more than 20 years experience, and has personally consulted to over 500 hundred public-sector organizations. Mr. Rujan's experience includes assisting governmental units with organizational and operational analyses, productivity improvement, and feasibility and ROI studies. He has developed specific expertise in assisting organizations understand, plan for and implement new technology. Mr. Rujan has significant experience assisting clients redesign complex processes to improve performance. His clients have included a wide range of local municipalities, counties, agencies and authorities, and state government. He is a frequent presenter and has authored numerous articles for a variety of professional organizations. Mr. Rujan earned an MBA from the University of Michigan, and holds a BS degree in engineering.*

# PART TWO:

# Leadership & Innovation

# 8. Barcelona 2.0, A Major Business Transformation

**ANDREU PUIG AND PILAR CONESA**

## 1. Barcelona, Mediterranean Metropolis

Barcelona is one of the largest European metropolises. Located on the shores of the Mediterranean Sea in the northeast of Spain, it lies at the center of an extensive metropolitan region of more than 217 municipalities. With just over 1.5 million inhabitants, but more than 4.5 million in its metropolitan area, the city is spearheading the use of new technologies as a strategic key element in its governance road map.

Barcelona is a reference point in relationships among the Mediterranean countries. In December 2008, the choice of Barcelona as the headquarters of the Union for the Mediterranean culminated the work carried out in the defense of Mediterranean cooperation. The Union for the Mediterranean comprises 43 countries, 27 of which are European Union Member States.

Activities such as services for businesses, cultural industries, audiovisual production, information and communication technologies (ICT), biotechnology or the aeronautics industry, are all on the rise in Barcelona. Similarly, trade, logistic services, restaurants and gastronomy, medical services, design and advertising, among others, are activities that enjoy a great tradition.

**Barcelona Metropolitan Region**
Surface: 3,236 km²
Inhabitants: 4.8 million
Municipalities: 217
6th metropolitan concentration of Europe
5th industrial concentration of Europe

**Barcelona City**
Surface: 100 km²
Inhabitants: 1.6 million

Barcelona is the European city that provides the best quality of life to its workers, according to the European Cities Monitor, which is published every year by the international consultants Cushman & Wakefield Healey & Baker. It has maintained this leading position for the last seven years.

Barcelona is an active, vital and dynamic city that reinvents itself year after year, and is always looking toward the future. Nowadays, the city is immersed in the most important urban and economic transformation in its recent history. The city never stops, and continues to address new projects for the future geared toward consolidating and expanding economic development in the new parameters of the Information Society, the international position, social cohesion and quality of life. The projects transcend the actual city and cover its metropolitan environment, in what is a clear commitment to the metropolitan city concept.

## 2. Evolution of the city management model

Barcelona always has been a pioneering city in terms of introducing changes to the management models of city councils of the major European cities.

Barcelona was the first city at the end of the 1980s to address, on one hand, a decentralized model based on districts and, on the other hand, the creation of a distinct executive structure to separate the responsibilities of political and executive powers.

Four main stages that have underpinned the management criteria may be identified:

- 1978–1983    First democratic reform
- 1984–1991    The age of efficacy
- 1992–1997    The age of efficiency
- 1998–2007    Maintenance of quality/cost equilibrium

Management criteria were focused in each stage, according to the established objectives. The key management instruments for accomplishing the objectives were adapted to each case:

| | BCN Stage | Priority City Council | Key Instrument |
|---|---|---|---|
| 1979–1983 | Creation democratic society | First democratic reform | Information |
| 1983–1991 | Preparation OG '92 | Efficacy | Deconcentration of structure (managerialization) |
| 1992–1997 | Economic crisis | Streamline and efficiency | Economic control |
| 1998–2007 | High standard of living and globalization | Quality/Cost equilibrium | Economic control |

**Figure 8-1.**

We will draw our attention to the two stages that led to the greatest number of changes in the management model: the efficacy and efficiency stages.

## The age of efficacy (1984-1991)

The age of efficacy began with the appearance of the democratic city councils that attach priority to providing more services to citizens, and to improving their quality, bringing policies closer to the citizens and bringing about an initial and radical transformation of the city.

Different processes may be distinguished in this stage, each one with its own timeline:

- The first wave of territorial decentralization (1984-1991)

    The most visible process of internal transformation was territorial decentralization, which had two objectives: to bring the political decision centers closer to citizens, and implement systems to improve relationships with citizens.

- Functional decentralization in companies and institutes

    Together with the territorial decentralization, another process was undertaken, consisting of creating new and more flexible and autonomous forms of management, to break away from the straitjacketed, centralized and bureaucratic model, due to a strict interpretation of the law and an overburdened central structure. Different forms of management were developed, ranging from the creation of companies, private municipal concerns and institutes, through to intermediate formulas, such as management centers.

The fundamental objective of the process was essentially the 'managerialization' of the organization. Every autonomous organization had self-organization capacities and powers for administration of their resources (with certain limitations), and their management could thus be held accountable, evaluated more by the results achieved than by bureaucratic activity.

♦ The improvement of the services provided to the citizen, the beginning of integrated attention (from 1985)

Coinciding with decentralization, a movement was undertaken to improve the efficacy of the services that were rendered to citizens. The idea was to provide services that improved their quality of life. It should be said that in many cases they did not fall—and do not fall—to the strict competence of the Barcelona City Council.

The 010 Service, a telephone information service, began to operate in 1985 and made a qualitative leap when, in 1990, citizens also were offered the possibility to carry out formalities related to the city council. That was the seed of what might be termed "integrated attention."

## The age of efficiency (1992-1997)

This period began with the idea of the post-Olympic municipality. The new technologies facilitated radical changes and made it possible to increase both productivity by reducing expenses, and efficacy by improving the quality of services. It was in this period when the greatest degree of decentralization was achieved, in which the new technologies played a decisive role.

The following processes merit special mention:

♦ Management control and cost containment (1991-1995)

From the initial lukewarm attempts at the implementation of managers in the functional divisions and the creation of management centers, it progressed with increasingly greater determination toward a company structure.

♦ The second wave of decentralization (1995-1998)

The second wave of decentralization went even further than the first, and many of the powers that were still with the central sectors were decentralized. Decentralization heralded a very important revolution in the city council's administrative procedures on different fronts at the same time: decentralization of powers and human resources; changes in formalities/procedures; streamlining and promotion of integrated attention; and harmonization and integration of information.

♦ The city council as a company: the first wave of process reengineering (as of 1995)

The only way to achieve harmonization and consistency was to formalize well protocolized procedures for the most frequent and well-established tasks. At the same time, the improvement of procedures and protocols had to render it possible to measure and increase service productivity, "industrializing" the process.

♦ Integrated attention: Citizens' Attention Offices (1993), the Internet and the city council online (as of 1994)

Progress was made in the concept of Citizens' Attention, taking it beyond mere centralized information. The objective was to make it easier for citizens to carry out their formalities all over the country through the creation of 11 Attention Offices. The back office and communication systems became critical elements of a good service to citizens.

The advent of the Internet offered a new technological opportunity to extend interaction between the citizens and the city council considerably. The web of the Barcelona City Council was started up in May 1995 and became a new channel alongside the 010 and the Citizens' Attention Offices. The Internet was set to become the channel that would render it possible to provide citizens with a high-quality information service, but it was also to help to do away with the paper phase in formalities.

## 3. The new city challenge

Throughout its history, Barcelona has demonstrated its great capacity to adapt and redefine itself in a changing environment. Certain aspects of the city's social and economic life have made a decisive contribution to what has been called the Barcelona model.

| **Barcelona City Council** | |
| --- | --- |
| Civil servants | 13,000 |
| 2009 budget | 2.438M€ |
| 2008-2011 Investment | 2.500M€ |

**Figure 8–2.**

This city model has combined growth with social cohesion, urban development with an in-depth remodeling of the neighborhoods, diversity with coexistence, the growth of employment with innovation, the recovery of traditions with a sound commitment to creativity, and a model of management and public services of proven efficacy, efficiency and responsibility in terms of results.

Now, the evolution of a model that includes the new challenges emerging from the city's new social, economic, cultural, technological and territorial realities must be tackled—challenges that are defined by the evolution of the Welfare Society, which requires major priority in service provision.

| | BCN Stage | Priority City Council | Key Instrument |
|---|---|---|---|
| **1979–1983** | Creation democratic society | First democratic reform | Information |
| **1983–1991** | Preparation OG '92 | Efficacy | Deconcentration of structure (managerialization) |
| **1992–1997** | Economic crisis | Streamline and efficiency | Economic control |
| **1998–2007** | High standard of living and globalization | Quality/Cost equilibrium | Economic control |
| **2008–2015** | **Welfare** | **Quality** | **Processes and people** |

Figure 8–3.

2008 heralded a new stage for the city, marked by the **Welfare Society,** with three main axes:

♦ **Social cohesion:** with the universalization and improvement of services and facilities, and the welfare of citizens and social and territorial quality as the main priorities.

♦ **Economic dynamism:** a city of opportunities, committed to innovation and creativity as the best guarantee moving forward.

♦ **Urban transformation:** building the city of tomorrow, equipping it with more and better infrastructures, managing the future.

The Municipal Action Program, approved following a participation-based process to mirror citizens' opinions, defines the challenges facing the city in the coming years:

| Strategic Line | Description | Challenges |
|---|---|---|
| Coexistence in proximity | Promote, expand and improve quality of services and public space in the neighborhoods | Neighborhood/district oriented planning |
| Social cohesion and inclusion | Guarantee equal opportunities for all citizens | Provide high-quality service |
| Sustainability | Achieve progress committed to sustainability, the environment and mobility | Social responsibility |
| Knowledge economy | Promote competitive economic development | Committed to the new technologies |
| Capitality | Consolidate Barcelona's international image and lead the economic and social development of Catalonia | Promote leadership & innovation |
| Good Governance | Implement good governance that leads change and the transformation of Barcelona | Objective-oriented management |

Figure 8–4.

# 4. The new management model: Barcelona 2.0

The new stage in the city is defined by quality objectives. In recent years, the services rendered to citizens have increased substantially, and the current challenge is to provide those services with excellence, focusing on quality versus quantity.

Over the last few years, society has evolved toward the Welfare Society, which has led citizens to become increasingly better informed and more demanding.

To be able to cater to this new scenario, the management model must also evolve and be oriented to:

♦ **Proximity**—The Barcelona City Council is organized in 10 districts, each one with administrative offices that manage the municipal services. The Municipal Action Program establishes the objective of rolling out infrastructures focused on the 73 neighborhoods to be able to address the particularities and special nature of each one.

♦ **Quality**—To increase service quality, it is necessary to rethink the way services are provided and make sure that citizens perceive the change and that their level of satisfaction increases.

♦ **Efficiency for the citizen**—The city council must be able to manage services, while also improving efficiency from the citizen's standpoint, sparing them unnecessary formalities. A proactive and innovative administration is called for.

To this end, Barcelona has implemented the **Barcelona** 2.0 Plan for the promotion of a new management model, led by the Mayor and the Deputy Mayor responsible for internal affairs and managed by the CEO.

The Barcelona 2.0 Plan focuses on:

♦ Improving municipal functions and services oriented toward the **citizen** and **quality**.

♦ Promoting **proximity** by defining a new **territorial model** that will leap from the 10 districts to the 73 neighborhoods with a new vision of proximity, physical and virtual.

It is not a question of deploying 73 administrative offices, but rather of reorganizing the city council, channeling both central and district services toward the neighborhoods. The new Territorial Model means centralizing certain functions to guarantee efficiency and homogeneity of quality in all points of the city.

It is a model based on centralized production and the rendering of services from the territory.

♦ **Innovating processes** through intensive use of ICT.

The improvement of quality and efficiency vis-à-vis the citizen requires a reengineering of processes to reduce formalities and simplify processes. Moreover, it should be remembered that this innovation in processes will call for legislative changes in order to adapt the legislation to the new scenario of the relation between citizens and the government: eGovernment.

♦ **Measurable management** with results-oriented objectives.

The new approach to achieve high-performance quality services requires a results-oriented culture.

The eventual accomplishment of those objectives means complete changes in the organization: it entails changes in the way services are provided, organizational changes, changes in the way public employees work, and changes at resource level.

Those changes are underpinned by two axes: the development of eGovernment and the new territorial model.

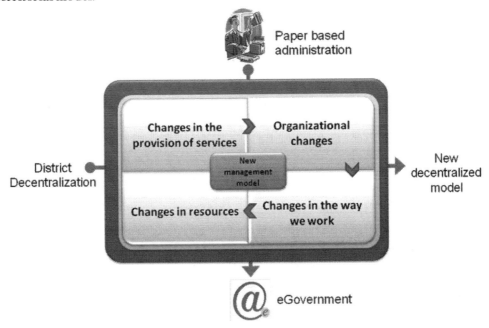

**Figure 8–5.**

♦ Changes in the provision of services:
  – Revamped and reinforced concept of proximity and decentralization.
  – Territory-oriented planning: producing services in a common and targeted fashion, with rugged and homogeneous processes, rendered from the territory, in proximity.

♦ Organizational changes:
  – The central sectors must exercise their management over the local authorities, companies and consortia reporting to them so that they can all move in the same direction: organizational verticalization.
  – The centralized units have to adapt in order to territorialize their action to provide service from the districts.
  – The districts must be geared toward the final provision of services based on proximity and make the leap from the 10 districts to the 73 neighborhoods.
♦ Changes in the way we work:
  – Reinventing processes: making them simpler, more flexible, with the citizens in mind.

– Establishing clear and measurable management objectives.
– Intranet with the information and services needed by every public employee and the promotion of collaborative tools.

♦ Changes in resources:
– Intensive use of ICT to innovate processes.
– Process-wide addition of electronic records, with an end-to-end approach.
– Promoting the ubiquity offered by technology, both in the work of the public employees and in their dealings with citizens.

## 5. The dynamo projects

In order to implement Barcelona 2.0, seven dynamo projects will be developed that will serve to promote and drive change.

The dynamo projects for change are instruments for the deployment of the Barcelona 2.0 model that will make it viable, afford it visibility and be fundamental to the construction of the new management model.

**Figure 8–6.**

| The 7 Projects | Lines of action | Objective |
| --- | --- | --- |
| **Management by objectives** | • Budget by programs<br>• Management by objectives<br>• Strategic Maps (PAM) | • To establish a municipal management methodology in accordance with the objectives of the project that enables an efficient allocation of resources and efficacious monitoring of municipal action. |
| **Catalogue of functions and services** | • Define the catalogue of functions and services<br>• Implement Service Level Agreements (ANS)<br>• Review processes and quality certification | • Classify municipal functions and services in a catalogue that illustrates activities, draw up the process map and establish the basic Service Level Agreements (SLA).<br>• Establish improvements in critical processes. |
| **Territorial model** | • Design the functions and organization of the districts<br>• Revise and adjust the methodology of relationship between districts and sectors | • Design the functions and services of the districts, their organization, resources and the model of interaction with the sectors. |
| **eGovernment** | • Application of ICT to administrative processes<br>• Electronic records and administrative simplification | • Application of information and communication technologies (ICT) to the administrative processes of the city council. |

| The 7 Projects | Lines of action | Objective |
| --- | --- | --- |
| **Interaction with the citizen** | • Major deployment of the multichannel and multimodal relationship with the citizen<br>• Homogenization of provision criteria and promotion of the city council brand | • Redesign and create the support systems needed to apply a new and more proactive culture of relationships, packaging formalities with a product-oriented approach and a transversal, multichannel and multimodal vocation.<br>• Establish the bases so that interaction with citizens is driven by innovative and common criteria of attention, communication and quality. |
| **Technology plan** | • Deployment of the new technologies as an instrument for innovating services and management with a view to accomplishing the quality, proximity and efficiency objectives | • Deployment of the new technologies as an instrument for innovating services and management with a view to accomplishing the quality, proximity and efficiency objectives based on an integrated vision.<br>• It encompasses the deployment of ICT to the other dynamo projects for change. |
| **Human Resource plan** | • Development of human resource management tools to develop the organization's human assets | • It is a project plan that comprises the review of the human resource structure of the city council, the management model for recruitment and people training and development, and the function of the human resource managers, based on the identification of determined strategic lines. |

# 6. The role of ICT in the transformation

The municipal government is opting for a citizen-oriented administration, where ICT must be the driving force of the transformation to achieve a more efficient and flexible administration that offers easier and simpler services to citizens, accessible to everyone and from anywhere. The new technologies are the instrument for innovating services and management, with the objectives of quality, proximity and efficiency.

ICT also are critical in achieving eGovernment, an administration that is closer to the citizen, guaranteeing transparency of management and widening channels of communication and participation. We must rethink processes, leveraging the advantages of technology and making service to the citizen the core of all activities. Innovation in processes and working methodology is unthinkable without the intensive use of ICT.

Technology also is the key to transforming the administration into a proactive administration, using citizens' knowledge and the different channels to make contact with the citizen, offering the services they may be interested in. One of the axes of innovation in the sphere of ICT is the convergence between IT and telecommunications, which is best embodied in:

- ♦ mobility services, which offer applications that are of great use to public municipal services operating in the public thoroughfare; and

- ♦ the integration of channels and devices using very different technologies (audio, video, television, radio, telephone, street panels and stands, etc)

that make it possible to render services anywhere, leveraging the ubiquity and immediacy provided by technology to make the u-city, the ubiquitous city, a reality.

The application of mobility is a clear example of ICT-based processes of transformation.

The two ICT-driven Barcelona 2.0 projects, eGovernment and Technology Plan, summarize the initiatives in four areas:

## Administration close to citizens

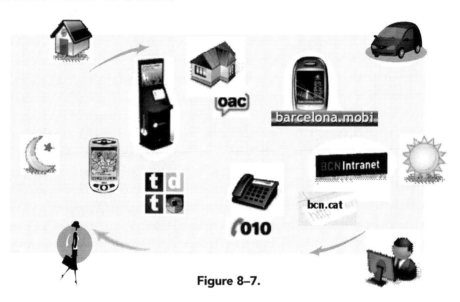

**Figure 8–7.**

Actions to improve attention to citizens by increasing the offer of services and their quality.

- ♦ **Integrated vision of eServices**

  Personalization of the offer for each target (citizen, company, intermediary) that interacts with the city council, taking the concept of multiple channels and multiple devices into account.

- ♦ Citizens' participation

  Exploring the channels of citizens' participation to enable the citizens to express their opinions and participate in municipal decisions. Promote the value of the web 2.0 to roll out social networks. One first step would be the citizens' consultation, via the electronic channel, on the reform of Diagonal Avenue.

- ♦ Interoperability

  Parallel to the availability of technology, there is another key element in facilitating formalities for citizens, namely interoperability between administrations, so that the administration can solve, at the internal level, access to information it already has.

## Flexible and efficacious administration

Actions targeting the improvement of municipal management based on efficient and integrated information systems.

◆ Process reengineering applying technology

Redesign of processes with an end-to-end view and leveraging the advantages of technology, to design the administration of the 21st century. Make the most of the advantages of technology to be flexible and efficacious: use mobility for public employees (police, technical inspectors, social assistants...) and electronic tools.

◆ Corporative management systems

Deployment of the economic and financial and human resource management system in the city council group in order to have a consolidated information system and a basis for the implementation of electronic records.

◆ Intranet and collaborative tools

Apply web 2.0 tools to develop a collaborative environment between public employees. It is a key factor in mobilizing the work force.

## Infrastructure

Actions targeting the improvement of telecommunications infrastructure, the mobility platform, integrated management of the territory and the guaranteed availability of the service.

◆ Deployment of the city telecommunications network

Deploy the city network based on a municipal fiber optic plus a municipal wireless network providing coverage to the municipal services that operate in the public thoroughfare.

## Information Society

Actions that facilitate access to the Information Society by citizens, minimizing the digital gap.

Special mention should be made of the deployment of 500 wireless access points for citizens in municipal spaces throughout the city.

## Conclusions

The intensive use of technology is key to the implementation of the City Council Business Transformation, the Barcelona 2.0 model, so technology is required in the success of nearly all dynamo projects.

ICT are a very powerful and indispensable tool for the development and universalization of efficient and quality public policies at the service of the citizens.

The Barcelona City Council is an international reference point in eGovernment, but efforts to transform management must be redoubled to achieve a more efficient and agile administration that offers easier and simpler services to the citizens, accessible to everyone and from anywhere.

Access to ICT is being configured as a citizen's right. Digital access is a pivotal tool in avoiding social exclusion and guaranteeing equal access to information by citizens. Technology has provided tools that permit new forms of interaction, opening up new horizons in democratic participation and the development of social networks.

The city's vision of the future is closely linked to the deployment of ICT at municipal management and city level. The implementation of the Barcelona 2.0 project entails intensifying the commitment to ICT, driven by a multidimensional and all-encompassing vision that straddles attention to the citizen, the deployment of new services, efficiency of municipal management, citizens' participation and city-oriented policies to guarantee access by citizens to the digital world.

In summary, ICT are a key tool for innovation and transformation to achieve a **proactive and innovative administration, pursuing the objectives of quality, proximity and efficiency.**

**Andreu Puig** *is the General Manager of the City of Barcelona. He is, by direct appointment of the Mayor of Barcelona, the leading executive officer of the Barcelona City Council. His responsibilities include the management of all the departments of the municipality and its holding of institutes and public enterprises, most of which he is a board member. He is also a member of the consulting commissions of several city institutions such as the Barcelona International Trade Fair, the Barcelona Free Trade Zone Consortium, and the Strategic Metropolitan Plan, among others.*

*He previously had developed his career in the fast-moving consumer goods sector in the Spanish multinational Corporación Agrolimen, in which he held several positions as director for Spain, China, the European area, and was in charge of the group's strategy and development from 1996 to 2007. He started his career in the German Henkel Group with different marketing responsibilities in Spain, Portugal and Eastern Europe from 1988 to 1996.*

*Mr. Puig obtained his combined bachelor/MBA degree in 1988 from the ESADE business school in Barcelona, Spain, of which he is currently a member of the board of ESADE Alumni association. The same year, he graduated in the Program of International Management from the University of Cologne, Germany. In 1991 he also obtained his MBA from NYU Stern School of Business, USA.*

**Pilar Conesa** *has held the position of Barcelona City Council CIO since October 2007, and is in charge of eGovernment and Process areas.*

*She holds different management positions in ICT sector companies and public organizations in Spain and abroad, the most relevant one being her former post as General Manager for Public Administration and Health in T-Systems Spain (Deutsche Telekom group). She was involved in the Barcelona Olympics '92 organization committee and worked in South America as CEO of AIS Chile. She has been involved in university organization, collaborating as External Quality Evaluator.*

*Ms. Conesa has a degree in Computer Sciences from the Polytechnic University of Catalonia, and studied Business Management in IESE, one of the most prestigious Business Schools in Europe.*

# 9. Innovation @ Work: Models that Drive Transparency, Engage Citizens and Lower the Cost of Government Operations

## VIVEK KUNDRA

### Apps for Democracy

I believe that true leadership is engaging citizens as co-creators of government. Bureaucratic government, developed as an answer to chaotic management during the Industrial Revolution, sacrificed its relationship with its constituents in the name of efficiency. With time, bureaucrats distanced themselves from citizens, becoming shrouded in secrecy for fear of the "mess" of citizen input. Notwithstanding its inherently anti-democratic characteristics, that style of governance has long outlived its usefulness and is known mostly for its infamous red tape. The democratic leanings of the information age, however, are rapidly putting pressure on government to open its doors and shine some light into its inner workings. It is my opinion that public servants, such as myself, are obligated to comply.

In the District of Columbia, we have embarked on a technological revolution to make government work for "we, the people." The corruption and dysfunction that has marked so many years of governance in the district is slowly beginning to unravel with leadership that believes in a transparent, accountable and responsive state. Citizens are not subjects to be governed; they should be a partner to government in a new era of participatory democracy. The mayor and I know all too well that government does not have a monopoly on good ideas, and thus we turn to the citizens and ask for their assistance in driving innovation in governance. With the philosophy of citizens as co-creators of government in mind, I created the Apps for Democracy contest.

The Apps for Democracy contest is part of our drive toward digital democracy.

Especially in these difficult economic times, it's crucial to the government's mission to find more efficient and impactful methods for delivering an even higher level of service for a fraction of the cost. DC Government's "Apps for Democracy" contest was held over the course of a month in fall 2008 as a part of our effort to enhance services through innovative technologies and engage citizens in what we like to call the "digital public square."

**Figure 9–1.**

Making government data public was one of my first actions in office; we took information on everything from building permits to contracts to crime incidents and made them available online in the form of 216 live data feeds. Shortly after they went public, we noticed that individuals and organizations were not only viewing our data, but were actually improving upon our work by analyzing and repurposing the information in useful ways. One innovative DC resident took it upon herself to aggregate government data on service requests, crimes, and building and public space permit applications to create an online information clearinghouse for her own neighborhood. Thanks to her, neighbors can use her site to track economic and real estate developments in their own backyard. I wanted to leverage the talent and interest of our technologically savvy citizens to co-create tools that deliver value for citizens, businesses and the government.

The contest, which was open to the public, invited technology developers across the nation to compete in creating applications for popular consumer technologies like the iPhone, Facebook, Map Mashups and others, using data from our online data catalog. The very first submission, submitted 24 hours from the contest kickoff, was from an individual who created a location-aware iPhone application that can identify the locations of crime incidents in the surrounding area, as well as tell the user where the nearest Metro station is and when the next train will arrive. The Apps for Democracy contest brought us 47 applications in 30 days, with an investment of $50,000. Had we pursued those terchnologies through the traditional procurement method, we would have spent millions of taxpayer dollars, and the process would have taken years.

## Stock market model

When Mayor Adrian Fenty appointed me to his cabinet as chief technology officer for the District of Columbia, I asked a simple question: Why can I find the real-time stock price and performance of any publicly traded company with a few keystrokes, but I can't get solid information on the performance of information technology projects in the government? My answer was to create a Wall Street model for managing the $950 million-plus district IT portfolio as a portfolio of stocks. In the model, each project is a "company," its team is company management, its schedule and financial status are captured in market reports, and customer satisfaction is the market reaction. The model allows us to balance riskier strategic IT investments with more conservative ones and re-balance the portfolio whenever necessary. The model also fosters government transparency and accountability—we deliver accurate, real-time performance data to officials using web reports, podcasts and videos.

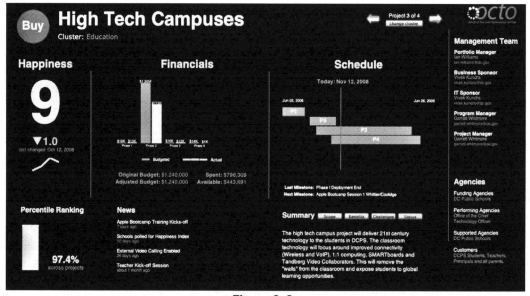

Figure 9–2.

I built a team of five portfolio managers to run the Wall Street model according to three core principles. First, apply the efficiency of the stock market to IT governance. In an environment of shrinking budgets and growing citizen expectations of government, evaluating the performance and promise of IT projects continuously and accurately is critical. With the Wall Street model, we can make fast and sound decisions to "buy," "hold" or "sell" an IT project—that is, invest more financial resources or change management to improve performance, maintain the current resource level or cancel a failing initiative.

Second, I wanted to capture quantitative and qualitative data. The IT stock model incorporates both quantitative and qualitative analysis to provide a holistic picture of the investment. Quantitatively, the portfolio managers analyze vital project statistics, including the schedule, what has been spent against budget, and return on investment. Qualitatively, the portfolio managers evaluate the management team, customer satisfaction and current project-related events to ensure a deep, integrated understanding of the project's drivers and results.

Finally, I told my team to treat taxpayers like investors. We define the portfolio managers' roles as guardians of taxpayer funds. Ultimately, these managers must ensure that all district agencies spend taxpayer dollars wisely on technology investments. The genius of the American stock market is to put capital to the most efficient use, continuously redirecting funds from low-performing companies to high performers. Our IT stock-market model infuses the same efficiency in government, assuring citizens the highest and best use of the tax dollars they entrust to us.

Here are just a few projects we've been able to adjust for millions in cost savings.

♦ **Intranet:** The district planned to invest $4 million to develop a government-wide Intranet using outdated technology. DC Government switched the technology to open-source software to reduce costs by 97.5 percent.

♦ **Report card system:** The city planned to build a new automated report card system for our public schools. However, we found the secondary schools already had automated report cards. We made a smaller $160,000 investment to install a primary school report card system and integrate it with the existing secondary school software

♦ **DC-Net:** A year ago, this state-of-the-art, fiber-optic network was a perfect example of excellent technology badly managed. It ran a $6.3 million annual deficit, it had not added new customers at the planned rate, and costly contract staff sat idle. A change of management and dismissal of the contract staff has resulted in a $4 million surplus, customer growth and high customer satisfaction.

## Cloud computing

No one would be surprised to hear that the District of Columbia government gets our electricity from wall outlets and our drinking water from the tap. What might cause some surprise, however, is our use of "cloud computing," a new approach to IT that treats the Internet as yet another utility.

"Cloud computing" is an innovative way for technology consumers—including governments—to obtain technology resources and services simply and cost-effectively. It's an approach to providing applications through the Internet using massively scalable data centers and a standardized computing platform that can help bring government IT into the 21st century.

Cloud computing is to technology what the electrical grid is to the delivery of electricity or the public water-supply system is to the delivery of water. Once, every household or every little town had its own generator; every farm or village once had its own well. Households or villages had to maintain their generators and wells and protect them from weather, theft and other harm. Today, consumers obtain electricity by simply plugging an appliance into a wall outlet and get clean water by simply turning on the tap—because large public utilities like the power company or the water and sewer company can meet these needs. In the same way, we can meet technology needs by reaching into the "cloud." In the cloud are companies like Google that maintain extensive technology resources, leveraging economies of scale to offer those resources to customers at a reasonable price.

Cloud computing allows us to move away from expensive contracts with software giants like Microsoft and procure information technology as a utility, paying for only what is needed, without the cost and burden associated with owning and operating hardware and software. Upgrades and maintenance on cloud applications are performed by the provider, thus getting the government out of the costly and time-consuming cycle of patching and keeping up with the latest versions of commercial technologies. That shift would allow the government to reallocate IT resources to focus on program missions, rather than providing commodity services. Government technologists can obtain services from the cloud instead of maintaining their own hardware, software, and facilities and staff to house and operate them.

Take email, for example. The district's email system serves 38,000 people. Previously, providing that basic technology service required us to purchase and maintain hundreds of servers, software to run on them, data centers to house the servers, security staff to protect the data centers, electricity to power them, and staff to operate and manage all the hardware, software and real estate. In addition to incurring tremendous cost, we always had to worry about strains on the capacity of our email system, and we were effectively in many other businesses besides technology—like power, real estate and security.

With cloud computing, we can now obtain virtually unlimited email capacity at a much lower cost. Our technologists can get out of the real estate, power and security businesses and instead focus on deploying technology solutions to meet our government service needs—like improving community policing, human services, education and "back office" government operations. Adopting cloud computing also allows the government to standardize computing platforms; increase agency information sharing and collaboration, storage capacity, and compute power; speed application development; and improve information security, continuity of operations and disaster recovery capabilities. By having that information hosted remotely, we ensure business continuity and the safety of data in the event of a disaster or disruption. There's also a significant cost-avoidance here; DC government is saving taxpayer dollars by avoiding taking an alternate route from the traditional e-government path, skipping costly software and security contracts.

In the background, cloud computing is transforming everyday work life for district employees by arming them with more flexible, convenient tools for doing their jobs. Our cloud computing tools now allow employees to connect to district systems from anywhere they have an Internet connection, and to use the consumer technology they know and like—cell phones, iPods, PDAs, YouTube, Facebook and more. Ultimately, cloud computing will help us create the mobile, "anytime, anywhere" workforce. Government employees like police officers, human services caseworkers, building inspectors, and teachers can spend more time—as they should—keeping people safe, caring for citizens in need, teaching our children, and keeping buildings up to code—and still have all the benefits of government technology resources.

As a result, customers from tenants to students will have much more immediate access to district employees and can make their needs known and voices heard more powerfully and effectively than in the past. Workers who need to telecommute or adopt flexible schedules will be able to do so even more easily without losing access to technology tools or compromising their effectiveness. Our ability to offer more innovative, flexible, customer-friendly technology also will help us meet the challenge of recruiting new employees.

Perhaps most importantly, cloud computing allows us to make smarter use of taxpayer dollars. Overall, the fees we'll pay for cloud computing services will be less than our costs of buying, maintaining, housing and operating hardware and software. In addition, our specific uses of cloud computing offer many opportunities for savings. To cite one simple example, with our new procurement wiki sites, we can upload videos of bidder conferences to YouTube quickly at no cost—whereas in the past, producing and posting a single video cost the government thousands of dollars. Multiply that savings by thousands of procurements each year, and the savings mount up fast.

A handful of Web-based applications have become valuable additions to our business processes. They provide savings in both cost and time, while providing services in a secure computing environment.

**Government operations.** Two areas government spends much of its time on are human resources management and procurement processes, but in the district, cloud computing has reduced both the cost and the time it takes to manage them.

♦ In the procurement arena, we created "wiki" sites to publish Requests for Proposals (RFPs) online. A wiki is a page or collection of web pages designed to enable anyone who accesses it to contribute or modify content. The wikis allow us to solicit feedback and share updates with vendors and the public for major procurements. We developed RFP wikis for an IT staff augmentation contract for our technology agency and a new evidence warehouse for the Metropolitan Police Department, allowing bidders to view all materials related to the RFP in one location. Users could not only read the RFPs in their entirety, but also view YouTube videos of pre-solicitation conferences. Updated consistently with new information, users also could get their questions answered in the "Q & A" section and watch the site for amendments to the RFPs and, finally, for awards. In the short amount of time we've used wikis and YouTube for procurement purposes, I've noticed an increased in the quality of proposals from vendors who say they have a greater understanding of the solicitations from the beginning. Our cloud computing tools also have helped us launch procurements faster by enabling government employees to collaborate in creating procurement documents online. The result is not just faster procurements, but more effective and more equitable ones. All interested parties get the same information at the same time, and a much broader range of potential vendors can participate than ever before. With more vendors participating, we extend procurement opportunities to more businesses, and government saves money through broader competition.

♦ We've also put wikis and YouTube to use in transforming the recruiting process. In advance of the mayor's annual Job Fair, we turned the traditional process on its head by posting announcements by video on a wiki page. Prospective applicants could hear from their potential supervisors before the fair and come to interviews better prepared with knowledge about the positions. We asked many leadership staffers to record their thoughts on working at the agency, describe

**Figure 9-3.**

the type of work they do, and discuss the best parts about their job to give applicants a feel for the working environment. That type of detail is above and beyond what is typically offered prior to any job interview, helping yield a better applicant pool, and is created using technology that is completely free and user-friendly.

**Education.** The development of software applications has long been an expensive and lengthy process. A normal application development process involves formal steps of requirements gathering, development, testing, deployment, etc. Unfortunately, there are a lot of business needs that are just not quite important or critical enough to justify the overhead of that software development process individually, but together are the cause of a lot of inefficiency and lost productivity. Tools like Intuit's Quickbase are targeted at that gap.

DC Public Schools had several projects that benefitted in terms of time and cost efficiency, as we were able to use Quickbase to quickly develop applications tailored to their needs. The web-based application allows business users to focus on improving their business process without being interrupted to focus on the system used to manage that process. The system follows the process and is flexible enough to deal with changes on the fly. By being implemented in the "cloud," it also inherently provides for collaboration and information sharing. Its ease of use means that business users are empowered to create their own systems rather than wait for technical resource availability, freeing those resources to focus on where they can truly add value.

DC Government agencies were able to implement 11 major applications and over 40 minor applications for everything from project and workflow management, to disseminating public data, to case resolution tracking, in less than eight months. Were the traditional application development model to be followed, a similar set of applications would have cost millions of dollars and taken years to deploy. At an average cost of $50,000 per application in cost alone, we saved approximately $2.45 million in a year by spending just $100,000 on a year-long license for Quickbase. DC Public Schools has since become highly engaged in creating its own Quickbase applications, some of which have become mission critical to the operations of the central office and others, which have allowed for greater transparency and communication to teaching staff and school administrators.

♦ The DCPS Office of the Ombudsman, for example, needed to track parent complaints to ensure timely response to constituents as well as report monthly and quarterly metrics to the mayor. Previously, the process for tracking was cumbersome and took nearly a year to develop. Generating reports was very difficult, and custom reports were not available. The application itself was very difficult to modify and meant months of work by an outside vendor. The system did capture data but did not drive workflow. With the new, Quickbase-based system, however, a solution was custom-created in-house within two days. It featured custom reports easily created by business users and did not require technical expertise to modify. The office was up and running on the new system, with legacy data imported in, within two weeks. The system tracked workflow and easily reported the status of any case at any point. Before Quickbase was in place, some of the business processes used Excel spreadsheets and Access databases, while the majority simply was not tracked at all. Quickbase allowed business users to drive systems development rather than be constrained by it. It allowed technical resources to focus on those tasks that truly required technical expertise, thus increasing productivity all around.

♦ The "Blackman-Jones" database now in use by DCPS refers to two court decisions against DCPS' Special Education Division. Complaints from parents of case mismanagement resulted in a court decision that requires DCPS to report statistics to the court monitor to ensure that complaints are being handled effectively and quickly. Before Quickbase, DCPS was using a simple spreadsheet to track cases. With multiple document owners, version control problems ran rampant, and workflow could not be tracked. With Quickbase, we were able to quickly develop a tailor-made application and import previous data. The current application not only allows the reporting of statistics to the court monitor, it also allows for workflow tracking to see how cases are being handled as they come in. Different users can now be assigned various permissions as well; principals and special education coordinators, for example, can only see the cases for students at their particular schools. The court monitor was assigned permissions that allow it to run reports itself, rather than waiting for DCPS to fill out a spreadsheet and send it in. Quickbase allowed DCPS to go from a two-dimensional spreadsheet with no data controls or data integrity to a full fledged, three-dimensional database with a full set or permissions and reporting capabilities.

**Public Safety.** Our first responders—and, as a result, citizens—have benefitted immensely from the use of cloud computing technologies. With over 2,000 employees, the district's Fire and Emergency Medical Services (FEMS) needed a scalable solution for quickly disseminating information. The FEMS Chief has been able to leverage the tools from Google Apps for both personnel and emergency management purposes. His staff needs no formal training to use Google Apps to create a web site and post training information and videos for access anywhere in the world. Employees don't need to have VPN access set up at home for a secure connection; They can simply sign on to Google from their home computer with their DC Government username and password, and we can rest assured that the data is secure and private on Google's servers.

Google also is helping first responders respond even faster during emergencies. With Google Earth, firefighters now determine the location of both functioning and non-functioning fire hydrants en route to an emergency, rather than scrambling for an operable hookup upon arrival. In advance of emergencies, FEMS can search for and locate community services and critical infrastructure, like dialysis centers, and notify incident commanders of their proximity to emergencies in case their services are needed. FEMS employees have access to Google Apps in their mobile units and, thus, are able to access unlimited amounts of critical, meaningful information within moments of a reported emergency. In short, we've turned from providing technology to providing services with the aid of cloud computing. Public safety is an area in which speed and access to information can truly save lives.

Cloud computing offers enormous opportunities to shift our government resources from maintaining basic technology support to creating innovative technology solutions that improve government services. Leveraging consumer technology for our own needs affords us valuable mobility and security, at a fraction of the cost. Cloud computing sits at the heart of our efforts to make government services more effective, accessible and transparent. By deploying this powerful new tool, we'll continue to transform the district government for the benefit of customers and employees alike.

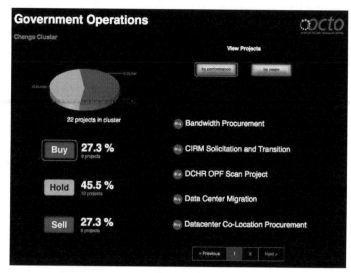

**Figure 9–4.**

**Vivek Kundra** *currently serves as Federal Chief Information Officer. Prior to that, and at the time he wrote this chapter, he served as the Chief Technology Officer, District of Columbia Government. Kundra was appointed by Mayor Adrian M. Fenty on March 27, 2007, to the cabinet post of Chief Technology Officer (CTO) for the District of Columbia. As CTO, Kundra led the Office of the Chief Technology Officer (OCTO), an organization of more than 600 staff that provides technology and telecommunications services and leadership for 86 agencies, 38,000 employees, residents, businesses, and millions of visitors. Before Kundra came to the district, Governor Timothy M. Kaine appointed him Assistant Secretary of Commerce and Technology for the Commonwealth of Virginia, the first dual cabinet role in the state's history.*

*In the private sector, Kundra led technology companies serving national and international customers. He served as Vice President of Marketing for Evincible Software, a company focused on electronic signatures and identity management for the financial services and defense sectors. As CEO of Creostar, he advised clients in government and industry on IT governance and strategy.*

*Earlier, Kundra served as Director of Infrastructure Technology for Arlington, Virginia. Kundra also has served as adjunct faculty at the University of Maryland, teaching courses in the theory and application of emerging and disruptive technologies ranging from wireless protocols to artificial intelligence. Kundra holds an M.S. in Information Technology and a B.S. in Psychology from the University of Maryland. He also is a graduate of University of Virginia's Sorensen Institute for Political Leadership.*

# 10. The Incredible Pace of Incredible Change

## DAVID BEHEN WITH JUDITH FOY

It wasn't enough that this position, the position of the Chief Information Officer, grew out of change—the relentless advance of technology. It would seem that today, we are facing another onslaught of change: the dramatic downturn in our economy. And, as I'm sure you know, the pace is unforgiving.

What I hope to accomplish in this chapter is an understanding that the evolution of the role of the CIO was, and is, inevitable. No matter the timeframe, no matter how we deal with our fiscal reality, it has become clear that understanding the worth of technology would lead the CIO from the *how* of information transfer to all the Ws: What, When, Where, Who and even Why.

*More and more, we see the CIO becoming the corporate-level strategist for the organization or the business. He or she is shifting focus to transforming the way we do business.*

In my own experience in the past five years as IT Director, then CIO/Support Services Director and now CIO/Deputy Administrator with Washtenaw County, Michigan, I have lived this evolution myself. It felt so intrinsic, this change from the small "i" big "T" to the big "I" and small "t" of Information Technology that it wasn't until I conducted a short survey of my PTI colleagues on the evolving role of the CIO that I realized how universal the progression had been.

> "You don't go through a computer science or engineering program and expect to come out with the skill set to drive business strategy"
>
> —*Mark Hall, Founding Manager, CIO Executive Council*

The survey was relatively small—about 40 CIOs or IT directors working in the public sector who answered 12 questions dealing with their roles as organizational leaders. At the time, I wanted to learn if other CIOs had experienced his or her position as a stepping stone to more mainstream higher organizational positions of Chief Executive or Chief Operations Officer—a path that seemed at odds with my thinking in the past.

There were certainly many variations on the theme but, in answer after answer, the survey showed the dismantling of the old stereotype—the pocket-protected techno-geek—as CIO. In fact, the survey findings offered no stereotypes that I could find. Just more evidence that knowledge is power and that innovation will drive organizations forward, especially as margins become non-existent, or worse. I believe that these conversations, strategic conversations, are the new home of today's CIO, or they should be.

That's where the speed bump is for most of us. To repurpose an Albert Einstein quote, "the skills that brought us to our position are very likely not the skills to keep us here."

Take a look at a couple of the following survey results from different organizations in the past couple of years. They indicate the best case for CIO evolution in coming years, and they show some of the challenges in getting there.

The CIO as an organizational leader:

> I consider myself and my IT team as "Thought Leaders" in the organization.
> **76%–Affirmed or Strongly Affirmed**

> The CIO or IT is ALWAYS at the table on strategic organizational decisions.
> **70%–Affirmed or Strongly Affirmed**

> *PTI/Behen—Evolving Role of the CIO—2007*

> I am regarded by my colleagues as a leader of change and transformation in my company.
> **80%–Affirmed or Strongly Affirmed**

> *Center for CIO Leadership—2008*

In fact, the Center of CIO Leadership recently published "The CIO Profession: Leaders of Change, Drivers of Innovation," which has brought together very timely survey results for largely private sector, quality research to produce a great report. Its survey findings begin with acknowledging where my survey ended: the role of today's CIO has changed. It continues to evolve, pulling in four new but basic competency areas:

- ◆ Leadership
- ◆ Business strategy and process
- ◆ Innovation and growth
- ◆ Organization and talent management

But the center's report indicated what was also apparent in our survey of public sector CIOs. There is a significant gap between the insight of leadership and the skill level—and organizational trust level—that CIOs presently have.

Take a look at these statistics from a Center of CIO Leadership/Harvard/MIT-Sloane Survey, 2007:

> **93%** of CIOs consider "promoting collaboration between IT and business units" to be a high or highest priority.

> **BUT, just 15%** *believe they are highly effective at doing so.*

> **78%** say that identifying and developing high potential IT staff is a high or highest priority.

> **BUT, just 8%** *feel they are highly effective at doing that.*

## My story

To appreciate those statistics—especially the perceived gap between what an organization needs in a CIO and the skills commensurate with that need, it might be useful to look at my own evolving journey.

I came to the position of IT director preceding a reorganization of Washtenaw County's support services in 2004. The moves we made at that time—painful yet regenerative—allowed me to see the broader call for strategic information dissemination in today's public organization. An entire IT department was laid off, new positions created and posted, management structure and technology infrastructure reassessed.

The scope of that change gave me the time and space to begin anew with information technology for the county. One of the key changes grew from the recognition of the danger of keeping technology isolated from the organization—in almost any way. Information is knowledge, and knowledge is power. It already had become apparent to me, to my Administrator Bob Guenzel and to his then-deputy, Frank Cambria, that our organization had made many successful strides at becoming a "knowledge organization." What had been missing was the thread of reliable communication, sustainable and accessible self-serve information and a shift in culture that would allow them.

To those ends, we expanded and decentralized our intranet, Employee Central, and created the position of Knowledge Manager. The position was an organizing center point for bringing about the development of our Project Management Team, our web content liaisons throughout the county and increased strategic communication for quicker, easier consumption.

Looking at those earlier days, I see that we were charged with the spirit of new ideas. If there is anything more powerful, I can't think of it—except, perhaps, for the team that worked and massaged those ideas every day. We were a team of individuals who saw the outcomes we needed and wanted, and we were able to create the ways to achieve them.

That is not to say that it was all easy; the pace of change and learning never allows it to be that easy. I was lucky to have the men and women around me whose backgrounds and whose passions shored up my credentials in technology. Developing relationships was key, for any success we enjoyed and mutual trust took time to grow after a pretty bruising reorganization.

At the same time that my role came more into focus, when I began to better understand the key role that the wise use of technology could have in furthering the main goals of the county, my responsibilities grew to include oversight and direction of Facilities, Strategy & Budget and Organizational Development. I took on the title of CIO in 2005 and slowly began to widen my gaze, partly as a strategy for business success and partly to follow my own passions that dovetailed with that success.

My personal affiliation with groups like Public Technology Institute (PTI), the International City/County Management Association (ICMA), the Society for Information Management (SIM) and the Alliance for Innovation (then, Innovation Groups,) became extraordinary windows on the wider world dealing with many of the same challenges and opportunities that we were experiencing at Washtenaw County. It was like having organizations in the wings working for me. Shared experiences, researched benchmarking of best practices and just conversations comparing our efforts with those of other organizations became invaluable tools to my professional development—and to my providing and nurturing better leadership in my own organization.

## What had we done?

We had accomplished a great deal in three years, and it was clear to me that the organization needed to make some effort to acknowledge those successes. "Celebrate your successes," say the business and leadership gurus. We had been in overdrive with the pace of change for so long, we hadn't really concentrated on affirming what we had been able to achieve.

I began looking for ways to acknowledge our achievements by adding award submissions to our list of strategic moves. Since then, the county has been honored five times as a Top Ten Digital County by the Center for Digital Government and the National Association of Counties, and named to CIO Magazine's *CIO 100* in 2006 and 2007. Along with other national, regional and state awards for excellence, our staff has been honored—and our wider organization made aware— multiple times.

For the first *CIO 100* award, I found a local consultant who crafted 35 handsome personalized box frames, with signed letters of appreciation to each IT staff person from our Administrator and Chair of the County Board of Commissioners. The cost was negligible—especially in light of the important impact the commemoratives had on our staff. Good ideas that lead to good outcomes need to become part of the group's story; it doesn't slow you down, it helps give the confidence you need to take the next steps.

## What do we want to do?

Personally, the recognition we received also helped me with my own confidence—part of the strategy I hadn't thought about really. When a casual conversation over coffee pertaining to the inequities of broadband availability came up in 2006, I took a large measure of that confidence to my Administrator and Board of Commissioners and soon began laying the groundwork for Wireless Washtenaw, an effort to provide free or very low-cost access to the Internet regardless of location or economic status. Wireless Washtenaw became an extraordinary collaboration of the private and public sectors to help construct a wireless network available countywide, with no taxpayer dollars spent on its construction, maintenance and operation.

As with the majority of municipal broadband efforts, Wireless Washtenaw has had its challenges, but continues to find its way. The initiative put the county in what has become a comfortable role as convener. For the project, we helped create governance and infrastructure through one of the most comprehensive private/public collaborative endeavors in our history.

My point though, is the cause and effect of taking action even slightly beyond what might normally be thought of as the "role of the CIO." With my own deep understanding of the goals and purpose of Washtenaw County government, the confidence I had gained from acknowledgements received, along with the vital support of a visionary administrator who found backing from the elected Board of Commissioners, I was able to step up and out into new territory.

Representing the county as a convener for this wireless initiative, I met and engaged private sector CEOs, university presidents and local and state public officials. The people I connected with through Wireless Washtenaw have become pivotal strategic partners in the creation or enhancement of other initiatives vital to the aims of the county, and our citizen customers:

♦ A high-profile and potentially fractious Police Services sub-committee with a large number of local municipal officials;
♦ Washtenaw County Literacy Coalition with strong local government and public sector representation;

♦ New economic development initiatives helping to provide new business incubators when we need them most; and

♦ A flourishing private/public Ann Arbor Region Success initiative to attract and retain new talent in the spreading downturn, and many more.

## The economy's turn: what will we be <u>able</u> to do?

In November 2006, when longtime Deputy Administrator Frank Cambria announced his retirement, I was named co-Deputy Administrator with Verna McDaniel. Then—when the housing, then credit, now general recession became keenly apparent in December 2007—it was clear that my evolution would be taking yet another stretch.

The State of Michigan predated the rest of the country with the economic downturn and, since losing the county's largest employer and non-profit funder, Pfizer, Inc., during 2008, there has been considerable effort locally to reassess and strategize. With its two high profile state universities—the University of Michigan and Eastern Michigan University—among other economic engines, Washtenaw County had long experienced a certain degree of immunity in its housing and property values. Property taxes make up nearly three quarters of the county's General Fund budget.

As of December of 2007, we were no longer immune.

The new numbers predicted that our property tax values—hence our tax revenue—would take a dip from 6% to nearly zero—unprecedented in 50 years of recordkeeping. Add to that a new mechanism that changed the timing of any realistic projections to six months later than in the past, and an already dwindling revenue sharing resource from the State of Michigan and you begin to see our situation.

The organization literally had finished its thorough and very inclusive planning process and passed our biennial budget for 2008/2009 in November, just a month earlier. By April of 2008, we had an amended and passed 2008 budget that included a hiring freeze, as many one-time reductions and contractions as we could find, and talks began in earnest with our 30-plus department and program directors about the more permanent, structural 10% reductions that needed to be met in 2009.

As I write this, we are still attempting to understand both the magnitude and impact of the financial crisis. We've begun the planning process for the 2010/2011 budget. Once again, we will call on technology to bring efficiencies to bear. With the feasibility of reduced services and further position loss, we also have chosen to promote web 2.0 technologies within the organization this year. Our hope is that administration and department head blogs, along with community of interest wikis will help us get information in and out more quickly and more transparently. Most important will be how the technologies will help build understanding of the financial situation and bring in concerns, questions and, especially, new ideas from our 1,300-plus employees whose collective knowledge we need to mine.

Not long ago, I wrote down a list of some of what I would call my "immutable truths" of any success I've had over the past five years. Even in a shattering economy, we just have to make room for trust and for new ideas. In my mind, I realized that my own evolution meant using those proven footholds that had pushed and pulled me forward as Chief Information Officer.

- The courage and temperament to begin anew
- Find the right people to do the right jobs
- Allow those people to do their jobs
- Build a supportive team through my office
- Acknowledge good work
- Communicate, communicate, communicate
- Share ideas and research best practices at a national level
- Seek out, and risk, both internal and external collaboration
- Find those unintended consequences (that aren't all bad)
- Look from different angles, and listen—alot

I suppose the most important point that I can make concerning this evolution of the CIO is to twist an old adage on its head. It turns out that, in fact, **_there is an "i" in "team:" information._**

Today's CIO, private or public sector, must take the lead in information as much as the technology that supports it. That means being ready to work as a team with top tier or "C-level" management in the organization. That means being strategic with how information is taken in and how it is shared. And, that may also mean a different mindset for the individual as CIO—and for the organization.

In this recession, seemingly bottomless as I write, everyone is out of their comfort zones; everyone is attempting to do more with less. No one has the resources for disengaged, unilateral use of technology. It has to be part of the wider strategy, aligned for outcomes in a very difficult economy. The role of CIO definitely has changed. It also has never been more important.

---

## Discussion questions

1. Most of today's CIOs have been trained in skills commensurate with the needs of their office.   True ___ False ✓

   *15% of today's CIOs believe they are highly effective at promoting collaboration between IT and business units, a high priority goal.*

   *8% of today's CIOs say they are highly effective at identifying and developing high-potential IT staff, another high priority goal.*

2. What needed educational concentration, or what skills development could you use today as CIO that might not have been part of your professional education thus far?
   - Strategic Planning?
   - Organizational Change principles?
   - Marketing?
   - Organizational Communication?
   - Personal Communication?
   - Other?

3. The current recession has forced any company and organization to rethink its priorities. Every CIO should focus on his or her own responsibilities for technology, adhering to the bottom line and making sure that what works stays working.  True ___ False ✓

*Keeping technology "working" is obviously a key responsibility for any Chief Information Officer. But today, with so much at stake, there is every reason for the CIO to take a broader look at ongoing "working" technologies in light of new, exigent circumstances in the organization.*

*The economic downturn should spur the changes already under way in the evolution of the CIO in more collaborative, strategic directions. It is most likely not a time for blinders and for hunkering down. This horrible economy should be a time for reinvention and creativity–for the individual CIO and for the organization.*

4. With so much changing so fast, with reductions taking the front seat in most conversations, can the CIO lead any important, future-oriented changes at this tumultuous time?
   ◆ Regionalizing services through merging or other means?
   ◆ Decentralize communication through a web 2.0 educational campaign within the organization, and perhaps with municipal partners (wikis, blogs and the like)?
   ◆ Move to Open Source applications?
   ◆ Develop technological expertise in non-IT employees to offset needed reductions?
   ◆ Other?

5. Tough economic times mean that team members should understand that public acknowledgement and commemoratives, like plaques and awards, must take a back seat.
   True \_\_\_ False ✓

*Though present economic circumstances would indicate that all areas of the organization need to be considered for reduction, the very fact that fewer people are doing more with fewer resources demonstrates a need for acknowledgement. That doesn't mean all-expenses-paid weekends in Aruba; it means taking time to see good work and single it out. A mention in a blog, an article on the intranet or organization's public web site or even a modest gift certificate will go a long way to encourage a sense of solidarity among your people.*

6. Can you think of a time when you understood the importance of personal acknowledgement in your work life? Perhaps a time when you felt good about receiving kudos–or maybe when you did not?

**David Behen** *is Deputy Administrator and Chief Information Officer for Washtenaw County, Michigan. In his nine years and three directorships with the county, Mr. Behen has been the consistent champion of the organization's drive toward reliable and accessible information, and fully integrated support for 1,300-plus employees. An important legacy for the county will be Mr. Behen's development of a knowledge management strategy that underpins internal communication and planning. Under his leadership in key roles in the organization, Washtenaw County has been named twice to the prestigious CIO100 list of the top 100 IT programs by CIO Magazine, and five times as one of the nation's Top Ten Digital Counties by the Center for Digital Government with the National Association of Counties (NACo). He was recently named to Crain's Detroit Business "40 Under 40" list for outstanding professional achievement before the age of 40.*

**Judith Ellen Foy** *is the founder and managing principal of "New Work Media" based in Ann Arbor, Michigan. Working chiefly with public and non-profit sector clients, Ms. Foy develops* *internal and external communication planning to maximize positive community impact. Her work in radio, television and online media has been acknowledged with numerous national awards.*

# 11. Leading Innovation: Creating Technology Foundations Through Regional Cooperation

**GEORGE DANILOVICS**

The terrorist acts of September 11, 2001, pointed out weaknesses in emergency communications and served as a catalyst to correct those weaknesses and improve capabilities across the nation. The National Capital Region (NCR) was a target of those attacks and has made it a priority to take steps to create a high-bandwidth, secure communication backbone that will serve the region on a day-to-day basis as well as in times of wide-scale emergency. While the project was initially proposed as a response to a catastrophe, the ongoing support of that network is further justified through daily use of the network by current and future planned applications. Through continued expansion of additional uses of the network, the regional chief information officers (CIOs) strengthen the initial justification for the network and can provide additional capabilities to the region.

The initial project to build a communication network for emergency communication needs has evolved to provide vital daily communication links between the independent governments and service partners. Because the basic, commercially available communications services did not prove to meet the availability requirements, especially supporting the intensity required to support emergency events, the regional leadership focused on leveraging locality communications infrastructures with opportunities for greater interconnectivity and security, and established the NCR-IP program. The regional CIOs followed a standard four-phase approach to projects:

1. Recognize the need
2. Set the vision
3. Assign leadership
4. Build on existing capabilities to add value

There are many project management methodologies that can be followed, and this article will not go into examining the detailed management of projects. However, when managing infrastructure projects across multiple information systems, simple project management methodologies—such as agile development, waterfall or even more complex methods—should be integrated within a formal IT service management framework, such as the Information Technology Infrastructure Library, in order to manage risks within a system of multiple interconnecting parts and stakeholders. The more complex the project, the greater the need for formal project management practices. Within this article I will explore some of the lessons learned from the creation of a regional fiber communication network and how the CIOs successfully added more to the region than just a fiber network.

## Background

The National Capital Region is made up of the cities and counties surrounding Washington, DC. The region has 11 jurisdictions in Maryland, nine from Virginia, and the District of Columbia. In order to facilitate collaboration within the region, the leaders in the region formed the Metropolitan Washington Council of Governments (MWCOG) in 1957. Policy leaders and jurisdictional department heads from the region come together to solve regional problems and work to improve life in the region.

The Chief Information Officers Committee at MWCOG is comprised of the head information technology officers from the member jurisdictions. In addition to sharing information technology best practices, the CIOs of the committee work to ensure the interoperability of technology within the National Capital Region. The CIOs work with other disciplines, such as traffic planners and emergency responders, and advise them on their technology needs.

Shortly after the attacks on September 11, 2001, public communication networks around the nation began to buckle. Cellular and landline phone networks became congested as families attempted to determine the safety of their loved ones. The Internet came to a crawl as everyone attempted to keep abreast on the unfolding events. News websites responded to the surge by changing their usually high graphic homepages to simple, faster-loading, text only links. Even with reduced size of webpages, users on the Internet still had to wait for pages to load as Internet links across the nation were fully saturated.

CIOs in the National Capital Region recognized that in future emergency situations, emergency responders and decision makers cannot depend on public communication networks for timely information delivery. The Internet is resilient and uses best-effort delivery protocols for information packets. The Internet can function even when some links are unavailable or saturated by choosing alternative routes with less traffic. But, during a large-scale event when a large number of critical links are overtaxed, there may be no alternative routes available, and communication across all links suffers. As a result, the CIOs determined that essential communications in the National Capital Region should be moved from the public networks to a private network.

## 1. Recognize the need

The National Capital Region has emergency responders and decision makers that need to communicate during an emergency. Systems that exchange information on a daily basis that utilize the Internet still need to exchange information during an emergency. Both people and systems require a reliable communication link to exchange information. The public networks perform that task well under normal circumstances, but their reliability and quality of service are subject to degradation during an emergency. As evident during the events of September 11, the public communications networks throughout the nation can be affected—not just the networks in close proximity to the event itself.

The regional CIOs recognized that they needed a way for their jurisdictions to communicate with one another that was not dependent on the publicly accessed networks. Commercial carriers can provide virtual private networks and other relatively secure network products, ranging from managed network services to building fiber optic "pipes," that the CIOs could control. However, recurring costs would quickly become prohibitive. The CIOs needed a physically separate network that did not share common equipment with the commercial networks.

The need cannot be a project born from within the information technology department and then released upon the jurisdiction or region. Like all projects, regional projects require a business case to justify their funding and implementation. The CIOs of the National Capital Region reached out to emergency support personnel to assess their needs for a communication network to support their applications and data exchanges. Some of the identified needs could be solved incrementally as jurisdictions got connected to the network. Other needs could only be realized when the entire network had been completed. The key point is that the needs were not solely those of the CIOs. The CIOs reached out first responders to determine which existing information systems could be candidates to take advantage of the fiber network. By using the shared regional private fiber network, the applications would not have to procure their own individual communication links.

## 2. Set the vision

The leaders in the region realized that they needed a physically separate network, but building a fiber network from the ground up would be extremely cost prohibitive. The National Capital Region is over 3,000 square miles. Wireless and microwave technologies had not yet matured to the point that they are today technologically and financially viable options. Furthermore, the wireless technologies are only as good as the underlying fiber infrastructure that supports them. The only medium that would provide the capacity and quality of service is fiber optic-based communication links.

Fortunately, the region is crisscrossed with fiber runs from multiple telecommunication entities. Many of the jurisdictions also had negotiated in their local cable franchise agreements additional fiber built to support governmental networks. Where already in place, those institutional networks, sometimes referred to as I-nets, were viewed as the baseline infrastructure and provided the opportunity to interconnect them in providing a seamless regional network.

Some of the different jurisdictional I-nets connected back to a shared telecommunications hub. The existence of fiber in the I-nets meant that, in many cases, only smaller sections of fiber would need to be laid or procured in order to connect the I-nets and jurisdictional networks together. The CIOs realized that by contributing some of those fiber optic resources to the joint network and by working together on the design and implementation, they could deliver an infrastructure that would be higher than the sum of its parts: a high-capacity, dedicated, secure and scalable, interconnected network that would accommodate a broad range of data and application exchange needs for emergency responders and government officials. The inter-connection of the I-nets would be referred to as NCRnet.

In 2004 the region submitted a grant request through the Department of Homeland Security's Urban Area Security Initiatives (UASI) program, to provide funding for the endeavor. UASI funds were established by the Department of Homeland Security to provide federal funds to assist first responder and emergency response capabilities. The CIOs fulfill the region's Emergency Support Function #2—Communications. The CIOs have been tasked to ensure that interoperable communication links are established and provide needed capability for emergency events. The requirement for a reliable private network for first responder use matched up with the grant requirements for the UASI federal funds.

## 3. Assign leadership

The Chief Information Officers Committee at the Metropolitan Washington Council of Governments developed the project that implemented a private fiber network utilizing the existing I-net footprint and making additional connections as necessary to fill out the region. The primary responsibility of the CIOs is to oversee the information technology systems of their own jurisdictions. Their support for regional projects, although important to the region, is an additional commitment that they took on in order to meet the tactical and strategic needs of the emergency response, mitigation and recovery. It was, therefore, doubly critical to delegate and assign leadership and leverage existing staff to dedicate the necessary support for regional projects.

The CIOs have relied on support from their information technology staff and established the Architectural Review Committee (ARC). The ARC engineers made technology selection and standards recommendations to the CIOs. By placing technology experts from across the region on the committee, the CIOs ensured that all jurisdictions would have the opportunity to provide input into the final network's design and operation. The ARC also would review communication needs of any application that would utilize NCRnet. That would allow the establishment of risk and security management on the network and the information systems of the participating jurisdictions, and ensure that the underlying architecture would support the requirements of application and data exchange. The CIOs were able to rely on the ARC to make technology decisions, which enabled the CIOs to keep their focus on the vision for the network.

In addition to the I-Net fiber transport, the CIOs also established a Data Exchange Hub (DEH) project and assigned a project team. The DEH team originally was tasked to develop application standards for information exchanges. The exchanges would use industry standards, such as XML, when possible and adapt standards to specific needs when needed. The team also created a project review process and service desk process. The service-oriented architecture created by the DEH team laid a foundation for any future application that would need to exchange information across the fiber network. NCRnet would be the physical means by which DEH applications would communicate.

The original NCRnet project plan relied on contractors to perform project management and delivery tasks. The contractors created the scope of work for the project, deliverables and time table. The contractors also drafted requests for proposals for procurement of required equipment and services to connect the I-nets. The project work included oversight of the deployment of the network and activation of the links. As sponsors, the CIOs provided overall oversight and policy guidance, however, the CIOs later decided that a full-time local jurisdictional employee was better suited to streamline governance and help insulate the contract teams from scope-stretching requests from multiple interested parties.

The decision to have a jurisdictional employee more familiar with the specifics of the jurisdictional intricacies head the technology projects provided greater accountability and trust in the minds of the CIOs. Instead of having a contractor managing itself, a government employee could better represent the needs of the region to the contractor. The federal grants allowed for that and either provided backfill funds for the position within the jurisdiction, or the employee's salary could be counted toward the grant's matching requirements. NCRnet and the DEH team were all led by full-time jurisdictional employees. The employees were responsible for reporting to the committee on project finance and deliverables. The employees also oversaw future grant requests for their projects. That methodology worked so well that, as emergency support groups began to explore utilizing the NCRnet for their applications, the project lead roles for the regional application projects were assigned to jurisdictional employees as well. Contractors were hired to complete the work and tasks associated with the project, but the ultimate responsibility for the success of the project was a jurisdictional employee.

## 4. Build on existing capabilities to add value

This final phase can become one of the most important for large projects. Most technology projects are started to serve a specific need. Infrastructure projects specifically provide undying enabling capability for other projects that need reliable and secure data and information interoperability. While they may not do something that the user community sees on a daily basis, they enable other applications that the users do see to work. Because infrastructure projects typically are not on the front minds of CIOs during dialogue about the benefits of technology, their importance is reinforced by business requirements and other projects.

The core premise of the NCRnet network was that numerous applications would need to use the network for their communication needs. At the outset, the CIOs engaged the emergency support personnel in the region to review their specific applications and needs. The first group to use NCRnet was the region's emergency managers. The emergency managers used a UASI grant to procure high-quality video conferencing equipment and deploy it over a leased frame relay network. The video conferencing equipment allowed the emergency managers to hold high-definition video and audio conferences and share presentations in the event of a regional emergency across the region.

The CIOs were instrumental not just in providing initial technical support for the project, but also in facilitating its migration from leased lines to NCRnet pipes. As jurisdictions were added to NCRnet, costly leased connections were replaced with the higher-bandwidth NCRnet links. The CIOs also have worked closely with the emergency managers to expand the capabilities of the video-conferencing infrastructure by interconnecting the regional video conferencing system with internal jurisdictional video conference systems running over jurisdictional networks. That allows government officials and emergency responders to participate from more sites and expands the potential user base.

The CIOs currently are engaged with the development and rollout of two more applications to run across NCRnet. The first is a computer aided dispatch exchange that would tie emergency response CAD systems together. The second is a geographic information system exchange to share geospatial data throughout the region.

The framework laid about by the DEH team provided the starting point, and the fiber network of NCRnet provided the communication link. The investments that the CIOs made in creating the standards with the DEH returns on that investment each time a new application wishes to exchange information. The NCRnet investment is justified as the number of applications running across NCRnet increases. It also has provided higher bandwidth needed by the modern applications that some localities would not have been able to afford through carriers.

CIOs working on large regional projects also should keep an eye on unintended benefits and opportunities arising from their projects. During the recent increases in fuel costs combined with cost-cutting by jurisdictions, the demand for telecommuting has increased in the National Capital Region. The video conference equipment that runs on NCRnet has been used to facilitate committee meetings at the Metropolitan Washington Council of Governments. Some committee members or project managers would drive over an hour to attend a one hour meeting and then spend another hour driving home. Many committees now offer video conference options, which allow participants to use their jurisdictional video conference equipment to join the meetings. That has engaged the committee members from the outer jurisdictions and increased participation in committee meetings. Some of the larger committees have even had participants using video conference links from Richmond, Virginia, and Annapolis, Maryland.

While NCRnet does not have fiber all the way to the two state capitals, the video conference bridge does allow inbound ISDN calls, which allows distant, non-NCRnet participants to join in. The most recent use of the extended video conference setup was used by the region's leadership to prioritize funding for the next year's UASI grant. That use was an excellent example to the leadership on how their initial investment for homeland security needs has added additional daily use capabilities to the region. Daily use also is important so that personnel in the region are familiar and comfortable with the technology. By hosting committee meetings on the video conference equipment, staff gain experience in joining conferences and troubleshooting problems. Those experiences undoubtedly will pay off when the system is used during a regional emergency.

Another capability being explored in the region is remote backup capabilities. Many of the smaller jurisdictions within the region cannot afford to pay for large colocation data center facilities. Those jurisdictions have a few servers in a server room that could be nothing more than an office that was later converted to house information technology equipment. Disaster recovery and continuity of operations plans also are lower on the priority scale for CIOs that are focused on daily operating expenses within their budget. The jurisdictions are exploring partnering with one another and putting colocation equipment in each other's data center. That would allow one jurisdiction to replicate data to the other for only the cost of the server hardware. The NCRnet network is capable of 1 gigabit per second and is modular to support future upgrades in speed. Even at the current 1 gigabit speed, the network is more than capable of supporting current disaster recovery options. Again, conformity of the backup solution to the published DEH standards and subsequent review by the ARC ensures that security and quality of service standards are adhered to.

Another way to build on the NCRnet investment is to promote the existence and capabilities of the network to other agencies within the region. When the network reached a majority of the jurisdictions, the CIOs began to reach out to other agencies to again assess their communication needs and to determine if the NCRnet network could provide them with a secure communication network. The continued marketing of capabilities to others in the region allows for other agencies and directors from public safety to public works to explore additional uses of the network. As the NCRnet network transitions from being funded by grants to being funded by jurisdictional coffers, it is important that the network be viewed as an essential piece to other projects and capabilities throughout the region. Without those additional buy-ins, the network could appear to be a technology system providing only limited value.

## Wrap up

Technology projects always require a clear business case and strong technology support. Cooperation between the users and technology leaders has to start at the beginning, when problems or potential improvements of existing capabilities are identified. Sometimes there is a clearly defined problem; other instances may require careful examination.

The first phase of recognize the need begins like all other projects: with an assessment of what the environment is like currently. Jurisdictional CIOs should engage their peers to see how technology is being used throughout different agencies and departments. Reducing duplicated efforts and infrastructure is one way to consolidate and reduce costs.

After a need has been identified, a CIO should work to set the vision. A CIO needs to understand how to manage technology systems and to position systems to serve needs into the future. The vision should not be just the CIO's vision, but rather a combined vision of what capabilities the jurisdiction wants to have and how technology can be a tool to reach those capabilities.

By assigning leadership, a CIO establishes a project charter, governance structure and appoints a capable project manager to lead the endeavors. The project manager always should follow industry standards for project management and service support. Project managers need a capable staff and the direct support from their CIO. The National Capital Region has found that jurisdictional project managers, as opposed to contractors, provide higher levels of accountability for their needs within the context of multiple stakeholders across the region, but that should be assessed on a case-by-case basis for each CIO.

And finally, a CIO needs to build on existing capabilities to add value. Information technology projects cannot be viewed as projects created by and only benefiting the information technology department. By engaging other agency and department heads, a CIO can promote existing capabilities and begin to assess opportunities to leverage those capabilities to aid other systems. The additional uses for a system increases the importance of that system and provides easier justifications for maintenance costs and expansions to add more capabilities.

A jurisdictional CIO is responsible for the information technology systems of their jurisdiction. By reaching across to other leaders in the jurisdiction in collaboration, a CIO is able to provide relevant technology advice to address needs and capability requirements. A CIO ultimately oversees the implementation of new systems and continues to show value for those already in place. A CIO can ensure that the jurisdiction will be prepared to handle future needs through strategic thinking that addresses today's needs and always keeping an eye for future opportunities.

## Discussion questions

1. Develop a list of obstacles that could complicate a local government's ability to partner with another local government or outside entity. Expand the list to include ways to mitigate those risks.
2. Managing expectations is a complex task associated with project management. What methods could be used to manage the expectations of multiple supporting agencies in a regional project that involves multiple entities?
3. What role should governance have in a regional project? When should governance be established?
4. What critical stakeholders should be identified in local government projects? Does the list change when projects become regional in scope?

5. How can local government projects provide for accountability and transparency with regard to information technology projects?

**George Danilovics** *is currently the Information Technology Chief at the Metropolitan Washington Council of Governments. In addition to his responsibility for MWCOG's information technology systems, George also staffs the regional Chief Information Officers Committee and Interoperability Council committees. In his current position, George assists CIOs and other leaders in the Washington, DC, area come together to work on regional technology projects. Before moving to Washington, George spent six years as the Information Technology Architect for National Church Residences in Columbus, Ohio. George possesses a Master's degree in Information Technology from Rochester Institute of Technology and serves as an adjunct professor at Devry University and Strayer University.*

# 12. Building an Award-winning County Web Portal: A Case Study in Architecture, Collaboration, Governance and Project Management

**IVAN GALIC**

The Montgomery County, Maryland (the "county") Internet web portal, http://www.montgomerycountymd.gov, provides a "one-stop shop" for county constituents to access an extensive and diverse portfolio of on-line services and information. The successful implementation of the county's web portal was made possible though strict adherence to four key principles:

1. Architecture
2. Collaboration
3. Governance
4. Project Management

This case study examines the county's application of those four principles and provides a model for other jurisdictions seeking to successfully implement programs of similar scope and complexity.

## Background

Before launching its award-winning web portal, http://www.montgomerycountymd.gov, the county operated two separate and distinct web sites. In 1995, the county launched the http://www.co.mo.md.us web site. That "informational" web site provided static web content about county government and related programs and services. By the year 2000, county leadership recognized the need to rapidly move county services online. As a result, a significant effort was undertaken to develop and deploy a new "transaction-oriented" web site, http://www.emontgomery.org, which came to be known as "eMontgomery." eMontgomery provided dynamic, interactive applications, including the ability for constituents to transact directly with the county via the Internet. Each of the two primary county government web sites had a distinct "look and feel," and each web site was operated, staffed and maintained by different work units within county government.

Compounding the challenges associated with the ongoing operation of two separate and distinct web sites was the fact that several county departments also operated their own web sites. Those departmental web sites, approximately 40 in total, promoted department-specific information and applications. In the aggregate, the web sites contained thousands of static web pages and several dozen interactive web applications. Further, the departmental web sites did not follow common standards, such as web page design and use of web addresses (URLs), to promote a consistent county web identity. Many departmental web sites failed to include navigation links back to either of the two primary county web sites. Additionally, few of the departmental web sites offered features or capabilities consistent with web site accessibility standards for persons with disabilities. Last, county departments continued to market and promote their own URLs, which increased web traffic to their departmental web sites rather than to either of the county's two primary web sites.

As a result of those challenges, the county completed an "outside-in" assessment (that is, reviewing the various web sites from the perspective of a county constituent) of its online presence to determine if constituent needs were being satisfactorily met by the current service offerings. Although the county offered an extensive and diverse portfolio of online services, information and applications, the assessment concluded that constituent needs were not being satisfactorily met. The county conducted several focus groups with community members to determine how the online services offering could be improved.

Upon completion of the focus group activities, county leadership decided to integrate the disparate pools of online services and information into a single, integrated web portal. Ultimately, the new portal would benefit county constituents by providing a single entry to county government information and services, presented in a consistent manner and following a set of well-defined and agreed-upon standards.

## Problem/solution

After approximately one year of planning and development, the county unveiled its new Internet web portal, http://www.montgomerycountymd.gov. The new county portal integrated the information and applications formerly provided by http://www.co.mo.md.us and http://www.emontgomery.org, which were subsequently retired.

The county's web portal provides constituents with a multitude of online interactive applications, including, but not limited to, the ability to pay property taxes and parking tickets, reserve ball fields, register for recreation classes, reserve library books, register service and infrastructure complaints, and obtain information on construction permits.

Under the leadership of Montgomery County Chief Information Officer (CIO) E. Steven Emanuel and Chief Technology Officer (CTO) Mike Knuppel, the county has deployed several "Web 2.0" applications, including blogs, mash-ups, web services and applications utilizing asynchronous javascript and XML (AJAX) technologies. The applications are provided and maintained by a number of county departments. In addition to those interactive applications, the county's portal maintains a database of thousands of informational web pages with links to hundreds of external web sites. Web content is maintained by more than 400 registered and authorized users of the county's web content management solution.

Although the first significant milestone of launching the new web portal was now complete, county leadership challenged the project's implementation team to further consolidate the approximately 40 remaining departmental web sites into the new portal. The consolidation would simplify and streamline the constituents' online experience by integrating the portfolio of information and services contained on the disparate departmental web sites into one portal with a common look and feel. County leadership directed the Department of Technology Services (DTS) and the Office of Public Information (OPI) to integrate the web sites into the county's portal. The integration of the web sites into the portal would improve service to county constituents by improving the accessibility and consistent delivery of on-line services and information. Further, program and technical staff across county government would leverage design policies and standards established by DTS and OPI, thereby improving productivity and overall quality and consistency of the portal. Within 14 months of the launch of the county's web portal, all departmental web sites were successfully integrated.

The successful implementation of the county's web portal was made possible though strict adherence to four key principles:

1. Architecture
2. Collaboration
3. Governance
4. Project Management

The following sections describe the county's implementation of those four principles.

## 1. Architecture

The consolidation of http://www.co.mo.md.us, http://www.emontgomery.org and approximately 40 departmental web sites into the new web portal was the county's first implementation of enterprise-level technology architecture.

During the planning and design phases for the implementation of the new portal, county staff reached consensus on a common set of design standards. The new design standards set forth the detailed requirements for county departmental web designers and content contributors. Further, the standards defined the policy for the use of URLs for marketing, branding, advertising and promotional purposes. County departments were expected to cease and desist use of their department specific URLs and to start utilizing the http://www.montgomerycountymd.gov "brand."

To better enable the transition to the new portal and to help enforce the new design standards, DTS developed a set of reusable templates to be leveraged by departmental staff in the implementation of their web sites. The new design standards were formally documented and posted to an online repository for easy access and retrieval by departmental staff. The repository contained useful and important technical documentation, design guidelines and best practices, interactive training materials and tutorials, and a feedback mechanism.

The web portal system utilizes several technologies. The search and language translation services are both powered by Google technology. The main pages are built using Microsoft Active Server Pages (ASP). Applications are written in several application server platforms. The database platform is mainly Microsoft SQL Server. The portal runs in a Windows server environment utilizing virtual server technologies. The portal supports multiple web browser platforms.

The county provides a text-only version of several web pages for persons with disabilities. The text version is created through use of ASP technology, allowing the county the ability to dynamically "read and filter" content into a template that can be read by screen reader technologies. Subsequent updates to the graphic version are "automatically" posted to the text version. That method avoids the necessity and difficulty of accurately maintaining two separate (i.e. "text-only" and "graphic") web sites. The county strives to continually enhance web site accessibility.

## 2. Collaboration

The web portal development and departmental website consolidation programs were executed in a highly collaborative manner. The success of the programs was due in large part to the "buy-in" of representatives from each county department that operated its own, distinct web site. Active stakeholder participation was a critical success factor for the web portal consolidation project.

The county made extensive use of public-private partnerships during the web portal development program. A local web design firm (Alias Design) was hired to prepare alternate web page designs. Over the course of several months, Alias Design presented several alternate designs for review by the county workgroup. Ultimately, the workgroup narrowed the selection to two finalists, which were then moved to the next stage for testing and approval.

Next, the county retained the services of UserWorks, a firm with specialized expertise in web site usability. UserWorks assembled a focus group consisting of county residents, members of the business community and members of the disabled community to assess the usability of the proposed web designs. UserWorks conducted a number of studies with the members of the focus group. The results of those studies were provided to the county in a detailed report, which contained recommendations relative to a final selection between the remaining design alternatives.

The county's use of focus groups to review and assess design alternatives represents a "best practice" that can be leveraged by other organizations considering undertaking similar initiatives. The focus groups provided a mechanism for the county to establish a framework by which department web sites could easily be integrated into the portal. The use of focus groups ensured that the portal was developed from the vantage point of a constituent and not from the vantage point of a county government employee. The objective of the focus group meetings was to discuss how to best organize—within the confines of a single-entry approach—the new web portal to make it easy to use and to ensure that information available on the existing web sites would be retained during the integration effort.

In addition to utilizing the services of Alias Design and UserWorks, the county contracted with Multimax and Advanced Software Systems for technical staff augmentation services. Collectively, those four firms brought forth a unique set of skills required by the county to implement the portal. Those skills included web site design, usability engineering, quality assurance testing, web development and systems administration.

## 3. Governance

The county established a three-tier governance model for the web portal development and consolidation programs. The governance model was conceived and implemented by Alisoun K. Moore, the county's former Chief Information Officer (CIO). The implementation of a functioning and effective governance model was viewed as a critical success factor that would make or break the initiative.

Following, each tier of the governance model is described in detail.

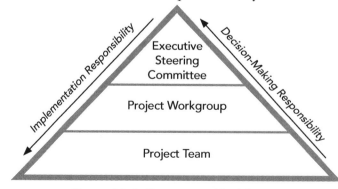

**Figure 11–1.** Governance Model

## Executive Steering Committee

The Executive Steering Committee (ESC) had broad decision-making responsibility for overall policy and execution of the program. Members of the ESC included Bruce F. Romer, the county's former Chief Administrative Officer; David Weaver, the county's former Director of the Office of Public Information; Paul Folkers, a former Assistant Chief Administrative Officer; and Ms. Moore. Major policy decisions were vetted through the Information Technology Policy Advisory Committee (IPAC), a group comprised of county government department heads. Further, Douglas M. Duncan, Montgomery County's Executive at the time of the implementation, and members of the Montgomery County Council were briefed at critical junctures and provided the opportunity to provide important feedback and direction throughout the program.

## Project Workgroup

The Project Workgroup was led by staff from DTS and PIO. The workgroup was responsible for the direct implementation and oversight of the program, and typically discussed implementation issues, as well as the pros and cons, and risks and consequences, of alternative solutions before presenting recommendations to the ESC. Representatives from the following departments participated on the project workgroup for the program:

- Commission for Women
- Department of Finance
- Department of Liquor Control
- Department of Public Works and Transportation
- Department of Recreation
- Fire and Rescue Services
- Office of Human Resources
- Office of Procurement
- Police Department
- Public Libraries

Major implementation issues were vetted through the Technical Operations Management Group (TOMG), a group comprised of technology leaders across county government.

## Project Team

The Project Team was directly responsible for the hands-on implementation and day-to-day execution of the program. The team was led by experienced senior project managers from DTS and PIO, and consisted of web content managers, application developers and technical and program staff from across county government. The program would not have been successful without the outstanding contributions of all project team participants, including the following core team members:

- Chris Daniel (DTS)
- Zelinda Fouant (DTS)
- Todd Harper (DTS)
- Donna Keating (DTS)
- Kevin Novak (DTS)
- Lola Pyne (Multimax Corporation)
- Rob Todd (PIO)

# 4. Project Management

The portal development and departmental web site consolidation programs represented Phases I and II of the overall multi-phase strategic plan for the county's web portal. Both of those phases were managed in accordance with industry standard project management practices. The project team developed a Work Breakdown Structure (WBS) and project budget. The WBS laid out the tasks, deliverables and critical milestones for the project. The WBS and project budget were both maintained by the project manager. The project manager conducted regular briefings for the ESC and Project Workgroup, and provided status reports on a consistent basis.

A team of programmers within DTS was assigned the task of technical construction of the web portal, including the conversion of dozens of interactive applications and thousands of static web pages from the old web sites to the new web portal design standards. Prototypes were developed and reviewed with members of the Project Team, Project Workgroup and ESC. Feedback from those stakeholder groups was worked into subsequent iterations of the prototypes.

Within six months, technical implementation activities were nearly complete. However, a key issue remained: the web site address, or URL, had not yet been determined. Senior county leadership felt that it was important that if a new web portal were to be released, it should have a new, fresh identity, and that visitors to existing county web sites should be redirected to the new portal immediately after launch, rather than after a transitional period. Therefore, DTS worked closely with the federal government to reserve a new URL using the new .gov extension and to implement the required redirects from the old web sites to the new web portal.

Before announcing the general availability of the new web portal to the public, the county unveiled the portal to all county employees in "soft-launch" mode. The soft-launch period lasted several weeks and was intended to catch any last minute errors and/or omissions.

Once the new portal was launched, the team enhanced the WBS to include the work requirements for Phase II of the program: the departmental web site conversion. The schedule defined the timelines by which departmental web sites would be converted and consolidated into the portal. The project team made technical and design resources available to the departments to assist with the technical conversion of the web sites. Over the course of the next 14 months, the project workgroup closely monitored the progress of the departmental web site consolidation until it was successfully completed.

## Results

According to the results of a customer satisfaction survey run continuously on the county's home page, the county has experienced a steady increase in customer satisfaction as a result of the ongoing enhancement and introduction of new online features and capabilities on the county's web portal. By directing all traffic through a single web portal instead of through a number of different and distinct web sites, the county has streamlined its constituents' online experience. All web pages have a consistent look and feel, leverage consistent technology and design standards, and promote the same brand. Further, maintaining a single web presence reduces the total cost of operations to the county while at the same time making it easier for constituents to obtain information about, and transact business with, county government.

Regarding customer satisfaction specifically, the percentage of survey respondents who agree that the county's web portal contains useful services and information, and is both visually appealing and well-designed, has risen in each of the three most recent fiscal years. *(Note: The county's fiscal year runs from July 1 through June 30.)*

The county also has realized improved employee productivity through the introduction of the new web portal and supporting tool sets. The use of the web site design standards has made it easier for departmental staff to build and deploy web content and applications. The development of the web policy and design guidelines have streamlined operations for the county's technical and program staff with web management and/or web content management responsibilities. Web designers now leverage the common repository of design templates to build and deploy web pages. Further, the centralized web content management system automates the content posting and approval workflow processes. The new web portal takes advantage of improving technology to make programs and services more accessible to county constituents and enhances constituent participation in local government.

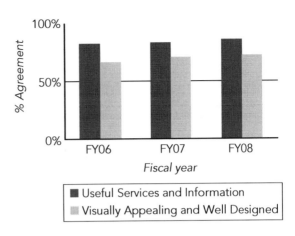

**Figure 11–2.** Customer Satisfaction Measures (FY06–FY08)

Over the same period of time during which the county has experienced a steady increase in customer satisfaction with the web portal, the county has also seen an increase in constituent utilization of the web portal. *(Note: The county utilizes WebTrends software to measure web utilization.)*

| | % increase from previous fiscal year | | |
|---|---|---|---|
| | FY06 | FY07 | FY08 |
| Visits | 13% | 21% | 8% |
| Hits | 8% | 8% | 25% |
| Unique visitors | 6% | | 13% |

**Figure 11–3.** Utilization Measures (FY06–FY08)

The increase in utilization of the web portal is attributable to several factors. Those include the introduction of new web sites and applications, changes to business processes (for example, effective in FY08, all applicants for county employment opportunities must apply using the online job application system instead of mailing or faxing job applications and resumes) and greater acceptance of the web as a viable and effective communication channel.

## Awards and recognition

Subsequent to its initial launch, the county web portal has received the following awards of distinction:

◆ *Computerworld Magazine*, Best e-Government Site, 2006
◆ MuniNet Guide and Review "Top Pick," 2004
◆ MuniNet Guide and Review "Top Pick," 2003
◆ Government Solutions Center "Pioneer" Award, 2003

- ◆ Center for Digital Government "Best of the Web" Award, 2003
- ◆ National Association of Telecommunications Officers and Advisors Award, 2003
- ◆ MuniNet Guide and Review "Top Pick," 2002

Further, the county's ranking in the Center for Digital Government's annual Digital Counties survey increased each year between 2004 (10th place) and 2007 (1st place–Top Digital County).

Last, several county e-Government web applications have been recognized with awards by prestigious organizations, including the Public Technology Institute and the National Association of Counties.

## Discussion questions

Undertaking a technically complex enterprise initiative is not for the faint of heart. Organizations considering such undertakings may consider its responses to the following questions prior to diving "head first" into such initiatives:

1. Is the program aligned with the organization's vision and mission?
2. To what extent is public engagement required? Are there processes to effectively engage internal and external constituents?
3. Does the organization have an effective governance model to enable successful execution of a complex enterprise initiative? Are roles and responsibilities, and decision making processes, well defined?
4. Is executive leadership fully committed to the effort, and have the required resources been provided?
5. Is the organization staffed with the skilled resources required to manage, implement and maintain a technically complex program?
6. Are there adequate controls to manage changes to: Scope? Schedule? Cost?
7. What is the projected ROI and total cost of ownership? Is the program affordable in the long term?
8. Is there an overall organizational change management strategy?
9. Have risks and consequences been documented, and is there an overall risk management plan? Have contingencies and mitigation plans been developed?
10. What does success look like? How is it measured?

**Ivan Galic** *joined Montgomery County's (Maryland) Department of Technology Services as the Division Chief for Enterprise Applications in June, 2002. Ivan held positions with General Electric, Verizon and American Management Systems prior to his tenure with the county. Ivan received his MBA from the University of Maryland and his B.S. degree from Penn State University.*

# PART THREE:

# Technology Practices

# Chapter 13. Resiliency Planning and Continuity of Operations: Beyond Disaster Planning

**LARRY CHASE**

Cities, regions and states rely on their voice and data resources to function on any given day. Data, voice and, today, even video capabilities make up the core infrastructure of economies and public services. Within government, the CIO is the primary steward of that infrastructure. The CIO is responsible for ensuring the network infrastructure is functional in order to enable all the departments to provide services on a daily basis. Despite that daily reliance on networks, however, the CIO often is thrust into a governance culture that does not always view those capabilities as core infrastructure.

When government officials talk about infrastructure, they usually mean roads, bridges, water lines, utility plants and other major physical assets dotting city landscapes. The term "disaster recovery" is rooted in that view of infrastructure. If a bridge collapses, a recovery operation is necessary.

When CIOs talk about infrastructure, they usually mean systems, networks, applications and other assets that thread through buildings and invisibly link various departments, services, command centers and mobile personnel. That infrastructure provides the foundation of daily government operations and economic transactions. The same infrastructure provides the basis of any crisis response. No disaster recovery operation will function without wired and wireless communications. It is like the "air" in any crisis. Nothing will happen without it.

"Recovery," then, is a misleading term in the context of this infrastructure category. Voice and data communications capabilities *must survive* a disaster to assist any recovery operation. Citizens must be able to call for help. First responders in the field must be able to coordinate efforts and be guided by dispatchers in a command center. This infrastructure enables all other recovery services and, thus, becomes a single point of failure for all services. Crisis situations expose the real role of the CIO and the infrastructure he or she protects. The CIO's role is to continuously maintain and protect the infrastructure *proactively* to make vital public services "resilient." Capabilities might bend, but they cannot break, or what comes after the hurricane, earthquake or explosion might actually be worse than the initial event.

Technology is the mechanism to deliver the various systems of government, such as health services. In concert, the CIO also works towards continuity of operations, which is often more regional in nature and encompasses collaboration between communities. The toggle point between ensuring daily operations and ensuring crisis response comes without warning. The CIO's charter is to build resiliency into the technology infrastructure on an ongoing basis so that the move from daily operations to crisis response is seamless.

For the CIO, network resiliency also must encompass contingencies for dealing with site-specific situations, such as a fire in a key healthcare facility. Too often, the many services provided by local government, especially counties, are overlooked. For instance, Los Angeles County Department of Health serves more than 10 million residents, providing healthcare to more than 700,000 people. That is a huge volume of daily traffic that would cause chaos if it were disrupted. Resiliency matters for that daily operation.

Elsewhere, Cook County's Bureau of Health Services has seven facilities serving its population. The ability to exchange medical data could be severely impacted if a fire occurs in just one facility. If servers and networks reside in each facility, what risk is associated with the loss of just one server? Residents who rely on county medical facilities may lose their entire medical history in one brief minute if resiliency planning is not in place. Rural counties may be more severely impacted in the face of their already slim budgets and limited service abilities as compared to urban counties.

Those real risks are part of daily operations for city, county and state agencies. Resiliency planning comprehends both daily needs and the absolute necessity for vital infrastructure to survive a natural or human-caused disaster. A paradigm change in the very nature of what constitutes a crisis demands resiliency planning in addition to disaster recovery. Hurricane Katrina, September 11, the threat of pandemics and other crises demand we become proactive in our thinking. The CIO's goal is to ensure the survival of critical infrastructure that maintains vital services throughout the crisis. Technically, that requires balancing the everyday usage of a system, the networks and applications against the infrequent crisis situations that may tax a system heavily but for a measured amount of time.

Toward that end, this chapter has three goals:

♦ Describe a resiliency planning process that takes an end-to-end view of the region as a holistic enterprise;
♦ Underscore the unique role of technology and the CIO within that process; and
♦ Call for a cultural transformation that embeds resiliency planning in the CIO's daily job responsibilities.

In that context, the CIO must argue for the resources necessary to bring together all the department and function leaders who will develop and implement the enterprise resiliency plan.

## The CIO's role

Technology infrastructure provides the backbone of operational flexibility and provides the foundation of crisis responses. Therefore, technology must fit into a larger plan, and the CIO must fight for stakeholder understanding on two different levels: the policy level to make governments aware of technology's role and what resiliency requires; and the field operational level to drive understanding of what is truly required in a crisis. Culturally, that means the CIO must build alliances with legislators, city controllers, agency heads, first responders and others to ensure that the critical nature of systems, applications and network infrastructure is well understood—and properly funded—by all stakeholders.

A growing vocabulary around disaster planning is useful, but definitions slide from context to context. For instance, what is "compliance" versus "readiness," and is one preferable over the other? Are "continuity" and "recovery" the same thing? The fact is that well-meaning people in this space use many words with great force even though precise definitions remain abstract and can easily shade into each other. The word "resiliency" is one such word—packed with meaning, yet difficult to pin down. This chapter defines "resiliency" as:

> The *capacity* to *ensure* that all *vital* public services *survive* in a crisis.

Certain items of infrastructure (e.g. key applications, servers, routers, radio networks) must function for anything else to happen. That is the essence of resiliency as used in this chapter. Resiliency planning carries implications for quality of life, economic development and the very nature of how a community sees itself. It also has policy and political implications that go well beyond networks and systems.

For the CIO, the best technology usage model is one where the technology is so naturally a part of the environment and an extension of the user's motivations that its usage becomes "second nature," whether the crisis is a major disaster or a fire in a key facility. This "second nature" philosophy underscores the key planning phases charted in this chapter:

♦ Risk and impact analysis
♦ Discovering dependencies
♦ Deploying the core capabilities of resiliency
♦ Practice, practice, practice
♦ Evolution

Resiliency is a process, a mode of thinking and a cultural practice. Cities, regions and states evolve over time, and the resiliency plan must keep pace. Likewise, infrastructure requires upgrades, maintenance and periodic re-thinking as new capabilities become available. Resiliency planning is a never-ending process. All the technology in the world cannot solve a problem that has not been identified and understood at the levels of daily business, strategic preparation and tactical operations. It begins with honestly analyzing the risks, establishing the priorities and determining where the interdependencies lay.

## Phase 1: Risk and impact analysis

The first step is to establish a holistic view of resiliency planning. Agency-by-agency planning is not a holistic process. The city, region or state must be viewed as a complete enterprise and approached with a comprehensive mindset. Only then can true risks be analyzed and meaningful priorities set. Taking this enterprise-wide perspective also facilitates buy-in amongst political leaders and local businesses, as well as aids breaking down cultural walls between various agencies. The CIO plays a crucial role in driving that holistic approach.

Resiliency planning starts with three basic questions that form the foundation of a plan:

1. What are the priorities—the critical services and functions that must survive disaster?
2. What, financially, is at risk (a city's economic engine, a costly major asset or a facility, etc.)?
3. What is the tolerance for disruption?

Unless you answer those questions, you have nothing to build a plan around. Without those answers, you could spend a lot of money on things that do not make a difference in a crisis. An enterprise-wide approach requires a thoughtful consideration of each question and its implications.

## 1. What are the priorities—the critical services and functions that must survive disaster?

The answers that will leap to mind are things such as human services, police, fire and rescue. Those answers contain many pre-suppositions, such as communications and transportation. First response services pre-suppose communications on at least two dimensions: dispatch and report. You have to be in contact with the first responders, and you have to be in contact with the public. From a transportation standpoint, you need to be able to deliver first responder services as a primary objective.

Secondly, for the local economy to survive, residents and businesses must be able to access transportation corridors, ship and receive materials and meet the daily demand for on-site service calls. You also need hospitals and shelters that can accept people once they are rescued, and you might need several backups for major disasters.

Planners must keep in mind that disasters take many forms. If a fire impacts one of the county medical facilities, it may strain the abilities of the other county medical facilities. Records will need to be shared, whether patient, pharmaceutical information or personnel data, and with equal priority placed on efficiency and the security of personnel information. Underlying those concerns, you are also assuming utilities will be functioning and backup power systems are operating.

A holistic approach to resiliency planning quickly demonstrates that hidden underneath the natural priorities are a series of dependencies that actually enable apparent priority functions. "Dependencies" in that context refers to infrastructure or processes that must function to enable some other capability, such as the pre-suppositions charted in the previous paragraph. Those dependency chains might be several layers deep and entail a web of human, physical and technological infrastructure. Understanding those dependency chains will lead you to where your real priorities lie. Those dependency chains also will become more important in a moment as the topic of "interdependency" enters the process.

## 2. What, financially, is at risk?

Once again, enterprise-wide thinking is critical to address that question. Businesses have assets and revenue at risk. Cities and counties have similar risks, but the question must be considered somewhat differently. Transportation hubs, such as airports or railroad lines, are assets of vital importance for reviving basic functions after a disaster. They also can be quite costly to rejuvenate if they are the sites of disaster. Likewise, key sites for data storage and transaction processing also are points of vulnerability for fires, power outages and less spectacular but no less important considerations. Such assets must play a role in resiliency planning, though only those in control of a plan can make the final risk assessment for such assets.

Regional economics also widens the scope of what should be considered at risk. For instance, the Gulf Coast often is pummeled by hurricanes that can wreak havoc with oil rigs and refinery operations potentially impacting the local economy directly and the entire nation indirectly as oil and gasoline production is curtailed during recovery. Those disruptions have ripple effects as it stresses the fuel supply chain across the nation, especially in states that might have mandated special fuel mixtures. If a major metropolitan area is unable to receive its necessary supply of fuel, for example, for its residents and businesses to travel to and from their jobs or produce and deliver goods, the impact extends beyond the actual area of the destruction. In an extreme case, the local government workforce, including first responders, could be hampered by inadequate fuel supplies. Those impacts come on top of the operational need to evacuate workers from those platforms and facilities ahead of the crisis.

The CIO must consider service disruption beyond the traditional perspective. Resiliency planning takes a holistic look at what is at risk and where the resources might be found to address those risks. For the CIO, the exercise expands the range of systems that must be linked beyond simply those within the walls of government agencies. For example, a social services department may need to re-establish itself temporarily at a warehouse to ensure access by those affected residents. That may require reaching beyond normal resource channels to ensure adequate supplies or support personnel.

While the answer to the "priorities" question might be largely similar between cities and regions, the "financial risk" question tailors a plan to the reality of a given location.

## 3. What is the tolerance for disruption?

A holistic thought process will identify assets and functions that must be considered in light of their importance to daily operations and their importance to crisis response. What if a pandemic flu caused the quarantine of a hospital? How will medical services continue uninterrupted across the region? What if fire or terrorist bombs crippled a power-generating facility? Those types of tough questions are a necessary component of a holistic view of resiliency planning.

Being able to respond to natural disasters is the top concern for public safety officials. (Source: APCO survey). Natural disasters bring their own considerations for what disruption can be temporarily tolerated. For instance, the disruption of feeder streets is more tolerable than a main artery that is blocked. For one locale, the city center might be less tolerant of disruption than the outer regions. For another city, maintaining a smooth connection to the suburbs might actually be more important than righting everything within the downtown core.

Different community services must be considered in the process as well as physical infrastructure. Courts and corrections agencies play a key role in everyday life and might be important in a disaster. Those judicial and penal functions implicate records management systems that must operate with impunity to process cases or the incarceration or release of individuals. Likewise, utility disruptions in one area might be more tolerable than in another area.

Disasters, by definition, will disrupt the normal rhythms of a city. Resiliency planning drives us to identify the rhythms that must be restored quickly and those that can wait. The answers to the above questions form the basis of a plan, but they constitute only the first step in the process. You now know your vulnerabilities and your core priorities. However, that knowledge alone does not meet the definition of resiliency. No one can yet confidently ensure key functions do not break. More work must be done, and here resiliency planning enters the realm of budgets and local/ regional politics. You must start taking the list of services and functions required and ask, "Who does that today?" "Who could do it if a backup were necessary?" "Where are my back-up facilities?" "What has to be functional before that service can be deployed?"

## Phase 2: Discovering dependencies

Two difficult things must happen in this phase of resiliency planning. First, the owners of functions, assets and public services identified as vital and vulnerable must make tough decisions on what action to take to address the vulnerability. Second, all the supporting factors that enable a vital function must be documented so that interdependencies can be targeted for resiliency assessment. Those are critical steps toward taking the priority baseline and building a plan around it. For the CIO engaged in resiliency planning, protecting systems and network infrastructure requires budget and cooperation from agencies and managers across the governmental and civic enterprise. Nothing happens in a vacuum. Resources must come from somewhere.

Of critical importance is a strong partnership between the CIO, public safety leaders and political leaders. The best overall results occur in those regions where those three entities are closely aligned. A good example of that is the State of Michigan, where the CIO/IT leader, state police and the political leaders are all very closely aligned. Most importantly, it has to be clear who really "owns" disaster preparedness from a technology perspective.

Faced with a known vulnerability, there are only three choices the owner of that priority function can make:

♦ Fix it
♦ Mitigate it
♦ Accept it

Putting off a decision is a tacit acceptance of risk. The holistic, enterprise-wide view requires open communication and cooperation, especially when different agency imperatives come into contact. Each choice carries a level of expenditure with it, either immediate or potentially at another point in time. Engaging the chief financial officer, the budget officer and procurement officer is crucial at this stage. Along with risk is an implied level of cost. Part of the CIO's educational role includes creating the understanding that these are not just investments for a potential disaster, but investments that will put daily operations on a more resilient footing, as well. The holistic view resists placing resiliency expenditures outside standard budgeting processes.

The reality is, however, that there are trade-offs government agencies will need to make with respect to levels of redundancy and back-up systems versus the economics and budget constraints. Those trade-offs should be clearly articulated to the political and public safety leaders with options, pros and cons, and recommended solutions so everyone understands the "calculated risk" that an agency may make due to budget constraints, such as not having a back-up master site. Trade-off decisions are made on a daily basis because there are severe budget constraints that government agencies are faced with every day. That further drives the need for more inter-local agreements, memorandums of understanding and sharing to achieve economies of scale.

For instance, the information security officer is responsible for the protection of data, including citizen records, business tax records, criminal records, employee personal health information and more. Media reports of data breaches and compromised privacy are numerous. Understanding the risks versus the investment of enhancing security measures is purely a business decision. How secure does an agency need to be, and what are the associated costs? With increasing instances of identity theft, businesses and residents will quickly lose faith in conducting transactions online, perhaps delaying revenue due to the city, county or state if security falters. Physical security and database back-up capability becomes more important in flood, earthquake, wildfire and hurricane regions. There is a cost to resiliency whether it is in the form of software or hardware, but it cannot be seen as an extraordinary cost. The CIO must create an environment in which technical infrastructure is rightly viewed as the basis of service delivery in all circumstances by all stakeholders.

Creating that environment might require CIOs to integrate stakeholder views outside their own experience. First responders have a special set of needs that must be considered. It is likely that most CIOs have never run into a burning building or faced down criminals in the street. Yet, they are responsible for ensuring the operation of the voice and data communication networks first responders require for coordinating rescue and police operations. Leaders of first responder services must make the harsh realities of their lives known to planners, and planners must recognize that there is more to resiliency than systems and networks.

Fortunately, more than one route presents itself to achieving resiliency. For key services, resiliency will require a backup strategy to avoid a single point of failure for the overall plan. To layer in backup capabilities and share costs, reciprocal agreements between neighboring communities, counties and states represent a growing trend. Those agreements can range from personnel to equipment. Reciprocal agreements stretch resources, budgets and the commitment to resiliency as a cultural underpinning of governance.

Even so, no simple solution exists for a problem that is not understood in its details. That takes us into the realm of dependency chaining: identifying the functions or services that depend on the smooth operation of another service or capability.

Most public-facing activities are dependent on other capabilities enabling them. Many of those individual support activities might carry their own dependencies. Resiliency lies in the details. In charting dependencies, you will no doubt identify interdependencies, singular enablers of multiple services and functions that present single points of failure in a crisis. Communications and human capital will no doubt emerge as crucial interdependencies and will be addressed in the next section to illustrate a dependency chaining exercise.

With dependencies and interdependencies fully documented and understood, you have the framework for a plan. It is time to begin putting tactical considerations into place.

## Phase 3: Deploying the core capabilities of resiliency

Vital functions that support all established priorities can bend, but they cannot break. They are not things that can be "recovered" after the crisis passes. They must survive the crisis, and that requires extensive planning and multiple backup contingency plans. One of those structural interdependencies is communications networks.

### *Communications networks*

Communications is the "air" in a crisis. It is consistently ranked by public safety administrators as their biggest worry in a crisis. Communications networks also provide the flow of data for normal functions in daily service delivery. Nothing happens without communications. It is a common enabling capacity across numerous dependency chains. Conversely, it is a single point of systemic failure in a crisis and an arena where the CIO can make a real difference in the planning process.

How do you make communications resilient? The dependency chain is the roadmap. Two key communications capabilities that will be stressed in a crisis are the 9-1-1 lines between government authorities and the public. The other is the private voice and data networks that enable first responders to coordinate. It is important to recognize first and foremost that those networks are used in the daily operation of public safety. They are mission critical at all times. Resiliency planning supports those functions through their daily roles as well as in their crisis roles. So, the budgets for ensuring resiliency naturally should be a part of the normal operations. That includes the ongoing maintenance and necessary upgrades required over the passage of time.

Likewise, the equipment—from radios to backup mobile sites on wheels—can and should be seen as the normal fabric of governance useful to coordinate civic functions as well as crisis response. Viewing those mission-critical pieces of infrastructure as only useful in a crisis is a step toward making personnel unfamiliar with them at a moment when lives are in the balance.

The convergence of voice, data and video on the networks creates various considerations that must be understood in advance of a crisis. Redundancy is one strategy toward resiliency. However, that strategy involves the dependency of *interoperability*. The CIO naturally will be well aware of interoperability as a technical and process issue. According to SAFECOM, a Department of Homeland Security agency, interoperability is both a technical and procedural imperative. Planners must recognize that while common systems across agencies and governmental units might be ideal, we are, at best, in transition toward that state, and we must accept that a special-needs situation might exist for one agency or locale that requires specialized applications support.

The SAFECOM recommendations specify common communications governance policies to reconcile processes and capabilities. Everyone sharing networks must operate by the same principles. That one compliance point leads to another dependency of common technical specifications for:

- ◆ Common communications applications where possible
- ◆ Customized interfaces that mask differences between applications
- ◆ Standards-based data interchange for *pulling* and *pushing* data across disparate networks and systems

Those data-oriented rules are just the beginning dependencies for ensuring interoperability. The tactical makeup of a disaster response varies from disaster to disaster. Fixed infrastructure (the first layer of service) might be damaged in unpredictable circumstances. Mobile solutions come in different categories of capability, supplementing and extending any fixed capability. Backup data networks can be established quickly to extend network capability into areas where fixed infrastructure has been damaged or overwhelmed with traffic. Likewise, CIOs should plan for a stock of critical components (routers, servers, etc.), backup fixed-site command and control centers, and mobile command and control vehicles that put the command and control function where it needs to be at a given point in time. One point easily overlooked, however, is that a significant portion of your mobile resources (though by no means all of them) are only useful if they are staged well outside the geographic scope of destruction or an impacted area, in the case of a pandemic.

## Human capital

The dependency chaining exercise cannot take anything for granted. For instance, it is easy to over-look the need for people—from first responders to medical professionals and beyond—to provide critical functions. To illustrate the point, the threat of pandemic flu and other viruses permeate public health literature and enter the headlines regularly. What happens if a facility is quaran-tined to control the public health impact? That quarantine might remove a hospital from servicing the public, but it also might shut down the building, which houses a vital public service. An entire agency affected by the disease quickly illustrates the importance of resiliency planning. In the case of medical facilities taken out of action, health and human services might quickly burst at the seams, unable to provide critical services to residents. Imagine the chaos if the staff providing human services also becomes ill, and the building becomes quarantined.

Network infrastructure also is implicated in those scenarios, both as problem and potential miti-gating factor. Challenges to access important records and information must be understood and quickly overcome. If a human services agency shuts down, the public quickly resorts to emer-gency rooms at county medical facilities. If those facilities can no longer accept patients, will the health facility in the neighboring county have access to patient medical histories?

A pandemic illustrates the interconnectedness of our world and the need for infrastructure that comprehends that interconnectedness. In a pandemic disease scenario, the issue quickly goes global. If you stockpile lifesaving medications in the most convenient spot in a city, for instance, those supplies may be in harm's way or inaccessible if roads are blocked or congested. The ability to interact quickly between various agencies is crucial. Having established relationships between the public and private sector under those conditions is crucial.

In either the structural interdependency (communications) or the human capital scenario, crisis agreements must be in place with all critical suppliers and vendors. Normal procurement pro-cesses may not work during times when urgency is critical. Establishing a quick-turn procure-ment process or contract with key suppliers can, in most cases, provide the means of getting what you need on a same-day priority basis. In some cases, making arrangements to lease equipment or establishing the timeframe to start building equipment as soon as you are aware of a pending major event or disaster such as a hurricane, may be the preferred option. A solid relationship with the financial controller and procurement officer will ensure that contracts are in place and that costs are understood and tracked—especially important for federal reimbursements.

This overview can be tailored to other interdependencies, such as utilities, transportation or pub-lic works functions such as mass transit. Upon completing Phase 3, the plan should be formalized, with those invested with triggering the plan's implementation fully empowered to do so. At that point, the basic underpinnings of a plan are in place. However, no one can yet ensure the plan works. It has not been tested.

## Phase 4: Practice, practice, practice

Practice and evaluation are absolutely necessary and must become so ingrained in the holistic enterprise-wide approach that responding to a crisis becomes "second nature." Yet, that can be one of the most difficult steps for the CIO to build momentum around. Staging a realistic disas-ter costs money, temporarily redirects personnel from their jobs and potentially disrupts traffic flows in populated areas. But, it's important that the CIO and CFO collaborate in making that happen. It can be considered an investment in the future; invest a little now to save a lot later. In a city or county, that is everyone's responsibility, but there must be one owner to make sure it happens.

Whether it's the CIO, city manager, purchasing director, county clerk, mayor, sheriff, police chief, there has to be agreement that formalizing the plan is only effective if everyone buys into it and practices it on a regular basis. Representatives from various agencies and even key vendor partners must be part of the resiliency planning process and also participate during any disaster scenario. Any exercise should include the operation of a "crisis response center" where all the agency heads, the CIO and critical vendors collaborate and practice the interactions of the response and recovery scenario.

At that point in the planning process, many scenarios have, no doubt, occurred to those involved, some of those fears perhaps haunting the process overall. One such scenario should be selected and staged. The behind-the-scenes directors of the scenario should be distinct from those in operational roles to preserve the legitimacy of surprises and the need to react in the moment. A full and painfully honest evaluation or "after action report" must then take place, with flaws highlighted and people tasked to address them. In an appropriate time and place, practice and training should take place once again. Updating the plan based on the learnings also is important.

You started with a blank sheet of paper staring at you. You have set priorities, gained buy-in from stakeholders, made tough decisions about disruption tolerance, laid in the backup systems and networks, and practiced. Assuming you have completed the process with open and honest commitment to improvement, you now have a resilient plan. You now face the challenge of maintaining resiliency as time passes and changes occur in the regional landscape and halls of power.

## Phase 5: Evolution

The final steps to formalizing the plan involve:

◆ Committing to regular training and practice. Document learnings and incorporate into the resiliency plan.
◆ Including ongoing maintenance and upgrades for all critical networks. Excluding that step only means taking on unnecessary risk that can be more costly in the long run.
◆ Committing to evolving the plan as time passes, new technologies or new priorities enter the planning horizon.

The resiliency philosophy requires documentation of the stages of response once a situation develops or occurs. Inherent in those stages is the goal of minimizing risk to people, assets and operational processes. You should think of it as a "script" that describes roles and responsibilities and the flow of the actions. No magic formula exists for how detailed that script should be. It is safe to say that it should be detailed enough to drive action, though not so detailed that the script itself becomes a barrier to triggering required activity. For some localities, a 20-page plan is appropriate. For another, 50 pages might be appropriate. The goal is to produce a document that will drive action when it is needed. Whether the CIO or another agency leader is responsible for the plan, the key leaders must have a copy and it must be used and continuously updated. It is a circular process by nature.

Part of the documenting process is the determination of who has the authority to trigger the plan's implementation. That could be a single official or a small group. Whoever holds that power must be willing and able to use it when necessary. Every second counts, and hesitation at the outset can have cascade effects throughout the emergency. Leaders must also recognize that cities, regions and states are not stagnant. They grow and evolve. New priorities can enter the picture. For the CIO, new technologies can alter dependency chains.

*Resiliency is the capacity to ensure that all vital services survive in a crisis.* The CIO is uniquely positioned to drive resiliency as an approach to crises because of technology's capabilities to collapse time and space, and connect disparate systems and processes. Of the planning stakeholders, the CIO is the one most comfortable with such a core capability of infrastructure. Even so, the CIO must be a force for bridging cultures, agencies and functions.

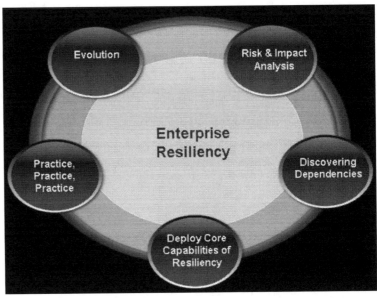

Figure 13-1.

This chapter provides one tool the CIO can use to drive a resiliency planning process, position technology's role within that process, and create a "resiliency" culture that practices regularly and evolves constantly. The CIO might not be the first person called when crisis erupts, but that first responder will rely on all networks functioning smoothly and the solid foundation of resiliency planning.

## Discussion questions

1. In what ways does enterprise resiliency compare and contrast to disaster planning?
2. How do you ensure that the resiliency plan of today is a usable resiliency plan in the future, whether it is six months, one year or five years in the future?
3. Have you ever experienced a natural disaster? How did it disrupt your daily family life? How did it disrupt the way your community runs? What did you learn from it?
4. If you were responsible for enterprise resiliency for your city, what measures would you take to minimize the impact on the economy (or productiveness) of your city?
5. Develop a list of priority services offered by your school, the company you work for or your city. In the event of a disaster, what is the financial impact associated with the disruption of those services? How well will the school administration, instructors and students (or the leaders of your business or city) be able to tolerate the disruption?

6. What are the functions or services that depend on each for a smooth operation of service? Use your school, business, city or county to identify functions or services that depend on each other. Do your dependencies link people to people or departments to departments? Which is a better dependency chain?

7. Your enterprise resiliency plan is complete. How do you ensure that all departments and all key people involved react according to plan?

## REFERENCES

Motorola/APCO Survey, February 2007. http://www.motorola.com/FutureTech

Los Angeles County website. http://lacounty.info

Cook County website. http://www.co.cook.il.us

SAFECOM website. http://www.safecomprogram.gov

"Workforce Continuity Defined." Gartner Research Report, 15 September 2008.

"Preparing for Natural Disaster." Motorola Position Paper, 2008.

Motorola interviews

**Larry Chase** *has 20 years of experience of global infrastructure engineering, including 15 years of operational Business Continuity & Disaster Recovery leadership in the Pharmaceutical, Banking and Technology Industries. In November 2007, Mr. Chase joined Motorola Information Protection Services as the Director of Enterprise Resiliency. He now leads a global team effort to institutionalize event management across the business and IT operations. Prior to his current position, Mr. Chase was responsible for the development of the Pfizer Worldwide Business Continuity Management program.*

*Mr. Chase is accredited as a Microsoft Certified Systems Engineer, Novell Certified Netware Engineer, and is a DRII Certified Business Continuity Professional. He served with the United States Air Force from 1983-1991 as an Intelligence Collections Officer. In April 2006, Mr. Chase was elected to the Strohl User Group Advisory Board and currently serves as one of three officers to the board.*

# 14. A CIO Perspective on Integrating Geo-Information Systems into IT

**ALAN LEIDNER**

## I. Introduction

As an everyday part of their jobs, CIOs of large county and city governments must integrate an ever-growing and evolving variety of capabilities and technologies to ensure the effective management of computer systems serving the enterprise needs of their jurisdictions. Over the past years, CIOs have had to contend with rapidly advancing Internet services, new generations of software and programming languages, high speed telecommunications technologies, wireless communications, and a proliferation of field computers and PDAs. Also, ever since microcomputers sparked an explosion of computer use outside the jurisdiction of the centralized mainframe world, CIOs have had to deal sensitively with a complex environment where agency-based IT managers who did not come under the CIO's direct control have a major hand in implementing departmental systems. Into this challenging environment, CIOs are also increasingly contending with geospatial information systems (GIS), trying to find the optimal balance between central control and *laissez faire* policies. The purpose of this chapter is to explore the synergies between central IT and GIS, and the role of the CIO in maximizing and measuring their benefits.

## II. Geospatial Information Systems hit the mainstream

Geospatial services are in the news. Millions of Internet users are flocking to Google Earth and Microsoft Maps, adding to those who regularly utilize Expedia.com and similar travel and direction-finding services on their desktops. Many municipal and state Internet portals feature detailed, interactive mapping applications. Cell phones and other PDAs are now routinely equipped with a global positioning system (GPS) capability. Many cars and boats come from the dealers with vehicle location systems installed. Those developments show that the public has an appetite for and increasing understanding of location-oriented services, heightening their expectations of government. Moreover, following the extensive use of geospatial systems to support response and recovery operations following 9/11 and subsequent disasters, GIS is being taken seriously as a strategic technology critical to national security. Geospatial systems have entered the mainstream, and there will be no looking back. Consequently, the posture taken by the CIO toward the systems is of increasing importance.

## III. A very brief and impressionistic history of location

**Beginnings:** The science of geography evolved from the human need to know where important resources could be located, where dangers were to be avoided and the best route to take when traveling from one place to another. The first maps were undoubtedly drawn on the ground with a stick and on the walls of caves with charcoal. They capitalized on the human genius to visually organize information as an aid to memory and as a means to grasp relationships and patterns. Ancient Egyptians, Greeks and Romans, through their development of mathematics and geometry, increased their understanding of the curved surface of the earth, and refined the art and science of map making. Navigational aids, from the compass to the sextant and the chronometer, revolutionized navigation and opened up the oceans for commerce.

Geography in combination with geology, the science of the structure and composition of the earth, were used to exploit important mineral deposits and other natural resources. Land survey methods and supportive technologies were developed to precisely demarcate property boundaries, delineate administrative districts and national borders, and plan the layout of roadways and cities. Geography was used in war time to "map" battlefield terrain, pinpoint the location of one's own forces and those of the enemy, and design strategies for attack and defense. As large bureaucracies came into existence, geographical functions served many agencies in support of property and asset management, taxation, zoning, engineering, and a variety of service delivery operations. In short, practical and valuable applications of the science of geography predate the development of the computer by thousands of years.

**Geography and the computer age:** As the value and importance of the IT function grew through the 1960s and 1970s, and as mainframe systems became increasingly essential, local governments began consolidating their IT operations into centralized departments with executive status. During that period, the application of computer technology to most geographic functions lagged because of the difficulty in digitally representing geographic information types, and because standard query languages could not accommodate critical spatial functions, such as measuring distance and calculating areas of overlap. Although addresses, parcels and similar location-oriented attribute data easily became fields within most databases, coordinate systems, photographic imagery and the digital representations of map features—such as points, lines and polygons—were not amenable to early computerization. Finally, in the 1980s, pioneering engineers and geographers created breakthrough software that could digitally represent and manipulate map and other graphical features, such as building structural elements. Those capabilities were designed to work on newly emergent stand-alone workstations and microcomputers and thus, GIS and Computer Assisted Design and Drafting (CADD) systems played an important role in the PC revolution that shook the IT world.

**GIS adopted for specialty functions:** Geospatial capabilities were rapidly adopted for use by professionals in a wide variety of fields for use in specialty systems usually at arms length from centralized mainstream shops. Geospatial practitioners also were able to utilize global positioning satellites for many non-military functions, from supporting aerial photography to allowing anyone with a GPS receiver to rapidly identify and communicate their exact location on the face of the earth.

Most geospatial practitioners saw themselves as engineers, environmental and health scientists, and planners first, and not as IT professionals. Culturally, it could be seen as crew cuts versus long hairs, sneakers and jeans versus white shirts and ties. (Note: These days CIOs are far hipper than they used to be!)

To many in the IT world, an address remained one field among many, albeit a particularly unreliable one where many errors were often found. To some GIS practitioners, enterprise practices and procedures were burdens to be ignored in pursuit of the cartographically perfect map.

**GIS catches on but finds success comes with problems:** Yet despite the divide between GIS users and the IT establishment, geospatial systems, often flying under the radar and funded by functional managers, caught on and grew. In particular, municipal agencies that directly delivered public services, managed facilities and infrastructure, or were responsible for planning services across large areas, recognized the importance of manipulating geo-enabled information to support their work.

When a municipal water utility repairs a distribution line, it can be guided by some combination of a unique infrastructure ID, a geographic coordinate, a map or sketch of house connections and customer address. When a local public safety dispatch center (PSAP) receives a distress call, a telephone number must be rapidly matched to the appropriate street address, which is then linked to the position of responders, and the location of travel routes and backup facilities. When a hurricane approaches, emergency managers want to rapidly identify areas likely to flood, at-risk infrastructure, evacuation routes, shelters and the location of at-risk individuals who may need assistance. When there is a disease outbreak, health scientists examine its geographic distribution to identify patterns that will help in the design of a containment strategy. When devising revenue-collection methods, governments need to look across all revenue-related databases to aggregate funds owed at the same address and within specific areas. Those are but a few instances where spatial systems enabling the rapid linking and combining of location information support essential government operations.

**Growing pains:** But the growth experienced by geospatial systems also led to problems. GIS application teams—not only in different agencies but often within the same agency—tended not to collaborate, and isolated geospatial data silos proliferated. Different agencies, at great expense, built duplicate and incompatible basemaps to suit their individual needs, then found to their dismay that data could not be easily or accurately related across systems. Moreover, most discovered they could not sustain the continuous flow of funding they required to keep their data up to date. Aware of the inefficiencies, GIS personnel started to band together to address enterprise-wide issues and opportunities, but because few—if any—held executive positions and could not command agency or city resources, it was often impossible for headway to be made. GIS began to acquire an unsavory reputation for producing flashy results in the short term that could not be sustained over time.

## IV. GIS into IT—A winning argument

The 1990s saw a combination of factors that led to the rapprochement between GIS committees and CIOs. Astute CIOs, watching the growing pains of geospatial initiatives often from afar, recognized the potential of the technology and were looking for opportunities to exert management control while also being wary of invading the turf of agencies with political clout. CIOs with a keen understanding of municipal operations grasped that there were aspects of GIS work that would greatly benefit from centralized authority. CIOs understood that geospatial information, no matter how exotic the object types, broke down into bits and bytes like all other data. They saw the folly of building duplicate networks to support geospatial systems and the inefficiency of acquiring GIS software in small, uncoordinated buys when the price could be significantly lowered through enterprise licensing. They noticed that the same street address might be collected independently by a dozen different divisions, with significant disparity in field structure, thwarting any hope that the address field could be used to cherry pick data from multiple databases to provide a complete picture of all activities going at any one location. They recognized that producing one authoritative ID for every building could solve a multitude of problems experienced by their jurisdiction—from police and fire responders not being able to find a location to boxes full of returned envelopes containing tax bills rejected by the Post Office because of bad addresses. Indeed, incomplete and contradictory location information introduces significant inefficiency and risk of failure into municipal operations. Many CIOs probably came to believe that the only thing more painful than getting location right was getting location wrong.

**GIS comes to the table:** On the other hand, astute geospatial practitioners, with increasing amounts of professional training and a broader perspective, recognized the inefficiencies of stand-alone and departmental systems, and understood the enormous benefits that could come from enterprise GIS (E-GIS). They imagined one most accurate basemap of the entire jurisdiction that was kept up to date and that everyone used, making all the information registered to the base fully compatible, and capable of being combined for analysis and operations support. They conceptualized a unified digital infrastructure that made it possible for bandwidth-intensive GIS data to be easily shipped between offices and even extended out to the field using wireless communications. They imagined a comprehensive address database incorporated into a geocoding engine that would ensure that all the key geospatial data elements in all databases were drawn from one, well-maintained source that guaranteed accuracy. They hoped for a powerful, highly placed champion willing to fight for their priorities.

While some dreamed about how that could come about through a totally independent GIS organization, many understood that integration with IT and the acceptance of the CIO as their leader made the most sense. Where reason did not prevail, there were instances where budget managers, fed up with waste, failure and duplication of effort, wielded the shotgun at the marriage of IT and GIS.

**A new environment emerges:** Fortunately, the IT organizations in the 1990s were different than the ones in the 1980s. Dealing with the proliferation of microcomputers and networked systems had taught CIOs that there needed to be a balance between centralized and decentralized systems management. Central control was needed to guarantee standards, efficient procurement, compatible architectures and the implementation of enterprise services and applications. Departments, if acting within enterprise guidelines, could then be given autonomy to develop systems that met specific business requirements and depended upon agency subject-matter expertise. That model worked when applied to GIS systems, especially when a CIO recognized the importance of hiring a highly qualified Geospatial Information Officer (GIO) as high-ranking deputy, who could serve as an expert champion for enterprise GIS efforts.

## V. Key elements in building enterprise GIS

While the nitty gritty of enterprise GIS development ought to be managed by the GIO, the CIO should have a clear understanding of some of the major elements that a successful effort must include.

**Building and maintaining the basemap:** One key to the development of enterprise GIS, and perhaps the most expensive, is the building of a spatial data infrastructure that encompasses the total area of a jurisdiction and includes all important physical and legal elements. Assuming that capable in-house or consultant staff is available for the up-front technical design work, building E-GIS usually begins with the acquisition of digital aerial photography with a pixel size of one foot or smaller. All the features seen in the imagery product—buildings, curblines, streets, water features, street furniture—will be in an accurate relationship with both the earth and with each other.

Concurrently, a jurisdiction should be developing a unified and comprehensive street name and address database, and assembling parcel maps for digital coversion and registration to the aerial basemap. Making sure that each structure and each parcel is tagged with its correct address and parcel ID ensures that all legacy databases containing address and parcel data can now be linked to the common basemap and, through the use of their location fields as indexing keys, to each other. Once base data has been built, data maintenance operations must be properly staffed. As base map products including a geocoding engine are distributed to municipal agencies, standards must be set to govern each department's data and application development activities. Also useful is an internal consulting service to help agencies harmonize their GIS development with the enterprise.

**Infrastructure upgrades:** CIOs, upon overcoming the sticker shock associated with building an E-GIS data infrastructure, will then be confronted with huge geospatial data sets that threaten to overwhelm IT infrastructures. Once more, it will be necessary for CIOs to take a big breath and push for the funds necessary to upgrade capacity. Fortunately, technology advances, such as the move toward high bandwidth fiber; the implementation of service-oriented, web-based architectures; exponential increases in processing power and memory; compression software, which can shrink the footprint of imagery and feature files; and new generations of database software that come with spatial extensions; are combining to keep costs in check while vastly expanding capabilities.

**Organizing, planning and financing:** Successful enterprise GIS requires the organization of a steering committee of agency GIS managers to help set GIS policies and priorities, and to promote data sharing and collaboration. The GIO must be an active member of the community if not its leader. The CIO will play a key role in being the overall champion for GIS initiatives with the clout to fight for new initiatives and funding for system and data maintenance.

In a hub/spoke organization design, a sensible division of labor between central and decentralized efforts will be required. Central IT must have sufficient staff and resources to develop enterprise applications serving everyone and maintain many of the common framework data sets, including regularly capturing new aerial photography, designing and enforcing standards, and ensuring that GIS requirements are part of the jurisdiction's IT planning and budgeting processes.

Many CIOs chronically strapped for funding often find themselves having to balance funding for their traditional systems with the insatiable appetite of geospatial systems for more. In the past, when the CIO asked the earnest GIS managers for a rationale for such expenditures, about all they received was a shrug of the shoulders that seemed to say, "We create maps, not business cases." That answer is not longer adequate. GIS priorities must compete with all other IT initiatives and deserve to be funded only if their worth can be proven. The following section provides a path for creating a cost benefit rationale for enterprise GIS and for individual GIS projects.

## VI. The payoff: New capabilities impact the bottom line

The build-out of an enterprise GIS will provide GIOs and CIOs with a number of capabilities that can have significant impact on municipal operations that can be shown to more than offset expenditures. GIS promotes **enterprise data integration** by making it possible for information from different datasets to be related to one another by keying on common spatial fields. The GIS capacity for **visualizing** information makes it easier for employees to organize and operationalize their field work, and for citizens to rapidly obtain useful information via highly intuitive mapping interfaces delivered over the Internet. The geocoding application made possible by enterprise GIS allows universal **address normalization and validation,** which guarantees the accuracy of address information upon which depends the efficient and timely delivery of critical services. GIS-based analysis enables **pattern recognition,** which allows government managers to identify trends, detect problems and find solutions in areas, including infrastructure protection, crime reduction and disease control. The **routing and distance calculation** capabilities of GIS permit more effective allocation of work and the more efficient design of work routes.

However, the true measure of benefits that can be realized by those and other geo-capabilities will remain unknown unless the CIO makes a conscious effort to quantify them. The next section outlines the specific kinds of quantifiable benefits achievable by GIS-enabled operations that can be documented and used to more than justify expenditures on E-GIS.

## VII. Return on investment: Proving that GIS is worth the extra price

The following are excellent areas to start looking for significant and measurable returns on your enterprise GIS investments.

**Improved revenues:** Many counties and cities depend upon property tax revenues based on the assessed value of land and structures. Although property tax operations have always been geospatial in nature, aerial photography, including oblique angle photos, can be used to identify property improvements missed by field inspectors. Benefits can range from a 0.5% to 2% or larger gain in assessed value. While seemingly small, when computed against the entire tax base, that benefit alone can totally offset the cost of building and maintaining an enterprise GIS. Similarly, if all revenue-oriented databases can be geo-enabled, jurisdictions can aggregate all outstanding taxes, fines and fees by individual, property and address, which can greatly assist collection efforts, a tactic used by Arlington County, Virginia, among others, with great success. Additionally, comprehensive and up-to-date GIS information about streets and houses supplied to the U.S. Census Bureau can increase population counts by 5% or more. If a jurisdiction of 100,000 receives $200 per capita in federal and state grants, a 5% census increase can result in an additional $1 million annually.

**Public safety:** E-911 emergency dispatch operations save thousands of lives annually and are supported by systems that depend on location information. At the core of the systems is the ability to pinpoint where an incident has occurred by matching phone number to address (or cell phone-provided coordinate), identify the nearest potential responder, and direct the responder to the scene by the shortest possible route. E-GIS can ensure that address and routing errors are kept to an absolute minimum. Efficient dispatch lowers response time, which is highly correlated to reduced deaths and injury.

GIS also is the key component of crime pattern analysis applications and aids the design of crime-fighting strategies. CompStat applications, a key component of the intelligence-led policing movement, have helped to dramatically reduce crime levels in a number of major counties and cities, including New York, which over the past 18 years has seen its murder rate reduced by more than 70 percent. Benefits measured in lives saved can have a significant impact on how GIS and IT funding requests are perceived by budget offices and CEOs.

**Productivity:** E-GIS data, when combined with automated vehicle location (AVL), mobile computers and wireless communications, can increase productivity of inspectors, social service workers and service crews by 10% or more. Geospatially equipping the mobile worker also can significantly increase the speed and improve quality of information collected in the field. Accurate field information can impact revenues by ensuring that data collected to support violations issuance and associated fines will stand up to challenge in court. Benefits can be quantified as time saved and in improved revenue collections.

**Greater information availability:** E-GIS gives a jurisdiction the ability to publish easy-to-understand information over the Internet to serve a variety of functions. Internet maps allow citizens and visitors to quickly locate key facilities, and identify services and areas of importance to them. During an emergency, maps posted to the Internet can direct the public to evacuation routes and to shelters. Additionally, a well-designed web site can highlight available sites that might be of interest to developers from across the county or around the world.

**Guidelines to coming up with numbers:** CIOs interested in coming up with solid numbers that document the benefits of enterprise GIS can utilize a number of tools. Public Technology Institute (PTI) has published guidelines, which include an ROI methodology to systematically identify and calculate benefits, that have been used successfully in a number of jurisdictions to justify expenditures. The Geospatial Information Technology Association (GITA) also has come out with a rigorous manual that guides ROI calculations with a focus on increased worker productivity.

## VIII. A national perspective

With GIS in their portfolios, CIOs now find themselves in a position not only to enable major improvements in their own jurisdictions but also to play a significant role in their region, their state and their nation. For as it turns out, the enterprise data built for municipal E-GIS have important applications beyond local boundaries.

The same factors that drive efforts to consolidate GIS within a local government also impel geo-data integration across regions, states, and the nation as a whole. When data is developed to common standards, there is no reason why it cannot be combined—LEGO®like—across jurisdictional borders to solve problems and support services. The federal government, aware of that potential has created institutions and programs that endeavor to realize the full potential of GIS for the nation. That mission has taken on added importance following 9/11 with the additional need to provide for national security and infrastructure protection. Most recently, the importance of the GIS mission has been heightened by the perception that national geo-data has a role in helping the nation dig out of its economic crisis by providing the information foundation for infrastructure rebuilding efforts. Those developments put CIOs and their GIS deputies at center stage of vital national efforts.

**Federal Geospatial Data Committee (FGDC):** The Federal Geographic Data Committee (FGDC: http://www.fgdc.gov/ ) is composed of high-ranking geospatial representatives from federal agencies that help to direct government geospatial policy. One of its programs, initated by the Office of Management and Budget, is the Geospatial Line of Business (GeoLoB: http://www.fgdc.gov/geospatial-lob ), which is striving to identify and eliminate redundancy in national geospatial initiatives, and is developing the National Spatial Data Infrastructure (NSDI). The Fifty States Initiative (http://www.fgdc.gov/policyandplanning/50states ) seeks to strengthen geospatial capabilities at the state and local level by providing grants for planning and data development.

The FGDC is working closely with the National States Geographic Information Council (NSGIC: www.nsgic.org ) composed of state geospatial representatives. Many NSGIC representatives have organized GIS Councils in their states that include local GIS directors.

Relatedly, the Department of the Interior recently established the National Geospatial Advisory Council (NGAC), under the Federal Advisory Committee Act (FACA). The role of NGAC is to provide advice on national geospatial policies. NGAC reports to the Chair of the FGDC and has a number of representatives drawn from local governments. Information about NGAC membership and activities can be found at: http://www.fgdc.gov/ngac.

**Homeland Infrastructure Foundation Level Data (HIFLD):** The HIFLD program (http://www.hifldwg.org/ ), jointly sponsored by the Department of Homeland Security, the National Geospatial-Intelligence Agency (NGA), Department of Defense, and the U.S. Geological Survey, has brought together GIS leaders from all levels of government and from the private sector, to identify GIS needs and data assets. The program has played an important role in the development of HSIP Gold infrastructure data, which now includes more than 400 critical infrastructure and key resources (CIKR) layers. HSIP Gold datasets relate to the 18 critical infrastructure and key resources (CIKR) categories identified and described in Homeland Security Presidential Directive #7 (HSPD7) and the National Infrastructure Protection Plan (NIPP). HSIP Freedom, a subset of the HSIP Gold datasets, is now being made available to state and local governments. The HIFLD program plans to increase collaboration with state and local governments over the coming year.

**DHS Office of Infrastructure Protection:** The Department of Homeland Security's Office of Infrastructure Protection (OIP: http://www.dhs.gov/xabout/structure/gc_1185203138955.shtm) within the National Planning and Programs Directorate (NPPD) not only plays a key role in developing and managing HSIP Gold data but also utilizes it to analyze infrastructure threats, vulnerabilities and interdependencies, and to develop protection programs. Additionally, DHS grant programs are being used to fund geospatial data and infrastructure programs and projects at the local level. CIOs may find it worthwhile to review a recent DHS publication entitled, "A Guide to Critical Infrastructure and Key Resources Protection at the State, Regional, Local, Tribal, and Territorial Level," issued in September 2008.

**National Geospatial Organizations:** CIOs also should be aware that there are a number of highly influential national organizations that bring together city and county geospatial practitioners and work to advance the use of geospatial technologies and systems. The organizations include the Geospatial Information Technology Association (GITA) and the Urban and Regional Information Systems Association (URISA). Also, PTI and the National Association of Counties (NACo) have active GIS forums and committees.

## IX. Conclusion

If you've gotten this far in the chapter and haven't skipped too many pages, then it is my hope that you have a deeper appreciation for GIS and your role as CIO in advancing its use and realizing its benefits for your jurisdiction. If your curiosity is peaked about GIS and you wish read more about this subject, I can personally recommend "The Mapmakers," by John Noble Wilford. Additionally, you can visit the web site of ESRI (www.esri.com), the world's largest GIS software company, which offers many good publications on geospatial subjects.

As CIO you may never become a black belt in the geospatial sciences, but if you can manipulate a digital map on the Internet, you are well on your way to being able to conceptualize most of the valuable functions that geospatial systems can perform and fit them into your overall vision for IT. What's more, your IT background gives you business management, enterprise architecture and strategic and business planning skills that your GIS operations dearly need.

With the hiring of a GIO as one of your key deputies, and with a firm adherence to the discipline of systematically measuring costs and benefits, you are on course to ensuring that your department will be able to serve your elected and appointed officials, fellow workers and citizens with state-of-the-art geospatial capabilities. You also will be in a position to guarantee that your jurisdiction takes its rightful place in efforts to advance the application of spatial technologies for the benefit of the nation as a whole.

## *Discussion questions*

1. Is the funding level for GIS in your jurisdiction calibrated to the potential ROI that GIS systems can provide?
2. Does GIS factor into your enterprise architecture and portfolio management initiatives?
3. Are the GIS practitioners in your jurisdiction appropriately organized and led to yield the most effective geo-services possible?
4. Is your jurisdiction systematically examining new spatially enabled technologies, like automated vehicle location, to determine which ones will work best for you?
5. When designing and building telecommunications and computer infrastructure, including wireless networks, do you keep in mind the high bandwidth requirements often needed to exchange geo-information, particularly to and from the field and remote offices?
6. Are you using highly expressive and attractive digital maps on your Internet site for a variety of public information, economic development and service delivery applications?
7. Are the key mapping layers in your jurisdiction edge-matched and integrated with those of adjoining jurisdictions to create regional coverages for strategic applications?
8. Is your jurisdiction participating in regional, state and national efforts to utilize geo-data and geo-systems for emergency management and homeland security?
9. Have you built jurisdiction-wide basemap layers and acquired or built a geocoding application to insure that all location information used across the enterprise can be validated, normalized and used for geo-enabled enterprise data integration?
10. Have you investigated how geospatial capabilities can enhance legacy systems by improving the accuracy and completeness of spatial data fields, and promoting data integration and visualization?
11. Have you hired a Geospatial Information Officer (GIO) as a high-ranking deputy to ensure the best possible leadership of your geospatial operations?

**Alan Leidner** *is a Senior Associate for Booz Allen Hamilton. With a Masters Degree in Urban Planning from Brooklyn's Pratt Institute, Mr. Leidner worked for 35 years as a planner and manager with New York City government. Starting in the late 1980s, he served as IT Director of the Department of Environmental Protection (DEP), where he initiated the city's Enterprise GIS Program and oversaw the development of the city's digital basemap. Mr. Leidner subsequently served as Assistant Commissioner in the Department of Information Technology and Telecommunications (DOITT), in charge of the city's GIS Utility. During that time, he organized and managed the Emergency Mapping and Data Center (EMDC), which provided information and mapping services to 9/11 responders. Mr. Leidner is a recipient of the 2001 Sloan Public Service Award, the 2002 ESRI Presidential Award, and was awarded a Medallion and Certificate of Appreciation from the National Geospatial-Intelligence Agency in January 2004. Mr. Leidner currently works for Booz Allen Hamilton as a senior associate within the Geospatial Services Team (GST). His current assignments focus on utilizing geospatially enabled information and systems to protect the nation's critical infrastructure.*

## REFERENCES

Wilford, John Noble. December, 2001. *The Mapmakers.* Second Vintage Books Edition. New York: Random House

Homeland Security Presidential Directive 7 (HSPD 7): www.whitehouse.gov/new/release/2003/12/20031217.html

National Infrastructure Protection Plan (NIPP): http://www.dhs.gov/xprevprot/programs/editorial_0827.shtm

A Guide to Critical Infrastructure and Key Resources Protection at the State, Regional, Local, Tribal, and Territorial Level, September, 2008 : http://www.dhs.gov/xprevprot/programs/editorial_0827.shtm

Geospatial Information Technology Association (GITA). *Building a Business Case for Geospatial Information Technology: A Practitioner's Guide to Strategic Financial Analysis.* http://gita.org/gita-in-action/roi_workbook.asp

Public Technology Incorporated (PTI). GIS ROI Tool Kit. http://www.pti.org/index.php/ptiee1/inside/C44

# 15. Network Operations and Security

**DR. ALAN R. SHARK**

There is no responsibility more critical than network security. It is a responsibility that simply cannot be delegated. This topic could easily fill an entire book, but the changing nature of network security and all its threats would require that same book to be updated so often as to make a print copy impractical. This chapter will highlight the basics of network security from the perspective of high-level management and oversight.

Last year, reported data breaches increased 47%, according to the nonprofit group, the Theft Resource Center. The Federal Trade Commission (FTC) received more than 800,000 consumer fraud and identity theft complaints, where consumers reported losses from fraud of more than $1.2 billion. Today's networks are constantly under attack, and some local governments report receiving more than 20,000 serious threats a day on average with well over 50% coming from foreign nations. Security threats from the "outside" are increasing in frequency and sophistication, but there also is an alarming trend that some of the greatest threats are coming from "within"—some of them knowingly and some of them unknowingly. This is one chapter were the key importance lies at the end with discussion questions. It is not the questions but the answers that will determine where you are in securing your network.

Before going further, it is important to review and understand the types of data that are obtained, validated, indexed and stored. Here are some typical government functions:

| | |
|---|---|
| ◆ Budget & Administration | ◆ Lottery |
| ◆ Community Affairs | ◆ Parks & Recreation |
| ◆ Corrections (prisons) | ◆ Pension Systems |
| ◆ Education (State Systems) | ◆ Prisons |
| ◆ Environmental Protection | ◆ Public Safety (Police & Emergency) |
| ◆ Employment Services | ◆ State Judicial Systems |
| ◆ Health Systems & Human Services | ◆ Social Services |
| ◆ Highways & Maintenance | ◆ Transportation |
| ◆ Insurance Administration | ◆ Taxation |
| ◆ Licensing (vehicles, registration, titles) | ◆ Vital Health Records |
| ◆ Justice & Court Systems | ◆ Voter Registration |

Given the amount of sensitive data that is collected and stored, it is imperative that the information is not only protected but the free flow of information is not compromised. Because critical public safety information plays a significant role in local government systems, they must be able to operate under almost any type of emergency. To protect and support local government networks, the need for sound polices and prevention systems is critical.

One also must understand and recognize the types of threats that network managers encounter. Not too long ago, it was acceptable to have a system rating of 99% up time. Now, applications demand a minimum up time of 99.9%, and network engineers will argue that there is a huge difference between the two.

When it comes to network threats, there are essentially four major areas that are interrelated but require separate strategies. They are (1) network security, (2) Web security, (3) e-mail security and (4) mobile workforce security.

The network could be viewed as the hub of all activities. Therefore, protecting the hub requires a multi-layer approach to security where the network is protected with smart firewalls, intrusion protection systems, secure and encrypted virtual private networks (VPN), and updated and secure user validation. The Internet increasingly is becoming the dominant source of two-way communication between cities and counties and the public they serve. Web security includes virus protection, content filtering and spyware protection. E-mail security includes virus protection, phishing protection and spam protection. The mobile environment includes both remote systems, such as satellite offices, or workers working from their homes or the field. Wireless communications also would be included where workers have laptops, portable storage devices and personal digital assistants (PDAs)—also referred to as smart phones. The mobile environment requires the same protections as the other forms except there is less control of the devices themselves. And, in the wireless arena, special precautions need to address encryption and remote monitoring.

Today's modern systems employ sophisticated network and traffic monitoring devices that help data managers see exactly how the network is functioning at any given point in time. Others employ ongoing vulnerability scanner or penetration tests. Policies must be updated continually and understood, and employee training must be part of any sound security plan.

When it comes to employees accessing government systems, most adhere to what is referred to the triple A's: access, authentication and authorization. Some favor the three D's: deter, detect, defend. Some localities issue physical devices that help in authentication. There, the emphasis is placed on trying to control who has permission to enter a network, and whether the person is whom he or she says they are.

An advantage of coming into a new local government jurisdiction provides an excellent opportunity to ask hard questions, such as what systems and policies are in place? When was the last time it was reviewed and or modified? When was the last time there was a major network security audit carried out by a reputable independent source? What kinds of historical data has been collected that can be used to better understand trends, patterns and possible abnormalities? Rather than wait for the next job to try that out, it might make sense for you to simply come in one day to work and pretend you are new to the enterprise and begin reviewing and asking all those questions. The answers may be scary because, perhaps, you thought all was well. But, most would trade scary answers any time for the opportunity to prevent a catastrophe.

Keeping employees up to date with the latest information also is tantamount to the success of any written policy. The need for ongoing training and education needs to be a continuous process of written guidelines, updates and hands-on demonstrations. Some will argue there is simply no time; Experts will argue that it is necessary and time well spent.

Not too long ago, most networks were relatively insulated from the outside environment. Today, with so many employees with network access and with an increasing number of public interfaces (due to enhanced e-government services), networks face an increased threat due to increased exposure as never before. With the growing use of videos and other forms of social media, network capacity and bandwidth issues will emerge. How can today's networks manage the predicted and dramatic increase in the need for more bandwidth? Certainly, network use will grow dramatically.

Early in the Obama presidency, the president and his staff learned first-hand what happens when a huge group of citizens tries to go to the White House Website as directed by the president himself, who had asked for input on his proposed policies. The result was the White House e-mail system crashed and was knocked out for several days. The White House system simply was unprepared for the overwhelming traffic—both legitimate and illegitimate.

Network threats begin with people. The first line of defense is sound poli-

## Examples of user training and education

- Data classification—public and non-public data
- Rules for adding "unauthorized" content or programs
- Rules for file sharing
- Rules for social networking Websites—do's and don'ts
- Files, backups and storage of data and how to ensure copies of your data
- Ethics and computer misuse
- Wireless communications technologies and security
- Rules for creation of passwords and changing passwords regularly
- Using the Internet—explanations of "Phishing," "Spyware" and other vulnerabilities
- Uses of e-mail, when to avoid e-mail and the use of attachments
- Physical security
- Rules for laptop data protection and encryption
- Providing users with lists of the most frequently asked questions

cies, followed by well-trained staff, followed by state-of-the art detection and prevention systems. The fast-growing mobile workforce is growing in complexity and usage. A police chief in a mid-sized western city, with the best of intentions, purchased new PDAs for his entire force without the input from the technology manager or anyone outside of the police department. The concern was that the new devices lacked known security features, was not supported by the city's network or IT staff, and required a time-consuming workaround for security and back-ups and more. Unfortunately, it happens all too often when departments make computer equipment or software application purchases without the knowledge or consent of IT security officials. Only when they turn for post-purchase help for support do people realize the need for better purchasing policies, greater security integration and oversight.

More local government employees are accessing applications from their homes or on the road. Questions are then raised as to how secure are wireless communications? And, peer to peer networking is becoming commonplace. How adequate is authentication protocols and encryption systems to protect both the data communications and entry into the network itself?

There are at least six areas of threats, and a surprising number may be found and growing *within* the enterprise itself.

## Malware: Denial of service, botnets and more....

The list of external dangers continues to grow both in number and sophistication. Even well-educated people get duped everyday and are tricked into turning over sensitive data, including passwords and bank account records. In simpler times, we just had to worry about computer viruses, then spam, then phishing and identity theft. Now, we see some of the same categories manifesting into monster applications. Added to the list, we worry about "botnets" and "denial of service requests"

A botnet, as its name implies, is a jargon term for a collection of software robots, or bots, that run autonomously and automatically, and controlled by someone with malicious intentions. According to PC Magazine, "A botnet is a large number of compromised computers that are used to create and send spam or viruses or flood a network with messages as a denial of service attack. The computer is compromised via a Trojan that often works by opening an Internet Relay Chat (IRC) channel that waits for commands from the person in control of the botnet. There is a thriving botnet business selling lists of compromised computers to hackers and spammers."

Denial of service, unlike a virus or worm, can cause severe damage to databases. A denial of service attack interrupts network service for some period of time. In a denial-of-service (DoS) attack, an attacker attempts to prevent legitimate users from accessing information or services. By targeting your computer and its network connection, or the computers and network of the sites you are trying to use, an attacker may be able to prevent you from accessing e-mail, Web sites, online accounts (banking, etc.), or other services that rely on the affected computer. Here, the network is flooded with information.

When you type a URL for a particular Web site into your browser, you are sending a request to that site's computer server to view the page. The server can only process a certain number of requests at once, so if an attacker overloads the server with requests, it can't process your request. It is a huge problem that has shut down many well-known Web sites from some very well-known companies. While there very few examples of local governments being attacked by denial of service threats, the principles are the same, and one must be prepared just the same. Because the attacks are almost impossible to prevent, network system engineers have developed secondary sites for just such an emergency. There also are procedures for minimizing both risks and damage.

**Malevolent intent from within.** First, there is a rising threat coming from what is called malevolent intent from employees within the enterprise. Here, local government employees could be the

---

## On any day of the week, your organization may encounter....

- **Denial of service**—An incident where an organization is deprived of the services of a resource
- **Social engineering attacks**—The use of influence and persuasion to deceive someone into believing you are someone you are not
- **Phishing attempts**—An attempt to acquire sensitive information, such as usernames or passwords, by masquerading as a trustworthy entity in an electronic communication
- **Pharming attempts**—An activity where criminals redirect users from a legitimate Web site to a fraudulent one where credit card numbers or bank accounts are requested to commit identity theft
- **Data leakage (intentional/non-intentional)**—Non-intentional could be a back door into your network where data can be removed; intentional can be data theft from within
- **Insider threats**—Deliberate malicious activity committed by an employee

SOURCE: STEVE JENNINGS, CIO, HARRIS COUNTY, TEXAS

greatest threat. Employees, after all, have access to sensitive data, including financial data and other forms of sensitive information. Embezzlement is not uncommon, and without sound checks and balances, crimes could go undetected for some time. However, malicious intent mostly deals with employees who are unhappy with their supervisor, the department or agency, or angry with the government itself. Not too long ago, an IT staff member held the entire city of San Francisco network operations at bay because the staff person was angered in not receiving a pay raise. He changed all the passwords and withheld them in a standoff and only offered them to the mayor while the employee was jailed. There need not be a seemingly rational reasoning to cause someone to hack into a network or cause harm for the "fun of it." No security system or policy can ignore threats from the inside, and there is growing evidence in the private sector to warn of the growing danger.

**Social media, or Web 2.0 applications and temptations.** The new media holds the promise of bringing people together into various social networks and interest groups. With benefits come threats, as well. Employees may be lured into revealing sensitive data or passwords because of leaving their guard down while online. That could manifest itself through clever e-mail or being lured into opening files, Web sites, or "reports" of interest that might contain Trojans, spybots or other security threats.

More people are sharing files and that, too, opens opportunities for unintentional consequences in carrying various security threats embedded in files and unknown to the user. Here, peer-to-peer networking through social networking sites has become a common routine for many, and that can become a gateway for unexpected intrusions.

Budget cuts. Because of the pressure for local governments to reduce costs, there could be greater staff turnover—with exiting employees taking invaluable knowledge with them. Budget reductions usually lead to less travel, training and, perhaps, system updates and monitoring systems. Finally, remaining staff often are asked to perform more, and there is a risk of not always being able to do the job as they normally would, leaving room for carelessness and costly mistakes. It is amazing how local governments don't always view network operations as something that is as essential as public safety and critical communications.

**Mobile workforce.** There is an increased danger of losing laptops, PDAs, cell phones and other mobile devices and the data they may contain. Even USB thumb drives—the small mobile storage devices that are used to exchange data between computers—can be a threat. And then, there are all the things that people download these days. Downloads of funny video clips, music or amusing pictures can contain embedded network threats once introduced into a system. The mobile environment and wireless environment requires strong VPN authentication, strong passwords, security manageability, encryption and remote-kill capabilities. The later is the ability for a network administrator to delete all data remotely on a laptop or PDA when online.

**Cloud computing and SaaS.** Cloud computing and software as a service (SaaS) is increasingly becoming popular with local governments. The upside is that both offer less day-to-day operational worries as the responsibility shifts to the provider. The downside is that some of the companies may not have the exacting standards needed for security and reliability. It also remains to be seen how the service providers will perform under various market conditions. What happens if a company goes out of business? How is the data returned? In what format? In what timeframe?

What are the security precautions taken by the service providers, and what is their guaranteed "up time?"

## Summary

Network operations and security also must take into consideration procedures for keeping systems operational during storms, power outages and other physical threats to network operations. It used to be completely adequate to have backup electrical support for up to 72 hours. Nowadays, experts are recommending backup systems that can operate for much longer periods of time. Individual employee and agency files and data require not only routine backups but redundant systems in case one system is down. Many local governments utilize remote storage systems and, in some cases, have relationships with other jurisdictions to store and retrieve critical data in case of emergencies.

Experts agree that we can never let our guard down. Every network must have a strategy for prevention, intervention and restoration.

---

### Discussion questions

1. When was the last time a network security audit was performed?
2. How often are passwords changed?
3. Do you have a "control panel" where passwords can be changed instantly?
4. Are your passwords generally considered "strong?"
5. What are your policies regarding downloads and adding software applications?
6. What are your polices regarding mobile devices?
7. When was your comprehensive security policy last reviewed?
8. How often do you perform staff training?
9. What are your policies for purchasing new IT equipment across the enterprise?
10. When installing security patches, do you have a system in place for trying them out before placing them on the network?

**Dr. Alan R. Shark** *currently serves as the Public Technology Institute's executive director/CEO. He also serves as Assistant Professor at Rutgers University's School of Public Affairs and Administration. As an author, lecturer and speaker on technology developments and applications for most of his distinguished career, Dr. Shark's experience both balances and embraces the business, government, education and technology sectors. His most recent book* Beyond e-Government & e-Democracy: A Global Perspective *is available from Amazon.com.*

*Dr. Shark has been elected as a Fellow of the National Academy of Public Administration (NAPA), as well as Fellow of the Radio Club of America (RCA) and Fellow of the American Society for Association Executives (ASAE).*

*Dr. Shark holds a doctorate in Public Administration from the University of Southern California's Washington Public Policy Center*

# 16. What Do CIOs Need to Know about Performance Measurement of E-Governance?

**DR. MARC HOLZER, AROON MANOHARAN AND YOUNHEE KIM**

## Introduction

Governments at all levels in the United States have been transitioning to e-government platforms for delivering better services, improving government efficiency and effectiveness, achieving transparency and accountability, and facilitating direct citizen participation. E-government is the application of Information and Communication Technologies (ICTs) within government to optimize its internal and external functions (UNDESA, 2003), as well as to foster e-democracy. It has the potential not only to improve the efficiency of internal processes, but also to change the relationship of government's interactions with individuals and organizations (Siew & Leng, 2003). E-government expands possibilities for direct democracy, focusing on transparency and openness. In the development of e-democracy, information disclosures and two-way communication are prerequisites for accelerating a high quality of political debate. To facilitate an informed citizenry, government websites should be evaluated to assure that they provide all the dimensions of e-governance effectively.

Many state governments—encouraged by the success of their federal counterparts, best practices in other states and in cities with populations over 100,000—had developed official websites by the spring of 1997 (Stowers, 1999). The phenomenon of linking technology and government was initially dominated by radio, cable television and telephone conferencing before the 1990s (Arterton, 1987, 1988; Becker, 1993; Christopher, 1987; McLean, 1989). Unlike televisions and radio, which typically rely on one-way interaction, computers enable citizens to access desired information interactively. Internet-based service applications may then help to satisfy citizens' complicated demands. The 2003 survey by the Pew Internet and American Life Project found that e-government is an increasingly popular tool for searching government information and obtaining government services (Horrigan, 2004). That practice clearly implies that e-government initiatives should go beyond the stationary "information lists-based" design to the customized "intentions-based" design in order to improve the functionality of websites.

Responding to demands from the citizen side, municipalities have focused on their e-government performance in terms of information dissemination, service delivery and government-citizen interaction. A sustainable methodology for e-governance performance is, therefore, required to measure essential aspects of the virtual state. As a methodological tool for a comprehensive evaluation of such performance, the Rutgers E-Governance Performance Index is one of the most wide-ranging instruments, focusing on five distinct categorical areas of e-governance: privacy, usability, content, services and citizen participation. Based on that instrument, an international survey of municipal websites in 2007 was conducted by the E-Governance Institute at Rutgers-Newark and the Global e-Policy e-Government Institute at Sungkyunkwan University. This paper discusses the performance measurement dimensions of e-governance on the basis of the Rutgers E-Governance Performance index and its application to the international survey. That is followed by a description of the best practices, identified by the international survey in 2007.

## Why does e-governance performance measurement matter?

Internet-based applications introduce a governmental landscape where information is more accessible, citizens feel more connected to their governments, and individuals are better able to participate in political processes. As ongoing development in ICTs has expanded the magnitude of e-governance capacities, measuring e-governance performance is increasingly emphasized to continuously improve information technology policies and strategies. The performance of e-government, especially at the local level, has been assessed by surveying administrators and technical staff who support the website. Studies by Reddick (2004) and Coursey & Norris (2008) have utilized data from the International City/County Management Association (ICMA) surveys that are based on the survey responses of chief administrative officers of municipalities and counties.

Research on e-government has long ignored the potential of websites in reaching out to citizen users. That is, websites often have been associated with merely providing information, advertising or attracting users to respective government agencies. In a significant study on the role of websites in state government electronic service delivery, Gant and Gant (2002) emphasize that such websites have the potential to integrate services and provide a higher quality of service to citizens. Initially, when portals began to appear on the scene, they were "...little more than dressed up search engines" (p.2). Since then, websites have rapidly improved, with multiple functions, and are today an important priority for governments investing in the digital delivery of services. Essentially, the websites are the new face of government, and are increasingly utilized to establish "electronic relationships between government and citizens, businesses, employees and other agencies" (Gant & Gant, 2002, p.2).

## E-governance categories in performance measurement

This section details the five e-governance categories and discusses specific measures that were used to evaluate websites. The discussion of security and privacy examines privacy policies and issues related to authentication. Discussion of the usability category involves traditional web pages, forms and search tools. The content category is addressed in terms of access to contact information, access to public documents and disability access, as well as access to multimedia and time-sensitive information. The section on services examines interactive services, services that allow users to purchase or pay for services, and the ability of users to apply or register for municipal events or services online. Finally, the measures for citizen participation involve examining how local governments are engaging citizens and providing mechanisms for citizens to participate in government online.

### Security/privacy

The analysis of security and privacy on municipal websites focused on two key issues: privacy policies and user authentication. With regard to municipal privacy policies, we first determined if the policy was available on every page that required data. We were particularly interested in determining whether privacy policies identified the agencies collecting the information, and whether the policy identified exactly what data were being collected on the site.

We also checked whether the website explained the intended use of data collected on the site, whether the privacy policy addressed its use by or sale to outside or third-party organizations, and whether third party agencies or organizations were governed by the same privacy policies as the municipal website. We also examined the privacy policies to determine whether the site offered a user option to decline disclosure of personal information to third parties, including other municipal agencies, state and local government offices, or private sector businesses. Additionally, we checked to ascertain if users had the ability to review personal data records and contest inaccurate or incomplete information.

In examining the factors affecting the security and privacy of local government websites, we addressed managerial measures that limit access to data and assure that it is not used for unauthorized purposes. Such examination also addressed the use of encryption in data transmission and the storage of personal information on secure servers. A growing e-governance trend at the local level is for municipalities to offer their website users access to public, and in some cases private, information online. Whereas other research has addressed the governance issues associated with sites that choose to charge citizens for access to public information (West, 2001), we are particularly concerned about the impact of the digital divide if public records are available only through the Internet or if municipalities insist on charging a fee for access to public records. Hence, our analysis specifically addressed online access to public databases by determining whether public information, like property tax assessments, or private information, like court documents, were available to municipal website users.

We also assessed whether websites used digital signatures to authenticate users and whether public or private information was accessible through a restricted area requiring a password and/or registration. An additional concern was that public agencies might use their websites to monitor citizens or create profiles based on information they access online. For example, many websites use cookies or web beacons to customize their sites for users; however, that technology also can be used to monitor Internet habits and profile website visitors. Thus, we examined municipal privacy policies to determine whether they addressed the use of cookies or web beacons.

## Usability

This research also examined municipal websites to determine whether they were, simply stated, user friendly. To address such usability concerns, we adapted several best practices and measures from other public and private sector research (Giga, 2000) and examined three types of websites: traditional web pages, forms and search tools.

To evaluate traditional web pages written using hypertext markup language (HTML), we examined issues like branding and structure (e.g., consistent color, font, graphics and page length). For example, we looked to see whether all pages used consistent color, formatting, default colors (e.g., blue links and purple visited links) and underlined text to indicate links. We also checked whether the website clearly described the system hardware and software requirements.

The examination also checked online forms to determine their usability in submitting data or searching municipal websites; most particularly, whether field labels aligned appropriately with each field, whether fields were accessible by keystroke (e.g., tabs), whether the cursor automatically placed itself in the first field, whether required fields were explicitly noted, and whether the tab order of fields was logical. For example, after a user filled out the first name and pressed the tab key, did the cursor automatically go to the surname field? Or did the page skip to another field such as zip code only to return to the surname later? We also looked to see whether form pages provided additional information about how to fix user errors; for example, did the user have to reenter information or did the site flag incomplete or erroneous forms before accepting them? Likewise, did the site give a confirmation page after a form was submitted, or did it return users to the homepage?

Our investigation also scrutinized each municipality's homepage to determine whether it was too long (two or more screen lengths) and/or whether it made available alternative versions of long documents, such as PDF or DOC files. We also looked for targeted audience links or channels that customize the website for specific groups, like citizens, businesses or other public agencies. Other considerations included the consistent use of navigation bars and links to the homepage on every page, the availability of a sitemap or hyperlinked outline of the entire website, and whether duplicated link names connected to the same content.

Finally, the usability analysis addressed search tools on municipal websites to determine whether help searching the site was available or whether the search scope could be limited to specific site areas. For instance, were users able to search only in "public works" or "the mayor's office," or did the search tool always search the entire site? We also looked for advanced search features like exact phrase searching, the ability to match all or any words, and Boolean searching capabilities (e.g., the ability to use AND/OR/NOT operators), as well as a site's ability to sort search results by relevance or other criteria.

## Content

Content is a critical component of any website no matter how technologically advanced the site's features. If site content is not current, if it is difficult to navigate, or if the information provided is incorrect, then it is not fulfilling its purpose. Hence, when examining website content, we examined five key areas: access to contact information (specifically, information about each agency represented on the website), public documents, access for those with disabilities, multimedia materials and time-sensitive information.

Accordingly, we looked not only for a schedule of agency offices hours and availability but also for online access to public documents, as well as a municipal code or charter and/or agency mission statements and the minutes of public meetings. We also determined whether users could access budget information and publications, whether the sites offered content in more than one language, and whether they provided access to disabled users through either "bobby compliance" (disability access for the blind, http://www.cast.org/bobby) or disability access for deaf users via a TDD phone service. To gauge the use of multimedia, we examined each site for the availability of audio or video files of public events, speeches or meetings. The time-sensitive information examined included the use of a municipal website for emergency management and/or as an alert mechanism (e.g., a terrorism or severe weather alert). We also checked for time-sensitive information, like job vacancies or a calendar of community events.

## Services

We divided municipal services provided online—a critical component of e-governance—into two different service types: those that allow citizens to interact with the municipality, which can be as basic as forms for requesting information or filing complaints, and those that allow users to register online for municipal events or services. As regards the first, because local governments worldwide provide advanced interactive services through which users can report crimes or violations, customize municipal homepages based on their needs (e.g., portal customization), and access private information like court, educational or medical records online, we evaluated municipal websites to determine whether they offered such services.

In terms of enabling citizens to register online for municipal services, many municipalities allow online application for a range of services as diverse as building permits and dog licenses. Some local governments also are using the Internet for procurement, allowing potential contractors to access requests for proposals or even bid online for municipal contracts. Others are chronicling the procurement process by listing the total number of bidders for a contract online and in some cases listing contact information for bidders.

Because many municipalities have developed the ability to accept payment for municipal services and taxes on their websites, we also examined whether the municipal websites had developed that capacity, exemplified across the U.S. by transactional services like online payment of public utility bills and parking tickets. Not only did cities and municipalities in many jurisdictions allow online users to file or pay local taxes or pay fines, in some cases around the world, cities are even allowing users to register or purchase tickets online for events in city halls or arenas.

## Citizen participation

Because, as noted in the 2003 survey, the Internet is a convenient mechanism through which citizen-users can engage their government, and also because of e-governance's potential to decentralize decision-making, online citizen participation in government recently has emerged as an important area of e-governance study. Hence, we strengthened our survey instrument in this area to identify the several ways in which public agencies at the local level were involving citizens, particularly through municipal use of the Internet to foster civic engagement and citizen participation in government. For example, we evaluated whether municipal websites allow users to provide online comments or feedback to individual agencies or elected officials. Once again, we found that the potential for online participation is still in its early stages of development: very few public agencies offer online opportunities for civic engagement.

We also looked at whether local governments offer current information about municipal governance online or through an online newsletter or e-mail listserv, and whether they use Internet-based polls about specific local issues. Likewise, we examined whether communities allow users to participate and view the results of citizen satisfaction surveys online. For example, some municipalities are using their websites to measure performance and publish the results of performance measurement activities online. Still others use online bulletin boards or other chat capabilities to gather input on public issues. Such online bulletin boards offer citizens the opportunity to post ideas, comments or opinions without stipulation of specific discussion topics, although in some cases, agencies were attempting to structure online discussions around policy issues or specific agencies.

## Survey design and methodology

The 2007 Digital Governance in Municipalities Worldwide Survey assessed the practice of digital governance in large municipalities worldwide and ranked them on a global scale. Because, fundamentally, digital governance includes both digital government (delivery of public service) and digital democracy (citizen participation in governance), we analyzed website security, usability and content; the type of online services currently offered; and citizen response and participation through websites established by municipal governments (Holzer & Kim, 2005) based on the 98-measure Rutgers Index.

## Website survey

For this research, we define the main city homepage as the official website on which the city provides information about city administration and online services. Nonetheless, even though municipalities worldwide are increasingly developing such sites to provide services online, e-government is more than simply construction of a website. Rather, the emphasis should be on using such technologies to effectively provide government services, as, for example, in the following initiatives: (a) providing 24/7 access to government information and public meetings; (b) providing mechanisms that enable citizens to comply with state and federal rules regarding drivers licenses, business licenses and so forth; (c) providing access to special benefits like welfare funds and pensions; (d) providing a network across various government agencies to enable collaborative approaches to serving citizens; and (e) providing various channels for digital democracy and citizen participation initiatives (Pardo, 2000). The fundamentals of government, which cannot be altered simply by introducing a website as government's new window (Pardo), should clearly extend beyond the textual listing of information to a more "intentions-based" design in which citizens can more effectively use websites (Howard, 2001).

In general, the city websites studied included information about the city council, the mayor and the executive branch. If there were also separate homepages for agencies, departments or the city council, our evaluators examined whether those sites were linked to the menu on the main city homepage. If the website was not linked, it was excluded from the evaluation.

## E-governance survey instrument and scale

The E-Governance Performance Measures table summarizes the 2007 survey instruments (see the overview of the criteria in Appendix A).

The survey instrument used 98 measures, of which 43 were dichotomous, for each of the five e-governance components; the research applied 18 to 20 measures. For questions that were not dichotomous, each measure was coded on a four-point scale: 0 - information about a given topic does not exist on the website; 1—information about a given topic exists on the website (including links to other information and e-mail addresses); 2—downloadable items are available on the website (forms, audio, video and other one-way transactions, popup boxes); 3—services, transactions or interactions can take place completely online (credit card transactions, applications for permits, searchable databases, use of cookies, digital signatures, restricted access).

## E-Governance Performance Measures

| E-governance category | Number of measures | Raw score | Weighted score | Key Concepts |
|---|---|---|---|---|
| Privacy/ Security | 18 | 25 | 20 | privacy policies, authentication, encryption, data management, cookies |
| Usability | 20 | 32 | 20 | user-friendly design, branding, length of homepage, targeted audience links or channels, and site search capabilities |
| Content | 20 | 48 | 20 | access to current accurate information, public documents, reports, publications, and multimedia materials |
| Services | 20 | 59 | 20 | transactional services — purchase or register, interaction between citizens, businesses and government |
| Citizen participation | 20 | 55 | 20 | online civic engagement/policy deliberation, citizen-based performance measurement |
| **Total** | **98** | **219** | **100** | |

To avoid skewing the research in favor of a particular category, in developing an overall score for each municipality, we weighted each of the five categories equally regardless of the number of questions each contained. The dichotomous measures in the services and citizen participation categories corresponded with the values on the four-point scale of 0 or 3, while the dichotomous measures on privacy and usability corresponded to ratings of 0 or 1 on the scale.

Nonetheless, because of the relative value of the different e-government services studied, our instrument placed a higher value on some dichotomous measures, For example, evaluators using our instrument in the service category were given the option of scoring websites as either 0 or 3 when assessing whether a site allowed users to access private information online (e.g., educational records, medical records, point total of driving violations, lost property). Hence, whereas no access equated to a rating of 0, allowing residents or employees to access private information online, a higher order task that requires more technical competence, is clearly an online service and was, therefore, rated at 3.

On the other hand, when assessing a site as to whether or not it had a privacy statement or policy—clearly a content issue that emphasizes the information placed online—evaluators were given the choice of scoring the site as a 0 or 1, for the absence or presence of a security policy, respectively. Obviously, the differential values assigned to such dichotomous categories were useful for comparing the different components of municipal websites with one another.

To ensure reliability, each municipal website was assessed by two evaluators, and in cases where significant variation (+ or – 10%) existed on the evaluators' weighted score between evaluators, the websites were analyzed a third time. Evaluators also were provided an example for each measure indicating how the variable should be scored and were given comprehensive written instructions for assessing the sites.

## Best practices in global municipal e-government performance

### Seoul, Republic of Korea (http://www.seoul.go.kr/)

Overall, Seoul has been ranked first in the international survey, owing to a well-developed website that has scored high across all five e-governance categories. It ranked first in the areas of privacy, service and citizen participation, and third in usability and content. A unique feature of Seoul's website is the Cyber Policy Forum, a result of the municipality's efforts toward enhancing online citizen participation. The Cyber Policy Forum strives to "provide citizens with opportunities to understand policy issues and to facilitate discussions; to encourage citizen participation in public administration and to obtain feedback about policy issues; and to reflect citizens' opinions in city policies and produce more tailored policy solutions for citizens." Seoul's homepage is very user-friendly, and provides appropriate targeted audience links and relevant privacy policy on each page. Citizens are able to participate in online governmental processes, including well-organized and systematic opportunities to submit their ideas and suggestions on proposed policies via policy forums. The website is offered in more than one language: Korean, English, Japanese, Chinese, French and Spanish.

### E-Governance Score for Seoul

| Year | Score | Privacy | Usability | Content | Service | Participation |
|------|-------|---------|-----------|---------|---------|---------------|
| 2007 | 87.74 | 17.60   | 18.13     | 16.00   | 19.83   | 16.18         |

### Hong Kong (http://www.gov.hk/)

Hong Kong recorded the second best practice in the international survey based on an overall score of 71.24. The city's homepage also is user-friendly, being less than two screens, along with targeted audience links available on each page. The webpage is marked by attractive, consistently sized font along with a searchable database for the city ordinance, city regulations and contact information. Information is posted periodically on the website on job opportunities along with a link to the calendar of events.

### E-Governance Score for Hong Kong

| Year | Score | Privacy | Usability | Content | Service | Participation |
|------|-------|---------|-----------|---------|---------|---------------|
| 2007 | 71.24 | 12.40   | 16.35     | 18.80   | 19.83   | 3.86          |

### Helsinki, Finland (http://www.hel.fi)

Helsinki scored third in the international survey with an overall score of 71.01. The website of Helsinki provides online forums for citizens to send feedback to government agencies and also circulates an online newsletter to keep the public informed of its activities. The website provides online survey/polls for specific issues and strives to engage the residents of Helsinki in community discussions like blogs, bulletin boards, e-discussions and policy forums The website allows users to report crimes, violations of administrative laws and regulations, as well as to register or purchase tickets to events in city/municipal halls, arenas or facilities of the city. The site offer access in Finnish, Swedish, English, German, French and Russian.

### E-Governance Score for Helsinki

| Year | Score | Privacy | Usability | Content | Service | Participation |
|------|-------|---------|-----------|---------|---------|---------------|
| 2007 | 71.01 | 15.60 | 17.82 | 14.60 | 11.36 | 11.64 |

## Singapore (http://www.gov.sg/)

The inclusion of Singapore as the third best practice for the 2007 is based on its overall score of 68.56. The high score for Singapore's website is a reflection of its increased performance throughout all five categories. The website is ranked fifth in privacy, sixth in usability, fifth in services and second in citizen participation. The website of Singapore provides users with discussion forums, online surveys and similar opportunities to participate in governmental processes online. The website also allows users to file taxes, pay for utilities, apply for permits, report crimes, violations of administrative laws and regulations, as well as to register or purchase tickets to events in city/municipal halls, arenas or facilities of the city.

### E-Governance Score for Singapore

| Year | Score | Privacy | Usability | Content | Service | Participation |
|------|-------|---------|-----------|---------|---------|---------------|
| 2007 | 68.56 | 14.00 | 16.57 | 12.20 | 12.88 | 12.91 |

## Madrid, Spain (www.munimadrid.es)

Madrid is ranked fifth overall with a score of 67.98 and first in the category of usability. The city's homepage is attractive and user-friendly along with targeted audience links available on each page. The website offers a searchable database that provides minutes of public meetings, budget documents in downloadable formats, city ordinance, city regulations and contact information for agencies and administrators.

### E-Governance Score for Madrid

| Year | Score | Privacy | Usability | Content | Service | Participation |
|------|-------|---------|-----------|---------|---------|---------------|
| 2007 | 67.98 | 12.80 | 18.75 | 16.4 | 14.58 | 5.45 |

## Conclusion

While the development and management of websites are important aspects of public management, little is known about the websites' overall performance and impact on governance. Moreover, public managers and chief information officers are being expected to provide a larger magnitude of e-government services through websites to an increasingly complex society. To achieve an overall quality and attain satisfaction from e-government functions internally and externally, e-government performance should be measured continuously by reliable and tangible instruments.

The Rutgers E-Governance Performance Index provides a well-described set of measures that maintains the balance between citizens' trust in government and the improvement of government services, focusing on five essential aspects: privacy, usability, content, services and citizen participation. The benefit of e-government performance evaluation based on the Rutgers E-Governance Performance instrument is to provide a unitary interpretation of the status of e-governance for both governments and citizens.

Moreover, every region has examples of best practices for overall performance and in each specific e-governance category. As governments seek to increase their e-governance performance, they need to search for models within their regions and identify e-governance benchmarks. Those agencies that serve as top performers in their respective regions can then look at the top-ranked government agencies throughout the nation, as continuous improvement should be the norm for every government online.

## Discussion questions

1. Does your agency have a performance measurement system for e-government? If so, what are key priorities addressed by the performance measurement index?
2. Can the Rutgers E-Governance Performance Index be applied in your agency and community settings? How can the five e-governance categories be incorporated into an agency's performance measurement system?
3. What are the most effective approaches for building a sustainable methodology for e-government performance?
4. What are the most effective strategies in using ICT applications to improve citizen access and encourage greater citizen participation?
5. What are the limitations and challenges in using ICT while interacting with citizens?
6. Discuss the organizational factors that enhance the performance of e-government in your jurisdiction?
7. To what extent does your agency outsource e-government technology to private contractors, and how has such contracting practices affected the performance of e-government?
8. What will the potential demand be for future e-government practices? How can you intertwine those demands into the e-government performance measurement?
9. Does your jurisdiction participate in regional, state and national forums, conferences on e-government and performance measurement issues?
10. Is it worthwhile to measure e-government performance in terms of quantitative return on investment (ROI) analysis?

**Dr. Marc Holzer,** *Dean of the Rutgers School of Public Affairs and Administration, is a leading expert in performance measurement, public management and e-governance. He is the founder and director of the National Center for Public Performance, a research and public service organization devoted to improving performance in the public sector. He also developed the E-Governance*

*Institute, created to explore the ongoing impact of the Internet and other information technologies on the productivity and performance of the public sector, and how e-government fosters new and deeper citizen involvement within the governing process.*

**Aroon Manoharan** *is Associate Director of the E-Governance Institute, Rutgers University-Newark. His research focuses on e-governance, performance measurement and reporting, organization management and comparative public administration.*

**Younhee Kim** *is Assistant Professor in the Department of Political Science at East Carolina University. Her current research interests focus on performance management, public sector entrepreneurship, and information technology policy and e-governance.*

## REFERENCES

Arterton, F. C. (1987). Can technology protect democracy? Newbury Park: SAGE Publications.

Arterton, F. C. (1988). Political participation and teledemocracy, PS: Political Science and Politics, 21(3), pp. 620-626.

Becker, T. (1993). Teledemocracy: Gathering momentum in state and local governance. Spectrum: The Journal of State and Government, 66(2), pp.14-19.

Christopher, A. F. (1987). Teledemocracy: Can technology protect democracy? Newbury Park: SAGE Publications

Coursey, D. and Norris, D. (2008). Models of E-Government: Are they correct? An empirical assessment, Public Administration Review, 68 (3), pp. 523–536.

Gant, J. P. and D. B. Gant. (2002) Web Portal Functionality and State Government E-Service. Proceedings of the 35th Annual Hawaii International Conference on System Science, pp. 1587-1596.

Giga Consulting. (2000). Scorecard Analysis of the New Jersey Department of Treasury. An unpublished report to the NJ Department of Treasury.

Holzer, M, & Kim, S.T., (2005) "Digital Governance in Municipalities Worldwide, A Longitudinal Assessment of Municipal Websites Throughout the World", the E-Governance Institute, Rutgers University, Newark and the Global e-policy e-government Institute, Sungkyunkwan, University.

Horrigan, J. B. (2004). How Americans get in touch with government: Internet users benefit from the efficiency of e-government, but multiple channels are still needed for citizens to reach agencies and solve problems. Washington, DC: Pew Internet & American Life Project.

Howard, M. (2001). e-Government across the globe: How will "e" change Government? Government Finance Review, (August) 6-9.

McLean, I. (1989). Democracy and the new technology. Cambridge: Polity Press.

Pardo, T. (2000). Realizing the promise of digital government: It's more than building a website. Albany, NY: Center for Technology in Government.

Reddick, C.G. (2004). A two-stage model for e-government growth: Theories and empirical evidence for U.S. cities, Government Information Quarterly, 21, pp. 51-64.

Siew, S.L. and L.Y. Leng. (2003). E-government in Action: Singapore Case Study, in The World of E-Government, G.G. Curtin, M.H. Sommer, and V. Vis-Sommer, Editors. The Havorth Press.

Stowers, G.N.L. (1999). Becoming cyberactive: state and local governments on the World Wide Web. Government Information Quarterly, 16 (2), pp. 111–127.

United Nations Department of Economic and Social Affairs (2003) e-Government Readiness Assessment Survey. Retrieved June 21, 2008: http://www.cabinet.gov.jm/docs/pdf/eGov_Readiness_Intro.pdf

West, D. M. 2001 - 2005. Global E-Government Survey, Available at http://www.insidepolitics.org/ Accessed March 16, 2006.

# APPENDIX A

| Category | Questions |
|---|---|
| Privacy/security | 1-2. A privacy or security statement/policy<br>3-6. Data collection<br>7. Option to have personal information used<br>8. Third-party disclosures<br>9. Ability to review personal data records<br>10. Managerial measures<br>11. Use of encryption<br>12. Secure server<br>13. Use of "cookies" or "web beacons"<br>14. Notification of privacy policy<br>15. Contact or e-mail address for inquiries<br>16. Public information through a restricted area<br>17. Access to nonpublic information for employees<br>18. Use of digital signatures |
| Usability | 19-20. Homepage, page length<br>21. Targeted audience<br>22-23. Navigation bar<br>24. Site map<br>25-27. Font color<br>30-31. Forms<br>32-37. Search tool<br>38. Update of website |
| Content | 39. Information about the location of offices<br>40. Listing of external links<br>41. Contact information<br>42. Minutes of public<br>43. City code and regulations<br>44. City charter and policy priority<br>45. Mission statements<br>46. Budget information<br>47-48. Documents, reports, or books<br>49. GIS capabilities<br>50. Emergency management or alert mechanism<br>51-52. Disability access<br>53. Wireless technology<br>54. Access in more than one language<br>55-56. Human resources information<br>57. Calendar of events<br>58. Downloadable documents |

*(continued)*

| Category | Questions | |
|---|---|---|
| Service | 59-61. Pay utilities, taxes, fines<br>62. Apply for permits<br>63. Online tracking system<br>64-65. Apply for licenses<br>66. E-procurement<br>67. Property assessments<br>68. Searchable databases<br>69. Complaints<br>70-71. Bulletin board about civil applications<br>72. FAQ<br>73. Request information<br>74. Customize the main city homepage<br>75. Access private information online<br>76. Purchase tickets<br>77. Webmaster response<br>78. Report violations of administrative laws and regulations | |
| Citizen participation | 79-80. Comments or feedback<br>81-83. Newsletter<br>84. Online bulletin board or chat capabilities<br>85-87. Online discussion forum on policy issues<br>88-89. Scheduled e-meetings for discussion<br>90-91. Online survey/ polls<br>92. Synchronous video<br>93-94. Citizen satisfaction survey<br>95. Online decision-making<br>96-98. Performance measures, standards, or benchmarks | |

# 17. Project and Performance Management Tools

**AVI DUVDEVANI WITH SEAN LAFFIN**

---

*The skills and success factors in project delivery are always based on the right people, with the right processes, utilizing the right tools.*

The content of this chapter was born out of experience. It is built on lessons learned at the New York City Housing Authority (NYCHA) as well Pcubed's decades of public sector CIO experience and best practices gleaned from thousands of enterprise project management tool implementations supporting billions of dollars worth of projects. Throughout the chapter, the NYCHA implementation of its award-winning project management tool, the NYCHA ePMO, is used as a case study to underscore the challenges and benefits of implementing a project management tool.

## Look before you leap: Do you have a firm foundation?

While it may be tempting to think that project management tools can be installed and deployed in fairly short order, the reality is that successfully implementing an enterprise project management tool is a significant culture adjustment, and requires deliberate planning and organizational change management.

Many organizations select their project management tool first and then allow the tool to drive the implementation. That common mistake can have undesired effects—instead of organizational objectives and best practices, software "bells and whistles" become the driving force behind the implementation.

Understanding where your organization stands is the critical first step. Following are key questions:

1. What is the project success rate of your organization?
2. What project management structures (PMO, established workflows and templates, required reports, etc.) are currently in place?
3. What is your organization's level of project management maturity?
4. Is there commitment to improve the organization's project management capability?
5. What does a successful enterprise project management tool implementation look like to you?

## What is the project success rate of your organization?

That is a loaded question. If you know the project success rate of your organization and can back it up with data, that means you have, at the very least, taken a project inventory and measured the projects' planned versus actual results. It also means that at a management level, oversight and accountability for project delivery exists. If you do not know the project success rate, then those basic measures have not been captured, bringing accountability for project delivery into question.

It is important to understand project accountability in an organization since that will indicate the extent of any required culture change when implementing an enterprise project management tool.

In early 2002, soon after coming on board as CIO at NYCHA, I recognized the project management challenges ahead of me. I used my understanding of those challenges as a springboard to help implement the ePMO solution. The challenges included:

- ♦ Projects did not meet their planned timeframes

- ♦ High rates of projects over budget

- ♦ Lack of transparency and visibility of the project plans and status
  – Management difficulty in mitigating delays and financial losses

In addition, NYCHA's lack of an enterprise-wide IT governance process hindered strategic alignment of its business and technology investments with its strategies. Compounding that, a lack of standardized business processes as well as limited reviews of IT funding, made it difficult to identify, initiate and execute strategic, multi-million dollar IT programs.

As a result, an Information Technology Strategic Plan (www.nyc.gov/html/nycha/html/about/it_strategic_plan.shtml) was developed and presented to NYCHA's Board of Commissioners. The purpose of the plan was to help reorganize NYCHA's Department of Information Technology organization into an enterprise service model, along with develop a robust governance, PMO and Enterprise Architecture program to help select and protect NYCHA's IT investments, and provide transparency and accountability.

## What project management structures (PMO, established workflows and templates, required reports, etc.) are currently in place?

The existence of project management structures in an organization will help to guide the strategy of the project management tool implementation and will greatly assist in planning the organizational change effort. If some structures do exist, an honest assessment of their adoption and reliability provides insight into which should be leveraged or scrapped. Organizations without reliable structures typically remain dependent on heroic project team members. While heroes may be able to deliver some of the most complex projects, outcomes are typically unpredictable. In those organizations, each project often starts with a blank slate, continuous reinvention is common and successful practices are rarely shared. It is the hero-type structure that likely will provide the most resistance in project management tool implementation.

NYCHA elected to use a phased approach when introducing project management structures to the organization. The initial phase consisted of the implementation of an enterprise-wide governance portal, which leveraged a shared server environment to create an online repository of tools and materials to support project managers. Far from a rudimentary framework to assist project managers, the structure of the portal was based on a specific project management methodology and provided carefully designed tools and templates. The initial phase introduced the project managers to the basic concepts of a project management tool: information sharing and adherence to a standard methodology.

# What is your organization's level of project management maturity?

An independent assessment of an organization's level of project management maturity will help the organization gain insight into current project management capabilities, determine gaps and find areas for potential improvement to project management competencies. Once that baseline has been established and levels of management agree on areas most needing improvement, priorities can be established on how to improve the effectiveness of project and program delivery throughout the enterprise. Those priorities will form the foundation on which to guide the project management tool implementation.

| PM Maturity Roadmap: People, Process, Tools and Governance | | | | |
|---|---|---|---|---|
| **LEVEL 1**<br>Initial/Ad Hoc | **LEVEL 2**<br>Planned/Repeatable | **LEVEL 3**<br>Defined/Organized | **LEVEL 4**<br>Integrated/Managed | **LEVEL 5**<br>Optimize/Sustain |
| **Overview** During crises, plans are often abandoned. Projects (especially non-critical ones) tend to be ad hoc & occasionally chaotic. | Basic PM disciplines have now been institutionalized, although execution may still differ considerably from project to project. | Formal project planning, process & controls are now institutionalized with a focus on consistent, but tailored project delivery. | Program & project performance have been integrated into management decision-making to better achieve business objectives. | Emphasis has shifted to continuous PM improvement & alignment with current business objectives as a strategic enabler. |
| **People** Project success often relies on the heroic effort of individuals & on-the-job training. | Guidelines exist for project roles & training, but this often conflicts with daily priorities. | Formal PM training & mentoring exists; right people & skills are assigned to projects. | PM competencies formally sponsored; projects perceived as "fast track" career path. | Corporate training promotes advanced PM skills; resources/ skills allocated by value. |
| **Process** Even if defined, PM processes tend to be discretionary & yield unpredictable results. | Compliance to minimum PM standards has been achieved; improved repeatability. | Enterprise processes enable consistent results & measurement with some flexibility. | Proven processes used to measure/analyze cost-benefits, resources & value delivery. | PM & core business processes are fully integrated with a focus on business value. |
| **Tools** Lack of consistent tools, process & training makes it hard to report on project status. | Consistent tool use improves collaboration & time/cost baselines for status reporting. | PM tools/training seen as corporate asset with focus on performance measurement. | PM & business systems integration improves forecasting, analysis & benchmarking. | PM, business & collaborative tools are fully integrated; used at all organization levels. |
| **Governance** Most projects managed in isolation with limited governance or executive sponsorship. | Key projects seen as strategic, but status data not yet geared to executive governance. | Enterprise PM data exists, but proactive analysis & decision-making is still limited. | Project objectives are managed quantitatively & support executive decision-making. | Projects managed as strategic portfolio; funding/priorities driven by corporate vision. |

Source: © Program Planning Professionals, Inc (Pcubed), 2008

**Figure 17–1.**

# Is there commitment to improve the organization's project management capability?

Enterprise project management tool implementations ultimately "lift the hood" and introduce transparency into an organization's ability to deliver projects. That is where the executive commitment level to improving project management capability plays a vital role. If, as was the case with NYCHA, the key stakeholders are dedicated to the transparency and accountability that accompanies a successful implementation, the organizational change effort will go more smoothly and hasten the return on investment. In addition, NYCHA's ePMO is built on an IT governance framework that allocates the project management responsibility to the *business owner*, further illustrating the level of transparency and accountability built into the foundation of the ePMO.

An extremely effective way to build organizational commitment to improving project management capability is through education. To build both commitment and capability, NYCHA took a four-phased approach to its comprehensive training program. The first phase covered project management fundamentals, which focused on balancing the triple constraints of project management: scope, time and cost. Once a solid project management foundation was built for the NYCHA project management community, the second phase focused on project scheduling, which covered both the basics of schedule development and utilizing project scheduling software. The third phase spotlighted the ePMO tool. In that phase, actual project teams collaborated on their projects by using the ePMO tool in a true working session. The fourth and final phase involved individual support and mentoring to drive the concepts home following the formal training sessions. To further foster learning and information sharing, NYCHA developed an eLearning module, which demonstrates the NYCHA IT Governance and PMO process. That is the only component of the ePMO tool that is accessible over the public Internet, and it can be accessed via: https://a996-housingauthority.nyc.gov/pmo/index.html.

*NYCHA's four-phased approach to building commitment and capability*

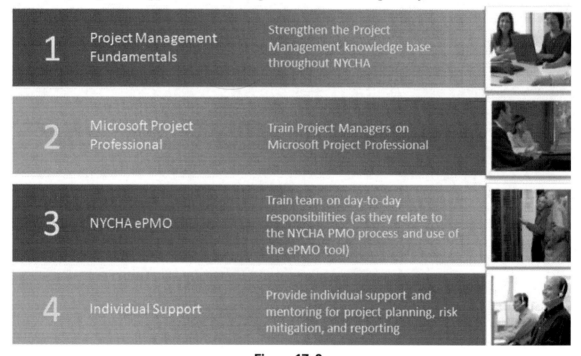

Figure 17–2.

## What does a successful enterprise project management tool implementation look like?

It is well known that at the outset of any enterprise software implementation, it is critical to understand its success criteria. When specifically thinking about a project management tool implementation and the organizational change involved, adoption is key, and is best facilitated by focusing on success criteria or benefits that carry the most weight—examples: visibility, resource management, deliverables management. Do not "boil the ocean"—focus on the right things; focus on the things that have the most leverage. In NYCHA's case, the organization focused its success criteria on increased productivity, reduced costs and improved resident satisfaction, with the parallel development of NYCHA's ability to make informed decisions about strategic, business-aligned IT programs.

Answering those questions will create an awareness of the sizable effort ahead and will set the stage for a successful implementation. Use that information to lay the foundation of project management structures and develop an implementation vision. That will not only expedite the tool selection process, but will jumpstart the change management process—drastically improving your chances of success.

## A trusted single source—manage by the facts

The selected project management tool must be the trusted single source of all project information. That trusted single source will provide visibility, drive consistency of project data and drive adherence to standards. A successful project management tool will do the following:

**Underpin complex project delivery**—A proven reporting and control solution to support project management by providing visibility, insight and control.

**Enable disciplined delivery capability**—A flexible project management toolkit that supports standard practices and required compliance.

**Improve business results**—A systemized toolkit that enables repeatable project success resulting in improved bottom line performance and control.

## Underpin complex project delivery

In simple terms, in order to "manage by the facts," the project management tool must actually provide the facts. The systems are only as good as the data that resides in them. They must store the correct types of data and that data must be of considerable quality. Thus, any project management tool should have the capability to securely store all of the following project management components:

- Project/program management teamwork capabilities
  - Onscreen ability to share project documents/meeting information across potentially geographically dispersed team members

- Schedule management
  - Project schedules based upon the chosen schedule templates as directed via any chosen methodology

- Risk management
  - Tracking and escalation of project risk data. Allow easily configurable reporting of risk data

- Issue management
  - Allows immediacy and close monitoring of issues that impact the project. Allow easily configurable reporting of issue data

- Resource management
  - Flexibility to identify resources and necessary skill sets, allowing for resource demand forecasting and management

– Change management
- Tracking and reporting any request for change as a project is in flight, not only the impact of change, but potentially any changes that may result in a fundamental adjustment to a project's deliverables

– Document management
- Capability to cost-effectively and securely allow the sharing of project documentation—one source for the truth, one source for all required project documentation

– Centralized reporting (standard/offline)
- Quick, "click" report generation as required by the project governance process. Immediate on-screen analysis in real-time or also stored with historical data to allow historical data trend analysis. Ability to quickly print as "packs" for offline use.

NYCHA's ePMO is the trusted single source of project information that drives the adoption of and compliance to NYCHA's Project Management (PM) framework. The following are key features:

♦ Document repositories and "collaboration spaces" that facilitate document storage and project communications

♦ Project schedule for planning and tracking—integrated with the collaboration space

♦ Risk and issue management tracking—integrated with the collaboration space and project schedule

♦ "Smart" templates and electronic project management forms

♦ Route-specific workflow automation

♦ Integrated reporting—Common reporting processes are automated and simplified by pre-loading data

## Enable disciplined delivery capability

As the trusted single source of project information for an organization, the project management tool must not only help the organization manage by the facts, but also help to drive a consistent project management process and methodology. There are an abundance of methodologies that are specific to industries, types of projects, regulatory requirements, etc. The project management tool must be flexible enough to incorporate any of those methodologies into its operation. Whatever methodology is adopted, or created for that matter, the fact that each project follows the same methodology will provide the mechanism for discipline, consistency and continuous improvement, and intelligible, trustworthy reports.

As noted above, NYCHA embeds its project management methodology into the tool. Depending on the project's risk level and type, project managers are required to complete specific project deliverables. The templates range from a project charter, to a risk management plan, to a software test plan and are available online as part of ePMO.

To enforce governance and standards, each form has built-in business rules that reinforce the corresponding NYCHA process for the form, including executive review and approval, email notifications and reporting. The forms are routed for approval using a simple and route-specific workflow automation. In addition, all of NYCHA's PM processes are illustrated online as "clickable" processes that bring a user to online help for the phase and provide any required forms.

*NYCHA's PM and deliverables processs*

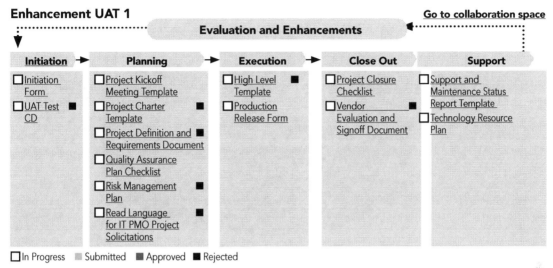

Figure 17–3.

## Improve business results

Building on the notions of "managing by facts" and driving disciplined delivery is the concept of repeatable project success. Having a trusted single source of information that provides the facts and enforces a standard methodology will drive the organizational learning curve and improve project delivery capability. Ideally, the processes that comprise the methodology become routine and part of "business as usual" for a project manager, the PMO or the project team. It adds constant value to the drive for project management consistency and continuous improvement of project delivery—this is *the gift that keeps on giving.*

The project management tool also drives accountability and responsibility. As the tool's core is based on the need for project management transparency ("manage by the facts"), the recognition and swift removal and reduction of "surprises" often leads to measurable increase in project benefits realization, even beyond the expected benefits identified in the business case, before project initiation.

At NYCHA that accountability and responsibility also is managed by a management structure, a PMO. As a result of a case study which Gartner had conducted with NYCHA, a PMO was defined as a center of expertise that can provide the organizational focus on improving the management of projects, programs and portfolios – the trusted single source of process. The case study demonstrated that PMOs are not always static and that they can evolve over time through three stages —a project management office, a program management office and finally a portfolio management office—even though the term "PMO" is used to refer to all three (see NYCHA's PMO approach in Figure 17–4, see next page).

Through its evolution, the scope of the NYCHA PMO changed from tactical to strategic, and the scope of initiatives changes from IT-intensive projects to combined business-IT programs and

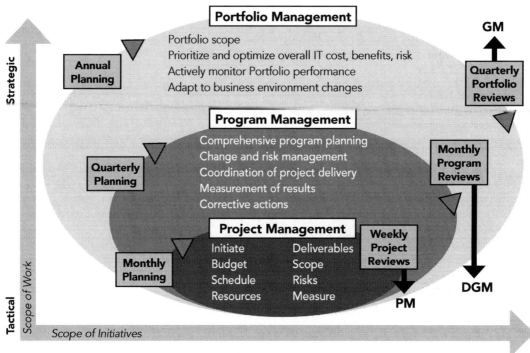

**Figure 17–4.**

finally to enterprise-wide initiatives. Yet, at each stage of the evolution, the PMO contributes significant benefits.

A project management office can reduce the risk of project schedule slippage, cost overruns and scope creep by focusing on a standard project management process, basic tools and project manager development. A program management office can improve resource management across business and IT projects and programs by combining related business and IS projects into programs. A portfolio management office can contribute to business growth by optimizing the mix of project and program investments and focusing on benefits realization and knowledge management.

CIOs must ensure that their PMOs have a firm foundation of their initial stage before they evolve them to the next stage. It also is important to recognize that the evolution must be supported by a strong IT governance process, which facilitates the strategic decisions and priority selections required by the PMO process at its later stages (see NYCHA's IT governance model in Figure 17–5.)

## Firm foundation...to trusted single source...to benefits realization

Setting a firm foundation—*understanding the organizational readiness and commitment, complimented by project management structures* —will help set the stage for successful change management. Ensuring that the project management tool is the single trusted source of all project information will enable an organization to "manage by facts," drive consistency of project data and drive adherence to standards.

*Firm foundation and trusted single source* enable the benefits realization of the project management tool. At a micro level, the facts may show that a large project is forecast to push far beyond the completion date, forcing management to analyze potential program interdependencies and

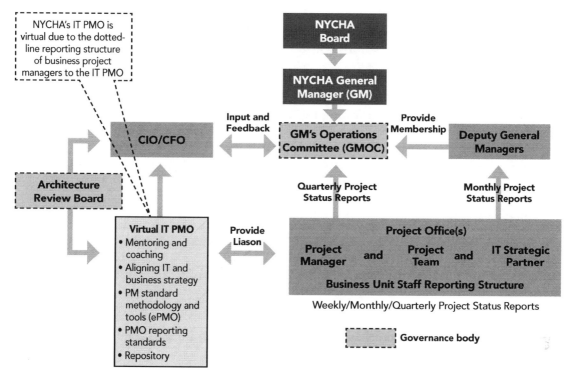

NYCHA's IT PMO is virtual due to the dotted-line reporting structure of business project managers to the IT PMO

NYCHA Board

NYCHA General Manager (GM)

Input and Feedback

CIO/CFO

Provide Membership

GM's Operations Committee (GMOC)

Deputy General Managers

Architecture Review Board

Quarterly Project Status Reports

Monthly Project Status Reports

Virtual IT PMO
• Mentoring and coaching
• Aligning IT and business strategy
• PM standard methodology and tools (ePMO)
• PMO reporting standards
• Repository

Provide Liason

Project Office(s)

Project Manager   and   Project Team   and   IT Strategic Partner

Business Unit Staff Reporting Structure

Weekly/Monthly/Quarterly Project Status Reports

Governance body

**Figure 17–5.**

de-scope the project in question. At a macro level, the organization now is positioned for long-term sustainable delivery, providing the organization with the ability to more effectively deliver projects and their accompanying business change required to achieve organizational strategies.

## From hero to zero

An organization will no longer be dependent on heroic project team members or unpredictable outcomes. Instead, the collective successful practices of the organization will be contained in a comprehensive foundation framework that can be repeated, continuously improved and leveraged across the organization. NYCHA leverages its PMO structure for the capture and reuse of best practices and enables those through the ePMO tool.

## Management insight

The organization will have valuable information for management decision making. The trusted single source will bring together critical portfolio information, providing an insightful snapshot of project portfolio performance and trends. The tool also will provide the capability for complex reporting requirements, building relationships between different activities recorded in disparate systems.

## Do more with less

The organization now will be better positioned to "do more with less." As the trusted single source of project information, the tool will provide the ability to connect day-to-day project delivery to progress toward organizational objectives. That will optimize resources across the organization's portfolio of projects and operational activities, ensuring the optimal alignment.

By starting with a firm foundation and creating a trusted single source of project information, NYCHA has realized the benefits above and more. Those benefits include:

- ◆ **Organizational benefits**
  - – Generated $1.2M in reductions through staff cost avoidance
  - – Increased business unit satisfaction and collaboration with IT
  - – Streamlined NYCHA business and IT five-year strategic planning process
  - – Improved level, quality, timeliness and cost effectiveness of strategic IT programs
  - – IT has demonstrated its ability to implement projects more efficiently, ultimately leading to more IT dollars available for more initiatives

- ◆ **Governance of IT projects**—The application organizes PM activities to understand the issues surrounding and the strategic importance of projects, such as:
  - – Efficient goal achievement
  - – Consistency in measuring project performance
  - – Organizational development and maturity
  - – Risk and opportunity assessment

- ◆ **Continuous improvement**—Project management practices reinforced by the tool have led to continuous process improvement in the areas of:
  - – Portfolio management—due to increased visibility and alignment with priorities
  - – Performance measurement
  - – Best practice documentation

- ◆ **Optimizing the PM environment**—Utilization of the ePMO Application improves visibility into the status and documentation for the project such as:
  - – Standardize processes
  - – Budget maintenance
  - – Quality control
  - – Goal alignment
  - – Monitor risks
  - – Organizational learning

Successful enterprise project management tool implementations involve a significant culture adjustment, and require deliberate planning and organizational change management. The change management effort is best facilitated by a thorough understanding of an organization's project management foundation—the current level of project management structures and commitment to improve project management capabilities. Regardless of the actual tool that is selected, processes and structures must be put in place so that the project management tool is the trusted single source of all project information. That trusted single source will be the platform to "manage by the facts" and provide visibility, drive consistency of project data and drive adherence to standards. As demonstrated by NYCHA's deployment of its ePMO tool, the concepts of *firm foundation* and *trusted single source* set the stage for benefits realization of the project management tool. NYCHA's benefits include cost savings, improved governance of IT projects and continuous improvement of project delivery.

## Discussion questions

1. Why is a project management tool implementation a significant culture change for an organization?
2. What do you consider the "cultural barriers" to implementing a project management tool in your organization? How did NYCHA overcome those barriers? How would your organization overcome those barriers?
3. What are the significant components that make up an organization's firm project management foundation?
4. Why is it critical that your project management tool is the *trusted single source* of project information?
5. What are the benefits to "managing by the facts" in a project organization?
6. How did the evolution of NYCHA's PMO benefit the organization? Why was the IT governance framework such an important component of that evolution?
7. Why is it important to gain a consolidated view of project information? How can that optimize your project portfolio?

**Avi Duvdevani,** *who was appointed Chief Information Officer and Deputy General Manager for Information Technology at the New York City Housing Authority in April 2002, has more than 30 years of public sector experience in IT planning, management and client services—27 years in dedicated government service to the City of New York. During his city career, Mr. Duvdevani has played a pivotal role in the city's technology history. Earlier in his tenure, he was a member of the leadership team that created the city's first technology agency, now known as The Department of Information Technology and Telecommunications (DoITT) and the city's first telecommunications network, CITYNET.*

*For the prior 12 years, Mr. Duvdevani had served in increasingly progressive technology management positions at DoITT, with primary responsibility for planning and managing the delivery of quality IT services by DoITT's Technology Center. Mr. Duvdevani played a critical role in the consolidation effort that combined three city agencies to create DoITT, the planning and design of the city's first Technology Center at MetroTech in Brooklyn, and most notably, the establishment of the city's presence on the Internet with its award-winning web site, NYC.gov. In 1998, he was appointed, by Mayor Giuliani to serve as First Deputy Commissioner of The Department of Information Technology and Telecommunications (DoITT), and he served for 12 months as DoITT's Acting Commissioner, and held that position for the remainder of the Giuliani administration, before, during and after the 9/11 tragedy.*

*Mr. Duvdevani was recognized for his "Demonstrated Leadership in the Management of IT" at the 2001 New York City Excellence in Technology Awards Program (ETAP), which applauds the contributions of IT managers in New York City government. Mr. Duvdevani also was honored for his post 9/11 leadership by the Fund for the City of New York's, 2002 Sloan Public Service Awards as well as by the New York City Managerial Employees Association, with a Distinguished Service Award as Manager of the Year "...for dedicated and exemplary service to the people of the City of New York in a year of profound crisis."*

*Written with assistance from* **Sean Laffin,** *PMP Managing Consultant with Program Planning Professionals, Inc. (Pcubed)(http://www.pcubed.com ), NYCHA's partner in the development of the award-winning project management tool, the NYCHA ePMO.*

# 18. Cloud Computing

**MARK CLEVERLEY**

## Introduction

Cloud computing uses Internet-based technology to deliver a variety of services. Dynamically scaleable and virtualized resources are made available over the Internet, as a service, often with a services-based business model. Service users do not need to know or have control of the technology infrastructure in the cloud that actually runs the service.

Wikipedia goes on:

> *"The concept incorporates <u>software as a service</u> (SaaS), <u>Web 2.0</u> and other recent, well-known technology trends, in which the common theme is reliance on the Internet for satisfying the computing needs of the users. Often-quoted examples are <u>Salesforce.com</u> and <u>Google Apps</u>, which provide common business applications online that are accessed from a <u>web browser</u>, while the <u>software</u> and <u>data</u> are stored on the servers. The cloud is a metaphor for the Internet... and is an abstraction for the complex infrastructure it conceals."*

Cloud, if you listen to the buzz, is either a disruptive trend representing the next stage in the evolution of the Internet, or it is a piece of hype that just describes a set of long-established computing technologies. Both of those ways of looking at cloud make it important to government.

## Why is cloud important for government?

The key points about cloud computing are not complex.

♦ For the user, cloud provides a way of acquiring computing services without requiring understanding of the underlying technology.

♦ For the government, cloud computing delivers services for employee, citizen and business needs in a simplified way, providing more or less unbounded scale and potential improvements in quality of service.

♦ For IT operations, cloud is a service acquisition and delivery model for IT resources and, if properly used within an overall strategy, can help improve business performance and control the costs of delivering IT resources to the organization.

Governments face accelerating pace of change. Economic disruption increases the need to do more with less. Global competitiveness pressures, environmental responsibility issues, the expectations of modern citizenry, all present severe challenges.

To help address those challenges, cloud computing offers a more dynamic computing model that can help to enable rapid innovation for applications, services and service delivery. Cloud's underlying technologies release applications and services from a fixed infrastructure, and can allow government to focus on creating a more dynamic and responsive enterprise, which adjusts more quickly and more effectively to change.

♦ Cloud computing can be a cost-effective model for provisioning processes, applications and services while making IT management simpler and increasing business responsiveness.

♦ Paying incrementally for services can directly save money. Replacing the need to manage thousands of email servers with a monthly payment to Google Apps can be an attractive option. In a cost-benefit analysis, a properly implemented and leveraged cloud computing model will drive lower cost-of-ownership, responsive delivery of services and higher service quality.

♦ Cloud computing can enable rapid innovation and higher service quality by delivering easy-to-use computing services to users on demand, regardless of their location or the type of device they are using. Users can access information wherever they are, rather than being bound to their office—a clear benefit for the workforce of tomorrow.

♦ Selecting the right use of cloud computing results in lower cost and greater flexibility by taking advantage of economies of scale and automated IT operations, optimizing investment in existing infrastructure, and allowing IT management to focus on core deliverables rather than on, say, maintenance.

♦ Solutions rapidly adjust to the volume of users as workload increases or decreases. Payment or internal chargeback for the services is more flexible and typically occurs on a usage basis. New business models are becoming more feasible and more swiftly available.

♦ Naturally, the cloud always will have more resources than the traditionally owned facility, whether it is storage, computing power, application scale, etc. And automation is increasingly more sophisticated, to the point of a tongue-in-cheek remark which looks more serious by the day: "If a human being manages it, it isn't a cloud, it's a data center."

## "Public" and "private" clouds

A cloud-based service can be "public," "private" or a combination of the two, sometimes referred to as a "hybrid cloud."

Much discussion of cloud computing is actually about the public clouds. Public cloud services are available to users from a service provider across the Internet. Different business models support them: from "free," or advertising-based, to user- or time-based subscription models.

A private cloud-based service provides many of the elements of public cloud, but data, applications and business processes are managed within the organization, which, thus, has more control over operational features—such as bandwidth, security posture and resilience—and allows appropriate deference to legal or politically desirable attributes of the service.

A private cloud could become an interesting part of today's government data center operations, offering a way to speed provisioning of certain kinds of capability to the disparate agencies that such centers support.

Combining public and private cloud-based services in configurations that reflect changing needs is likely to be a successful strategy. So, we should expect to see new business models develop that integrate public and private cloud-based capability to support new and pressing needs.

"Needs must when the devil drives" is an old expression that highlights part of the quandary that we face today. There are institutional, historical and political reasons that mean governments have been slower than other sectors to adopt principles of shared services.

In these peculiarly stressed times, however, new and more radical approaches might become more feasible. Cloud computing is one such, as part of a broad set of cost-reduction strategies. So, as well as central IT departments taking on the private cloud role to support their users, we might expect to see different government jurisdictions agreeing to come together in new ways to share certain services.

Either way, cloud computing brings more options to the table in thinking about how to achieve those goals.

## Technology behind cloud computing

If you don't like the weather, people say in certain climatically interesting parts of the world, wait a while and some new weather will arrive. Technology is like that, and we have seen some of the challenges around assimilation of new technology into the traditional structures that provide government with its IT.

So, a discussion of cloud technology is more importantly about the top-level attributes and much less about specifically what servers are where—broadly speaking, it no longer matters. Assimilating new technology is part and parcel of what the cloud providers do.

So, let's dig into the attributes that cloud computing, whether public, private or a combination, typically will demonstrate.

### Services-focused

Cloud computing is about providing services to any authorized user, anywhere, from any device. So cloud computing must be built on a service-oriented architecture and deployed with industry standards and best practices for service management. It might not be overstatement to say that, as Irving Wladawsky-Berger, Chairman Emeritus, IBM Academy of Technology, has stated, "SOA is to cloud computing as HTML is to the Internet."

### Shared, highly scalable, networked infrastructure

New IT infrastructure, application and business process services are made available leveraging the Internet paradigm. That means standardized, highly efficient, shared, virtualized compute resources (servers, storage, network, data, middleware, applications and business processes) can be rapidly scaled up and down, with elasticity through automated workload management, in a secure way, to deliver high-quality service and meet fast-changing needs.

And, it isn't just about those traditional computing components. Technology is enabling opportunities for innovation in such disparate areas as high-speed wireless connectivity, social networking, global positioning systems, radio frequency identification (RFID), intelligent appliances, utility meters, building control systems, mobile banking, automobiles and even our own homes. Cloud can bring access to innovations in those areas, too.

### Automated service delivery

Service management is request-driven and strives for near-zero incremental labor costs. Cloud computing supports business processes, applications and IT infrastructure collaboratively and cohesively. It can allocate services, dynamically move and optimize workloads and data across the shared infrastructure, and integrate added resources to scale with very little, if any, intervention by the cloud service provider personnel. Those same resources are returned to the cloud environment and are immediately made available to others when they are no longer needed. The service management supporting the cloud service also tracks usage for purposes of billing or usage chargeback.

## *Enhanced, standardized and familiar user experience*

Typical of cloud applications are their adoption of easy-to-use interfaces and straightforward information access methods, allowing users to more quickly accustom themselves to new capabilities.

## What kinds of activities are under way?

There are too many to chronicle, of course, as cloud computing forces it way into the mainstream. But a few examples illustrate:

- ◆ Google and Amazon as a platform, Salesforce.com and 37 Signals as application services, are among those making the headlines and moving fast in offering cloud based services, including to government.

- ◆ More and more software vendors are working to make their applications "cloud-ready."

- ◆ We are all increasingly familiar with the cloud paradigm, using servers and storage the location of which we do not know, but trusting our capabilities and data to such operations as Facebook, LinkedIn, MySpace, etc.

- ◆ IBM Research uses a private cloud to provision resources to researchers around the world. Its global Technology Adoption Program has 90,000 cloud users (Business Week, 8/07).

- ◆ Some financial institutions deployed an enterprise cloud to dynamically manage resources and improve utilization of the infrastructure. Automated provisioning has reduced the time required to provision from up to two days to less than one hour.

- ◆ A major U.S. university built an infrastructure cloud computing service to share computing resources across as many as 10 campuses, optimizing computing power, storage, service and data center labor across the university system, and delivering services across its constituency.

- ◆ A Ministry in Vietnam links researchers, students and potential startups with incubation and collaboration services on a cloud platform.

- ◆ A city in China plans a data center to support growing 200,000 software developers as part of its economic development strategy. The data center will reside in the cloud.

- ◆ Cloud applications are proliferating—whether it's a collaboration company assembling and providing patient information on demand from connected healthcare systems, or a social network for educators to perform peer reviews of upcoming published works.

## Government uses for cloud?

So, cloud can provide benefits and options for many different situations. What kinds of things does it promise for government?

- Sophisticated government data centers can use cloud to help optimize their delivery of services to internal users.

- Smaller governments might use cloud to facilitate incremental moves toward shared services environments.

- State or regional governments might adopt cloud as a way to help their small and medium businesses, who might benefit from gaining more sophisticated processes and applications without heavy capital investment, allowing them to invest more in other parts of their business.

- Emerging nations might not need to replicate the investment in IT infrastructure of the developed world.

- International organizations could use cloud to help emerging markets to develop valuable government processes through access to systems they could otherwise not afford.

Consider some key questions as you think about how cloud can be used in your own environment:

- Can we create and deliver innovative internal and external services at higher quality, lower cost, and shorter cycle time?

  Use of cloud computing, public or private, can enable greater innovation through collaboration, rapid deployment and lower costs. Many future innovations will integrate innovative application and information services from different sources, as government leverages suppliers, partners, voluntary sector and citizens (citizen-generated applications).

- Can cloud computing help to more quickly achieve goals for IT optimization, cost savings and faster deployment?

  Cloud computing can provide access to standardized IT resources from a provider that can enable you to rapidly deploy new applications, services or computing resources without re-engineering your infrastructure. Cloud computing provides a set of core services or building blocks that can be rapidly assembled into higher level business services for quick deployment. In some cases, organizations will purchase cloud-based services to augment or replace their existing infrastructure. Other organizations will look for ways to retool their infrastructure to support being a deliverer of cloud-based services.

  Of course, in some cases, you might not need to have an infrastructure at all. Cloud computing is in some ways about the industrialization of IT infrastructure, including the data center, to reduce costs while improving quality and time to delivery. Businesses used to generate their own electricity, until the world started to build the grid. Perhaps we are witnessing the beginning of the computing equivalent. Why, you might pose the question speculatively, would an agency or a regional government need a data center at all, five or 10 years from now?

- Can we gain advantage in achieving our strategic missions by using cloud computing?

  Cloud approaches can lead to more rapid innovation, massive scalability (up and down) to optimize resources and costs and access to resources otherwise not readily available. Speed of implementation and degree of cost savings will be impacted by the degree of customization required by the organization. The key is an organization's ability to integrate cloud computing into a broader strategy and architected plan to align IT resources closely with overall business goals, objectives and needs.

In some cases, cloud computing may be the answer for receiving and/or delivering services. In other cases, that will not be the case, which leads us to think about the challenges that come along with the opportunities.

## Challenges

Cloud operations bring challenges to government that go beyond the issues the private sector sees.

♦ Government runs mission-critical and life-critical systems, which might not be ready for cloud-based provision.

Citizens place trust in government in ways that go beyond their experiences with, say, retail or auction clouds. Allowing a cloud-based service to answer a citizen's question might be acceptable—or it might not. A service that runs in the cloud is often beyond the control of government; at certain times that might matter less than at others. If it absolutely needs to be available, there are sure to be some hard discussions to be had with cloud providers. Not all software of value in government is "cloud-ready:" able in the short term to really take advantage of the cloud's architecture and processes. Political considerations, as they have a habit of doing, may intervene. Cloud services may operate beyond the boundaries of a jurisdiction, or data may reside outside those limits, and that can become a political issue.

But, all those challenges just mean that there is something here to be worked through—over time, and in specific cases—to prove or disprove the benefits of cloud in a specific government environment. Government has done that before with technology—on every innovation from outsourcing all the way back to the telephone. It's time to have a similar discussion on cloud.

---

### Discussion questions

1. Can you assess your environment for "readiness for cloud?" Consider different kinds of applications, and different kinds of users, that might lend themselves more readily to a cloud-based approach.
2. Are your people already using cloud capabilities? Are they perhaps using them for business purposes? Many "Web 2.0" capabilities in the cloud today are already in the hands of your employees in their private lives. Are they using them to facilitate collaboration or knowledge sharing, perhaps because internal systems are not effective? (Think especially about your younger workers.)
3. Do you have applicable policies and/or legislation that would support or inhibit adoption of cloud paradigms?
4. Have you educated your key stakeholders on the potential impacts of the power of cloud computing?

**Mark Cleverley** *is IBM's Global Director for Government Strategy, helping governments with technology-enabled transformation. He advises IBM's public sector customers and IBM teams on potentials, challenges and best practices in the evolving use of new technologies. He has consulted* *widely for IBM's government projects, and has written and spoken publicly extensively in the USA and abroad. He has worked with governments in many nations and many areas of information systems. For some years he was responsible for IBM's Public Safety, Justice and related clients in Europe, the Middle East and Africa. Earlier, he led technology-enabled innovation projects in the oil, aviation and financial services industries, in Western Europe, the USA and Russia. They ranged from consolidating European data centres, through implementing core airline systems, and included one of the earliest (pre-web) public access kiosk developments.*

*Before joining IBM, Mr Cleverley was trained as an air traffic controller. He has a joint honours degree in Psychology and Philosophy from Oxford University. A British citizen now living in the USA, he is fluent in French, and has a working knowledge of Russian.*

# 19. Enterprise Resource Planning (ERP)

**MICHAEL H. JOHNSON, SR.**

Enterprise Resource Planning (ERP) implementations are difficult. By their very nature, they can affect the daily lives of thousands of people. The systems can affect everyone one from a warehouse dock worker to the chief financial officer. Governments spend millions of dollars hiring the best and brightest ERP companies and individuals to assist them, yet many of the projects fail to achieve the benefits originally envisioned, cost significantly more than expected or, in the worst case scenario, they are never implemented at all. There are well-defined methodologies, metrics, strategies and approaches for ERP projects. There is a right way and a wrong way to execute an ERP implementation. The role of the CIO is help the organization avoid the common pitfalls inherent in ERP projects. This chapter articulates some common themes for ERP project success and failures.

## They are people projects, not technology projects

ERP implementations require advanced technology. Load-balanced servers, sophisticated programmers and high-speed networks are expected. What often is not expected is the impact the projects have on people. A department was implementing a large-scale ERP system to replace multiple existing systems. It had a clerk whose job was to reconcile the various systems and record journal entries between the systems. She had worked for the department for 20 years performing that task. Early in the project, it was determined that her function would be eliminated. The department worked with her to redefine her role, and over the 12 month course of the project, she was able to adjust to the change and get ready for her new role. A year after the implementation, she was performing analytical tasks, reviewing the general ledger for discrepancies and helping the business units adjust to the new system. Her role and value to the organization had increased immensely.

Another organization had a division with the sole purpose of reconciling in the outstanding treasury warrants (essentially checks). The new ERP completely automated the reconciliation process and replaced all of the existing reconciliation systems. Although the functions and requirements of the new system were well documented and understood within the project team, no one—client or consultant—had identified that significant impact on the organization. During the cutover meeting with the reconciliation staff, the head of the division realized the impact that the new ERP would have on him and his staff and literally broke into tears. Within a few months, the reconciliation process was out of control and required significant resources to get it back on track.

In both instances, the technology worked as designed. The servers processed their transactions, the network delivered information and programmers addressed any bugs or performance issues. The major difference between the two outcomes is early identification of the impact the system would have on the daily lives of the employees.

# Failure to dedicate resources

Governments typically implement new ERP systems because the existing systems are failing and resources are strained. The new system is supposed to allow more efficient processing of transactions and require fewer resources to operate. Almost by definition, the existing staff is over worked. There are several common approaches to addressing the additional resources requirements for an ERP implementation:

**Hire new resources**—Often, governments will be able to get new positions dedicated to the ERP projects. The individuals may be fresh out of college or have a few years of experience. They are generally excited about learning a new system and working with new technology. What they typically lack is institutional knowledge. A large state was implementing a major ERP. The project director hired eight relatively junior staff and assigned them responsibility for specific modules in the system. The junior staff worked side-by-side with the integrator throughout the project. At the end of the project, the staff continued to support their modules and maintain the system. They could write new reports, update the system configuration table and train new users without having to rely on the integrator. That was a relatively inexpensive and effective solution.

**Dedicate experienced resources**—Another approach is for the customer to dedicate senior, experienced resources. That requires a significant dedication on the part of the organization but can result in significant benefits. A major county department was preparing for a new system implementation. The project had been under way for more than a year and had six months left to implementation. There was continued resistance from existing staff and a general lack of support for the new system. When the executive sponsor approached the integrator to ask what could be done to address the issue, the integrator suggested he dedicate his most senior resources, full-time, to the project. Although those resources had been involved in the project from the beginning, they still maintained their day-to-day operating responsibilities. Dedicating them full-time to the project would require backfilling their existing positions. He agreed. Five of his top people were relocated to the project area. Their replacements sat in their old offices. The replacements were individuals in the organization that were more junior, but understood the operation and were eager for a new challenge. For the next six months, senior resources learned the new system, conducted acceptance testing, and wrote the new policies and procedures. The backfill resources learned their supervisor's roles and significantly increased their value to the organization.

ERP projects are hard. People generally will resist working on difficult tasks unless that is their primary responsibility. Regardless of whether the people assigned to the project are relatively new or highly experienced, it is critical that the project have dedicated staff.

# Lack of executive commitment

ERP implementations require tough decisions. They will require organizations to cooperate in ways they never have before. For example, procurement may not have worked with accounting often in the past, but the new ERP will require accounting information to be entered by procurement on the requisition. That type of change requires coordinated leadership and an executive sponsor that will make a decision when conflicts arise. Here are some techniques to build the executive commitment that will be necessary for a successful implementation:

**Establish a steering committee**—A steering committee is an important part of an ERP implementation. It serves as an escalation point for key issues and provides a communication method for project progress. For example, a large organization that served as a service bureau for multiple smaller regional districts was installing a new ERP system. The service bureau provided accounting and support services for the districts, but also had oversight responsibility. The service bureau never had a group of end users who provided advice and input. The implementer suggested to the chief financial officer that a steering committee be formed for the new system. She was concerned, but ultimately agreed to form the committee. Within a few months, the committee was providing valuable input, assisting with key decisions and helping to improve the service bureaus image. The service bureau had not given up their oversight responsibility, but they now had a direct communication path to their end users.

**Brief the executive sponsor**—ERP implementations for governments can be publicity nightmares. Incorrect paychecks, late vendor payments or system outages can be major public relations issues for an organization. It is imperative that the individuals who are ultimately responsible for the implementations are involved from the beginning. The executive sponsor for an ERP project may be an elected or appointed official. Individuals in the organization may not be accustomed to coordinating activities with someone at that level, but ERP projects require that level of involvement.

Early in the implementation of a new payroll system for a large county, the implementer informed the auditor/controller that the existing payroll system was most likely incorrectly calculating paychecks for the county employees. She was somewhat surprised at the statement because it was so early in the project and asked what evidence supported such a bold statement. The implementer said it was based on experience and, given the complexity of their payroll and the age of their systems, they almost certainly were not conforming to the existing labor agreements.

Because of the likelihood of that issue, the auditor/controller and her staff reached out to the unions early, established contacts to address the issues should they arise and waited for parallel testing. Within the first parallel payroll, multiple overpayment and underpayment issues had been identified. Although it took several months to work out the issues with the unions, neither the auditor/controller nor the unions were surprised, and ultimately the issues were resolved without a major publicity issue. The key to resolving those issues was early involvement of the elected official.

In another instance, the director of a large department was briefed monthly on the project. When training started for the system implementation, attendance for the classes was low. An email from the director to the staff that stressed the importance of training and requested that any staff who could not attend training contact him directly significantly increased the attendance numbers.

## Outside change

ERP projects operate in complex environments. Many factors, internal and external, can affect the outcome of the project. Some of those factors can be anticipated, and some cannot. War, natural disasters, fires and floods cannot be anticipated, but some external factors can be anticipated. Common, predictable external factors for governments include:

**Elections**—Elections that occur during an ERP implementation can significantly impact the project. One significant impact occurred to a multi-year effort that required millions of dollars and literally affected hundreds of people. Eighteen months into the project, the executive sponsor changed due to an election. It took an additional year to complete the implementation while the new executive sponsor became comfortable with the project. While the change in leadership could not be anticipated, the election was predictable. If the project had been delayed a year, it would have saved the taxpayers millions of dollars.

**Budget cycles**–Governments go through regular, planned budget cycles. ERP projects typically cross multiple budget cycles. Project leaders often make the mistake of not anticipating the effect those cycles can have on the project. Regular briefings to the legislative body can help prepare for the budget cycle. If the legislative body has been briefed quarterly on the project, its members should not be surprised by the additional funding necessary to complete the project for the following years. Projects should have discreet, measurable milestones that show progress through the multiple budget cycles that may be necessary to complete the project.

**Fiscal and calendar year end**–ERP systems typically require significant finance and human resource personnel involvement. The systems also typically go live on a calendar or fiscal year end. Understanding the need to augment resources during those cycles can be critical to a successful implementation. Governments typically cannot add resources quickly. One county department negotiated contracts with temporary agencies in advance of the implementation and set up funding in case the resources were needed. Another department added contingency in their project budget and negotiated a clause in the implementation contract that allowed the integrator to provide additional resources. The important factor is that the need should be anticipated in advance.

While all external factors cannot be controlled or predicted, it is important that those common factors be considered during the ERP project planning process.

## Involving the users

Many ERP system users will interact with the system virtually full-time during the course of a business day. Involving those users early is critical to the success of the project. Multiple techniques may be used to solicit that involvement, including:

**Conduct a large, inclusive kickoff meeting**–The start of the project sets the tone for the entire project. If the kickoff meeting is a small group of people, it leaves the impression that the project is somewhat closed. The kickoff meeting should include anyone that will be affected by the system. The meetings can be conducted in the city council chambers, large conference rooms and even convention halls holding thousands of people. If the project is large enough, it may make sense to have multiple meetings in different locations so a wider audience can attend.

**Continue regular communication with the users**–Some projects make the mistake of having a kickoff meeting and then going silent for months. That leaves the end users to speculate on what is going on with the project. Many methods may be used to continue communication, including brown bag lunches, email bulletins and a project website. One project had monthly coffee and donuts in the county boardroom for the users. The meetings were well attended, and it gave the users a chance to interact with the project team. It also gave the project team a chance to show the users new functions and features as they were available.

**Have users assist with testing**– There are some risks associated with having end users assist with testing. They may see issues with the system and get the impression that the system is flawed. If you establish expectations, those risks can be mitigated, and the benefits are tremendous. For instance, the best person to test accounts payable processing is an accounts payable clerk. You need to pick an individual who is seen as a leader by their peers. Their input will be extremely valuable to the process, and they can serve as a project advocate for their area.

**Use internal trainers**—Many organizations make the mistake of having external trainers conduct all of the training for their end users. While it may make sense to have professional trainers, the result of that approach is that there are no internal resources skilled to continue training after the implementation. One county department selected a group on internal resources based on their interest and abilities. Although the individuals had never conducted formal training sessions, they wanted to learn, and felt it would be an advantage to their career development. The department hired a firm that specialized in public speaking training and had onsite training, including videotaping the trainers and providing feedback. The internal trainers were paired with professional trainers for the first few training sessions and then, when they were comfortable, they conducted the classes on their own. The client was left with an internal training staff to continue to support the system long-term.

**Training does not stop when the system goes live**—Many projects make the mistake of assuming that because the users have been trained, everything should be fine at go-live. Nothing could be further from the truth. One of the most critical components to a new system implementation is monitoring user adoption. Simple metrics (payment vouchers processed, timesheets entered, requisitions initiated, etc.) can be powerful tools. Inevitably, users will have different levels of system adoption. One very effective technique for improving user adoption is having post go-live training. That technique involves having users come to a site dedicated to helping them process actual transactions on the system after go-live. The room should have trainers and system experts to guide the users as they process transactions. A few sessions, and most users are comfortable with the new system.

Continuous involvement of the users recognizes the critical importance they have to the project and helps improve the likelihood of success.

## Understanding the connections

ERP systems depend on many factors for success. They often replace complex software environments that have developed over years. The interdependencies of those systems often are not documented or well understood. Changing those environments requires care and diligence. Some common areas to consider include:

**Conduct existing system surveys**—Regardless of the anticipated scope of the ERP system, there may be expectations that the system will or will not replace certain systems that operate for the organization. If the system will be replaced, then the new ERP must be configured to support its function. If the system will not be replaced, then it may require an interface to the new system. Cataloging those systems early in the process is critical to planning the system implementation.

**Start external interfaces**—Finance and human resource systems typically have multiple interfaces to external entities. Those interfaces may include banks, governments, vendors and customers. Coordinating efforts to test the new interfaces for the ERP with those organizations early allows those organizations to properly plan their resources to support the system implementation.

**Don't forget the network**—ERP systems require high-speed networks and properly configured user workstations. Reviewing the network needs and workstation configuration is important early in the process. One of the first steps is to create a list of anticipated end users for the system. That list can be used to assist with training and outreach during the system implementation. A network map should be created for all locations with users. The map should be used to analyze the network and workstation requirements for each site. In one instance, a government had to delay implementation of an ERP for several months due to late identification of network needs.

ERP project teams can become insular. Many operate at separate project sites and can fail to realize the interdependencies the project has with other internal and external resources. Identifying those interdependencies early is critical to ERP project success.

## Paving the cow path

ERP projects can be extremely painful. The best analogy is open heart surgery. A good ERP implementation will require significant organizational change, a shifting of roles and tremendous effort. Similar to open heart surgery, the patient typically will not be pleased immediately following the surgery, but after a year or two, the patient should see significant improvements. If the ERP is implemented and the organization does not change, there will be limited or no benefits. The role of the CIO and other leaders is to guide the organization into making the tough changes that will be necessary to realize the benefits.

Often the contract with the integrator will include a term that requires the new system to have the same or similar functions to the old system. That can be a major area of contention between the integrator and the client. That contractual term is intended to protect the client so they are not left with a gap in feature or function. One contract for a large county department had such a term, but had been modified to include the requirement that process be reengineered to support the software whenever practical.

For the department, the goal for procurements was to have a virtually paperless process. The existing process required hardcopy signatures, multiple purchase orders copies and weeks to complete. The procurement staff was not convinced that the goal of a paperless system was achievable. Existing policy required approval, and they were concerned about electronic signatures. By demonstrating the system capabilities, working with the staff to modify procedures and involving the procurement director in the process, the department was able to achieve the goal and provide significant benefits to the organization. Now, field personnel could initiate purchase orders online, and the process was streamlined from requisition to check. If they had simply automated the old paper process, the organization would have seen little or no benefit.

## Think outside the box

As mentioned earlier, organizations involve bright people in the ERP implementations. Those people will generate ideas during the process that may provide a significant benefit to the organization. It is important that those ideas be vetted and adopted when appropriate. Some examples include:

**Use your organization's expertise**—One county department was significantly involved in curriculum development for school districts within the county. The project team felt it would be helpful to have some of the department curriculum experts assist with developing the training. They were involved early in the project and were able to provide significant value during the process.

**Find a different solution**—One large ERP implementation was set to train thousands of users. The training team felt that a good student registration system would speed the registration process and provide a method for managing the large number of classes a registrants. A relatively inexpensive solution was procured that allowed the organization to smoothly handle the large number of students.

**Change the law**—During the review of a complex, time-intensive contracting process, it was discovered that one of the major reasons the process was so complex was because of specific regulations that required the process. The organization approached the legislative body, explained the cost of the regulation, and they were able to get the law changed.

**Celebrate**—Overtime, late nights, weekend and pizza in the office are common in ERP projects. Employees in governments rarely get extra, direct compensation for their effort. A little recognition goes a long way in keeping the team happy. Some governments have had a banquet at the end of the project hosted by senior officials to recognize the team. Other governments have done something as simple as a bowling tournament or coffee mugs. Recognizing the team lets them know their efforts are appreciated by the organization.

## Conclusion

The CIO is the technology leader for a government. Typically, the CIO will be heavily involved in, if not leading, the ERP project. The success or failure of the ERP project will impact the career of the CIO negatively or positively. Understanding common techniques and pitfalls of an ERP implementation can help the CIO successfully lead the project. Make the hard decisions, give the tough advice and reap the benefits!

---

### Discussion questions

1. How would implementation of a new ERP affect your organization?
2. What level of change is appropriate for your organization's culture?
3. Could your organization dedicate the necessary resources to accomplish a project of this scale?
4. What implementation alternatives (phasing, decreasing scoping, less customization, etc.) would be appropriate to help your organization achieve a project such as this?
5. Do you have a strong executive team that could support large-scale organizational change?
6. What steps would you need to take to prepare the executive team?
7. What members of your leadership team would need to be a part of the steering committee?
8. What external factors could impact implementation of an ERP project in your organization?
9. What techniques would be effective for involving your users?
10. What interdependencies exist in your organization for an ERP implementation?
11. How would existing business processes be affected by an ERP implementation?
12. What unique approaches could your organization bring to an ERP project?

**Michael H. Johnson, Sr.,** *CPA, began his career at Peat Marwick Mitchell & Co. as a staff auditor. After two years in audit, he joined the consulting practice for the firm assisting with large-scale ERP implementations for governments. Michael spent the following 20 years with KPMG and then BearingPoint, implementing ERP systems for states, cities, counties, school districts and other governmental entities. His experience includes custom financial system development and package implementation for various ERP vendors. Michael currently leads the information technology consulting practice for Bridgepoint Consulting, LLC in Austin, where he assists public and private organizations with strategic information technology planning and system implementations. Michael has a Bachelor of Arts degree from Austin College with an emphasis on accounting and information technology, and is a Certified Public Accountant in the State of Texas.*

# 20. Outsourcing vs. Insourcing— How to Assess, Manage and Evaluate

**CLIFFORD CLARKE**

Today, senior leaders are faced with many information technology-related challenges. The nature of information technology requires a rapid response to threats and opportunities. The public sector Chief Information Officer generally faces a magnified set of circumstances different from those in the private sector.

As an example, all could agree that budgets are constricting. Unlike the private sector where marketers identify new products and sales opportunities, the public sector's revenue model has changed very little. Taxes of one sort or another continue to be the main source of operating income. More municipalities are trying to identify ways of reducing the tax burden on their constituents, further exacerbating the challenges of responding to threats and opportunities.

Public sector Chief Information Officers must evaluate the alignment of their information technology operation with the business needs. To achieve the desired alignment and performance, the CIO may review the sourcing model. The obvious choices are to insource, outsource or have some hybrid model. A review of the sourcing model requires significant evaluation. Changing the model is not something to be taken lightly. Below is a brief discussion of the basic factors influencing the decision to outsource and some of the issues that must be evaluated that are unique to the public sector.

## Outsourcing is not new

Critical to a rational discussion is the acknowledgment that outsourcing is not new. Although this is no attempt to pinpoint the first example of outsourcing, it is fair to say that as soon as individuals started to trade goods and services, the outsourcing marketplace was created.

Work is outsourced every day. It is an element of our daily lives and has proven healthy for business. Outsourcing, when done successfully, allows entities to focus or specialize on their core competencies. That focus generally has had a positive effect for the customer by spawning innovation of new products and services, reductions in cost through competition, improved quality and enhancements to existing features. Outsourcing is an integral part of how products and services are delivered today, and there is no realistic chance to reverse that model. The conversation must then change to why would you choose to outsource, and when is it appropriate.

## Why look at outsourcing

The traditional reasons for outsourcing have not changed. It is expected that goods and services would be produced better, quicker or more cost effectively than the in-sourced model. Organizations can choose one or more of those reasons to outsource. It is difficult, but not impossible, to do well in all three categories at once. In the case where all three categories cannot be achieved, the choice to outsource should produce some strategic advantage or reasonably resolve some operating deficiency.

As mentioned earlier, the public sector generally has a limited revenue stream. Taxes are the predominate source, but fines and fee for services also provide significant revenue opportunities. Less significant are allocations, like from the federal government, grants and gifts. The important fact is that the revenue model was designed to be stable, if not predictable, showing modest changes over time. That designed stability does not reflect the rapidly changing environment of information technology. That financial limitation affects all of the traditional rationale for outsourcing.

Entities improve their products and services through continuous improvement and honing their most important tool. That tool is the knowledge worker, human talent, the employees. The CIO may recognize the organization's core competencies are not aligned with the needs, and the time or cost required to bridge that gap maybe prohibitive. Limited flexibility in the revenue model affects the talent pool. Still, today relatively few municipalities invest in keeping that tool sharp through the promotion of advanced degrees and continuing education requirements and reimbursement. Additionally, the compensation for the public sector work is generally below a comparable job in the private sector.

Many public sector information technology workers choose to leave and find employment in the private sector for financial rewards, other opportunities and continued development. With retention as a challenge, today's public sector Chief Information Officers can leverage strategies to ensure the information technology staff remain current with tools, techniques, opportunities and threats in the rapidly changing landscape. Some such strategies could be to mandate the knowledge currency of the outsource partner, require certifications for key positions, or require the outsource partner demonstrate that it can remain on the leading edge of information technology change environment. Some outsourcing contracts have requirements for mandated training hours for each worker at the vendor's expense. Today's outsourced contracts may state a reasonable expectation for talent acquisition at some known quantity. Those strategies are generally well accepted by the taxpayers because it is perceived as having a predictable and fixed cost relative to the expected return.

Outsourcing has another advantage in the speed to market, faster, scenario. Traditionally, employees view municipalities as stable in comparison to the private sector. Cities do not move out of town or generally merge, forcing massive layoffs. Usually the term nimble is not used to describe government. In fact, bureaucracy is intentionally built into the decision process as a way to retard rash decision making. Unfortunately, the rest of the world does not care about the planned pace of government. As it relates to information technology security and trends, many municipalities find themselves ill prepared for the rapid pace of change. Outsourcing can provide for a rapid redeployment of the toolset where the entity can turn off one type of developer and turn on another.

Additionally, the entity need only acquire the fractional amount of talent needed to complete the task at hand. Information technology outsourcing contracts of today seek to build in the flexibility, without penalty, to quickly scale up or down within a reasonable period of time. That is designed to reduce time and cap, if not totally eliminate, the cost of acquiring and trading resources to meet the changing demands of the enterprise, such as a flat rate for staff augmentation, or a predefined bench or reserve strength. Superior contracts tie service level expectations to the out-sourcer's performance in the deliverable. Additionally, though not often discussed, there is the ability to make the necessary changes and maintain the entity's goodwill by pushing the hiring and firing issue squarely on the outsourcer.

Cost is the third major reason to consider outsourcing. Entities seeking to reduce the cost of the delivery structure look at outsourcing as a solution. It seems contradictory that municipalities with a lower employee compensation model could be more expensive than an outsource model, but in many cases they are. The lack of speed mentioned above comes with overhead cost. The acquisition of fractional resources is another reason for an improved cost model with outsourcing. Many times, the ability of an outsourcing organization to focus on a core competency produces innovation and cost efficiencies. Public sector Chief Information Officers can leverage a quality request for proposal to attain a competitive cost for the required services.

## Outsourcing versus offshoring

Soon after organizations figured out how to outsource goods and services, someone began think-ing about offshoring. This discussion will focus on outsourcing versus insourcing, but the exer-cise would not be complete without a brief definition of offshoring. The reasons for offshoring are primarily the same as outsourcing. Offshoring is where the work is physically completed outside your territory or country. In the public sector, offshoring is generally perceived as bad. The thought of losing work to another country regardless of the cost, quality or speed does not sit well with most taxpayers. The perceived security and economic issues have cast a negative connotation on offshoring. One complicating fact of our global economy is the convergence of companies and their physical locations. The major U.S. information technology firms operate with significant presence in other parts of the world. That generally does not concern the U.S. taxpayer. Work can move freely across borders within a firm. Taxpayers view foreign companies and, therefore, coun-tries working on public sector information as a challenge. As it relates to homeland security, pub-lic safety or public information, the offshoring model is not yet mature in the public eye.

## Why look to insourcing

Insourcing is the traditional information technology model. Outsourcing usually happens due to some threat or market opportunity, and the reaction is to outsource to reduce the threat or capi-talize on an opportunity. It may seem that the scales are tilted very heavily in favor of outsourcing, but insourcing provides a key element: the perception of greater control. Control over the re-sources, projects, security or other areas can be driving factors for remaining or returning to an insourced model. Outsourcing could be seen as a solution looking for a problem. A well-run in-sourced information technology operation should not move away from that model. An entity may be comfortable with the current insource model, and no compelling reason to change exists. Change is disruptive. Change for the sake of change without a clear expectation or vision for the end game should be avoided.

## New criteria for the public sector

Outsourcing is a viable and valid option in today's information technology management model, but the public sector CIO should consider the additional issues that will affect the outsourcing decision-making process. As discussed briefly above, ownership (foreign or domestic) should be part of the evaluation. Another new wrinkle is location (local, regional or national). The political cycle (election year or not) can be an influencer. Additionally, one should consider the economic climate (job loss and shrinkage versus job growth and booming) and the political climate. Those criteria should be evaluated along with the questions of better, faster, cheaper.

As mentioned above, the major U.S.-based information technology firms—like IBM, Dell, CSC, ACS and Unisys just to name a few—all have a significant operational presence in other parts of the world. Non-U.S. companies wish to benefit from the flattening of the world. Companies from India, Ireland, the Pacific Rim and the UK have set up shop on U.S. soil with hopes of supplying the marketplace. Taxpayers have not warmed up to that idea. The perception of who benefits is often inaccurate. Taxpayers believe all their dollars are moving to another country and feel that is a threat to our economy. The reality is that the largest cost of those operations is in human talent. With work onshore, the majority of the money stays within the country. Strategically, the Chief Information Officer must evaluate just how progressive the community may be and be prepared to educate the public. Several municipalities have incorporated bonus points for domestic firms. That is not without peril. Some weighting scales have been challenged as prohibiting free trade.

Only a little less sensitive is the location of the work. When the tech bubble burst, many qualified information technology professionals left their companies. Additionally, the practice of offshoring matured and increased in popularity. That changing face of the business environment has created many start-up information technology firms. The public sector Chief Information Officer should be concerned with the number of local or regional firms available and competing for the opportunity to provide services to the government sector. When outsourcing, selecting a local firm is generally viewed as a more acceptable direction for taxpayers. The availability of local resources should not short circuit the due diligence process. The CIO still must ensure that the firm or consortium of firms will be well managed, have an ongoing concern, is financially viable and have a clearly articulated reporting structure.

Viewed in a vacuum, the political cycle is neutral, but today's CIO cannot ignore how the stresses of changing the information technology environment can affect key elected officials. Consider whether flipping, moving from insourced to outsourced or reverse, helps or hurts the cause. Consider whether changing the model will negatively affect the chances of re-election. The CIO must be in alignment with key elected officials, as they may have campaigned on a specific model. Strategically, the CIO must be aligned with the organization, its leadership and customers. That is not to suggest that if the information strongly supports a change that it should be avoided simply for the election cycle. It does suggest that a more aggressive approach to educating the officials and, thus, the public on the issues will be required. The potential for leadership change is mandated by the laws of the electoral process, therefore, a careful evaluation of the timing is critical.

Although there always will be a degree of distrust and cynicism toward government, consider whether the taxpayers feel local government is making good choices or whether the public harbors a mistrust of their elected officials. Also consider whether the population generally believes in the direction of the administration, whether the administration enjoys a positive approval rating, and whether the decisions of the administration are viewed as helping or hurting the economy. When the public agrees with the general direction, they will be more apt to support changes in the delivery model for government goods and services. Prosperity has a calming affect. Although the economic and political environments also are neutral viewed in isolation, the public sector

CIO cannot under estimate how modifying the information technology delivery system will be perceived and the effect on the administration.

## Hybrids

Choosing to outsource your information technology operation is no small undertaking. The general components of an outsourced contract are help desk management, operations, application development and maintenance, telecommunication and network infrastructure, and the asset move add change process. If it is determined that the organization wishes to pursue the outsourced model, then the CIO should consider whether outsourcing a fraction of the organization will achieve the desired results. That is a viable option and can prove to be less disruptive to the organization. It also can serve as a jumping off point for additional outsourcing. Strategically, the CIO should plan ahead by selecting firms that can scale up to the other components or, at minimum, understand how the partner fits in the larger model.

## Ensuring success in any model

Either model can work and does work, depending on the climate. Whether the organization chooses to keep an insourced model or outsource the information technology environment, the CIO must look to the following components for success:

♦ Alignment
♦ Process
♦ Measurement
♦ Talent
♦ Tools
♦ Alignment

### *Alignment*

Alignment can be difficult to attain. Information technology by its nature is rapidly changing. The information technology environment must service many and typically very diverse stakeholders. A key to successful alignment is being engaged and in the loop. Private sector organizations like Wal-Mart and Dell have embraced the competitive advantage that an innovative information technology organization can provide. Most public sector entities still view information technology as a necessary evil, a cost center and something only the propeller heads in the basement need to understand. Thus, many government units never leverage the strategic advantage that information technology can provide, therefore, limit it to the tactical roles of printing reports and delivering email. The public sector has been resistant to change and has not leveraged the strategic advantage of an aligned technology delivery system. It is the responsibility of the CIO to identify ways to engage the senior staff, to be part of the decision process and demonstrate value. Business intelligence, business process re-engineering and workflow optimization, policy and procedure development, network and data center optimization, and project selection and governance are just a few ways a strategically aligned information technology operation can improve the performance of the organization. The CIO must be at the decision-making table and provide valued information to the leadership body.

Organizational alignment, by default, requires strong communication and feedback. Although feedback is a subset of the communication system, it is important to capture that valued information must flow freely from the CIO's office to the stakeholders. Feedback allows for course correction. Success can be dependent on anticipating the needs of the stakeholders and monitoring the formal and informal feedback loops. The feedback system gives clues to the organizational readiness for change. Before undertaking a significant change, make sure the stakeholders are onboard.

## Process

Process is another underrated element of a successful information technology organization. Process denotes a systematic series of actions directed to some end. Taken to the highest level of performance, process must be controlled, predictable. The connotation is that the process is well documented, clearly articulated, and there is organizational compliance. Without a stable process, success is unpredictable at best and, in many cases, unrepeatable. Again, processes like outage notification, work assignment notices and project initiation are expected. High-performance organizations are strong in governance, the system development lifecycle, lean, information technology infrastructure library, and other processes that take a more scientific approach to information technology.

## Measurements

Information technology organizations must measure their effectiveness. Typical statistics like call resolution rates and time to ticket closure are great but should be considered the price for admission. Those stats are purely tactical. The gold is hidden in the multi-million dollar project. The CIO must know that the effort is achieving the expected results. Information technology must help the elected officials demonstrate the value for the dollars spent. Most organizations use the "Ronco" model for project implementation, where the organization takes a "set it and forget it" approach. As soon as the project is completed, the resources and attention are turned to the next assignment. High-performance organizations review their work periodically to ensure the justifications for the engagement are being met. Whether information technology is insourced or outsourced, it must establish service level expectations that are clearly stated, monitored and adjusted.

## Talent

Talent acquisition and retention has been discussed above, and it remains problematic and a serious issue in the public sector. Compensation can be restrictive, but that is only part of the talent acquisition and retention model. Due to limited and contracting budgets, training often is limited. Internal opportunities for advancement are few. Some public sector entities place additional talent restrictions on themselves, like residence requirements and non-compete clauses with their consultants and contractors.

Talent is such an important asset, the public sector should take a cue from the private sector by leveraging the flat world and revisit the reasoning for residency requires. Aside for the perceived employment stability, many seek work in the public sector because they have a calling for public service. Some municipalities have created attractive retention programs that offset the lower compensation model.

## Tools

The operation must add the right tools to the mix of aforementioned components to be a successful information technology organization. Although there has been improvement in the currency, often the tools are outdated in the public sector. The replacement schedule is on breakage only and maintenance is non-existent.

Tied with a measurement process, the CIO must evaluate when it is time to refresh the tools being used even if that means an accelerated replacement. Equipment failures should undergo a root cause analysis and a determination should be made as to the true cost of being unproductive. A maintenance schedule should be implemented to keep the equipment in tip top condition. We have become accustomed to security and features patching. We need to become accustomed to database management and network closet inspections.

## Added factors exclusive to successful outsourcing

An added dimension that exists in the outsource model is the exit strategy. It is said that the best defense is a strong offense. The same is true in outsourcing. As a CIO, you must understand how to reverse the gears if it becomes necessary. Entering into an outsourcing contract is a time-consuming process and is not easily reversed. Contractually, it may be easy to identify a breach, but organizations should be willing to spend considerable time and efforts to resolve the challenges. The CIO is responsible for being prepared if all efforts to resolve the issues are not working. A fully developed exit strategy will include managing hardware and software ownership issues, human capital transfer, play fair agreements and management of transfer of other intellectual property assets developed for the account.

Additionally, if the organization chooses a hybrid or fully outsourced model, it can not escape the ownership, responsibility and accountability issues. It is important that the organization retain enough of a management or governance team to manage and audit the performance of the outsourcer. Simply handing over the keys to the shop rarely works. Outsourcing should be approached in a spirit of partnership, not as a planned opportunity to blame the vendor for failures. That will only ensure breakage.

The organization may choose to keep an insource model, outsource information technology or have some hybrid model. A review of the sourcing model requires significant evaluation and cooperation. Changing the model is not something to be taken lightly. All models can and do work in the public sector. The organization must review those issues and evaluate its situation to adopt the best fit.

---

### Discussion questions

1. Is there a governmental application that should never be outsourced?
2. How does the municipality ensure it has the maturity in governance to manage an outsource relationship? Consider the organization's ability to select projects, measure its success, and communicate and report progress.
3. What steps can a public sector CIO take to ensure that upon termination (early or normal) it can assume the work? Consider factors like intellectual capital and application currency.
4. Aside from breach of contractual service level agreements, and understanding early termination penalties could apply, what would be a case to terminate without cause and bring the work back in house?

5. How does the public sector CIO integrate and balance the election process and the high potential for a rapid change in strategic direction against a long term outsourcing agreement and maturing service level goals?
6. What things can a public sector CIO do to ensure the organization remains engaged and accountable for the success of the outsourced relationship versus engaging finger pointing?

**Clifford Clarke** *is currently the President and CEO of* **C2 IT Advisors**, *a company dedicated to serving growing companies with information technology strategy and optimization, generally in the middle tier. Mr. Clarke is the former Chief Information Officer / Chief Technology Officer for the City of Fort Wayne, Indiana. Clifford has more than 20 years of information technology experience. He has worked with several Fortune 500 companies, including Lincoln Financial Group, Aon Corp. and General Motors. Clarke is a Certified Project Management Professional, Certified Information Security Manager, Certified in the Governance of Enterprise Information Technology, and holds an MBA.*

# 21. The Greening of IT and Local Government

**MARK CLEVERLEY AND CURTIS CLARK**

Today, public and private organizations are focused on environmental and energy issues from a variety of perspectives—political, social and economic. That focus is challenging government organizations to develop strategies and programs that effectively address issues ranging from clean water to their carbon footprints. To a significant degree, regardless of your views concerning the environmental issues and the causes, the debate over whether we should be concerned about those issues has been replaced with a "call to action." Understanding the challenges, the political and policy priorities, and developing comprehensive responses will take a collaborative approach from both the public and private sector. The focus today should be around being good stewards of our environment and the public resources we use.

In this paper, we will explore the green agenda and the critical leadership role that CIOs and their organizations can play in shaping and implementing effective, sustainable models of green government.

## A perspective

In 2008, IBM published "Government 2020 and the perpetual collaboration mandate."[1] The report, based on IBM's experience with our public sector clients globally and our ongoing research, focuses on six drivers that will require governments to fundamentally rethink their strategies and operations. Rising environmental concerns form one of the six drivers and provide an enlightening perspective as we explore the focus on green government.

An excerpt from "Government 2020," IBM Institute for Business Value, April 2008:

> *Natural resource availability can reshape nations, societies and peoples' daily lives. Governments are realizing that individual and national behavior will ultimately impact all humanity. This issue is gaining political and scientific attention and the consideration of environmental impacts is increasingly critical to public and private economic discussion. As a result, the "greening" of government policies is taking place around the world.*
>
> *In varying degrees, governments face pressure to deal with the effects of global warming, a foreseeable decline in fossil fuel and gas supplies, steeply rising energy costs and the scarcity of fresh water. Often, the cycle times from action to impact to remediation are quite long. These and related concerns have led to the rise of new green industries, including a push toward the use of alternative and renewable energy sources. Among recent responses to environmental challenges, some cities have begun implementing creative strategies to reduce road traffic and its pollution.*

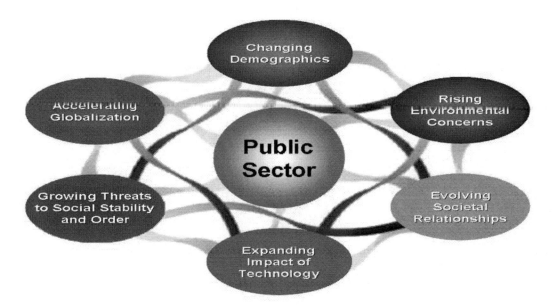

**Figure 21–1.** The drivers of change facing governments globally.

The CIO's organization can provide critical leadership in the formulation of solutions and the deployment of enabling technologies to address the environmental and energy agenda. We believe it is critical for our technology leaders to understand the broader policy issues, so before we examine specific strategies and actions that a CIO's organization might consider to facilitate the green government agenda, it is informative to see the focus and range of priorities that governments and their national organizations are advocating.

## The government response

While governments at all levels have a range of programs in place or under consideration to respond to their environmental and energy issues, several national government organizations in the United States have taken on the green agenda as a serious policy area. Those initiatives can serve as a valuable resource by bringing together thought leadership and experience that can be shared as models for other governments.

For example, the National Association of Counties (NACo) has created a Green Government Initiative[2], made up of leading county governments that are actively working on green initiatives, along with private sector companies that are helping support and facilitate the work. The collaborative initiative is designed to provide education, share best practices and facilitate open discussions around critical environmental and energy issues. The initiative has a broad focus around the following areas:

♦ Green Buildings and Energy Efficiency
♦ Green Fleets and Alternative Fuels
♦ Climate Protection and Air Quality
♦ Purchasing and Procurement
♦ Waste Management and Recycling
♦ Land Use and Conservation
♦ Water Quality and Conservations

Driving the Green Government Initiative are three principles about "Why go green?"

♦ **Economic Reasons:** Going green can save taxpayer dollars, create jobs and improve the local economy. For example, one finding suggests that up to 30% of energy consumed in commercial (including government) buildings often is used unnecessarily or inefficiently.

♦ **Environmental Reasons:** From understanding the "carbon footprint" of government buildings, and implementing policies and systems to reduce the footprint, to establishing overarching policies around the use of renewable, recycled or recyclable materials, government can lead in a variety of ways to improve the environment.

♦ **Social Reasons:** As we have seen, the growing awareness of the need to protect our environment makes green government good for all citizens and can have a positive impact on creating regions that are environmentally friendly and vibrant places to live, work and play.

Clearly, NACo has taken a leadership position concerning green government, and their work will provide valuable insights to political and government leaders who want to move forward on that important policy initiative, but they are not alone. A range of other organizations are taking equally significant steps.

Governor Tim Pawlenty, National Governors Association's (NGA) Chair for 2007-2008, established the Securing a Clean Energy Future task force as a major initiative for his term and challenged the task force to identify approaches that:[3]

♦ Use our energy resources better through efficiency and conservation;
♦ Promote non-petroleum based fuels, such as ethanol and biodiesel;
♦ Take reasonable steps to reduce greenhouse gas emissions; and,
♦ Accelerate research and development of advanced, clean energy technologies.

The NGA is calling for bold and collaborative actions by the states to address those issues. In fact, the NGA's 2008 report on the Governors' State of the State Addresses revealed that nearly 90% of the governors identified policies focused on energy, the environment and natural resources as top priorities, ranking them with economic development, education and health care in the top tier of priorities. While significant components of Securing a Clean Energy Future focus on policy issues, economic strategies and research approaches, governments will be called on to lead by example.

In 2008, the National Association of State Chief Information Officers (NASCIO) published a white paper entitled "Green IT in Enterprise Practices: The Essential Role of the State CIO,"[4] where they used terms like "moral imperative," "ethical obligation" and "global duty" to frame the discussion about the challenges the environmental issues are creating, and the need for everyone, including governments, to collaboratively address those challenges. The call for the CIOs is to bring their knowledge and expertise to focus on green IT, not only within their enterprise IT practices, but on "how IT support of state government functions can reduce overall environmental impact." In October 2008, NASCIO released the CIO's top 10 priorities for 2009. Green IT—with a focus on policies, energy efficiency, power management, green procurement, green technologies/solutions and e-waste—was identified as one of their top 10 priorities.

All three organizations have taken clear positions on the environment and energy, and the role that government can and must assume in addressing those issues. While our elected leaders, academics and government officials may debate specifics around those initiatives, there is little debate today that the environment and energy issues are a top policy area of focus, and governments need to proactively adopt strategies and practices that begin to address those challenges.

On an international level, similar actions are being supported:

♦ The Intergovernmental Panel on Climate Change (IPCC) calls for a 50-85% reduction in $CO_2$ emissions by 2050 to mitigate the risks of climate change. That will require more than turning out the lights when you leave the kitchen. There need to be dramatic changes in behavior, and the deployment of technologies and energy sources to help us reach these goals.

♦ The G-8 countries recently agreed early in July 2008 to a 50% reduction in greenhouse gas emissions by 2050.

## The role of the CIO: *An opportunity for leadership*

The CIO is in a unique position to assure that his or her IT organization has adopted strategies and implemented practices that embrace the green agenda, and to provide leadership throughout government.

## Getting started—Taking care of basics

CIOs have a range of options available to them to formulate and drive a green IT environment. Leveraging those capabilities can lead to more environmentally sensitive practices within their organization and throughout government, as well as to reduced cost.

♦ **Enterprise architecture standards:** By incorporating green IT standards into the architecture, the CIO's organization can work collaboratively with procurement officials to assure that future IT procurements are considering environmentally friendly provisions as decisions are made. Leveraging metrics such as Energy Star and the Electronic Product Environmental Assessment Tool can provide a guide to IT procurements. For example, New York is beginning to incorporate such metrics when purchasing hardware.

♦ **Management:** The data center represents a major opportunity to assess and introduce green strategies. Data center power and cooling requirements top the list of today's green IT initiatives. An EPA report to Congress in 2007 highlights the value of proactive management of the data center. Understanding and implementing advanced practices can directly impact cost, operational efficiency and significantly reduce the environmental impact of data center operations.

♦ **Consolidation:** Enterprise management of IT resources represents another significant step in reducing the government's carbon footprint. While creating shared services centers for IT has been an emerging priority for governments over the last several years, the green government initiative has renewed interest in those enterprise approaches because they can reduce the level of IT infrastructure necessary to deliver services, directly impacting the cost of operations while delivering a positive impact on the environment.

| Scenario | IT Equipment | Site Infrastructure (Power and Cooling) |
|---|---|---|
| Improved operation: 20% energy savings | • Continue current trends for server consolidation<br>• Eliminate unused servers<br>• Adopt "energy-efficient" servers to modest level<br>• Enable power management on 100% of applicable servers<br>• Assume modest decline in energy use of enterprise storage equipment | 30% improvement in infrastructure energy efficiency from improved airflow management |
| Best practice: 45% energy savings | • Consolidate servers to moderate extent<br>• Aggressively adopt "energy-efficient" servers<br>• Assume moderate storage consolidation | Up to 70% improvement in infrastructure energy efficiency from all measures in "improved operation" scenario, plus:<br>• Improved transformers and uninterruptible power supplies<br>• Improved efficiency chillers, fans, and pumps<br>• Free cooling |
| State-of-the-art: 55% energy savings | • Aggressively consolidate servers<br>• Aggressively consolidate storage<br>• Enable power management at data center level of applications, servers, and equipment for networking and storage | Up to 80% improvement in infrastructure energy efficiency, due to all measures in "Best practice" scenario, plus:<br>• Direct liquid cooling<br>• Combined heat and power |

*EPA Response to Congress for Public Law 109-431, August 7, 2007*

**Figure 21–2.**

♦ **Virtualization:** Virtualization, where one physical server can function as multiple virtual servers, represents another major strategy within an enterprise IT program, with several significant benefits, including reduction in capital and cooling cost, reduced floor space requirements, and increased utilization of IT assets.

♦ **E-waste:** Gartner estimates that by 2010 over 1 billion computers could become scrap. Developing a comprehensive strategy around recycling, refurbishing and safe disposal should be a component of the CIO's strategy. Some governments are beginning to explore buyback provisions from manufacturers at the time of procurement or are establishing recycling contracts to assure the reuse or the appropriate disposal of IT equipment.

As CIOs consider an appropriate Green IT framework, the following model can provide a useful guide to assure that a comprehensive, enterprise approach is taken.

Diagnose — Facilities — Compute Resources — Cooling Innovations — Virtualization

Active Energy Management — Distributed IT — Responsible Disposal — Demand-side Efficiency — Monitoring & Verification

© 2008 IBM Corporation

**Figure 21–3.** IBM's Approach to Green IT

# Best practices: *Learning from government peers*[5]

Not surprisingly, governments at all levels and throughout the world are moving forward with a range of initiatives. Understanding their initiatives, their experiences and lessons learned can serve as a valuable resource as you consider the development of your green government strategies. We have highlighted some leading examples as a way to get the conversation going.

## Harris County, Texas—Converged Information Utility

Harris County's enterprise IT services are designed around three core concepts—a utility "on demand" computing platform, virtualization and convergence—to create a shared services infrastructure that has modernized the IT environment, enhanced the quality of services to constituents, and introduced a more cost-effective management model. Harris County's move to a Converged Information Utility was driven by a number of pressures the county was facing, including declining revenues, increasing cost and the need to improve citizen services. While the green agenda was not a direct driver in the creation of the utility, the impact of those innovative actions in the county has clearly contributed to a more environmentally friendly model for IT management and has positively contributed to the reduction of the county's carbon footprint.

## Howard County, Maryland—Office of Environmental Sustainability

The office has a comprehensive set of responsibilities focused on green government for the county, including policy formulation, energy management, environmental compliance, education and outreach, and financial management. In addition, the office has an advisory commission in place to work with the county on its environmental future.

## State of North Carolina—Consolidation of the IT environment

The State of North Carolina has initiated a multiyear IT consolidation program that will reduce the number of data centers, servers and associated IT infrastructure. In the second phase of the program, eight agencies will eliminate their local data centers and reduce the number of physical servers by 35%. The program will reduce the state's carbon footprint as well as create a more cost-effective environment to operate the state's IT infrastructure.

## State of California—Energy Consumption Executive Order

In response to the Governor's Executive Order S-20-04, the California Department of Technology Services undertook a major modernization project to improve the data center facility. Improvements included an upgrade in the energy management system and development of an energy management plan for the data center. The project resulted in an 8.8% reduction in annual electric power consumption and a 69% reduction in annual natural gas usage. In addition to meeting the goals of the executive order to directly reduce energy consumption, there was a corresponding 9% reduction in the facility's energy cost. The project also identified future projects that, as funding becomes available, could reduce the facilities energy consumption by an additional 10%.

Resources such as NGA, NACo and NASCIO will be very valuable as you move through your green government strategies, and we encourage you to stay in touch with those, and other organizations—public and private—that are leading the green government initiative. For example, NASCIO has released a webcast series on Green IT.[6] IBM has created a "green" portal where we will maintain current insights, research and best practices.[7] Experience from other transformational initiatives demonstrates that peer experiences can provide valuable insights and lessons learned.

## Some closing thoughts

As we have mentioned throughout, the green government agenda extends beyond the CIO's office and IT. However, since information technology will be a critical enabler to a wide range of green initiatives, the CIO is in a unique position to be a leader in the transformation journey to a green government model. For example, mobile employees, carbon management, intelligent transportation, web 2.0 in government, to name a few initiatives, all represent areas where CIOs and their organizations will be critical in evaluating strategies and implementing appropriate solutions.

The following recommendations, based on a 2008 report from IBM's Institute for Electronic Government concerning the trends around green government,[8] are relevant not only to the CIO organizations, but for elected officials and senior government executives as well.

## Be proactive and get started

There is no excuse for doing nothing. Recognize that it may take time for formal enterprise-wide green strategies and management structures to catch up. In the meantime, plenty of best practices already exist at all levels of government and in most functional areas that can be replicated readily. Take the initiative to launch meaningful green efforts.

## Put someone in charge

Successful execution requires leadership and accountability to achieve results. Ultimately, an enterprise-wide green leader is ideal, with similar leaders identified within departments. Consider a cross-boundary steering or advisory committee to institutionalize green and facilitate government-wide execution of green initiatives. Leadership and an appropriate governance structure/collaboration strategy will be critical to implementing a successful strategy.[9]

## Develop a clear green agenda with quantifiable goals

Develop your green agenda with specific energy-reduction targets and other environmentally friendly goals for your organizations. Take inventory of green initiatives and adopt new initiatives to fill gaps. Create a portfolio that includes both relatively easy "low-hanging fruit" initiatives to achieve early successes in the near term as well as more difficult, ambitious initiatives that will stretch the organization but deliver significant long-term energy reductions, cost savings and environmental benefits. And, remember to set goals, measure results and report progress.

## Identify your stage of development

Assess your organization against a green roadmap. Where are you now, and where do you want to be within your own time targets? The stage of development may vary department-by-department or even initiative-by-initiative within one government. Continue to benchmark best practices at each development stage.

## Close the knowledge gap—educate and communicate

First of all ... educate yourself. Devote time to become informed about green and stay abreast of rapidly changing developments. Educate employees and citizens about what green means, how the government is responding on an operational, day-to-day basis and what benefits are expected. Then maintain ongoing communication.

## Employ proven change management techniques and cross pollinate

Take communication a step further and start to change behavior. Encourage a sense of individual employee responsibility for success of the green agenda. Encourage grassroots green efforts, and replicate innovative successes across agencies. Leveraging web 2.0 tools, such as blogs, encourages employees to share ideas and creates opportunities for citizen engagement through new social networking capabilities. Remember, the best ideas may come from sources you least expect; Be open to those opportunities.

## Look for promising voluntary and private sector sources of ideas and action

The voluntary sector and a variety of advocacy groups on many aspects of the environment and energy are extremely active and encompass a number of sources of ideas and practical advice for taking action and communicating the green messages. Don't hesitate to discover who they are and research them. Then encourage them, especially if they are local to you, to join you in your endeavors.

---

### Discussion questions

1. Do you have someone in charge of your green government agenda?
2. Have you developed a set of goals for green government?
3. Have you developed an education program for your organization so your employees are actively engaged in driving green government?
4. Have you established a process for measuring and reporting progress?

**Mark Cleverley** *is IBM's Global Director for Government Strategy, helping governments with technology-enabled transformation. He advises IBM's public sector customers and IBM teams on potentials, challenges and best practices in the evolving use of new technologies. He has consulted widely for IBM's government projects, and has written and spoken publicly extensively in the USA and abroad. He has worked with governments in many nations and many areas of information systems. For some years, he was responsible for IBM's Public Safety, Justice, and related clients in Europe, the Middle East and Africa. Earlier, he led technology-enabled innovation projects in the oil, aviation and financial services industries in Western Europe, the USA and Russia. Those ranged from consolidating European data centres, through implementing core airline systems, and included one of the earliest (pre-web) public access kiosk developments.*

*Before joining IBM, Mr. Cleverley was trained as an air traffic controller. He has a joint honours degree in Psychology and Philosophy from Oxford University. A British citizen now living in the USA, he is fluent in French and has a working knowledge of Russian.*

**Curtis Clark** *is IBM's Global Director for Government Innovation. In that role, Mr. Clark focuses on trends and directions in the public sector and works with public sector organizations globally on strategies for developing and implementing innovative programs, services and operations* *that more effectively and efficiently meet the needs of citizens, businesses and government employees. He also is responsible for IBM's Institute for Electronic Government Briefing Center in Washington D.C. Prior to joining IBM in 1997, Mr. Clark spent more than 17 years with the State of North Carolina, where he held various executive and legislative positions, including: Deputy State Controller for Information Resource Management, Executive Director of the North Carolina Statewide Performance Audit and Director of the Performance Audit Division of the State Auditor's Office. He is a Graduate of the University of North Carolina at Chapel Hill with a degree in Political Science, did post graduate work in accounting and is a Certified Public Accountant.*

## REFERENCES

1 Government 2020 and the Perpetual Collaboration Mandate, IBM Institute for Business Value, April 2008

2 National Association of Counties Green Government Initiative Web Site http:// www.green-counties.com

3 National Governor's Association, Chair's Initiative, 2008 http://www.nga.org/portal/site/nga/menuitem.50aeae5ff70b817ae8ebb856a11010a0/

4 Green IT in Enterprise Practices: The Essential Role of the State CIO, National Association of State Chief Information Officers, 2008

5 NACo Green Government Initiative and NASCIO's Green IT in the Enterprise: The essential role of the State CIO, 2008

6 Green IT: CIOs Speak Out, NASCIO, http://www.nascio.org/committees/green/ciosSpeak-Out.cfm

7 IBM green portal: http://www.ibm.com/ibm/green/index.shtml?cm_site=swggreenit

8 The Greening of Government: A Study of How Governments Define the Green Agenda, Institute for Electronic Government, IBM Corporation, 2008.

9 Keon S. Chi, "Four Strategies to Transform State Governance," IBM Center for The Business of Government, 2008

# 22. Communications Law Issues in Technology Projects and Contract Negotiations

**FREDERICK E. ELLROD III AND GAIL A. KARISH**

## Introduction

Today's CIO may be asked to enhance communications capabilities to improve the effectiveness of local emergency response, to save money on government operations or to improve broadband connectivity options available to citizens. Whatever the project goal may be, technology is not the only matter to consider in a new deployment. Just as each communications technology has technical capabilities and limitations, each also involves regulatory requirements. Some of those requirements are tied to the technology (for example, whether wireless spectrum will be used). Others will come into play depending on the types of services made available (for example, whether services will be offered to the public or only to employees).

The first step in any evaluation of regulatory requirements is to determine whether the proposed technologies are subject to federal, state or local regulation, or some combination. Generally, communications technology issues are regulated at the federal level, principally by the Federal Communications Commission (FCC). At the state level, the regulator is typically a state public utilities commission. The regulatory authority of local governments is closely related to their control over public rights-of-way.

This chapter will focus primarily on federal communications laws and regulations that can affect project structure and contract negotiations. The laws must be considered, for example, when choosing between government operation and contracting out to a third party. The chapter will highlight major areas to be aware of in project planning and negotiations.

Although this chapter does not address state laws, they also may need to be considered in structuring a project. For example, some states restrict the activities that local governments may undertake or impose special requirements on public projects that may compete with the private sector. In addition, state laws may require local governments to treat all providers in nondiscriminatory fashion. A community must consider those laws in, for example, structuring public-private partnerships.

## Communications law issues in technology projects

Communications law issues arise when a local government engages in activities that are subject to federal communications regulation. A convenient way to classify such activities is to divide them by type of system (wireless or wireline) and by "client" – internal (i.e., services self-provisioned by the local government), or external (services to third-party customers). Examples are on the following page.

| | Internal services | External services (to third parties) |
|---|---|---|
| Wireline | VoIP telephone system for internal use | Municipally owned cable or (wireline) telecommunications system |
| Wireless | Public safety radio system | Wi-Fi system providing public Internet access |

Because different rules apply to the different types of systems, different regulatory issues will arise. The chart below illustrates which are likely to arise in the four examples.

| Issues raised | VoIP (internal use only) | Public safety radio | Wi-Fi public Internet access | Municipally owned cable or telecom system |
|---|---|---|---|---|
| **Spectrum issues** | | | | |
| 800 MHz re-banding | | ✓ | | |
| 700 MHz public safety spectrum | | ✓ | | |
| Unlicensed spectrum | | ✓ | ✓ | |
| **Law enforcement and emergencies** | | | | |
| CALEA | ✓ | | ✓ | ✓ |
| E911 | ✓ | | ✓ | ✓ |
| Emergency Alert System | | | | ✓ |
| **Non-discrimination** | | | | |
| Section 253 (barriers to entry) | | | ✓ | ✓ |
| Section 332 (wireless zoning/siting) | | ✓ | ✓ | |
| Pole Attachments Act | | | ✓ | ✓ |
| Net neutrality | | | ✓ | ✓ |
| **Data collection and information** | | | | |
| Privacy – subscriber communications | | | ✓ | ✓ |
| CPNI | | | ✓ | ✓ |
| FTC "Red Flag" rules | | | ✓ | ✓ |
| Broadband information collection | | | ✓ | ✓ |
| **Third-party service issues** | | | | |
| Issues arising from the provision of service to end users generally | | | ✓ | ✓ |

A community that provides information to the general public over communications networks—for example, via a municipal cable system—may become involved with many other content-specific regulations. For example, a municipal cable operator will need to deal with the federal rules for must-carry and retransmission consent, program access, customer service and the like. Similarly, a community that offers content to the public via online applications such as blogs, wikis, social networking sites or virtual worlds may have to consider issues such as intellectual property and libel. This chapter does not address such content-specific issues.

## Spectrum-related issues

Most of the wireless spectrum is subject to FCC regulation and licensing requirements. Specialized issues, such as radio frequency licensing and interference, arise if a community operates wireless installations. This section provides background on the issues related to public safety spectrum (800 MHz and 700 MHz) and the unregulated spectrum typically used by Wi-Fi systems.

### 800 MHz public safety spectrum re-banding

The FCC grants licenses to state and local governments for public safety radio systems in the 800 MHz band. With the growth of commercial wireless services in the same 800 MHz band, serious interference problems have arisen, hampering the operation of the public safety radio systems.

In 2004, the FCC released an ambitious plan to mitigate the interference nationwide by re-banding or relocating the public safety radio systems. Improving Public Safety Communications in the 800 MHz Band, WT Docket 02-55 etc., Report and Order, Fifth Report and Order, Fourth Memorandum Opinion and Order, and Order, FCC 04-168, 19 FCC Rcd 14969 (2004).[1] If a community uses the affected channels, it may already have been involved in frequency relocations. Even if its channels are not directly affected, interoperability agreements with neighbors may have indirect consequences.

The FCC's plan principally involves the reconfiguration, or "re-banding," of spectrum lying between 806 and 824 MHz (mobile and control station frequencies) and 851 and 869 (base station frequencies). The re-banding aims to consolidate public safety spectrum between 806/851 and 816/861 MHz, and to move other users higher up in the band or outside it altogether. In return for giving up the 800 MHz frequencies and getting replacement channels elsewhere, Sprint Nextel, the primary private-sector user, compensates the public safety users that are forced to change channels.

The FCC appointed a Transition Administrator and established a Regional Prioritization Plan creating four "waves" or groups of states for successive re-banding. Communities in those states negotiate funding for the necessary system replacements with Sprint Nextel.

In addition, the FCC established a set of procedures for expeditious resolution of interference. For the first time, public safety licensees meeting certain signal-level thresholds can be guaranteed relief from interference. See 47 C.F.R. §§ 90.672-675.

Spectrum reconfiguration is complex and expensive. Public safety radio systems cannot afford to be "down"—in whole or part—for any great length of time.[2] Re-banding often needs to be coordinated with neighboring systems that inter-operate during emergencies. Sprint Nextel's negotiations with public safety entities under the re-banding plan thus far has been a time-consuming, though generally successful, enterprise.

In 2004, the FCC expected the re-banding effort to be completed by mid-2008. However, the commercial operators failed to meet their benchmarks, and that deadline could not be achieved. In September 2007 the FCC issued a new order, In the Matter of Improving Public Safety Communications in the 800 MHz Band, WT Docket 02-55, Third Memorandum Opinion and Order, FCC 07-167, 22 FCC Rcd 17209 (2007). That order generally maintained the same overall deadline, but established new benchmarks and permitted participants to seek waivers or extensions. The response has been a flurry of waiver requests. The re-banding process appears to be set to continue for several more years to come. Thus, public safety radio projects need to plan ahead for the frequencies they eventually will be using and for any transitional actions and costs that may be required to change to the new frequencies.

**Links:**

- ◆ 800 MHz Transition Administrator website: www.800ta.org
- ◆ FCC's 800 MHz site: http://www.fcc.gov/pshs/public-safety-spectrum/800-MHz/
- ◆ Third Memorandum Opinion and Order in WT Docket 02-55 (2007):
- ◆ http://hraunfoss.fcc.gov/edocs_public/attachmatch/FCC-07-167A1.pdf
- ◆ Report and Order in WT Docket 02-55 (2004):
- ◆ http://hraunfoss.fcc.gov/edocs_public/attachmatch/FCC-04-168A1.pdf

## 700 MHz public safety spectrum

The 700 MHz spectrum, which runs from 698-806 MHz, currently is occupied primarily by television broadcasters in TV channels 52-69. In February 2009, that spectrum will be vacated by the broadcasters as part of the digital television ("DTV") transition, and a significant portion will be made available to develop a national broadband public safety system. The Digital Television and Public Safety Act of 2005 set a firm deadline of February 17, 2009, for the DTV transition. Section 337 of the Communications Act, 47 U.S.C. § 337(a), directs the FCC to set aside 24 MHz of spectrum in the 700 MHz band for public safety as well as 36 MHz for commercial use.

Public safety users currently have some 700 MHz allocations for narrowband uses. In July 2007 the FCC revised the licensing scheme and established a time frame for transitioning the existing narrowband operations to the upper band with a completion deadline no later than February 17, 2009. In order to implement the narrowband relocation, each of the 55 Regional Planning Committees ("RPC") must submit to the FCC its updated plan for the assignment of licenses for general use spectrum. The RPCs must ensure that their plans reflect the needs of all public safety entities in their regions by providing notice of meetings, opportunity for comment and reasonable consideration of views expressed.

For the broadband segment, the FCC initially appointed a single nationwide licensee for public safety, the Public Safety Broadband Licensee. The national license approach was a departure from the FCC's traditional practice of licensing individual state and local jurisdictions on a site-by-site basis.[3] The FCC's plan, however, depended on the successful auction of another portion of the 700 MHz spectrum, the "D Block" (758-763/788-793 MHz), to a commercial entity. The FCC's first attempt to auction that spectrum failed to attract any successful bids. In September 2008, based on further comments received over the summer, the FCC issued for comment a new set of proposed rules governing the auction of the D Block spectrum. At time of writing, those rules had not been finalized.

Despite the difficulties with the auction process to date, the physical characteristics of the 700 MHz band make it extremely valuable for advanced services. Signals using those frequencies penetrate buildings and foliage, and fill in around terrain features and other obstacles very effectively. They also travel farther at low power. That means fewer cell sites are needed to reach a desired level of coverage. Basically, a 700 MHz system can do more with less. All of those characteristics suggest that 700 MHz technology may be a better solution for many local government needs than the Wi-Fi networks many communities have been pursuing.

In addition, FCC rules allow governmental and approved non-governmental uses of public safety spectrum beyond the immediate demands of responding to and resolving emergencies. The "sole or principal purpose" of a public safety service must be "to protect the safety of life, health, or property." 47 U.S.C. § 337(f)(1)(A). That criterion can be interpreted to include a broader range of users and uses than those typically associated with "public safety." For example, the FCC has stated that utilities and pipelines might be eligible for licenses to use public safety spectrum. The FCC also has ruled that a state department of transportation provides public safety services, because its function is to maintain safe roadways.

If the FCC does appoint a single national broadband licensee for the 700 MHz band, the licensee would need to be kept attuned to the needs and views of the communities that keep their communities safe. That would not happen automatically. Local governments would need to figure out how to make their views known to the licensee.

**Link:**

♦ FCC's 700 MHz site: http://www.fcc.gov/pshs/public-safety-spectrum/700-MHz/

## *Unlicensed spectrum (such as Wi-Fi)*

Wi-Fi networks operate in the 2.4 GHz band, which is not subject to FCC licensing requirements. That does not mean, however, that it is entirely free from regulation. On the contrary, regulatory obligations, such as compliance with radio frequency interference and over-the-air-reception-device rules, may be applicable.

## Radio frequency interference (RFI)

Radio frequency interference (RFI) poses potential compliance and liability issues, as well as public safety concerns. Deployment of unlicensed community-wide networks by local governments or by commercial operators (in partnership with local governments or alone) could interfere with the operation of individual hot spots by retail businesses and residential users, and with existing municipal wireless applications.

Unlicensed users have no protection from interference; if they suffer interference from other sources, they must accept the consequences. On the other hand, if they cause interference with licensed users operating in compliance with their licenses, the licensee may seek relief from the FCC.

Proponents of commercial Wi-Fi projects often seek citywide authority to install equipment in municipal rights-of-way, on rooftops and on other facilities. Because the FCC generally will not adjudicate disputes solely involving unlicensed frequencies, such access contracts should include contractual remedies for interference.

Should RFI become a greater concern with the growing availability of competing Wi-Fi networks, the FCC could impose new restrictions on their operation that would affect their technical or commercial viability. Monitoring the FCC's agenda for relevant regulatory initiatives should be a routine part of system operation.

## Over-the-air reception devices (OTARD)

When granting rights to install facilities, the local government should pay careful attention to the FCC's Over-the-Air Reception Devices ("OTARD") Rule, 47 C.F.R. § 1.4000. The rule preempts all kinds of restrictions that limit the placement not only of satellite TV antennas but also of other fixed wireless facilities, such as Wi-Fi antennas. The rule applies to facilities installed on property under the "exclusive use or control" of the antenna user, including leased property. Thus, if a community grants a provider an exclusive right to use space on poles or rooftops, the OTARD rule could operate to preempt restrictions in the agreement between the community and the provider. Agreements, therefore, must be drafted carefully to guard against inadvertently allowing the provider to claim exclusive rights and, thus, preempting restrictions under the OTARD rule. For example, the wireless provider should waive the application of OTARD and should explicitly state that no exclusive rights are being granted.

**Links:**

- ◆ FCC Tower Siting website: http://wireless.fcc.gov/siting/otard.html (OTARD)
- ◆ http://wireless.fcc.gov/siting/interference.html (RFI)
- ◆ FCC Fact Sheet on OTARD http://www.fcc.gov/mb/facts/otard.html

## Law enforcement and emergency services

If a local government plans to operate a system to provide communications services to the public, it must address rules that enable law enforcement to engage in wiretapping, give service users enhanced 911 capabilities, and permit broadcasts by emergency alert systems.

## Communications Assistance for Law Enforcement Act of 1994 (CALEA)

In 1994, Congress enacted CALEA "to preserve the ability of law enforcement agencies to conduct electronic surveillance by requiring that telecommunications carriers and manufacturers of telecommunications equipment modify and design their equipment, facilities, and services to ensure that they have the necessary surveillance capabilities."[4] The law ensures that law enforcement officials can, when issued warrants, perform wiretapping and the like in advanced communications systems. In 2004, the FCC issued a Notice of Proposed Rulemaking ("NPRM") on extending CALEA to new communications technologies. The FCC concluded that all broadband Internet access services and "interconnected" voice over IP (VoIP) services were subject to CALEA.[5] *First CALEA Order* at ¶ 8. A subsequent FCC order addressed issues related to the implementation of the new requirements. Second Report and Order and Memorandum Opinion and Order, *In the Matter of Communications Assistance for Law Enforcement Act and Broadband Access and Services,* ET Docket No. 04-295, FCC 06-56, (released May 12, 2006) (*"Second CALEA Order"*).

CALEA clearly applies to traditional telephone companies and other entities that offer telecommunications services to the public.[6] On the other hand, purely private networks are exempt; see

47 C.F.R. § 1002(b)(2)(B). Do the CALEA rules apply to facilities owned or used by a local government? The difficulty is in determining whether networks that do not fit squarely in one or the other category must comply with CALEA. The answer can turn on subtle differences in the network architecture. The FCC and the FBI presume that performing any kind of switching or routing is sufficient to render a person a telecommunications carrier for CALEA purposes, because the agency needs to be able to capture a given user's traffic at the switch. Essentially, then, any network that is connected to the Internet or the public switched telephone network ("PSTN") is subject to CALEA.

If CALEA applies, the network architecture must enable law enforcement surveillance. The statute does create a safe harbor for systems that adopt technical solutions approved by "appropriate associations and standard-setting organizations."[7] The Telecommunications Industry Association and the National Cable and Telecommunications Association have issued such standards.[8] They were developed with the large telephone and cable companies in mind and may not be practical for smaller networks. The Wireless Internet Service Providers Association recently issued its own standards, which may be useful for entities operating smaller networks.[9] Contracting with a third party to provide the service may insulate a local government from some compliance requirements, but not necessarily all of them.

Not only should existing government networks be evaluated, but as new technology projects are presented, the potential CALEA implications must be considered. Compliance can be expensive even if incorporated into the original plan; having to retrofit would increase costs. Non-compliance can lead to fines and civil penalties of up to $10,000 per day. See 47 C.F.R. §§ 1.20008, 1.80; 47 U.S.C. § 503(b)(2)(C).

## Enhanced 911 (E911)

The FCC was directed in 1999 to make 911 the universal emergency number for all telephone services. The capability to include the location of the caller and the callback number is referred to as enhanced 911 or E-911. Basically, if a system allows telephony (including VoIP) and interconnects with the PSTN, it is subject to E-911 rules. First Report and Order and Notice of Proposed Rulemaking, *In the Matter of E911 Requirements for IP-Enabled Service Providers*, WC Docket 05-196, FCC 05-116 (released June 3, 2005), ¶¶ 24, 47. The service provider must be able to transmit 911 calls, call-back number, and "Registered Location" to the public safety answering point (PSAP) (¶¶ 36, 46). Those requirements may be satisfied by interconnecting through a third party (¶ 38).

For mobile technologies, providing that information can be challenging. For example, a given VoIP user may use the service from different locations at different times. And, as new technologies are adopted, new rules for compliance are being developed.

The New and Emerging Technologies (NET) 911 Improvement Act of 2008 ("Net 911 Act") specifically requires interconnected VoIP providers to provide 911 and E911 service. On October 21, 2008, the FCC issued its implementing order in WC Docket No. 08-171, *In the Matter of implementation of the NET 911 Improvement Act of 2008*, FCC 08-249. In that order, the FCC issued rules to ensure that VoIP providers have access to all the capabilities needed to comply with 911 and E911 service requirements.

**Links:**

- ♦ FCC's Net 911 Report and Order:
- ♦ http://hraunfoss.fcc.gov/edocs_public/attachmatch/FCC-08-249A1.pdf

## Emergency Alert System

Some form of national emergency warning system has been in place since the 1960s, with periodic updates and modernization efforts. The current Emergency Alert System (EAS) requires broadcasters, cable operators, wireless cable systems and others to enable the president to address the public during a national emergency. In 2006, Congress enacted the Warning, Alert, and Response Network (WARN) Act (10/13/06), providing for a national alert system covering a broad range of communications providers.

The FCC's Second Report and Order and Further Notice of Proposed Rulemaking, *In the Matter of Review of the Emergency Alert System*, EB Docket No. 04-296, FCC 07-109 (released July 12, 2007) revised rules to provide for "Next Generation EAS". Wireline video systems must participate. See Order at ¶50; 47 C.F.R. § 11.2(c). In April 2008, the FCC adopted technical requirements for a Commercial Mobile Alert System (CMAS), by which commercial mobile service providers may transmit emergency alerts to their subscribers if they choose. Municipal communications systems that fall within those categories will need to examine the rules to see whether they need to establish those capabilities.

**Links:**

- ♦ FCC's CALEA website http://www.fcc.gov/calea/
- ♦ FBI's CALEA website http://www.askcalea.net/
- ♦ FCC's 911 website http://www.fcc.gov/pshs/services/911-services/Welcome.html
- ♦ DOT's NG 911 website http://www.its.dot.gov/ng911/index.htm
- ♦ FCC's EAS website http://www.fcc.gov/pshs/services/eas/

## Non-discrimination and related issues

Governments with strained budgets are increasingly willing to consider entering into public-private partnerships to implement new technologies. In creating such a partnership, or in contracting out certain communications systems to the private sector, it is necessary to bear in mind the impact of laws that prohibit favoring one provider over another. Some of the laws also may apply to purely municipal projects that compete with privately owned systems.

## Section 253 (telecommunications)

When Congress passed the Telecommunications Act of 1996, it adopted a new provision entitled "Removal of Barriers to Entry," 47 U.S.C. § 253. Section 253(a) preempts state or local statutes, regulations or other requirements that prohibit or have the effect of prohibiting the ability of any entity to provide a telecommunications service. The provision also has two "safe harbors," Section 253(b) and (c), which provide that notwithstanding the preemption in Section 253(a), certain state and local rights can still be exercised, such as the right to manage public rights-of-way on a "competitively neutral" basis.

To the extent that a local community might treat private telecommunications users differently from the way it treats a municipal utility, the competitor could seek to argue that a competitive disadvantage constituted a "barrier to entry" under Section 253 and question whether the city was applying its right-of-way management policies on a "competitively neutral and nondiscriminatory" basis pursuant to the exception in § 253(c). Such a claim would face numerous hurdles in practice. However, the possibility of having to contend with such a challenge does argue for careful consideration of a community's right-of-way policies in this respect.

**Links:**

- Frederick E. Ellrod III and Nicholas P. Miller, *Property Rights, Federalism, and the Public Rights-of-Way,* 26 Seattle U. L. Rev. 475 (2003)
- http://www.millervaneaton.com/pdf_docs/SeattleLawArticle.PDF
- 9th Circuit Reverses Auburn Section 253 Decision:
- http://www.millervaneaton.com/content.agent?page_name=HT%3A++9th+Circuit+Reverses+Auburn+Section+253+Decision

## Section 332 (wireless)

In the Telecommunications Act of 1996, Congress also adopted a new provision entitled "Preservation of Local Zoning Authority," 47 U.S.C. § 332(c)(7). That section ensured that local governments could regulate the placement and construction of those towers consistent with normal land use planning processes. To promote deployment of wireless services, however, Congress also placed certain conditions on the exercise of local zoning authority.

Regulation of the "placement, construction and modification" of cell towers:

- Cannot unreasonably discriminate among providers of functionally equivalent services;
- Cannot prohibit or have the effect of prohibiting the provision of personal wireless services.

Certain procedural requirements also must be satisfied:

- A request for a tower authorization must be acted on within a reasonable period of time.
- Any denial must be supported by "substantial evidence" contained in a "written record" in a written decision
- Placement, construction or modification of towers may not be regulated on the basis of RF emissions if the facility complies with FCC regulations.

If a local government sets up wireless facilities as part of its own network—particularly if it is in partnership with a private company—it will want to keep in mind the nondiscrimination requirement of Section 332 so as not to give other parties any excuse for objection.

## Pole attachments

Deployment of communications infrastructure often involves installation of facilities on poles or in ducts, conduits or rights-of-way owned by utilities. Under Section 224 of the Communications Act, the "Pole Attachment Act," the FCC has authority to regulate the rates charged and other aspects of the contractual relationship between utilities and the telecommunications and cable providers desiring to attach facilities to their poles. The FCC is to ensure that such rates, terms and conditions are just and reasonable, and to make certain that access to the utilities' poles, ducts, conduits and rights-of-way is provided in a nondiscriminatory manner.

The Pole Attachment Act and the FCC's rules do not apply if the pole owner is a federal, state or local government. However, if a project involves the use of other entities' poles—for example, poles belonging to a power or telephone company—the terms under which those poles can be used may be governed by the Pole Attachment Act (or state regulation, if the state has certified to regulate pole attachments in place of the FCC).

**Links:**

- ◆ FCC's Pole Attachment Enforcement website: http://www.fcc.gov/eb/mdrd/PoleAtt.html
- ◆ FCC's State Regulators List: http://www.fcc.gov/eb/Public_Notices/DA-08-653A1.html
- ◆ FCC's Pole Attachment Notice of Proposed Rulemaking (FCC 07-187):
- ◆ http://fjallfoss.fcc.gov/edocs_public/attachmatch/FCC-07-187A1.pdf

## Net neutrality

When widespread public use of the Internet began in the 1990s, access to the Internet was typically via dial-up modem, over telephone lines that were treated as common carrier facilities. As more and more Internet traffic moved to proprietary cable and telecommunications networks, the network owners began to express an interest in prioritizing traffic from certain sites, perhaps in exchange for compensation from the site owners. Network owners also argued that they needed ways to manage the traffic on their networks, including blocking or degrading access to user applications that consume a great deal of capacity, such as peer-to-peer applications. Those activities have generated a debate on whether such techniques may undermine "net neutrality," the concept that the Internet is a neutral network where the network owners do not exercise control over the content, platforms and sites that can be accessed by users.

In August 2008, the FCC took its first enforcement action in the area with the issuance of an order requiring Comcast to replace its existing techniques for manipulating subscribers' Internet traffic with a protocol-agnostic network management technique, and to report to the FCC on its compliance. Further developments may be expected in this area. Some may affect networks managed by local governments, particularly those that may be open to the public.

**Link:**

- ◆ FCC's Comcast order (8/20/08): http://hraunfoss.fcc.gov/edocs_public/attachmatch/FCC-08-183A1.pdf

## Data collection and privacy

## Subscriber privacy

There are a variety of subscriber privacy rules that must be considered in structuring a communications project, particularly one that involves offering services to the public. The rules include:

- ◆ Electronic Communications Privacy Act (ECPA), 18 U.S.C. § 2510 *et seq.*, which imposes penalties for intentional interception of communications, but largely shields communications service providers.

- ◆ Rules under 47 U.S.C. § 222 that protect Customer Proprietary Network Information (CPNI), the information that a telecommunications carrier has about its customers solely by virtue of the carrier-customer relationship.[10] A telecommunications carrier, including a VoIP provider, must have a plan to protect that information. If a local government has access to CPNI, it must make periodic filings with the FCC describing its compliance plan for ensuring CPNI security.

♦ Fair and Accurate Credit Transactions (FACT) Act of 2003 and the implementing "Red Flag" rules of the Federal Trade Commission (FTC) on protection against identity theft. These rules require "creditors" (defined broadly enough to include government and non-profit entities, if they defer payment for goods or services) to have "identity theft prevention programs to identify, detect, and respond to patterns, practices, or specific activities that could indicate identity theft." Thus, if a system bills users for some services in arrears, it needs to have a Red Flag compliance program. As of the time of writing, the new compliance requirements were scheduled to take effect May 1, 2009.

♦ Cable Act, 47 U.S.C. § 551, which restricts the uses cable operators can make of personally identifiable information from subscribers.

In connection with the applicable privacy requirements, local governments offering communications services to the public should carefully review their state's applicable freedom of information laws and public meeting laws. Private-sector competitors may seek to use those mechanisms to obtain local government information to gain competitive advantage. A given state's laws may or may not protect competitively sensitive data from public disclosure.

**Links:**

- ♦ FCC's Small Entity Compliance Guide for CPNI, DA 08-1321:
- ♦ http://hraunfoss.fcc.gov/edocs_public/attachmatch/DA-08-1321A1.pdf
- ♦ FTC's explanation of Red Flag rules:
- ♦ www.ftc.gov/bcp/edu/pubs/business/alerts/alt050.shtm
- ♦ FTC press release on extended deadline: www.ftc.gov/opa/2008/10/redflags.shtm

## Broadband information collection requirements

Federal and state governments have made efforts recently to collect better information on broadband deployment by requiring providers to make periodic reports. For example, the FCC initiated a new program for collecting information on access to broadband by order dated June 12, 2008 in its Report and Order and Further Notice of Proposed Rulemaking, *In the Matter of Development of Nationwide Broadband Data to Evaluate Reasonable and Timely Deployment of Advanced Services to All Americans, Improvement of Wireless Broadband Subscribership Data, and Development of Data on Interconnected Voice over Internet Protocol (VoIP) Subscribership,* WC Docket No. 07-38, (FCC 08-89). That order modified the FCC's existing Form 477 to require "facilities-based providers of broadband connections to end users," including local governments, to report. See Order at ¶ 5, 14; 47 C.F.R. §§ 1.7001(b), 43.11(a). Providers of interconnected VoIP services also must report (Order at ¶ 30). Thus, data may be required both from systems offering Internet access to end users, and from systems that merely offer interconnected VoIP services.

## Issues regarding provision of service to third parties

If a local government sells communications services to end users, it must deal with a number of specialized issues as a carrier or service provider, over and above those issues regarding end-user information that were addressed in the preceding section. For example, providing interconnected VoIP service may raise issues such as:

- **Universal Service Fund (USF)**: Interconnected VoIP providers are required to report and contribute to the federal USF on their interstate and international end-user telecommunications revenues. Some states also have imposed USF contribution requirements on VoIP providers' intrastate revenues.

- **Disability access and telecommunications relay services ("TRS") capabilities:** The FCC requires interconnected VoIP providers to comply with all disability access requirements that currently apply to telecommunications carriers and to make contributions to the TRS fund.

- **Payment of FCC regulatory fees:** The FCC charges communications providers fees to support the FCC's regulatory efforts. Interconnected VoIP providers generally must pay the FCC regulatory fees. However, governmental entities, as defined in the commission's rules, are exempt from payment of the fees.

- **Local number portability ("LNP") capabilities:** LNP rules give interconnected VoIP providers a right to transfer customer numbers from other providers and a duty to transfer numbers to other providers, so that customers who change carriers can take their phone numbers with them. The rules applicable to different types of carriers vary somewhat, and a VoIP provider must comply with the rules applicable to its numbering partner (the carrier from which the VoIP provider obtains numbering resources). Contributions also must be made to the numbering plan administration.

- **Abbreviated number dialing capabilities:** VoIP providers must support "abbreviated" dialing capabilities for short-form numbers such as 911 (the national emergency number) and 711 (for access to TRS). The FCC is considering whether to require other abbreviated number dialing capabilities (such as 411 for directory assistance) as well.

- **Interconnection rights:** Section 251 of the Communications Act gives telecommunications providers the right to interconnect and exchange traffic with other telecommunications providers. While the FCC has not yet extended that right to VoIP providers, it has indicated that telecommunications providers do have the right to interconnect even if the purpose of their interconnection is in turn to provide wholesale telecommunications services to a VoIP provider.

- **Intercarrier compensation for exchange of traffic between networks:** This issue continues to evolve, and VoIP systems may come to be subject to such compensation for traffic that originates in the community and terminates elsewhere, or vice versa.

- **State law tax issues:** Telephone sales taxes or excise taxes may apply to VoIP revenues, depending on how the tax code is drawn.

## Conclusion

The complex and flexible information systems demanded by local communities today bring CIOs into contact with regulatory requirements that in earlier years would have been important only to communications carriers. The issues can be addressed with careful preparation and planning. Understanding the legal rights and responsibilities involved in various project structures and roles, knowing the priorities of the community and elected officials, and keeping abreast of changes in the law that can affect the project are essential tasks to avoid pitfalls and make the most of limited time and resources.

**Frederick E. Ellrod III** *represents public and private sector telecommunications clients. He is expert in cable television and telecommunications matters, including cable franchise renewal, transfer, enforcement and rate regulation; right-of-way issues; and wireless zoning and siting. His experience includes major FCC rulemakings, such as the open video systems, video dialtone and cable rate regulation proceedings, and related litigation. He has represented private sector clients at the FCC in licensing for satellite and other wireless communications systems, and drafted contracts for communications and computer-based information systems, particularly as they address confidentiality issues. In addition to his telecommunications work, he has participated in major litigation in energy, environmental law and transportation matters. Mr. Ellrod has worked extensively with information systems professionals to develop computerized support systems for litigation and legal analysis. He is admitted to practice in the District of Columbia. He holds a Ph.D. from Boston University and received his law degree, cum laude, from Harvard Law School. He was affiliated with Miller & Holbrooke before the firm merged with Miller Canfield in 1994, and now practices with Miller & Van Eaton (MVE).*

*Gail A. Karish assists clients with state and federal regulatory matters, contract negotiations and litigation. She has a broad range of domestic and international experience advising public and private sector entities in the telecommunications and electricity sectors in the United States, Canada and Latin America. Her experience includes regulatory compliance, corporate and commercial transactions, mergers and acquisitions, and litigation.*

*Since joining MVE, Ms. Karish has assisted clients affected by the Adelphia bankruptcy and the subsequent sale to Time Warner and Comcast with their analysis of the associated franchise transfer applications, participation in settlement negotiations, and submissions to the bankruptcy court. She also has assisted clients with analysis of and litigation involving the constitutionality and application of local, state and federal communications laws and regulations.*

## REFERENCES

1 FCC orders may be found by their document numbers (FCC- or DA-) through the EDOCS search system on the FCC's Web site at http://hraunfoss.fcc.gov/edocs_public.

2 Down time, in this case, refers not just to changing the operating characteristics of antennas and other parts of system infrastructure, but also to "retuning" (changing frequencies) or reprogramming—if not replacing—those "subscriber units" (vehicle mobiles or personal portable radios) in daily use by police, fire, medical and other public safety personnel.

3 The FCC rules did permit broadband licensing to a local entity in at least one case, that of the District of Columbia. See Order Granting Request by National Capital Region for Special Temporary Authority to Operate a Broadband Network in the 700 MHz Public Safety Band, DA 07-4850 (November 29, 2007).

4 First Report and Order and Further Notice of Proposed Rulemaking, *Communications Assistance for Law Enforcement Act and Broadband Access and Services*, ET Docket No. 04-295, FCC 05-153, ¶ 4, released Sept. 23. 2005 (*"First CALEA Order"*).

5 "An interconnected Voice over Internet Protocol (VoIP) service is a service that: (1) Enables real-time, two-way voice communications; (2) Requires a broadband connection from the user's location; (3) Requires Internet protocol-compatible customer premises equipment (CPE); and (4) Permits users generally to receive calls that originate on the public switched telephone network and to terminate calls to the public switched telephone network." 47 C.F.R. § 9.3. Thus, for example, any VoIP system that allows the user to make or receive conventional telephone calls is "interconnected."

6 *Communications Assistance for Law Enforcement Act*, Second Report and Order, 15 F.C.C.R. 7105 (2000) at 7110, ¶ 9.

7 47 U.S.C. § 1006; 47 C.F.R. § 1.2006(a).

8 Telecommunications Industry Association and Alliance for Telecommunications Industry Standards, *Lawfully Authorized Electronic Surveillance*, ANSI/J-STD-025-B-2006 (2006); Cable Television Laboratories, Inc., *Cable Broadband Intercept Specification*, CM-SP-CBI2.0-I02-071206 (Dec. 6, 2007)

9 Wireless Internet Service Providers Ass'n, *WISPA CALEA Standard Version 2.0* (effective May 1, 2009) (available at http://www.wispa.org/calea/WCS/WISPA-CS-IPNA-2.0.pdf).

10 See 47 U.S.C. § 222(h)(1).

# 23. SaaS Gov: A Viable Public Sector Solution for Risky Times

**AJ MALIK**

*Civilization advances by extending the number of important operations
which we can perform without thinking of them.*
— Alfred North Whitehead

*Change alone is eternal, perpetual, immortal.*
— Arthur Schopenhauer

*You affect the world by what you browse.*
— Tim Berners-Lee

Change manifests opportunities. Today's rapidly changing economic, technical and social landscapes are forcing the public sector to become both more nimble and responsive. In turn, public sector IT organizations are being pushed to become more innovative with shrinking budgets and diminishing resources. To ensure organization agility, rapid adoption of new technology paradigms that can better manage the inherent risks of uncertain times is required. Now is not the time to cling to traditional technology paradigms that may likely fail during today's challenging times. Rather, now is when organizations need to be innovative, rather than hunkering down to survive.

Software as a Service (SaaS), a rising web applications delivery model, is just such an emerging technology paradigm. What exactly is SaaS? Gartner Research's SaaS model definition is "hosted software based on a single set of common code and data definitions that are consumed in a one-to-many model by all contracted customers, at any time, on a pay-for-use basis, or as a subscription based on usage metrics."

SaaS is confused frequently with its precursor, the Application Services Provider (ASP), as being simply "hosted applications." The ASP model dedicates hosted server hardware to organizations. The SaaS model dedicates collective server hardware to multi-user applications, accessed by multiple organizations. ASPs can be more cost prohibitive over time; whereas SaaS attains economies of scale more rapidly as all costs are spread among its global user base. SaaS also has a unique single instance, one-to-many, "multi-tenancy" attribute that provides users to experience the same instance of the application. Multi-tenancy allows for more efficient server usage, especially when coupled with server virtualization technology and the virtualized cloud computing environment.

Server virtualization separates application software from the physical hardware on which it runs, enabling server hardware to support multiple applications simultaneously, more efficiently, and for lower cost. In turn, data centers can use server virtualization to reduce their hardware footprint, which results in substantial hardware, power and cooling cost savings. Standardized server virtualization platforms also enable data centers to facilitate disaster recovery whenever the occasion arises.

A common SaaS misconception lies with data "control issues" concerning ownership, stewardship and security. The traditional "on premises" software data remains within an organization's domain. With SaaS, enterprise data is entrusted to an outside party for access, storage and disaster recovery purposes. That paradigm shift creates a sense of insecurity for many CIOs. However, be assured that SaaS data centers have evolved considerably since ASPs first materialized over a decade ago. The proliferation and reliability of the Internet has made SaaS as highly available as "on premises" software applications.

Furthermore, today's commercial data centers integrate industrial strength security, disaster recovery, redundancy and reliability controls to be able to attract (and retain) corporate enterprises, especially security-centric financial institutions and health care organizations. Furthermore, service level agreements (SLA) insure precise provider service level delivery for data security, disaster recovery and global accessibility 24/7. Because the SaaS model is geared toward economies of scale, SaaS providers can provide specialized mission-critical application and data services at substantially less cost than an internal IT organization. A less-burdened IT organization can then free up its IT resources to be deployed for other important enterprise tasks.

Because technology is rapidly changing, substantial investments in technology are risky, especially during these expense- and budget-cutting times. SaaS offers substantial financial benefits to be considered. Traditional "on premises" software requires substantial up front capital due to its complex licensing models. SaaS, on the other hand, requires no large up front costs to be implemented, allowing systems deployment without substantial capital investment. SaaS utilizes a subscription based, turnkey pricing model, based on the number of an organization's active users. Therefore, as a variable cost, SaaS minimizes financial risk by minimizing capital investment, cash flow impact and potential sunk costs if the application is abandoned in the future.

It is always difficult to predict before-hand, how much system capacity will be required in the future. SaaS offers scalability, system capacity engineered into the solution, to better manage growing future demands. Scalability makes it difficult to outgrow application capacity. Scalability also provides piloting new systems on a small test scale, a "sandbox," for evaluation and justification for large scale deployment.

SaaS provides centralized software maintenance and upgrades that are more seamless and less disruptive to users than traditional "on premises" application deployment. The integration of SaaS with Web 2.0 and intuitive interfaces flatten learning curves, thereby reducing user training costs and increasing user adoption. Furthermore, SaaS tends to be more innovative than "on premises" software, with more frequent product updates that usually are driven by an engaged online user community.

Popular SaaS offerings include ERP, CRM, Content Management, Web Analytics, Social Networks, etc. Salesforce.com, a leading online CRM provider, also is an SaaS pioneer. However, new, more innovative SaaS offerings will materialize within the next few years. Recently, more than half of software developers polled indicated they were focusing on creating new SaaS products. IDC recently reported that the "global SaaS market is projected to hit $10.7 in 2009." It is apparent that the SaaS model continues to be very compelling for many reasons, including connectivity, functionality and cost savings. Public sector CIOs that understand the SaaS paradigm shift already are moving forward toward an SaaS Gov world. The question is, will they move fast enough?

## Discussion questions

1. Availability/SLAs: Can the SaaS provider show that they are meeting their uptime targets? What are the credit or refund consequences if the SaaS provider does not live up to their service level agreements (SLAs)?
2. Customization/integration: How easy is it to integrate the SaaS application with other applications? Is there a standard interface to enable integrations? How can the SaaS application be customized to meet our needs?
3. Support/upgrades/enhancements: What is the SaaS application product road map? How are application enhancements deployed and how frequently? What are the SaaS provider's technical support offerings (e.g. FAQs, Knowledge Base, Phone, E-mail, Live chat support, etc.) and respective support response times?
4. Disaster recovery: What systems do the SaaS data centers have in place to protect data (e.g. collocation, redundancy, backups, etc.)?
5. Termination and data ownership: Will the SaaS provider provide data access or data exports in popular formats if the contract is terminated? If so, for how long after the contract is terminated?

**AJ Malik** *is a business technologist with over 25 years of direct experience with technical information services. Mr. Malik has provided professional technical guidance to public, private, nonprofit and healthcare sector clients. Mr. Malik successfully implemented one of the first customer relationship management (CRM) solutions for a leading economic development organization. His CRM solution has been adopted by more than a dozen other local and national economic development organizations. Mr. Malik has successfully managed electronic medical record (EMR) implementations, with web, electronic data interchange (EDI) and office automation integration, to create "paperless" health care organizations. Mr. Malik is currently a collaboration strategist, guiding public sector organizations with emerging social media and other collaboration technologies.*

# PART FOUR:

# Human Resource Leadership & Management

# 24. Human Resource Management: Selecting and Maintaining Great Staff

**SUSAN ALLEN**

## Introduction

**Speculation:** The retirement of the baby boomers over the next five years is going to create a shortage of about 3 million workers in the US.

**Fact:** Declared computer science majors have declined by 50% in the US since 1998.

The bottom line is that you soon will have no choice but to recruit and retain workers any way you can. It is time to get creative and be flexible—you can bet your competitors are; in fact, even the federal government is. The following discussion will get you started and enhance any efforts you already have under way.

## Recruiting exceptional staff

### Why work in government?

Let us start by throwing those newspaper job advertisements out the window. Does anyone even read them anymore? Granted, the job posting on your website is a step in the right direction, but that approach assumes a candidate knows that they want to work in government. Then, if the candidates do make it to your webpage, what are the chances that they actually are going to understand what the job entails and what you are looking for?

The first thing to do is scale those job descriptions down to verbiage that has tangible meaning. Make them easy to read, as a resume should be. Use bullet points to outline the specific skills needed, clearly state the details of the technology they will work with and accentuate any potential new projects they may work on. Clarify key terms that may have different meanings to people with different backgrounds. For example, an inventory system for a government warehouse is substantially different from an inventory system used in manufacturing. The job title should be updated to reflect titles commonly used in the current industry. It also may be helpful to review your education and experience requirements—are the levels you set really necessary? Make sure the opening statements of the job description portray the excitement that exists within your department.

Keep an open mind, and do not box yourself into a limited number of candidates. Avoid favoring employees with more experience over employees with more potential. There is a big difference between the two, particularly when it comes to innovation. A common pitfall of many HR departments is that they lack the knowledge to interpret IT experience and education when reviewing a candidates qualifications. As such, it is no surprise that capable candidates that you might consider based on potential rather than experience often are turned away. Lastly, keep in mind you need new employees as much as they need you. The more exciting and challenging the job is the better candidates you are going to recruit.

Chances are you will be recruiting someone who is currently employed elsewhere. As such, you must convey the advantages and opportunities your organization has to offer over the candidate's current place of employment. Ensure that your organization's website conveys the message of an exciting place to work. Emphasize the extraordinary benefits government employment has to offer. In markets where it is difficult for government to compete with private sector salaries, it is essential that the associated cost of the benefits staff receive be advertised.

For example, a worker making $40,000 in government can save approximately 45% of his or her salary in pre-tax retirement accounts, whereas a private sector employee can save only about 18% (estimates include matching contributions). Another significant difference to share is the cost of health insurance that is usually substantially lower for government employees. In times of economic downturn, job and retirement security also are great motivators for entry into the government workforce. Other advantages to government employment generally include fewer work hours than the private sector: 40 hours versus 60 to 80 hours.

Most importantly for younger generations, it fulfills the need/want for public service. For older workers who have worked only in one industry, it provides the opportunity to interact with many different types of businesses, as local governments provide such a wide variety of services. And, for some people, it may even be an opportunity for a career change. If your organization has numerous vacancies or expects to have many, tout the ability to promote within the organization more quickly than in the private sector and without the nuisance of having to job hop.

Work with your HR department to develop a snazzy flyer that provides a synopsis of benefits such as vacation leave, sick leave, personal leave, health insurance, pension plans, 457 plans, flexible work schedules, telecommuting, career development (training and formal education), career progression, and on and on and on. Post them on your website and provide a link to them from each job description for easy reference by the candidates. You may even want to provide a hard copy to the candidates you interview. Answering as many benefit questions as possible before the interview will save time throughout the hiring process. Candidates who are just surfing the job market (not sure if they really want to make a change or not—generally the more loyal staff that are worth having) will do a salary and benefits comparison between their current employer and your organization before they even submit a resume.

Another key ingredient to effective recruiting is an efficient application process. Gather as much information as possible on candidates during the application process. Make sure you are ready to conduct interviews within a reasonable amount of time before the job is posted. Consider noting on the job description the expected duration of the hiring process. If you solicit an application from someone and then do not make an offer for another six months, you can expect him or her to decline. For recruiting purposes, design sections of your website to highlight the various programs in place to retain staff and provide a link back to that page from each job posting. For example, if your staff is fortunate enough to have cool workspaces, show pictures of that, or if staff telecommute, post pictures of someone working from home. The first impression you leave with a candidate is just as important as the first impression they leave with you. Recruiting is no different than selling your own self in a job interview. You have to sell, sell and then sell your organization some more.

## Selling your biz

Everyone knows government does not pay well and their technology is years behind the rest of the world. Not true? Then, spread the word! Job fairs provide an excellent advertising opportunity for you to inform potential employees about the opportunities available within your organization. Develop some handouts on the technologies you use to distribute at job fairs. Also, take copies of that benefits flyer HR helped you create earlier. Send one or two of your more enthusiastic staff members to the fair regardless of whether HR is available to join you or not. With their enthusiasm, some creativity and a bit of positive communication coaching, they will spark interest among a potential candidate or two.

The current generation expects you to come looking for them. As such, college job fairs and placement offices are the best bet for recruiting students who have graduated recently. Studies show that the current generation is looking for challenging and meaningful work. Again, create flyers advertising your current technologies and list some future technologies you are interested in recruiting for or building an in-house skill set for. Recent college graduates have just spent the past four years learning about the latest technology and want to utilize that knowledge right away. Take advantage of their eagerness. If your technology is exciting enough, salary will not be much of a consideration for them. Post job openings on university career websites and job lists as soon as they become available.

In a true effort to recruit, make the effort to review the resumes uploaded on such sites as Career Builder or Monster. On a regular basis, people upload their resumes to job sites and then forget to remove them once they have found a job. Browsing those resumes will put some candidates in front of you that may not be actively job hunting but will consider a reasonable offer. If you still are not having much luck, utilize tools such as Myspace, Facebook, Stickcam and Second Life. Social networks such as those will provide great exposure to a global market for your organization while advertising your organization as the 'in' place to work.

## Alternatives to traditional staffing

In today's world, there is no such a thing as a computer illiterate child anymore. High schools have realized a need for developing a more challenging technological curriculum. In fact, there is probably a high school in your area that offers some IT classes (if not an entire training program) on PC repair, website design, etc. Make contact with those schools. During their senior year, many students participate in a Cooperative Education (Co-op) Program where they go to school half a day and work half a day. What a great opportunity this provides you! Co-op students can be utilized to augment the support desk if you want to extend services or hours or work in a particular area where there is not enough work to hire someone full time. If the students do not have the skills needed, use them as substitutes for entry-level positions while you train current staff in more advanced areas. Not only can you find a solution in a high school student, but you can also hire them for well under the going rate of consultants and may even recruit a future employee for yourself in the process.

As with high school co-op students, there are plenty of opportunities for you to recruit college students part time or full time. Only on rare occasions will you find a college student who is not willing to learn something new for those situations in which you do not have adequate expertise on staff. As an added benefit, they will spread the word among their classmates about the exciting work they are doing in government. An additional advantage for hiring college students is they are a resource you will have access to for about four years. Furthermore, the student may be able to use some of the projects they complete as class work or college credit. Be sure to discuss your needs with the college or university before you make contact with students. After all, it can be a win-win situation for all three parties. Although you may have to be rather flexible with their work schedule, they are employees you can hire for a significantly lower cost than the going market value.

Job sharing also is becoming popular as the baby boomers begin to consider retirement. Two issues they face are the cost of health insurance and pure boredom. A part-time salary will allow them to draw their retirement and, yet, live comfortably with a bit of extra income to cover the cost of health insurance. It also will benefit the organization by reducing the costs of overhead associated with a full-time employee and reduce insurance costs by keeping older employees active. For others, having the financial ability to retire at such a younger age than previous generations leaves many of them wondering what to do with themselves. In that instance of job sharing, you have the opportunity to transfer institutional knowledge to a college intern or entry-level employee before the employee fully retires.

Regardless of what approach you take to recruiting, start a database or just a simple list of people who have expressed an interest in government work in the past. Include people you have interviewed that just were not the right fit for the job you were interviewing for at the time. Add to the list anyone who contacts you mentioning an interest to move back home. The database should include not only personal contact information but also a friend or relative you can follow up with if they have moved before you reach out to them. Additionally, include specific skills they have, positions they might be a good fit for, and interests they may have, such as part-time, job sharing, contract work, etc. The best thing about that approach is that no HR rules will ever be broken; simply call people up who meet the qualifications of an opening and ask them to apply.

## Finding Mr./Ms. Right

Structure, structure, structure is the most important aspect of a productive interview. The use of an interview panel is highly recommended, as each interviewer will rate the candidate from a different perspective resulting in a more global view of the candidate. It may prove useful to include various levels of your department on the interview panel, such as the expected supervisor, subordinate and peer. If it is a position that will deal primarily with customers (user departments), include a departmental representative, as well. Make sure that each of your interviewers is positive, open minded and enthusiastic. The last thing you want to do is scare a candidate away before the interview process is even finished.

Interview questions should be open-ended to promote discussions and follow-up questions. Determine whether the position requires an innovation- or maintenance-focused individual. Using correct questions can bring those preferences out of a candidate. Hiring an innovative employee into a maintenance-type position will only prove financially disastrous to the organization, as they likely will not stay around very long after they have mastered the job. The use of "what would you do" or "what have you done" questions will provide predictive behavior models indicative of the behavior you can expect from the candidate if you do hire them.

Eventually, the time will come when you have to gauge experience against potential. The most successful way to do that is through testing. Basic knowledge tests have an expected answer regardless of whether they are a simple question or a task to be performed. Such tests are only valuable when comparing levels of experience and/or knowledge between candidates.

To compare candidates' potential, they must be presented with an exercise that neither one knows the answer to. For example, create a training manual and give each candidate four hours to complete a business case in a system (use a training or test environment) the candidates have never used before. For a more technical position, structure the business case so that something breaks, and they have to look at database tables to figure out what broke and then identify a solution. Other options may include adjusting the configuration settings on a system or migrating data from one platform to another. Allow candidates to use any resources they see fit. Wrap up the process with a presentation to show what they did—good tool for insight into soft skills. The use of various resources shows ingenuity, self-teaching abilities and conceptual thinking.

Testing for potential does require a lot of effort to be put forth by both parties. On a positive note, though, the test only has to be designed once and then it can be used repeatedly with a few modifications. Consider using that same technique for promotions. If you decide to perform tests, make sure the requirement of a test is stated specifically in the job description. Consider scheduling the tests on Saturday due to the length of time required.

As important as skills, knowledge and experience are, cultural fit is just as important. When it comes time to consider cultural fit, think of what the "to be" culture is that you are targeting rather than the "as is." New staff can be instrumental in changing the culture by spurring a little healthy competitiveness. Unfortunately, new staff that does not fit well within the culture of your organization can contribute to a decrease in office morale and potentially a loss of productivity amongst their team members. Furthermore, never settle for mediocrity just because you have a vacancy that needs to be filled. If you find yourself facing such a situation, take a step back and reevaluate the potential of candidates rather than their experience.

## Retaining superior staff

### Build it, they will come
The foundation for a retainable workforce is common purpose. Without a cohesive team, staff ends up going in different directions, and nothing is ever accomplished. Common purpose exists on teams when each individual has a clear sense of the reason the team exists, their individual role on the team and the importance of that role to the team. To create a common purpose for your department, involve everyone in the process of establishing guiding principals on how staff will interact with each other. The guiding principals will then help the team identify their values. In turn, the team values establish direction for which decisions can be based upon. Once the team knows the direction they are headed in, a common purpose has been established.

### Capitalize on strengths
Leadership development programs correlate strongly with retention, but more important than providing leadership opportunities is assisting your staff in identifying the future of their career. Most people concentrate on improving their weaknesses rather than further developing their strengths. Observe your staff interacting with others and working on projects. With a little bit of practice you will notice easily what their strengths are. Discuss those strengths with the individ-

ual while you discuss the direction they want to take their career. In some cases, a conflict may exist between their strengths and the direction they have in mind for their career. If you feel that to be the case, then discuss with them the various possibilities available for them to utilize their strengths to see if they "enjoy" using that strength. Utilizing a strength will bring success, and success generally leads to more productive employees.

The next step is to pair up that newly self-enlightened employee with a mentor who can help them further develop that strength. By pairing them up with a mentor, you have just created a succession plan. You soon will have someone to replace a retiring employee while having successfully created a career path for a less experienced employee. To avoid the appearance of favoritism, pair two or three people up with one mentor, if possible. When that mentor does retire, you will have a few candidates from which to choose a replacement. In the meantime, the mentor will have a renewed sense of purpose and stay around a little longer. Word of caution: Do not confuse a mentor with a supervisor. For such a plan to work, that mentor has to be a leader rather than just a supervisor. A supervisor gives directives; a mentor coaches an employee on how to develop good decision-making habits and encourages the employee to make decisions on their own. It is important for employees (just as it is for children) to make mistakes so they can learn. Fortunately, mentors can mitigate the risk associated with those mistakes.

## Dangle a carrot!

A major shortcoming in any organization is the staff's comprehension of their benefits. Just because someone chooses to participate in a 457-investment plan does not mean he/she fully understands all of the benefits of such a plan. Be sure providers meet with staff one on one who sign up for such a program and have them provide a quick reference sheet that can be used five years from now when the need arises for someone to withdraw hardship funds.

Make sure staff really know how to use their Flex Benefit Account, what the benefits of the account are, what the tax advantages are, and what it can and cannot be used for. Explain to them how they can save twice as much, if not more, for retirement in public sector versus private. Make sure they understand what the co-pays for surgery or the birth of a child are. Provide them with information detailing the differences between short-term, long-term and social security disability. Discuss their needs for life insurance relative to such expenses as a funeral, education of children, care of spouse, etc. If you hold sessions rather than one on one meetings, have the employees invite their spouse or other relatives to join them.

All of those suggestions sound like stuff the HR department should do, but what usually happens is that employees are corralled into large organizational meetings on benefit education and are too shy to ask the questions most important to them. Educating your staff (and yourself) on their benefits package makes staff aware of the tangible benefits they normally do not consider relative to their paycheck. For most, it will be a revelation. Moreover, as you improve employee perception of the value of government employment you will increase the quality of your applicants (word of mouth is the best form of advertisement). With a little bit of luck, HR will take over the program for organization-wide implementation once they realize the impact it has had on your department. Why is this so important? Chances are that if you do not understand what your benefits are, then your staff does not either; thus, the benefits really are not a benefit at all.

Have you been to the offices of a software development company lately? Did you notice how casual and comfortable the workspaces were? If you sat in front of a computer screen all day writing code, would you prefer your current office or an office with a beanbag chair and a mini basketball hoop? Next time the department is in need of furniture let your staff design their own working area. They may end up distracted for a few days (by excitement), but such a simple exercise will show them how much you trust them and value their individuality. Moreover, a comfortable workspace conducive to their lifestyle is sure to increase productivity. Furthermore, when it comes to retention, why would they settle for a drab cubicle elsewhere over the flashy new one they now have? If you do not have the funds to upgrade everyone's office, start with the break room or an empty space in the data center. Make it comfortable so staff will take breaks and eat lunch together. That will help build a feeling of oneness among the group and may even spur a little innovative brainstorming on occasion. If you do not have money to lighten the mood even in the break room, allow staff to donate items collecting dust in their garage (everyone has something to spare in their garage).

While many companies offer training in technology that is currently used, very few places take a long-term approach by investing in staff for technologies or career opportunities on the horizon. Hiring high school or college students for part-time work can help remedy some staffing issues for the immediate future, but if you have younger employees that you want to retain until retirement, it would be wise to start investing in them now for the technology of tomorrow. Most successful IT organizations place organizational development at the center of their IT recruiting and retention strategies. Several studies have found that the biggest driver of turnover for employees under age 30 is dissatisfaction with job content and career opportunities. One easy approach to providing satisfaction with job content is to present those workers with a variety of interesting work assignments and challenges. Ultimately, they will tailor their own growth and development to the assignments they have been given regardless of how great the challenge. Those are the workers that will work 36 hours straight to restore a database that even the vendor said could not be resurrected.

Work environments that allow for telecommuting or flexible work schedules are extremely attractive for employees under the age of 35 or 40. Telecommuting can provide many benefits not only to the employee, but to the organization as well. Most organizations find that employees who telecommute are more effective and productive when working from home. To start with, employees who work from home have fewer distractions and interruptions than in the office and are subject to fewer internal stressors. The establishment of a sound work-life balance increases quality of life by allowing more flexibility for running daytime errands, lowering personal costs and freeing up more time for family with the elimination of a commute. If you were offered a 5% pay raise versus two more hours a day with your family, which would you choose? Keeping your employees happy ultimately will help reduce your recruiting, training, real estate and relocation costs. That approach will also lay the foundation for good business continuity and disaster recovery plans by geographically dispersing staff. Lastly, you will be expanding your pool of applicants, as employees will not necessarily have to live within the local area.

Word of mouth always will be the number one advertising tool of any organization. If employees are happy, they will do the recruiting for you. So, keep them happy! Additional retention approaches utilized by federal government, state government, local government and the private sector follow on the next page.

- ◆ Breakfast with managers
- ◆ Loan forgiveness
- ◆ College loan repayment
- ◆ Moving expenses
- ◆ Sign on bonus
- ◆ Retraining existing staff
- ◆ Emergency child care centers
- ◆ Leave for school events
- ◆ Voluntary reduction in work days
- ◆ Domestic violence leave
- ◆ Bringing infants to work
- ◆ Part-time with full benefits
- ◆ Mentor new staff before retiring
- ◆ Reduced workload until retired
- ◆ Deferred retirement option
- ◆ Voluntary job sharing
- ◆ Dual career ladder (management vs. technical)
- ◆ Streamline internal transfer process
- ◆ Meaningful evaluations with merit pay
- ◆ Meet with supervisor's supervisor
- ◆ Continuing education and license payments
- ◆ Provide retirement education
- ◆ Provide instant feedback
- ◆ Keep staff informed
- ◆ Offer eldercare and home care assistance
- ◆ Referral bonus
- ◆ Child care stipend
- ◆ Internships
- ◆ Parking expenses
- ◆ Redesign work space
- ◆ Retention bonus
- ◆ Spot bonuses
- ◆ Increased vacation time
- ◆ Concierge
- ◆ Gym membership
- ◆ Onsite fitness center
- ◆ Pension portability
- ◆ Exit interviews
- ◆ Job rotation
- ◆ Domestic partner benefits
- ◆ Home loans
- ◆ Promotion options
- ◆ Educational leave
- ◆ Career coaching
- ◆ Employee attitude surveys
- ◆ Travel options
- ◆ Sabbatical
- ◆ Vary assignments
- ◆ Reduce hierarchy

## Staff augmentation

### The big 'O'

After all that effort has been put forth to recruit and retain excellent staff, the economy goes south, tax revenues drop and someone decides the shortfall in this year's budget can be offset by the cost savings associated with the outsourcing of IT operations. Unfortunately, it is not very realistic to assume that the entire IT department can be outsourced. To do so would take years of preparatory work and transition efforts. The immediate savings that the budget department is looking for would be years to come. Rather than biting off more than the organization can chew, try examining the departmental divisions separately. Determine where the largest investments and shortcomings are. For example, if application development, deployment and upgrades require substantial investments annually, customers are asking for 24-hour support from the help desk for desktop issues, or a new data center is needed and hardware is aging, consider outsourcing just those individual functions. As every agency has different business processes and regulations in practice, it is unlikely that functional support for enterprise applications can be outsourced.

When the decision has been made to outsource a specific area, it is imperative for an agency to clearly identify the services they wish to have performed in order for an outsourcing arrangement to be successful. In doing so, service level agreements (SLAs), key performance metrics and penalties for failure to deliver services must be documented in the contract. Identification of each of those items is crucial, as the vendor you will negotiate the contract with has undertaken the effort many times before, and it will be your first attempt.

Having completed the work of identifying the services, SLAs and metrics to be incorporated into a contract, the foundation for re-engineering the department has been laid. The question then becomes: Do you pay a vendor (out to make a profit) to do the work for you, or do you begin the re-engineering process yourself? Other key considerations include the impact on current employees, the management of the new contract, existing investments that will be lost, the vendor's business continuity/disaster recovery plan, security of data, vendor personnel background checks, and the process for bringing new services and technologies online.

## Contract for hire

Hiring staff on a contract basis may be another avenue to consider. The practice can provide quick access to expertise and the means to complete large projects quicker, and bottom-line cost savings can be made in regards to benefits.

Unfortunately, there are a few drawbacks to the approach, as well. If the contract employee has to travel, you will pay those costs either directly or as overhead on top of their salary. In order to mitigate risk, insurance requirements of the agency may make it cost prohibitive for a contractor to work without the umbrella of a larger company (hence rate goes up to cover overhead). If the contract employee is not contracted on a full-time basis, your agency eventually will have to compete with other clients. In the long run, the agency may face some more problematic issues, such as the lack of in-house expertise, potentially poor knowledge transfer, and the jeopardy of existing staff becoming resentful. The biggest area of concern ultimately will be that certain business assumptions made by the contract employee may adversely affect the line of business in the end. To avoid that, it may prove more beneficial to invest in current staff to meet future needs.

# Conclusion

## Be a leader

According to various studies, employees place a great deal of importance on the "intangibles" of work, such as having a good supervisor, a pleasant work environment and interesting work regardless of what their age is. It is human nature to seek, crave and strive for acknowledgement. Civil servants often feel satisfaction in knowing they are helping deliver vital citizen services and contributing to the advancement of their community.

Request that external departments share letters from citizens complimenting a service they provided that is directly supported by technology. Generation XY seeks immediate gratification for accomplishments, whereas Baby Boomers are content with just an occasional "good job" comment.

To be fair though, treat all workers the same. Start by publicizing accomplishments within the department (post a quarterly newsletter on the website), organization and maybe even the industry if the opportunity arises. Consider having staff nominate each other for a job well done and then vote at the end of the year for employee of the year. Display the employee's picture in an open area for visitors to admire. Another option is to designate a special parking space for the employee of the month. Efforts that dramatic ultimately will spur some healthy competitiveness and encourage creativity in solution providing. You might also try rewarding the over-achievers with an assignment on a special project of interest (yes, it will work, particularly for anyone interested in career advancement). It can be a project within your department, such as a security audit team if they like to hack, or delegate your role on an organization-wide team to them. Alternatively, you can kill two birds with one stone by rewarding staff who are interested with a trip to a job fair as a recruiter. For less astounding accomplishments, try handing out items from a goodie bag (useless freebie items collected at conferences, which also make great door prizes at departmental meetings). We all spend too much time at work not to have some fun every now and then.

## Only great leadership retains great staff

The best advice you will ever get is to treat employees and potential employees the way you would want to be treated. Practice what you preach, learn something special about each employee and engage your staff as often as possible. If you are not sure how to interact with someone of a different generation, think about how you would treat someone in your own family of that generation. Make a commitment to your employees if you expect them to commit to you. Your success can only be built upon theirs.

---

### Discussion questions

1. What is the common purpose of our department?
2. How can we update our job descriptions to be more exciting and appealing?
3. What are some new advertising and recruiting avenues we can use?
4. Will the use of interns allow us to cut staffing costs (salaries or over time)?
5. Will the use of interns allow us to expand our service offerings in any way?
6. Are there any local universities, colleges or high schools we can work with to develop some internship opportunities? If so, what areas would benefit from the use of interns?
7. What technology do we utilize that is uncommon? Should we outsource support for that technology?
8. Do we have any projects in the pipeline that are noteworthy from an innovation perspective or require special skill sets?
9. How can I address immediate, near and long term staffing needs?
10. What efforts have we put toward succession planning thus far?
11. What benefits and incentives can we provide existing and potential staff for retention and recruitment purposes?
12. How can we reward staff when they perform exceptionally well?
13. Would the utilization of contract employees or outsourcing of specific functions be feasible for our organization? If so, what should we consider?

**Susan Allen** *is a Business Unit Manager (Program Manager) with the City of Corpus Christi. She joined the organization at the age of 25 as the equivalent of a Business Analyst for the Financial Services Department supporting PeopleSoft Financials. Within two years, she was promoted to Business Unit Manager in the Municipal Information Systems Department. Along the way, she had doubled her salary in less than four years. Two years ago, Susan was the application and database support team manager leading a team of 24 focused on providing services to utilities, public safety and administrative departments. After eight years of service in local government, Susan is now the Program Manager focusing on strategic development for the City of Corpus Christi Municipal Information Systems Department. She attributes her success to prior experience in the private sector as a project implementation manager for a software development company (from which she took a 50% pay cut to join the city). Susan is not only passionate about good customer service, but good employee service as well.*

# 25. The Selection and Retention of Information Technology (IT) Staff

**DON DELOACH**

The selection and retention of Information Technology (IT) staff is one of the most important aspects of a Chief Information Officer's (CIO) job. The ability to recruit, motivate and retain great employees could be the difference in whether a CIO's plan or vision is successful. Employee retention is one of the challenges facing many business organizations today. For many organizations, strategic staffing has become a concern because the ability to hold on to highly talented employees can be crucial to future success. Employee turnover costs can be staggering and can range from two to five times the annual wages of the replaced worker; not to mention the training costs spent to train another employee. On average, in Tallahassee, it takes eight weeks to hire a new employee. For eight to 10 weeks, other employees have to pick up the remaining workload, which can lead to morale problems in the organization. What can a CIO do to lessen the impact to organizations? This chapter will discuss proven techniques that can enhance a CIO's ability to recruit, retain and motivate great staff members.

All of us can remember the Dot-Com boon when IT professionals were leaving the security of public sector life and chasing the six-figure salaries of the private sector. Subsequent staff turnover in the public sector caused many projects to run behind schedule and, more importantly, over budget. In 1998, the City of Tallahassee decided to purchase PeopleSoft Human Resources software to manage its payroll and human resource function. A project team was formed, and each was sent to PeopleSoft training to become acclimated in the PeopleSoft methodology. The project was progressing smoothly: We trained employees who were making significant progress on the project; we purchased software that was meeting our business requirements; we had executive management support and life was good!! Then it happened, headhunters from the private sector started to hover like mosquitoes in a Florida swamp. One by one, the project team was depleted to the point that we had to start the project all over. What a learning experience!

The end result was that we put policies and procedures in place to prevent that type of event from happening again. We established a policy called the training reimbursement policy. The policy directed that the employee who has accepted training from the city and departs the city within a two-year window must repay the city for the training. If the employee leaves after one year, then the expense is cut in half. That was not a popular policy among employees, and many complaints were lodged because of the policy. From the city's perspective, we had to protect our training dollar investment and could not continue to be a training ground for head-hunters to cherry pick our best and brightest employees. One never knows what is going to happen in your organization. We went from productivity being very high to no productivity at all. Be prepared to deal with the unexpected.

If CIOs had the answer to the question of retention, then this would not be a discussion item.

However, there are tools and techniques that can help reduce the anxiety and apprehension that CIOs feel when turnover increases. One must remember that retention is personal in nature, which means that the employee is the decision maker and has control of the decision-making process. They determine whether they stay or leave. You cannot expect 100% retention nor should you want it. You, as the CIO, must focus on what you can control and influence, and that leads to the tools and techniques that I have tried over the years and have found successful.

## Develop a succession plan and cross train

The first technique is you have to decide who needs to be retained and which jobs are important. That should be documented in a succession plan. The plan should address not only the critical positions for your organization but the knowledge, skills and abilities associated with making the position successful. When you are designing the plan, put names to the positions and make sure that you have more than one name associated with each position. Do not rely on one "expert" to carry you. Suppose that "expert" gets sick or wants to go visit their relatives over seas. Can you afford that? Probably not. Cross training has become one of the most important management objectives, and we will continue to keep young talent ready to take over if the situation presents itself.

After a plan has been established, the second part of the process is to utilize some managerial techniques to keep employees excited about coming to their jobs. A good manager understands that you have to earn an employee's respect, not demand it. I see too many managers that use position power as if it were a divine right. Position power could be utilized with the loyal Baby Boomer employees, but Generation X and Y's could really care less. You must engage with your employees. Develop a rapport with them. Understand what motivates each and every one of them. I can hear the dissenters now: "I don't have time to sit down and chit chat with employees." Well, if you really want to make a difference and build a team that works well together, get to know your employees. Watch how they respond to your questions, because they can give you keen insight on just exactly what is happening in your organization. Challenge your senior managers to listen to their employees and find out exactly what is happening on the front lines of customer support. Talk to employees on your help desk. The help desk is the first level of support for your IT department, but more important, the help desk is the customer's first impression of IT. Make sure the help desk employees are customer-oriented and have a pleasant demeanor with customers. That might take some extra training but is well worth the training dollars.

## Refresh your talent pool

Another technique that has been useful in retaining employees is to refresh your talent pool. Give your older employees a chance to recharge their batteries. Different challenges motivate people to get things done. If you let the work force become stale and stagnant, the results might not be what you want or expect. For example, suppose you have an employee that has worked in one area for the entire time they have been employed. You stop by to see how things are going, and the employee tells you that they are not happy with the work they are performing and sure could use a change. You take that input into consideration and work a reorganization plan that moves the employee to an entirely different section with an entirely different customer base. A few months later, the employee is producing at a tremendous rate again. That example actually happened in my organization. Listening to your employees can give you the input you need to organize them in a way that everyone can be happy and productive. Don't be apprehensive about changing things and shaking things up. Sometimes organizations need some shaking to make sure productivity stays high.

There will be failures, also. Don't get caught up in why things fail; learn from the experience and keep moving forward. I will always remember one of my first supervisors used to say, "If you are not making mistakes, you aren't doing anything." Those words inspired me to step out and try to make things better. We can always go back and fix things, the learning experience starts when we make a mistake, and the key is to learn from the mistake and not make the same mistake again. If you can get your employees to that level, you have a very mature work force that will pay huge dividends in providing customer service to your internal operating departments.

## Analyze benefits

Another technique that can be used is organizational in nature. The technique will be an analysis of current benefits and rewards programs your current employer offers. What type of benefit plans does your organization have that would attract high-quality applicants to your organization? Do you use intrinsic motivational programs to lure good workers? Do you use sign-on bonuses or reward your employees for good work? The IT workforce is global now, and organizations' ability to lure workers that can produce results is getting harder and harder. Competition for good IT talent has never been greater, and those organizations that put programs in place to compete for the talent are the organizations that will succeed in the future.

Gartner Group has performed studies that define what types of company attributes motivate employees to want to work for them. The following table was taken from a research report that interviewed 152 applicants to find out what types of programs would be enticing for prospective applicants.[1]

| Attribute | Percentage of respondents rated as effective |
|---|---|
| Benefit programs | 89.5% |
| Company reputation | 86.8% |
| Base compensation | 82.9% |
| Challenging work environment | 81.6% |
| Career advancement opportunities | 81.6% |
| IT organization culture | 78.9% |
| Casual work environment | 75.0% |
| Flexible work arrangements | 67.1% |
| Training and development programs | 65.1% |
| Employee recognition programs | 59.9% |
| Short-term incentives/bonuses | 52.6% |
| Coaching/mentoring programs | 48.7% |
| Sign-on bonuses | 44.7% |
| Stock options | 15.8% |

Notice that base compensation is not the number one attribute. It must be noted that "challenging work environment" and "career advancement opportunities" are attributes that most everyone says are important to employees, but I always felt that those attributes led to more base compensation, which is why those attributes show up on every survey. In my experience, I have found that base compensation is an important attribute. Younger staff that are just starting out in their careers are base compensation-motivated. I feel there is a perfectly good reason for that. Most young employees just starting out are looking to purchase homes and start their own families. Money motivates them. As time goes by and their money needs are met, the employee starts to look at job satisfiers more closely.

Remember Maslow's Hierarchy of Needs? Maslow's Hierarchy of Needs is often depicted as a pyramid consisting of five levels: the four lower levels are grouped together as being associated with physiological needs, while the top level is termed growth needs associated with psychological needs. Deficiency needs must be met first. Once those are met, seeking to satisfy growth needs drives personal growth. The higher needs in the hierarchy only come into focus when the lower needs in the pyramid are satisfied. Once an individual has moved upward to the next level, needs in the lower level will no longer be prioritized. If a lower set of needs is no longer being met, the individual will temporarily re-prioritize those needs by focusing attention on the unfulfilled needs but will not permanently regress to the lower level. For instance, a businessman at the esteem level who is diagnosed with cancer will spend a great deal of time concentrating on his health (physiological needs) but will continue to value his work performance (esteem needs) and likely will return to work during periods of remission. My analogy is very similar.

The following table depicts what I feel is the most accurate account of recruitment attributes for employees. The table, produced by Gartner in 2007, depicts by age group the most effective recruitment attributes and verifies what I have experienced in my 27-year career. As you see from the table, the degree of importance of a particular attribute to each employee varies according to where they are in their professional careers. The employees surveyed that were under 25 were more base compensation-motivated, and those that were over 46 were more concerned with the benefit packages available to them. This data should help you target marketing strategies to recruit new talent to your organizations. By remembering what motivates employees, you can devise strategies to make sure your strategies are designed to meet the basic needs of the employee.

## Most effective recruitment attributes by age group

| Attribute Rank | <25 | 25–35 | 36–45 | 46 or older |
|---|---|---|---|---|
| #1 | Base Compensation | Career Advancement Opportunities | Base Compensation | Benefit Programs |
| #2 | Challenging Work Environment | Base Compensation | Benefit Programs | Base Compensation and Company Reputation |
| #3 | Career Advancement Opportunities | Challenging Work Environment | Challenging Work Environment | Challenging Work Environment |

When hiring new applicants, one must select people who are right for the job; employee selection curtails employee turnover. It is extremely important to hire quality people and, most of all, hire quality people the first time. Too many times, employers fill positions to get a warm body in the position when they know that the hire is not going to make it. Do not hire someone unless you are comfortable knowing the employee will add value to your staff. If you hire the wrong person, you will live to regret it, because most of the time, the employee will be challenged to perform when they are not really ready for the position. What happens is you end up spending a lot of energy trying to get the employee up to speed. In reality, the employee should have never been hired.

A word of advice: hire for the long term. If you have a pressing need and need somebody immediately, think about staff augmentation with a private provider. At the City of Tallahassee, we have used that strategy to our advantage. Let me illustrate. Most every year, we are in the process of doing an Enterprise Resource Planning (ERP) system upgrade. The upgrades are time-consuming and require many hours of staff support to get through. We currently do not have the staff to do an upgrade and then also perform the day-to-day work associated with maintaining an ERP. Because of that dilemma, we hire professional help to get us through the upgrade process. We let our staff members manage the project but have hired guns helping us get over the upgrade hump. That strategy has proven very successful and has been utilized for every upgrade. It is much to our advantage to continue to maintain and provide great customer service to our fellow employees. If we were constantly performing upgrades, we would not be able to provide great customer service. It is very important for IT to be out in the business units learning the business so that we can recommend technology solutions that will add value to our business unit's mission.

## Hire for character

The final technique that will be the deciding factor in successful retention of your top employees is that of hiring people with character. Character is defined as, "The qualities built into an individual's life that determines his or her response, regardless of circumstances. The most accurate predictor of a person's behavior is his or her character."[4] Let's illustrate. At this year Master's golf tournament, a young amateur golfer from Alabama University named Michael Thompson was playing in his first Master's tournament. Michael was playing extremely well and had a great chance to make the cut and play on Saturday and Sunday. That would have been quite the accomplishment for such a young golfer. Michael was standing over his putt to make a birdie on hole 15. It was the biggest moment of his young life. He was about to make the cut at the Masters. It could easily propel him into a promising career on the professional golf tour. His future vocation may have even been at stake. But, as he set up to make his putt and he set his putter on the ground, the ball moved on its own ever so slightly! Other players were on the green with him. Television cameras were rolling. No one saw it!

You might not think that is a big deal, but golf is a game about rules. Rule 18 -2b states, "If a player's *ball in play moves* after he has *addressed* it (other than as a result of a *stroke*), the player is deemed to have *moved* the ball and incurs a penalty of one stroke." Michael kept his composure, called the rules official over and penalized himself a stroke. What was going to be a birdie became a bogey, and he was out for the weekend! That difference meant making the cut or not making the cut! No one had seen the ball move but him! Even as they replayed it in slow motion you could barely see it move. But it did, ever so slightly and he had penalized himself. For young Michael

Thompson, character mattered. It mattered more than career or fame. In a world where cheating is commonplace, it was refreshing to see this man "doing the right thing!"

Think about the people who work for you, and put them into that same situation. What would they do? You should strive to surround yourself with employees that will always do the right thing. Employees that have good character are less likely to call in sick, less likely to steal time from the organization, and are more likely to be productive. Disciplinary problems are less frequent, and a "can do" attitude permeates through your entire organization.

There are many reasons why people do what is right, but fear, personal gain and doing it just because it is the right thing to do are a few of the most prevalent reasons. Fear is a tremendous motivator. I can say from experience that the fear of failure drove me to accomplish things that I thought were unattainable. For example, in athletics, the fear of losing or failing motivates some players to achieve at the highest level. Many employees are motivated by personal gain. Those type of employees are always looking to climb up the corporate ladder sometimes at the expense of others. Those employees are high achievers and producers because they are looking for accolades and promotions that will further their climb. Those that are motivated because it is the "right thing to do" are the employees that have a high ethical standard and are usually employees you can count on when things are tough. They are not swayed by promotions or accolades and are more concerned about doing the right thing.

The point of this topic is that many different things motivate employees, and their attitudes can be influenced by the leadership you provide. People of great character are able to improve the quality of their work, they increase their productivity and, more importantly, develop customer relationships that have a dramatic positive effect on the service they provide.

## Conclusion

Let's recap the tools and techniques discussed in this chapter. First, develop a succession plan that can also be used as a cross-training device. Second, refresh your talent pool. Give veterans of your staff a new beginning, and watch their efforts increase. Third, analyze your current benefit plans and work with your human resource department to make them competitive with other organizations. Finally, hire for character. Find people of great character and hire them so that you limit the amount of resources you spend hiring employees. Those techniques will be useful and help you retain your IT talent. Remember, you are not in control of individuals, but you can influence the outcome of whether people want to continue working for you and your organization.

---

### Discussion questions

1. What tools and techniques does your organization use to recruit and retain great talent?
2. Is your IT unit organized for success, or does it need tweaking for better performance?
3. Is your organization's benefits package comparable to other organizations in your region?
4. Has your succession plan taken into account employee character?
5. Does the economic recession hinder or help you retain your best employees?

6. What does the future hold for your organization in regards to recruitment of great employees?
7. Are you prepared to lead?

*A native of Tallahassee,* **Don DeLoach** *obtained his undergraduate degree from The Florida State University in 1981. He received his Masters Degree in Public Administration from Florida State in 1994.*

*His professional experience includes 27 years in the technology industry, of which the last 17 have been in management. Mr. DeLoach has worked on numerous projects involving systems application design, system selection, implementation and contract management. Currently, Mr. DeLoach is the Chief Information Systems Officer for the City of Tallahassee responsible for all of the technology needs of the city, including the management of the 800 MHz communication system. His staff of 87 employees maintains a state-of-the-art Oracle/PeopleSoft ERP and numerous mission critical applications necessary for the city to operate.*

*Mr. DeLoach is a former President of the Florida Local Government Information Systems Association, a current member of the Board of Directors for Public Technology Institute and was recognized this year as a "Premier 100" CIO by Computer World magazine.*

## REFERENCES

1 IT Recruitment and Retention Practices 2007 Gartner IT Market Compensation Study, Page 47

2 (http;//en.wikipedia.org/wiki/Maslow's_hierarchy_of_needs)

3 IT Recruitment and Retention Practices 2007 Gartner IT Market Compensation Study, Page 48

4 Character First!–Management Training Seminar Page 3. Character Council PO box 840 Marianna, Florida 32447

# 26. Navigating the Grey Areas: Ethical Actions and Decisions

**LIZA LOWERY MASSEY**

## Introduction

High ethical standards are especially important in the public sector because they are key to credibility and lead to increased support for government agencies and political leaders.[1] While most people would agree that ethics are important, the term means different things to different people: principles, judgments, right or wrong, rules, conduct, consequences, values and decisions. Ethics are more than just *not* doing the wrong things. While most people do not need a code of conduct to keep them from doing obviously bad things, not all situations are black and white—grey areas exist everywhere.

In addition to personally following ethical standards, public sector employees and organizations must avoid even the appearance of wrongful actions in order to maintain public trust. Personal ethics are not enough for public sector leaders who must also ensure ethical behavior by the people for whom they have responsibility and the organization as a whole. Finally, advances in technology have raised new ethical questions and issues regarding privacy, access, analysis and monitoring. This environment makes being an ethical public sector information technology (IT) leader more challenging than ever before.

## Ethics defined

To better understand ethics, it is important to first know what ethics are *not*.

- ♦ Ethics are not feelings, because not everyone feels badly when they do something wrong.
- ♦ Ethics are not only following laws, which can deviate from ethics, and not all situations are addressed by laws.

- ♦ Ethics are not just following societal norms, because cultures can be corrupt or turn a blind eye to unethical behavior.

- ♦ Ethics are not science, because, although it can provide explanations and data, science does not tell us what we should do.[2]

The word "ethics" is derived from the Greek root "ethos," which means "the persuasive appeal of one's character." An official definition of ethics is "a code of behavior, especially of a particular group, profession, or individual" and "the moral fitness of a decision or course of action."[3] Ethics equal action—doing the right things—not just knowing what is right. Therefore, ethics can best be defined as standards of conduct that direct how one should act based on moral duties, and derived from principles of right and wrong.[4]

## Survey says

According to a recent Ethics Resource Center (ERC) National Government Ethics Survey

(NGES), the public sector is at a high risk of experiencing major ethics scandals because many local and state entities, in particular, are failing to establish strong ethics programs. ERC finds that the programs have a direct correlation to ethical behavior. "Almost one-quarter of public sector employees identify their work environments as conducive to misconduct—places where there is strong pressure to compromise standards, where situations invite wrongdoing and/or employees' personal values conflict with the values espoused at work," says ERC President Patricia Harned, Ph.D.[5]

While the federal government fared somewhat better than state and local government workplaces, only 30% of federal workers surveyed believe their organizations have well-implemented ethics and compliance programs, and 10% believe a strong ethical culture exists in their federal workplace. The results are considerably worse at the state level—where 14% believe their work place has a strong ethics programs, and a mere 7% perceive a truly ethical culture—and in local government, where the figures are 14% and 9%, respectively. While 57% of public servants responded that they witnessed at least one type of misconduct in the previous year, only 34% of local and 29% of state workers actually reported the misconduct. The reasons behind the lack of reporting of misconduct in the public sector mirror those stated by private sector workers, and center around feelings of futility and fear of retaliation. Whistleblower hotlines do not help, with only 1% of public sector workers using them to report misconduct.[6]

The issues mentioned most often by public sector workers include:

♦ Government not being socially responsible by failing to consider its impact on the environment or future generations;

♦ An increase in situations that invite misconduct; and

♦ Fraudulent conduct, such as document and financial record alteration; lying to customers, vendors, the public and employees; and misreporting of hours worked.[7]

## Technology and ethics

The IT field is not immune to ethical dilemmas. A 2002 poll found that more than half of responding IT managers have been asked to do something unethical by their supervisors. A similar poll of IT consultants found that nearly 20% of them have been asked repeatedly to do something unethical, with 40% being asked to do so on rare occasions.[8] As such, IT leaders are faced with many ethical dilemmas as a function of their job responsibilities. Consider the following questions.

♦ Should I grant access to a system or data if I'm unsure that the requestor has a legitimate reason to ask for it? What if my boss or some other leader is asking?

♦ Should I set up a single account that is shared by many users to "get around" license requirements if directed to do so by my boss?

♦ How do I ensure that end users follow policies and procedures to protect the organization's digital assets? To what extent do I "take it out of their hands" by using technology to control it?

♦ Should we charge for access to public data? If so, under what circumstances?

♦ Should I look the other way if my boss or other leader in the organization has unlicensed software or potentially inappropriate material on his/her computer? What about personal data and programs?

♦ Should I push for new systems that potentially eliminate jobs and/or change the working environment in a potentially negative way?

♦ How do I determine what is intellectual property versus freely available program code, documents, etc.? If I'm unsure, should I use the resource or not?

Technology itself has raised many new ethical questions and issues related to privacy, access, control, analysis, monitoring and security. While legislation is just beginning to address some of the issues, an organization's leadership—not just the IT leader—must determine how to address them and other technology-related ethical questions. Consider the following.

♦ How much information should we collect and maintain? Should we let our customers know what is being collected and allow them to determine how it is used?

♦ Should electronic information be used just because it is readily available?

♦ How much should we spend to protect confidential electronic data?

♦ How much should we spend to ensure accuracy and prevent errors in our electronic information?

♦ How much should we spend to secure our systems?

♦ Are managers liable when systems and/or electronic information are compromised? If so, under what circumstances?

♦ Whom should we notify, and how quickly should we do it if personal and confidential information is compromised?

♦ Should we use technology to monitor our employees, and if so, to what extent, and how much do we tell them about what we are doing?

♦ Should we search social networking sites like Facebook and MySpace when conducting background checks?

♦ To what extent do we use our resources to ensure that every copy of software in use in our organization is legally licensed?

♦ What do we do if our analysis of seemingly unrelated electronic data identifies potential relationships or activities that are questionable or potentially illegal? What if we're wrong?

♦ Do we have an obligation to share negative data with other organizations, i.e., have data follow individuals or businesses? If so, under what circumstances?

## Principles and rules

With those grim statistics regarding the public sector workplace and ethical dilemmas introduced by technology as context, how do today's public sector IT leaders make ethical decisions? How do they help their employees behave ethically and maintain public trust? Understanding basic ethical standards is the foundation for answering those questions and implementing a strong ethics program. Experts suggest the following five ethical standards.[9]

## The Utilitarian Principle

This principle requires determination if the action will provide the most good or does the least harm to all who are impacted—customers, employees, stakeholders and the community. It is a consequences approach, where one attempts to increase good and decrease harm done.

## The Rights Principle

This principle requires determination if the action best protects and respects basic human rights of those impacted. Human rights include the right to be treated as an "end" not just a means to an end, to be told the truth, not to be injured, to a degree of privacy, etc.

## The Fairness Principle

This principle requires determination if the action treats all parties equally, or in the absence of equality, if they are treated fairly based on a defensible standard. For instance, people who work harder are paid more.

## The Common Good Principle

This principle requires determination if the action contributes to the overall good of the community. It is built upon common conditions that are important to everyone's welfare, including laws, public services and educational resources.

## The Virtue Principle

This principle requires determination if the action is consistent with certain ideal virtues that support fully developing our humanity to allow us to act in accordance with our highest potential of character. It is based on virtues such as beauty, truth, courage, compassion, generosity, love, integrity, fairness, etc.

Other practical ethical standards are rule-based and include the following.

## Disclosure Rule

This approach focuses on considering how one would feel explaining their decision or action to peers, colleagues, family and friends, or how the decision would look on the front page of the paper or on the evening news.

## Golden Rule

This approach focuses on putting one's self in the other person's place when making a decision or taking an action, and considering how that person would feel.

## Overnight Rule

This approach focuses on delaying making the decision or taking action for 24 hours or at least overnight—sleeping on it—to see if the action or decision remains the best course of action.

Using one or more of those standards or rules as a foundation when faced with an ethical dilemma helps public sector IT leaders respond in an ethical manner. Ensuring our employees understand and use the standards and rules ensures that they have the foundation for making ethical decisions and taking ethical actions, too.

## Responding ethically

With ethical standards and rules as the foundation, how does one go about making ethical decisions or taking ethical actions? How do today's public sector IT leaders ensure that their employees behave ethically? While experts suggest a variety of ways to respond ethically, the following steps outline a solid approach.

### Know your temptations

Identifying and understanding your particular temptations before you encounter an ethical dilemma helps you resist them, especially when you are in a stressful or crisis situation.

### The 6 W's of Escalation

Understanding the appropriate way to escalate an issue can mean the difference between disaster and success.

1. **Who?** Your immediate supervisor, working up the chain of command, and other pertinent people as needed, e.g., human resources

2. **What?** Issues that have clear political or customer fallout or based on the level or breadth of impact

3. **Where?** In the most appropriate setting and as privately or confidentially as possible

4. **Why?** To avoid eroding public trust and surprising officials

5. **When?** ASAP—as quickly as PRACTICAL—with time for consideration if possible

6. **How?** With all pertinent facts and a recommendation for action

### Recognize ethical dilemmas

The first step in responding in an ethical manner is learning to recognize ethical issues. This approach means perceiving when an action or decision might be damaging to the organization, stakeholders, employees or the community before responding. It also means identifying and addressing those situations where an action or decision might be legal or correct but will appear wrong to the public and media.

### Consider the facts and responses

The next step is to gather facts and information regarding the situation to the extent possible based upon the time available and identify several potential responses.

### Use tactics that illuminate ethical choices

Next, apply one or more ethical standards or rules to the potential responses to see how each fairs when examined more closely.

### Seek input

If the choice is still unclear, seek input regarding the situation by talking to a boss, trusted colleague or other trusted advisor.

### Avoid surprises

If the situation is particularly sensitive, notify your boss, elected officials, etc., as soon as practical to ensure that they are not caught off guard should the situation escalate, or your action or decision causes problems or garners negative publicity.

## Ethical leadership

Being a public sector leader means that every decision or action taken in the work place is carefully watched and often imitated by subordinates and peers. Leaders who make ethical decisions and take ethical actions serve as good personal examples for others. So, how does a public sector IT leader set the right example for ethical workplace behavior?

◆ **Define it**
Create a personal ethics statement.

◆ **Publicize it**
Share the ethics statement with your employees, stakeholders and vendors.

◆ **Live it**
Act in accordance with your ethics statement, setting the example for others.

◆ **Evaluate it**
Periodically consider your actions and decisions to ensure that they are in alignment with your personal ethics statement, and invite evaluation and feedback from others, such as your boss, peers and employees.

## Credibility killers

Unethical behavior is a surefire credibility killer and can damage or even kill your public sector career. Recently, Michael S. Wade outlined 10 ways to erode trust. The list is a valuable reminder of unethical behaviors to avoid.[10]

◆ **Fail to honor commitments**
Make a commitment to another person and later switch your position without giving that person timely and explicit notice.

◆ **Over-promise and under-deliver**
Make grand promises then skimp on delivery or fail to deliver at all.

◆ **Don't return phone calls**
It is the silent way of saying that you don't count. If you're that busy, leave a quick message to buy time for a more lengthy response.

◆ **Don't return e-mail messages**
Technology gives us new and faster ways to show our indifference. An automated response to buy time is better than no response at all.

◆ **Inflate words of praise**
Your words are your currency. Don't devalue them.

◆ **Take credit for the work of others**
Everyone will notice, and you'll stop receiving credit even when you do something.

- ◆ **Don't admit mistakes**

  This may be both a denial of responsibility and of reality. Gain credibility by promptly "fessing up" to your blunders.

- ◆ **Fail to provide reasonable support to others**

  The resentment this creates may last for years.

- ◆ **Be hypocritical (pretend to have ethical principles)**

  The gap between your words and your actions can be detected in nanoseconds.

- ◆ **Deceive others**

  Even well-intentioned lies possess the potential to explode and damage credibility. Ethicist Michael Josephson asks, "How many times do you have to lie to be a liar?" One time can be sufficient to sink a career.

## Ethics in action

If a strong ethics program leads to more ethical behavior, how does a public sector IT leader implement one in the workplace? A recommended course of action that builds on the information presented in this chapter follows.

- ◆ **Collaborate to create**

  Involve all stakeholders in designing a program that includes a code of ethics for the organization. Include recommendations for education, publicity, practice and evaluation.

- ◆ **Make it public**

  Publicly announce the program, explaining the code of ethics, outlining the program requirements and components, and stressing its importance.

- ◆ **Show commitment**

  Provide adequate time and resources to plan, implement and manage the ethics program.

- ◆ **Hold each other accountable**

  Create an environment that rewards ethical behavior, encourages shining the light on questionable behavior and swiftly addresses unethical behavior.

- ◆ **Implement it**

  Include a strategy for making ethics an integral part of the workplace through education, practice and feedback.

- ◆ **Reflect, review and renew**

  Implement a process for ongoing assessment that includes an annual review and re-adoption of the code of ethics, evaluation of recent ethical dilemmas and responses—focusing on lessons learned—and identification of ways to communicate it to new employees and stakeholders.

The City of Los Angeles provides a good example of a strong ethics program. In 2006, Mayor Antonio Villaraigosa issued an Executive Directive on Ethics that required appointment of a high-level Ethics Liaison for each city department, instructed each department to assess and update their Conflict of Interest Code, and required all city officials to complete a two-hour ethics course. The mandate built upon the first ethics-related directive he issued shortly after taking office in

2005, which outlined a series of steps for city officials to take in maintaining and enhancing public confidence. An Ethics Pledge also was developed and distributed to all department heads. Additionally, the city has a documented Code of Ethics, an active Ethics Commission and staff, and an abundant amount of ethics-related information and resources available on its website.[11]

---

### Permission or Forgiveness?

Is it better to ask for permission or forgiveness? The following lists can help you and your employees decide when to seek approval for an action or decision in advance, or when to take the action and, hopefully, avoid the necessity of asking for forgiveness.

| PERMISSION | FORGIVENESS |
|---|---|
| • Outside your scope of responsibility | • Within your authority/responsibility |
| • Impacts a large number of people | • Time sensitive, e.g., severe consequences if not done right away |
| • Funds are requested beyond your authority | • Is an emergency or threat to safety or health |
| • Goes against established agreements | • Need to act, and benefits clearly outweigh the costs |
| • Impacts a sensitive area, e.g., safety, politics | • Must act, and you are reasonably certain your boss would make the same decision |
| • May be illegal, unsafe, immoral | • Must act, and it holds up to tests, e.g., ethical standards and rules |
| • Has never been addressed before | • Must act, makes sense—is a calculated risk |
| • May violate a rule, policy or established procedure | • The outcome is predictable |
| • Not sure if you should go ahead | |
| • Expected to get permission in advance | |
| • Unplanned use or commitment of resources | |

---

## Putting it all together

By using the standard ethical principles and rules, and following the ethical response process outlined in this chapter, public sector IT leaders can confront workplace issues and respond in an ethical manner. By implementing a strong ethics program and setting the example in all that they do, public sector IT leaders also can extend their personal ethics to their employees and the organization. Through those efforts, credibility and public support are maintained and potentially enhanced.

> *"Public confidence in the integrity of the government is in-dispensable to faith in democracy, and when we lose faith in the system, we lose faith in everything we fight and spend for."*
>
> — Adlai Stevenson, Former Governor of Illinois

## Discussion questions

1. Identify an ethical dilemma that has arisen in your organization in the recent past due to the introduction of technology. What made it an ethical dilemma? Identify the stakeholders and the type of dilemma, e.g., legal, policy and procedure-related, employee morale, damaging to public trust, appearance only, etc.

2. Considering the ethical dilemma from question #1, apply two ethical principles or rules to develop a response to it. Evaluate how this response differs or is similar to what was done?

3. Develop or update your own personal ethics statement. How will it assist you in the workplace? Does it address or assist you with dealing with your personal ethical temptations.

4. Consider how you would escalate an ethical dilemma related to technology, such as excessive personal use of business resources by your immediate supervisor. Do you have policies in place to address the situation? Would you confront your supervisor? Do you involve his/her boss, human resources, etc.? Should you explain the situation to your employees? If so, how?

5. Describe what you would do if an IT employee brought "evidence" to you that another high placed employee in your organization was accessing personal data for fraudulent reasons. Assume the activity is taking place as the matter is brought to your attention. Further assume that the "evidence" is not conclusive but looks very damaging. Do you act immediately to stop the access or seek permission? Do you escalate the issue or try to obtain additional evidence? What do you tell the employee who brought the evidence forward?

6. Does your IT department have a Code of Ethics? If so, what updates are needed. If not, outline a Code of Ethics for your IT department.

**Liza Lowery Massey** *left public service in 2005 to establish The CIO Collaborative to provide CIO advisory and consulting services. She also is an adjunct professor in the College of Business for the Executive MBA program at the University of Nevada, Las Vegas, a Senior Fellow with the Center for Digital Government, and a columnist for Public CIO Magazine. Previously, Ms. Lowery Massey served as the CIO for the City of Los Angeles and, prior to that, the City/County of San Francisco. During her public sector career, she was recognized in the Top 25 Doers, Dreamers & Drivers of IT in Government. Ms. Lowery Massey can be reached at liza@ciocollaborative.com. Visit www.ciocollaborative.com for more information about The CIO Collaborative.*

## REFERENCES

1 http://www.scu.edu/ethics/practicing/focusareas/government_ethics/publc-sector-ethics.html

2 http://www.scu.edu/ethics/practicing/decision/framework.html

3 http://www.thefreedictionary.com/ethics

4 http://www.esec.pt/veem/materials/pdf/aditionalreadings/makingethicaldecisions.pdf

5 https://www.ethics.org/about-erc/press-releases.asp?aid=1148

6 ditto

7 ditto

8 http://articles.techrepublic.com.com/5100-10878_11-1054036.html?tag=rbxccnbtr1

9 http://www.scu.edu/ethics/practicing/decision/framework.html

10 http://www.usnews.com/blogs/outside-voices-careers/2008/6/27/10-ways-youll-erode-trust.html

11 http://ethics.lacity.org/MayorExecDirec.cfm

# PART FIVE:

# Knowledge & Records Management

# 27. Knowledge Retention

**LINDA BLANKENSHIP**

## Introduction

In every organization, including those in the government sector, intellectual capital has become a key enabler of providing products and services to customers. In the past several decades, intellectual capital in organizations has advanced greatly, in part because information technologies have played a key role in enhancing the knowledge cycle. Knowledge retention and management has become a field of its own. Retaining critical knowledge certainly will improve service delivery, enhance customer satisfaction and enable organizational innovation.

Information technology can be a key enabler in retaining the data, information, knowledge and even wisdom of the organization. Figure 27-1 illustrates the knowledge value pyramid.

Because the chief information officer "holds the keys" to the organization's technology, CIOs must play a leading role in facilitating the management of organizational knowledge. Local, state and federal government, like every other segment of employment, is facing a situation of unprecedented knowledge loss. In the next 10 years, most organizations will see an influx of new, largely unseasoned workers at the same time as the knowledge that they have paid decades to accumulate walks out the door. Research has shown that managers who plan now can reap the benefits of retaining valuable worker knowledge at the same time as they position their organizations to leverage new knowledge to meet new ways of doing business; those who don't will be forced to recreate knowledge at substantial cost to their organizations.[1]

Organizational knowledge consists of a wide variety of types, some of which is written, but most of which is unwritten. The written portion consists of documented knowledge that can range from simple staff directories, online policies, meeting minutes and reports, to databases with detailed information on the organization's customer base, as well as key operational information. Such knowledge is termed "explicit knowledge" because it has been captured in a written format.

It is important to note that not all "written" documents specifically comprise important knowledge of the organization that needs to be maintained. Knowledge retention is accomplished

**Figure 27-1.** The Knowledge Pyramid

at a cost to the organization. Therefore, organizations must determine what knowledge is critical by considering the value, or business case, for maintaining it.

However, there is another type of knowledge that comprises the vast majority of organizational knowledge that is learned over time and, therefore, is "hard won." That knowledge is termed "tacit knowledge," and it includes knowledge accumulated by experience over time, from experience, lessons learned from conducting business operations over time. Tacit knowledge is comprised of unwritten knowledge that experienced staff have in their heads—lessons learned from conducting business operations over a period of time.

A very simple example of tacit knowledge is "know who" knowledge, in the sense that over time, experienced workers "know who" to go to to get things done. A more complex example of tacit knowledge is the infrequent but highly important processes that operational staff know to use to recover from an emergency event, for example, an experienced water treatment plant operator who knows how to recover a filter that is clogged from highly turbid source water, such as during spring runoff.

Given that systems are constantly changing and associated business operations and practices are constantly changing, when combined with the previously noted staff turnover and retirement, illustrates the very real potential for a knowledge loss of crisis proportions.

Knowledge management is a field that approaches the management of knowledge systematically to ensure its retention, transfer and reuse. However, not all knowledge can or should be retained, so wise CIOs need to strategically and deliberately plan what needs to be retained. The approaches to knowledge retention are widely varied, ranging from simple documentation methods, such as developing document repositories, to people-oriented approaches, such as mentoring, storytelling and organizational learning and training. A blend of approaches likely will be needed to retain the most valuable organizational approaches, and those approaches will be interrelated and, therefore, must support and complement one other.

## The role of information technology

Information technology is a critical enabler for knowledge retention. Information technology can be leveraged to store vast amounts of information about local government operations and assets. Governments deliver vital health, social, security, education and countless other services. In addition, governments are responsible for the stewardship of assets worth trillions of dollars: roads, schools, emergency facilities, water and sewer systems, and so on. Workers will have large amounts of undocumented knowledge about the services and assets that are critical to carrying out the day-to-day and emergency services that taxpayers expect and are vital to our economy and way of life.

Standard operating procedures, policies and other critical documents can be kept in a repository as a source of "organizational knowledge" for new workers.

Well-established content management systems can reduce the amount of time wasted on fruitless searches for information and subsequent "re-creation of the wheel," allowing workers to focus on innovating instead.

## A range of solutions will be needed, supported by the appropriate information technology

However, managers must understand that, while information technology will be required, it will not be sufficient alone to ensure critical knowledge is retained. Research has shown that a blend of approaches, combining technology, processes and people, supported by technology, will be required to successfully manage knowledge.

Note: It is important to understand that public agencies are subject to the provisions of state and federal freedom of information acts, which may prohibit destruction of public records without authorization from the central agency. In addition, there are other sources of guidelines for records retention, such as those published by International Standards Organization on records management."[2]

However, records management is only one small component of knowledge management. Therefore, CIOs should be prepared to be part of and even lead a corporate effort to retain, manage and transfer knowledge readily in the organization.

## How to get started

CIOs should ensure that well-developed processes and policies are in place for knowledge management. Such policies should address what types of documents need to be archived and maintained, and what methods are appropriate to archive them.

If such processes and policies have not yet been well-established or well-executed, a program will need to be designed. Given the scope of such an undertaking, it is easy to imagine that establishing a program can easily crumble under the sheer weight of it. CIOs should consider starting with a modest effort to get the organizational ball rolling, gain momentum and expand as experience and success dictate. If possible, given the needs of the organization, it is best to start with a relatively small type of pilot project. Such an approach allows the greatest chance of success. "Quick wins" can be achieved and used to build momentum, tailor the program based on lessons learned and expand it accordingly.

Like many projects, executive sponsorship and a project champion are needed. Very often, the strategies to be put in place should be supported by the elected or appointed leadership of the organization.

In terms of selecting the type of project, start where the organization's "energy" is—where the most critical business need exists.

Pilot projects offer the opportunity to learn, adapt and grow the program.

Communicating success will be important to keep the momentum going and enable expansion. Rewards can be important reinforcements and should be in keeping with the organization's approach. Non-monetary incentives, such as a certificates, recognition on an employee website or newsletter, and letters of recommendation, can go a long way toward providing positive reinforcement.

A business case can be developed by estimating benefits and identifying costs for the program.

## Conduct a knowledge audit

Organizations looking to establish a document or content management system should conduct a knowledge audit. The first step involves identifying what the important business processes are. That step helps to define the boundaries of what is important to create and/or maintain.

The next step involves rigorous examination of sources of content. Sources include articles of incorporation, by-laws, policies, standard operating procedures, master plan documents, etc. A good standard archive should be in place to collect those documents and place them in a central repository. Then, senior managers can assess what is available, and more importantly, what is missing.

Process owners, subject matter experts, operators and users, as well as new hires can potentially be involved.

## Develop a good taxonomy

A taxonomy is needed to categorize and catalog information in a logical and accessible manner for users. A taxonomy is a classification methodology based on relationships. Examples of common taxonomies include the Dewey Decimal system, Library of Congress classification system and Linnaeus' taxonomy for classifying plants and animals. If a good taxonomy is not created, users may not be able to find the information that they need, resulting in the need for time wasted searching for and recreating knowledge. Search capabilities can only go so far in helping users find relevant content.

A good taxonomy will use terms that are well-understood by the user community. Organization-wide information should be organized using a common taxonomy. However, for individual business units, it is not necessary to organize information in the exact same way for each unit.

Ideally, content depth within the classification system should be relatively uniform. Categories should be mutually exclusive to the greatest extent possible, again, to facilitate easy location of relevant content.

Finally, a good taxonomy should be comprehensive so that use of categories that comprise miscellaneous or unrelated information is minimized, again, to facilitate retrieval of information by users. It should not be too narrow, nor changed too frequently.

## Develop a process to keep content updated

Organizations with effective content management systems must develop a rigorous process to ensure that information is kept up-to-date. Users must be able to feel confident that they can rely on the system to find accurate, current content; otherwise, the organization will quickly devolve to creating new content. Further, most knowledge typically has a "shelf life." Therefore, the process must include a periodic but regular review cycle by subject matter experts to review and update the content of the key documents.

## Knowledge retention methods supported by IT

As previously noted, deep tacit knowledge will not get written down easily or archived using methods that are primarily driven by information technology. Those knowledge retention approaches will require the active involvement of people, and information technology will play a minor or possibly even no role. It is important for the CIO to realize, support and even champion the whole range of knowledge retention approaches, including the following.

## Mentoring

Mentoring is often thought about in terms of leadership development as well as succession planning. However, mentoring can play a significant role in retaining organization knowledge. For example, mentoring is an excellent approach for transferring cultural knowledge, such as the experience of the organization in "how we get things done around here." Mentoring also can readily transfer "know-who" knowledge, particularly of the type that does not lend itself to capturing in a written format. There are many resources that are readily available on how to design mentoring programs.

## Storytelling

Storytelling also can be a powerful tool for retaining tacit knowledge, such as cultural and historical knowledge. Native Americans and other cultures have used storytelling as a way of archiving their history in absence of a written form of language. Stories can convey a rich set of information, such as organization history, great successes and failures, highly complex tasks, or otherwise dry technical material. Information technology can play a role in archiving the stories of experienced workers by videotaping or digitally recording such stories. Generally, they will need rigorous editing to be truly useful as knowledge retention tools.

## Approaches to using retirees

Retiring or retired employees have great amounts of tacit knowledge, some of which can be converted to explicit knowledge through information technology approaches. Restrictions on the ability to continue to use retirees vary widely by locality and state. Governments that rely on retired employees need to plan specifically for capturing and retaining knowledge, or else they are merely delaying the loss of that knowledge. Retired workers can document a whole host of information, ranging from location of specific assets to standard operating procedures to best practices to training. Some agencies use databases to track retiree expertise.

CIOs should recognize that such workers may need specific support to be able to use certain information technologies because they are not comfortable or adept at using them, and so the information technology itself can be a barrier to knowledge capture. For example, a knowledgeable field worker who understands the location and condition of certain infrastructure may find that using a keyboard to document information in a Geographic Information System is an unfamiliar skill.

## Supporting communities of practice

Communities of practice are groups of individuals that come together to interact regularly using face-to-face and virtual methods for purposes of providing assistance, knowledge sharing, developing best practices, and conducting research and innovation. Information technology can help support communities of practice, particularly in large organizations where the opportunity for face-to-face meetings is less. Approaches such as blogs, SharePoint sites and other social networking approaches can greatly assist such communities in transferring tacit knowledge and capturing such knowledge to make it explicit for future uses.

## Organizational learning and training

Organizational learning and training for purposes of knowledge retention must specifically be designed to shorten the cycle between training and application of knowledge. Here again, however, IT also can help support knowledge transfer through training programs using a wide variety of online and computer-based training systems. When appropriately combined with more traditional classroom and on-the-job training, this approach creates a rich blend of training, learning and knowledge retention opportunities.

Lastly, knowledge must be applied and can be applied only if it is truly "learned." Such learning often occurs through employee development programs. The Kirkpatrick Model of training developed by Donald Kirkpatrick in the 1950s proposes a four-step learning process: Reaction, Learning, Behavior Change and Results. The first step is Reaction to a training process. The fourth step, Results, in which the organization realizes the benefit of the knowledge, can only occur through opportunities to apply knowledge. Employee training and development must incorporate "teachable moments" to reduce the cycle time between learning and application in order for the organization to realize the benefits.

## Creating a knowledge sharing culture

CIOs and other C-suite executives should not wait for the culture to change to support knowledge retention efforts. Rather, the knowledge-retention efforts can be used to help change the culture by getting people to share—and not hoard—knowledge, even as experienced workers are retiring and being replaced by new staff.

---

### Discussion questions

1. What are the two principal types of knowledge that organizations must manage?
2. How can organizations best organize their written knowledge?
3. What approaches and methods can be used to develop a content management system?
4. Give four methods that can be used to retain and transfer organization's unwritten knowledge.
5. What role does IT play in managing unwritten knowledge?

**Linda Blankenship** *is Principal Consultant with EMA, Inc. where she consults on a range of management topics, including asset management, knowledge management, strategic planning, operations optimization, benchmarking and other continuous improvement efforts. She has more than 25 years experience working with local government and utilities as a consultant, association executive and staff member. Linda has a B.A.Sc. in Civil Engineering from the University of Waterloo, an MBA in International Finance from The American University, Washington, D.C., and is a licensed professional engineer in the Province of Ontario. She is an affiliate member of the American Society of Civil Engineers and a member of the American Water Works Association and the Water Environment Federation. She is a Board Certified Environmental Engineer.*

## REFERENCES

1 AwwaRF (now the Water Research Foundation), Strategies to Help Drinking Water Utilities Ensure Effective Retention of Knowledge. 2008.

2 See the following on the ISO website, www.iso.org:

ISO 15489-1:2001
Information and documentation—Records management—Part 1: General

ISO/TR 26122:2008
Information and documentation—Work process analysis for records

ISO/TS 23081-2:2007
Information and documentation—Records management processes—Metadata for records—Part 2: Conceptual and implementation issues

# 28. Evolving State of Records Management

**KIMBERLY NELSON**

Anyone who has read a newspaper recently has seen any number of stories about government officials having to admit to emails and other documents being deleted and lost. Countless records across the country are being lost every day because government employees, faced with a staggering growth in electronic documents, do not understand how to preserve the electronic documents they create. It is astonishing to think that 100 years from now historians are more likely to have better records documenting the Civil War than the Gulf War.

While government officials have looked to technology and the Internet to transform their processes, improve customer service and drive efficiencies, there often has been insufficient regard for how to manage the electronic content in both the short and long term. All too often, the records and content management aspects of a project were afterthoughts, if addressed at all. The failure to do so has resulted in too many government officials being unprepared to meet public scrutiny of their actions. When questioned about emails or other documents that cannot be produced, government officials find themselves in the position of having to admit to incompetence or malfeasance—not a choice any government official wants to face. And now because of recent federal changes, the failure to produce relevant documents in civil court proceedings may carry with it excessive penalties if the officials cannot demonstrate a good faith effort to appropriately preserve important documents and records.

## What is records management?

All too often there seems to be confusion among government employees to the requirements for public records preservation, disclosure and discovery. Therefore, the first step in preserving important records is to understand what needs to be preserved.

At Microsoft, we define Enterprise Content Management (ECM) as "the orderly management of information." *Information* may be found in both physical and digital artifacts. *Management* means knowing what to do with those artifacts, when to do so, and ultimately knowing the state and location of the artifacts. And lastly, *orderly* means proactive rather than reactive management. As indicated by the diagram below, records are a subset of all documents that must be managed by an agency.

Records, which memorialize a government decision, policy or activity, may take many forms (e.g., video, voice or electronic mail or word processing documents). Like traditional paper records, electronic records have to be located, retrieved and stored according to established records retention schedules. They also should be destroyed according to the same retention schedules, unless litigation or other extenuating circumstances dictate otherwise. The final preservation of the artifacts ultimately becomes the responsibility of the government's archivists.

Records management was never easy, but further complicating the issue are the explosion in electronic information and the legal, policy and social changes that have increasingly expanded the scope of content and records.

## New uses of technology continue to stress records managers

Government officials are facing unprecedented drivers that are rapidly changing the face of government and the way governments manage records. One needs only to look to the recent presidential election and the adoption of social networking concepts in government to appreciate that the technology driver

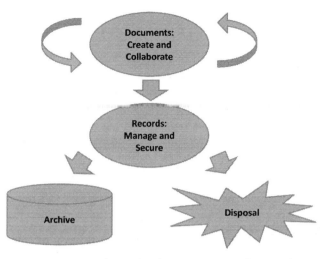

**Figure 28–1.** Life Cycle of Documents and Records Management. ECM means managing the full lifecycle in an electronic fashion.

that pushed government processes onto the Internet over a decade ago is showing no sign of slowing. Officials have yet to understand how to proactively manage the explosion of information driven by the first generation of the Internet, let alone that produced in a Web 2.0 environment. As more government content moves to websites, the number of documents in electronic format only and the ephemeral nature of websites will increasingly challenge records managers. At the same time, new legal, regulatory and social changes are further challenging records managers. Recently enacted requirements, like the Federal Rules of Civil Procedure, and legislative and public oversight of government activities during disasters like Katrina have increased the pressure on government officials to better manage broader sets of documents.

The amount of electronically generated information is growing at an alarming rate due to the ease with which documents can be created today. According to Ferris Research, 35% to 60% of today's critical information is stored in email systems. Moreover, roughly 97% of all information is stored electronically and as little as 3% of information is converted to paper form.[1] The National Association of State CIOs issued a report in October 2008 citing similar concerns.[2]

Traditionally, paper documents were created with the assistance of clerical staff and stored in local or centrally managed filing cabinets managed by clerical staff. As professionals began creating their own documents, agencies reduced or eliminated full-time professional clerical staff. While document creation didn't suffer, document retention and preservation most certainly did. After all, even in the days of professional clerical staff, "filing" was often the last task to get done. Little has changed today. Most employees find it far easier to maintain a document on their own computer, rather than try to understand the complex rules around records management and retention. Consequently, sending properly tagged electronic documents to centralized repositories just doesn't happen often enough.

The ubiquitous nature of the Internet has made document publication easier than ever. As a cost-saving measure, many government officials now favor creating documents in electronic form only and posting those documents on their websites.[3] Not only are electronic reports cheaper to produce, but they also can be more easily corrected or updated. Electronic documents do not require large and costly physical storage facilities, minimize wasteful paper usage and reduce transportation and packaging costs—all favorable characteristics in an increasingly environmentally friendly world.

While technology has driven those efficiencies, there is a downside. What constitutes an official version of a government report? What happens when the electronic version is taken off a website? What assurance do we have that documents will be in readable format 50 years from now? Those and other questions have to be addressed by a responsible records management program.

Contemporary communications, collaboration and networking tools further complicate records management issues. As government officials use podcasts, blogs and video streaming to announce and describe decisions, it becomes more difficult to identify and preserve "the official record" of a decision or action. If the official government announcement takes the form of a streamed video, are agencies preserving the record appropriately?

As employees work collaboratively and create wikis and share sites, which employees are responsible for purging and preserving documents? As the government creates more new interactive web sites with government officials responding to questions and issues online, how do those forms of communication fit into the traditional records retention schedules?

There is also the more recent phenomenon of government officials choosing to use "personal" email accounts for some work-related correspondence. Who is making decisions as to whether those electronic files should be preserved as official government records? Regardless of whether the correspondence constitutes official government business, there may be an important historical perspective that most certainly will be lost because personal email is not preserved.

Consider the rich perspective we have from reading the personal letters between John and Abigail Adams. Now, imagine the kinds of texts and emails that will be sent between President Obama and his wife, Michelle, now the president is carrying a mobile device of his own. Fortunately, the White House has made the decision to preserve those messages as records where appropriate. Just days after the inauguration, David Gibbs, the president's press secretary stated, "The presumption is that any email Obama sends will be subject to the Presidential Records Act."[4] He further added that there are some "narrow exemptions" in the law for "strictly personal communications." Decisions like that one are important to ensuring the preservation of our nation's rich history.

## Electronic discovery raises the demand for accountability and performance

Further complicating traditional Enterprise Content Management is the fact that the federal government in December 2006 issued new Federal Rules of Civil Procedure that recognize the importance of electronic documents to legal proceedings. The rules outline the requirements for electronic discovery (eDiscovery), which is the discovery of information in electronic format during civil litigation. Electronically stored information includes "... writings, drawings, graphs, charts, photographs, sound recordings, images and other data or data compilations stored in any medium from which information can be obtained..."[5] In the process of eDiscovery, data of all types can serve as evidence in a civil court proceeding.

The new federal rules require that parties in a civil proceeding discuss what types of content will be searched and how parties will preserve, format and access relevant content at the outset of litigation. Judges and parties in the proceeding expect government agencies to have knowledge about and control over all electronically stored information. In those situations it is important that an agency be able to implement appropriate notifications quickly and to place litigation "holds" on data in order to preserve any information that may be evidence and, thus, relevant or material to the proceeding.

For many years, government agencies relied on only hard copy formats for official record keeping purposes. The most common method of preserving important email messages and attachments was, and is, to print them on paper and store them in paper files. That was certainly the case during my years in government. In fact, until just recently, the United States Environmental Protection Agency did not allow for the electronic storage of official records. Should those paper based agencies become involved in litigation, they may, under the new federal rules of civil procedure, find it difficult to explain why they cannot retrieve electronic versions of documents in their "native" or proprietary form. All agencies, regardless of the propensity for litigation, should consider how they will move to some form of electronic record keeping or archiving solutions. Organizations of a more litigious nature should be particularly concerned, as the failure to take proactive steps can result in severe penalties.

Like Freedom of Information laws, the new eDiscovery requirements apply to a broad scope of documents within an agency, not just preserved records. Therefore, it is paramount that an agency has a governance process for managing all content—not just preserved records.

## Records often lost despite records management efforts

A 2008 survey by Kahn Consulting, Inc., in association with other industry partners, indicates companies are implementing records management programs, but significant work is necessary in order to realize the full value of those efforts. While 90% of companies were already addressing governance, risk management and compliance (GRC), electronic discovery and records and information management issues, 70% expected to make changes in those areas within 18 months.[6] Like private sector organizations, government organizations at all levels are expected to focus increased attention on these matters. Recent surveys of both state and federal CIOs placed records management in the top 10 lists of issues for both groups, due in large part to the issues discussed above.

Despite the increased importance of the issue and the increased attention by senior officials, records management programs often fail because they are not designed with the end user in mind. While executive attention can be extremely helpful to the overall solution, without end user support and cooperation, the best records management solution will fail. It is important to understand why so many records management systems have failed so it can be prevented in the future.

Some users cannot properly define a record, and those that can often find records management solutions unnecessarily time consuming and confusing. Some agencies have hundreds of different retention schedules, making it difficult to remember what has to be maintained and for how long. Many systems require time-consuming document tagging and confusing processes for filing records. Rather than try to understand complex agency policies, many users arbitrarily document with little regard for the official policies.

The New York Times recently referenced a report by the Government Accountability Office that described widespread violations of federal record-keeping requirements. According to the article, "Email records of senior officials were not consistently preserved." The article further noted that some officials keep tens of thousands of messages in their email accounts, where they "cannot be efficiently searched" and are not accessible to others.[7]

Records managers often have found themselves in the unenviable position of establishing and overseeing policies for what most employees considered a mundane aspect of the job. Historically, records managers received little oversight from senior executives and little regard from individual workers. Like that old Rodney Dangerfield remark: Records managers often felt as though they just can't get any respect. Fortunately, those days are changing.

Today, responsible senior career and elected officials fully understand that the public expects a high level of transparency and that a well-managed records management solution, for both paper and electronic records, is pivotal to providing that transparency and maintaining the public trust. They also understand that the absence of such a program puts the agency at risk for litigation. The failure to locate, retrieve and present material records during litigation can result not only in significant penalties, but also the eventual erosion of public trust. Unfortunately, too many public officials learned that the hard way after public reports or court cases uncovered records mismanagement.

## Moving to an enterprise-wide content management solution

It is somewhat counterintuitive to talk about widespread records management problems when, in fact, government has been performing the function for hundreds of years. We are all accustomed to government's role in maintaining records of the most important milestones and events in our lives: births and deaths, land purchases and court proceedings, weddings and divorces. "County governments serve many public service roles on behalf of their respective constituencies," explains Ross King, deputy director of the Association County Commissioners of Georgia (ACCG). "One of the least mentioned, yet vitally important roles, is that of public records management. Property records, court records, personal records are all officially 'managed' by dedicated and professionally trained elected and appointed county government officials."

Why is it, then, that we now read and hear so much about government's inability to manage today's records?

Historically, governments maintained a large volume of records, but those records represented a fairly narrow set of the overall agency content. Today, the amount of content expected to be managed is much broader. The narrow, yet deep, set of content is depicted as the "head" of the curve on the left side of Figure 28–2, and the new broader set of content is the "long and growing tail of unmanaged content"[8] in today's organizations.

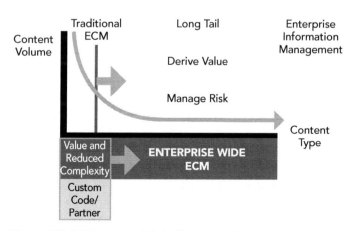

**Figure 28–2.** Enterprise Wide Electronic Content Management

The documents at the head of the curve typically represent those that are "process-centric," such as birth and death records, while those at the tail of the curve represent documents that are "user centric," such as email.[9] The process-centric records are often managed because they have been long-standing government functions and have had customized solutions for capturing and recording transactions. The only real downside to those customized solutions is that they have been costly and difficult to implement. Because of the cost and complexity of the solutions, we now see the long and growing problem of unmanaged content, as traditional solutions are cost prohibitive for wide-scale implementation. It's that aspect that today represents the challenge to government agencies and creates the greatest degree of vulnerability, particularly with the new rules of civil procedure mentioned above.

Most government officials now realize that traditional records management solutions are simply impractical for the enterprise; they are too costly, too customized and too complex. Government officials must look for solutions that will cover the broad spectrum of content—from the head to the tail—and engage all end users in the solution.

"As technology evolves, the opportunity to effectively and efficiently manage current and historical records in a digital format is available and strongly recommended," King says. "That is why ACCG is working with the Georgia State Archives staff as well as with qualified private sector vendors to help address these identified county government records management needs."

## Getting the end user in the new records management game

Getting the end user involved requires a shift in thinking. Instead of thinking of records management as a reactive, after-the-fact process, responsible officials need to instrument records management tasks into the overall process of information lifecycle management. Tasks such as metadata entry, categorization and record declaration are all steps that can be driven down to the users creating and managing the content proactively, rather than relying on a small team of records managers to perform clean-up on all the content once it arrives at the organization's official record repository.

Over the years, it was acceptable to educate staff using a more traditional, and thus narrow, view of records management concepts, including how to define a record and how to file and preserve it accordingly. Inherent in that approach was the inevitable and acceptable fact that the remainder of content would go largely unmanaged. Often, documents were sent to records centers years after creation only as files were being purged. Now that all information is discoverable, all information must be treated like a record throughout the document lifecycle process from creation to eventual destruction or archival. Failure to do so puts the organization at tremendous risk, and ignoring the problem only increases unnecessary liability. In the table (see next page), we look at the various aspects of effective information management and characterize the aspects according to the traditional way (Head) records are managed versus the emerging way (Tail).

As noted in the table, approximately 99% of all content is undefined as a record. Given the new discovery requirements, it is apparent records managers cannot be solely responsible for managing the full extent of an organization's content. Equally unrealistic, however, is the expectation that those same users can be expected to manage the content without an efficient and effective governance framework. Therefore, the role of records managers must include the creation of a governance structure that covers document lifecycles and agency workflows. That

| | Head | Tail |
|---|---|---|
| Governance | Control | Manage |
| Information | Defined | Undefined |
| Classification Schema | Classified | Flexible |
| Metadata | Taxonomy | Folksonomy |
| Content Type | Mechanism for record content | Mechanism to scale policy and process |
| Business Process | Transactional—managed by IT | Interactive with need to decentralize management |
| Participants | ~1% | ~99% |

framework must be seamlessly integrated into the workflow, using an interface that is common across the organization and familiar to the users. The approach must be easy to use and support the management of records created via standard processes, as well as those created for ad hoc purposes.

## Government solution fundamentals

### Implement a lifecycle management approach

Organizations should consider solutions that streamline and improve core government business processes by applying rules *throughout* the record's lifecycle, particularly categorizing records *early* in the creation process. That can be done for both process- and user-centric situations. The enterprise governance framework should cover the full spectrum of content created by an organization and fully integrate all vertical business applications, capturing records from business applications, as well as those created by end users independently with automatically created metadata. That will reduce risk created by user error. In addition, users should be encouraged to create metadata at the time a document is being created and not wait until such time that the document is filed in a records management system.

### Tightly control and monitor access

Inappropriate access to and modification of documents can undermine historical accuracy and have negative and costly litigation consequences. Records management solutions should limit access to authorized users to prevent document tampering or unintended alterations. An appropriate solution should define access rights with an appropriate degree of flexibility to meet agency business needs and statutory requirements, including privacy protections. The dual and sometimes competing goals of preserving records for public review and access and protecting privacy of constituent, employee and confidential information require a solution with built-in rights management and policy enforcement. The solution should incorporate activity auditing to track and allow access and alterations according to policies. Finally, rights management policies must be enforced throughout the lifecycle to protect against inappropriate reviews, particularly for confidential or classified documents.

## Store and search more efficiently

A centralized storage repository helps ensure the integrity of documents, but to be fully embraced by the end users, the repository should be seamlessly integrated into the work processes with a familiar look and feel for the users. Recognizing that organizations may have multiple repositories of structured, semi-structured and unstructured information that the new eDiscovery rules require to be available, internal search functions have become more important and complex. To prevent unnecessary wasted time, a records management solution should incorporate a single search engine that works across the centralized repository and other business applications. The search engine should find the right material based on content and metadata, and allow for the placement of legal holds for relevant records.

## Options abound

Government officials today should not feel constrained by traditional highly customized, on-site solutions. Today, more governments are looking to extend the use of commercial off-the-shelf products and are also looking for creative and efficient ways of applying those products. Among the options government should consider today are hosted or shared services, instead of running an on-premise records management solution. Because records management is a ubiquitous requirement, more governments are considering a hosted solution. Both public and private sector entities can offer highly secured, scalable and compliant solutions that often can be implemented more quickly and at a lower cost than traditional on-site solutions. Consideration should be given to a shared services solution managed by a government agency or even a non-profit non-governmental organization. Shared service solutions can mean a lower infrastructure investment for each agency and improved service delivery for employees and citizens alike. Multi-agency sharing can begin to offer significant economies of scale as more agencies join in the solution.

## Summary

Recent legal, social and technology trends are altering the records management landscape. Government officials considering records management solutions need to address those trends and understand their impact on the organization's mission. The solution must protect government records by automating and enforcing agency, regulatory and legal requirements. The solution must enable users to find the records regardless of origin and then control and track access for audit purposes. Ultimately, the solution must reduce the overall complexity of records management and protect an agency during legal discoveries. Finally, government officials should keep an open mind about the implementation strategy, whether it is a customized on-site solution, a hosted solution provided by private party or a hosted shared service solution.

---

### Discussion questions

1. What and how much agency content currently is managed or unmanaged?
2. What is the impact of blogs, wikis, video and other Web 2.0 media on your records management program?
3. What is the level of risk for litigation within your agency?
4. Do you have an official policy and process for responding to eDiscovery requirements?

5. Do you know how much time your staff is spending responding to eDiscovery requests?
6. Have you ever lost valuable government records due to natural disaster?
7. Do you train employees annually on their records management responsibilities, and have you measured their awareness level of records management responsibilities?
8. If you are considering a records management solution, have you thought about the full spectrum of information including that found at the head and the tail?
9. How involved have your end users been in designing your system?
10. Will your solution easily scale to include new programs or content types?
11. Should you consider a hosted service provider?
12. Are there multiple counties that may want to participate in shared service?

**Kimberly Nelson** *is Executive Director of eGovernment and manages a government solutions team in Microsoft's U.S. Public Sector organization. Before joining Microsoft in 2006, Ms. Nelson spent 22 years with the Commonwealth of Pennsylvania in a variety of positions and most recently served four years as the Assistant Administrator for Environmental Information and CIO at the U.S. Environmental Protection Agency.*

## REFERENCES

1 NASCIO report: http://www.nascio.org/publications/documents/NASCIO-RecordsManagement.pdf. See presentation by Debbie Gearhart, CRM, Director of Records Management Services, State of Michigan, retrieved on October 31, 2006, from: http://media-govtech.net/Events/2005Events/2005Michigan/12_1030_InformationLifeCycleManagement_GEARHART.ppt

2 http://www.nascio.org/publications/documents/NASCIO-E-RecordsChallenges.pdf

3 I made the decision in 2005 to stop printing the Environmental Protection Agency's annual Toxics Release Inventory report. The printed versions of the report had always been released months after the official report was released electronically, and the printed versions always contained errors that had to be corrected through errata sheets. It became apparent that the online version was easier to update, more accurate and most often used by concerned citizens, and that printing the several hundred page document was not a good use of taxpayer dollars.

4 http://www.cnn.com/2009/POLITICS/01/22/gibbs.presser/index.html?iref=newssearch

5 Federal Rules of Civil Procedure, December 1, 2006, http://judiciary.house.gov/media/pdfs/printers/109th/31308.pdf

6 http://www.hahnconsultinginc.com/library/KCR-GRC-RIM-EDD-survey.pdf

7 *New York Times,* In Digital Age, Federal Files Blip Into Oblivion; September 13, 2008

8 *Moving Beyond Traditional Records Management,* Managing a Broader Set of Content, a Microsoft U.S. Public Sector Whitepaper; May 2008

9 Ibid

10 Microsoft Records Management PowerPoint presentation, Evan Richman, Microsoft SharePoint Group Product Manager

# 29. E-Discovery

## GAIL A. KARISH AND KENNETH A. BRUNETTI

## Introduction

As record-keeping has moved increasingly from paper to electronic format, specialized legal rules have developed for dealing with access to those electronic records. As CIO at a local government, you are no doubt aware of applicable public records act (PRA) requirements, which typically apply to records in many formats, including electronic records. If you have not already done so, you should take steps to ensure that electronic records are preserved and are accessible to comply with disclosure requests that may be made under the applicable PRA. What you may not have considered, however, is what your obligations are with respect to requests for electronic records that are made in the course of litigation. Discovery means the exchange of documents and evidence between the parties to a lawsuit prior to trial. The term e-discovery is the shorthand reference to discovery of electronic records.

This chapter will focus primarily on the laws that have developed in connection with e-discovery in federal courts. The chapter will highlight major issues and rules to be aware of, and how to handle those issues as part of your electronic records management system. Although this chapter does not address e-discovery requirements in state courts, it is worth noting that state requirements do vary and also will need to be considered when developing internal protocols and procedures for maintaining electronic records. Your procedures also should be flexible enough to be tailored to any particular requirements that might arise in a particular case.

## The basics: Major differences between records requests pursuant to public records acts and for discovery purposes

By way of background, it is useful to consider the major differences between a request for government records made under a PRA regime and one made through discovery in a lawsuit. The discussion in this section and in the chart below highlights the major differences.

**Public Records Act (PRA):** The main purpose of a PRA is to provide a process and rules for public disclosure of government records. Public access is viewed as a necessary means of ensuring that government decision-making is open and accountable. As such, just about anyone can make a request under a PRA. The person requesting information can make a request at any time and need not give a reason for making the request. Keeping with the notion of open government, the grounds for refusing disclosure are narrow and limited.

**Discovery:** In litigation, discovery is the process used by the parties to obtain information used to prepare their case and, ultimately, which may be used as evidence at trial. The purpose of discovery is fact-finding related to the potential claims and defenses made in the lawsuit. Hence, only parties to a lawsuit are permitted to make discovery requests, and court rules govern when and how the requests can be made. The grounds for refusing to comply with a discovery request are limited to whether the request is relevant to the claims or defenses raised in the lawsuit or whether the requested information is protected under a privilege, such as the attorney-client privilege. One should not assume that just because a record is exempt from disclosure under a PRA request that it will not have to be disclosed in litigation. For example, PRA rules may exempt drafts of documents from disclosure, but the discovery rules typically require disclosure of drafts, if they are requested.

## Summary table

| | Public Records Act | Discovery |
|---|---|---|
| WHO makes a request? | Anyone | Party to lawsuit |
| WHY can records be requested? | No reason is required for the request. The PRA promotes open government. | Relevant to claims and defenses raised in lawsuit. Discovery aids fact-finding. |
| WHAT can be requested? | Any record (exempt records are defined narrowly) | Non-privileged records relevant to the matters being litigated. |
| WHEN can a request be made? | Anytime | Pre-trial only during discovery period specified by court rules and orders. |

Finally, it is worth noting that because PRA requests and discovery requests serve different purposes, you may be subject to both in regard to the same types of information and even from the same parties at the same time. Depending on the wording of your particular PRA, you may be required to respond to both types of requests separately and simultaneously even though there will be some inevitable overlap. In other words, you should seek legal advice on how to respond to PRA requests that appear to have a litigation-related purpose. It is prudent to track the responses to those requests separately.

## E-discovery process

As noted above, discovery is the formal process by which the parties obtain information used to prepare their cases and to introduce as evidence at trial. Parties who receive formal discovery requests are required to produce all information in their possession or control that is responsive the request, unless the information is not relevant to the issues in the lawsuit or is protected under a privilege. The term "relevant" is construed broadly. It includes not only information directly related to an issue in the lawsuit but also information that is reasonably calculated to lead to admissible evidence.

Traditionally, when most records were kept in paper form, the process of gathering information responsive to a discovery request typically was straightforward, although it could be time-consuming. As technology has advanced, however, and more records are made and kept electronically, the discovery process has necessarily evolved to include electronic records, and new rules have had to be adopted to regulate the disclosure of those electronic records. In this section, we highlight some of the major steps in the discovery process as they apply in particular to disclosure of electronic records.

### Preservation of evidence—Litigation hold

When litigation arises, there is a duty on all parties to ensure that all evidence pertinent to the litigation is preserved. A failure to do so can risk the imposition of court sanctions, which can be severe, including fines, payment of the opposing party's attorneys' fees caused by the failure to produce, exclusion of evidence favorable to your side, the imposition of adverse inferences through jury instructions, dismissing a party's claims or defenses, and even a default judgment against the party who refused to preserve and/or produce the evidence. Fed. R. Civ. P. 37.

In many circumstances, that will require you to take action to override your regular document retention and destruction processes and protocols. This is commonly referred to as a "litigation hold." For example, if you routinely "clean" the hard drives of departing employees, that should not be done if the computers may have information pertinent to a potential lawsuit. Similarly, if your employer deletes back-up files on a regular basis, there may be an obligation to preserve records pertaining to key employees who might have information pertinent to a potential lawsuit.

One might assume that discovery rules do not apply until a lawsuit is actually commenced. That assumption would be wrong. In fact, parties to potential litigation need to be prepared to act even before a lawsuit begins because the duty arises the moment potential litigation is foreseeable. A demand letter is an obvious sign of foreseeable litigation, but it could be something as simple as an email exchange reflecting a potential dispute. Your attorney and staff involved in the potential dispute should make the call on when a litigation hold should be implemented and will determine the extent of the hold (e.g., which employees, computers and other systems it should apply to), but you can expect to be called upon to assist in the technical aspects of the analysis and to devise a way to ensure that it is properly and consistently implemented.

## Meeting on proposed discovery plan

The parties to a lawsuit typically are required to hold a conference early on in the case to discuss and attempt to agree on a discovery plan, including the issues upon which discovery may be had, how to address e-discovery and timing. Fed. R. Civ. P. 26(f). Your attorney likely will seek your input on a number of matters that will come up for discussion at this conference. For example, issues are likely to arise with respect to electronically stored information, including the form or forms in which it should be produced. (The definition of "electronically stored information" and the common items covered by e-discovery requests are discussed in the next section.) You should be prepared to discuss with your attorney the procedures you use for storing electronic information, including the formats used to store such information, the different software programs used, back-up retention and deletion procedures, the time and cost of retrieval and production in different forms, and any other pertinent information about your electronic records management system. Your attorney also may need advice on preferable forms for receiving electronically stored information from opposing counsel. Obviously, you will be better prepared to address those issues if you have a thorough understanding of the procedures and systems used by your employer to maintain and delete electronically stored information.

## Making disclosures

The collection, review and production of information in response to discovery requests can be onerous. The more detailed the discussions and agreements in the discovery plan, the easier it will be to know how to respond to the requests. As a general rule, the requesting party may specify the form or forms of production of electronically stored information. Fed. R. Civ. P. 34(b)(1)(C). However, it is possible to object to the requested form, and state the alternative forms of production you intend to use. Fed. R. Civ. P. 34(b)(2)(D). If the parties cannot reach agreement, the court may be called on to resolve the dispute. If there is no applicable agreement or court order, and the request does not specify the form of production, you have some flexibility. You are required to produce the electronically stored information "in a form or forms in which it is ordinarily maintained or in a reasonably usable form or forms." Fed. R. Civ. P. 34(b)(2)(E)(ii). There is no obligation to produce the same electronically stored information in more than one form. Fed. R. Civ. P. 34(b)(2)(E)(iii).

## Depositions

You also should be aware that in some instances, a party may seek to depose the IT manager (you or one representing an opposing party) to better understand the procedures and systems used in the maintenance of electronically stored information, including operating systems being used, the forms of storage, document retention systems and search capabilities, and other technical information related to electronically stored information. Your attorney will help you prepare if you are called on to be deposed.

## Common sources of e-discovery materials

In its original formulation, discovery rules typically applied to "documents" and "things." In 1970, recognizing the advent of computers, the Federal Rules of Civil Procedure added the term "data compilations" to the list of items that were discoverable. As technology advanced over the years, that list proved to be too limited. The current version of the Federal Rules of Civil Procedure contains a broad definition of "electronically stored information." "Electronically stored information" is defined to include: "writings, drawings, graphs, charts, photographs, sound recordings, images, and other data or data compilations—stored in any medium from which information can be obtained either directly or, if necessary, after translation by the responding party into a reasonably usable form." Fed. R. Civ. P. 34(a)(1)(A).

In this section, we discuss some of the common types of electronically stored information that may be subject to a discovery request.

### Electronic mail/Instant messages

Electronic mail and instant messages are now ubiquitous in the work environment. Thus, they are routinely sought in discovery. You should not assume, however, that only printed emails will be requested, or that the request can necessarily be met by printing out and delivering stored emails. Electronic versions may be sought to reveal information contained only in the metadata, such as whether anyone was blind copied (BCC'd). In addition, back up tapes and other storage locations may be sought to recover emails that may have been deleted intentionally or through automated processes.

### Voicemail and other audio recordings

Sound recordings also may be the subject of a discovery request. There are multiple sources to search for audio recordings that may be relevant, including voicemail, teleconferences, recordings from call centers and dictation. And, the same information may be located in different places. For example, depending on how your voicemail storage and retrieval system is configured and backed up, there may be multiple locations where voicemails may be stored, including on .wav files attached to emails.

## Spreadsheets and databases

Excel and similar files and databases that are commonly used are routinely requested through discovery. Printouts of those types of documents can be difficult to follow and are of limited use, especially when the information presented in the electronic source is dynamic, linked to multiple information sources, and is constantly being updated. As a result, requesting parties may seek to perform their own searches in a dynamic environment. Thus, it is not uncommon for parties to seek production of or access to the electronic source itself.

As one can imagine, electronic disclosure may raise a number of technical and other concerns. For example, formulas embedded in spreadsheets may be proprietary and confidential property of a third party, which may need to be protected from disclosure. Databases also may contain other irrelevant or privileged information that should not be disclosed. Your attorney will need assistance in understanding the size and content of the database, its functionality and possible ways to permit access to more limited types of information contained within it.

## Grounds for excusing requirement of e-disclosure

The general rule, interpreted broadly, is that parties may obtain discovery of any non-privileged matter that is relevant to any party's claim or defense. Fed. R. Civ. P. 26(b)(1). As noted above, the term "relevant" is construed broadly by courts and includes any information reasonably calculated to lead to admissible evidence. However, when it comes to e-discovery, there are specific limitations on the extent of permissible discovery. They are discussed below.

## Sources not reasonably accessible

One possible ground for refusing e-discovery is that the electronically stored information is being sought from a source that the party from whom discovery is sought identifies as "not reasonably accessible because of undue burden or cost." Fed. R. Civ. P. 26(b)(2)(B). An example of a type of electronically stored information that may not be reasonably accessible is deleted information that is retrievable only through substantial effort and expense. Backup tapes also may pose similar cost and time concerns.

The burden is on the party from whom discovery is sought to prove that the standard has been met. *Id.* Your attorney will need information and examples of what data is contained in those sources and the burden involved in producing it in a reasonably usable form in order to make the case to opposing counsel and, if necessary, a judge, that the sources of electronic information are truly inaccessible, or that the burden or cost outweighs the benefit. However, even if the court agrees that the required burden of proof is met, it may still order disclosure and establish conditions for the discovery, if the requesting party shows good cause. *Id.*

In considering whether there is good cause to require some discovery of inaccessible sources of data, the court will consider a range of factors, such as the likelihood that the source will contain any relevant information, the benefits of obtaining the data and the costs of production (and which party may pay them). And, the court may impose limitations or conditions on the discovery of data from inaccessible sources. *Semsroth v. City of Wichita,* 239 F.R.D. 630 (D. Kan. 2006) (Court found the estimated cost of $1,950 to $2,625 of restoring emails from the city's back-up tape was not unreasonable, but nevertheless limited the search terms and number of mailboxes to be searched.)

## Routine, good faith operation

One valid reason for refusing to produce electronically stored information is if the information was destroyed "as a result of routine, good-faith operation of an electronic information system." Fed. R. Civ. P. 37(e). For example, the routine destruction of emails pursuant to a document retention and destruction policy may be a valid excuse, particularly if there is little likelihood that the records would have contained pertinent evidence. *Escobar v. City of Houston*, 2007 WL 2900581 (S.D. Tex. Sept. 29, 2007).

You must be very careful about relying on that exception, however. As noted earlier, there is a very serious obligation to preserve relevant evidence, and the sanctions for failing to preserve evidence can be severe. The purpose of this rule is simply to protect parties from sanctions when they are acting in good faith in the routine operation of an information system. The courts recognize that good faith "may involve a party's intervention to modify or suspend certain features of that routine operation to prevent the loss of information, if that information is subject to a preservation obligation." *Disability Rights Council of Greater Wash. v. Wash. Metro. Area Transit Auth.*, 2007 WL 1585452 (D.D.C. June 1, 2007).

## Conclusion

As our society increasingly relies on the retention of records in an electronic format, the rules of discovery have changed. More formal rules and requirements have evolved with respect to the retention and production of electronically stored information. IT managers and employees must be aware of the rules and requirements in order to protect their employers in the event of a lawsuit. Failure to comply with the rules could result in severe sanctions, including entry of a default judgment against a non-complying party.

The best way to avoid being overwhelmed by time-consuming and costly disclosure obligations is to plan ahead. Don't wait for the first litigation hold request to arrive in your office before you consider how to address e-discovery issues. You need to be proactive in discussions with attorneys and other departments. And, you need to make sure your shop is in order. That means being well-versed in the scope, capabilities and limitations of your various sources of electronic records. Knowing what is out there and being able to explain the systems to your attorneys and others can go a long way to assisting them in developing reasonable e-discovery plans that satisfy the rules of the court and recognize the capabilities and limitations of your sources of electronically stored information.

---

### Discussion questions

1. To what extent are you familiar with the PRA?
2. To what extent are you familiar with any state or jurisdictional law or regulation in this area?
3. Who should be in charge of carrying this responsibility out?
4. How accessible is your data stored and retrievable?
5. What policies might you institute, anticipating the future?
6. What budget considerations might you recommend in carrying out these responsibilities moving forward?

**Gail A. Karish** *assists clients with state and federal regulatory matters, contract negotiations and litigation. She has a broad range of domestic and international experience advising public and private sector entities in the telecommunications and electricity sectors in the United States, Canada and Latin America. Her experience includes regulatory compliance, corporate and commercial transactions, mergers and acquisitions, and litigation.*

*Since joining Miller & Van Eaton, p.l.l.c., Ms. Karish has assisted clients affected by the Adelphia bankruptcy and the subsequent sale to Time Warner and Comcast with their analysis of the associated franchise transfer applications, participation in settlement negotiations, and submissions to the bankruptcy court. She also has assisted clients with analysis of and litigation involving the constitutionality and application of local, state and federal communications laws and regulations.*

**Kenneth A. Brunetti** *counsels and represents local governments in cable television and telecommunications matters. He specializes in complex litigation and bankruptcy related to cable television, telecommunications and rights-of-way management issues. Since joining the firm in 2000, Mr. Brunetti has represented municipalities in a variety of forums throughout the country, including state and federal courts, as well as state regulatory commissions. He also assists communities in cable television and telecommunications franchise and license renewals and transfers, and in drafting telecommunications ordinances. He brings to the firm's clients a specialized expertise in bankruptcy and secured transactions, which is critical in establishing both enforcement and protective strategies in the new competitive telecommunications environment. In that regard, Mr. Brunetti has represented communities in several major bankruptcy proceedings involving telecommunications providers. Prior to joining the firm, Mr. Brunetti specialized in complex commercial litigation and bankruptcy law. Mr. Brunetti received his law degree magna cum laude from the University of California, Hastings College of the Law in 1991 and his Bachelor of Arts in Psychology from the University of Pennsylvania in 1986. He is admitted to practice in California, and is resident in the firm's San Francisco office. He is the author of "Telecom and Cable Bankruptcy—A Primer for Municipalities,"* Municipal Lawyer, *January/February 2003.*

# 30. Proper Management of Electronically Stored Information (ESI) Requires Collaboration of Technical and Legal Expertise

*Unfamiliarity with Electronic Statutes, Regulations and Court Rulings and Amendments to the Federal Rules of Civil Procedure poses increased Management Risk when Converting from Paper to Electronic Transactions*

**FRANK MAGUIRE**

## Overview

Electronic liabilities abound in both private and public sectors, and by allowing employees access to e-mail systems without proper rules and procedures put into place, the likelihood of costly e-mail disaster increases. Changing technology and the evolving legal and regulatory governance of electronically stored information (ESI) compound the problem. Effective operating rules and policy controls require a cohesive team effort of not only IT and legal departments but also HR, Finance and Compliance in addressing ESI strategy/management initiatives to protect against successful challenges.

Unfortunately, the evolution of digital information and its underlying statutes is today probably the least understood area of law. Lack of knowledge is seldom an acceptable legal defense, and so the information accumulated in this chapter is offered as a broad overview of source material and in no way is meant to serve as legal advice. The intent is to acquaint the reader with background and relevant reference material to assist in more detailed analyses of the complexities involved in managing ESI properly.

## Background

Love them or hate them, regulations are put into place to help implement the underlying statute from which their authority ensues. However, due to an excess of caution on the part of those involved with the drafting and passage of federal electronic law, the decision was made to forgo the mandate of implementing regulations for fear that they would be too long in coming and too confusing and, therefore, counterproductive to the goal of boosting e-commerce/communication. Also, that lack of a mandate for implementing rules was in line with the priority of the time to keep online regulation light in order to foster innovation. Instead, industry felt obliged to design best practices standards and procedures as detailed in a 2003 private initiative relating to the 2000 ESIGN statute, whose passage proved to be somewhat obscure—"Standards and Procedures for Electronic Records and Signatures," www.spers.org.[1]

Those standards and procedures were intended to fill the regulatory void with practical user instruction, but dissemination proved to be a daunting task and the public/legal knowledge of

ESIGN provisions proved to be limited. Generally, regulations provide a blueprint to follow while acquainting readers with the thrust of the underlying law, but in this instance there were none, and federal electronic law was slow to take hold despite its many benefits. [Aside: it is likely that the dot.com explosion and the onset of a recession were additional impediments to the underlying goal of replacing piles of paper with efficient electronic counterparts, which delayed further the full benefits of e-commerce law.]

The end result of that sequence of events has created an environment in which the general public and legal/tech specialists have yet to fully embrace the many efficiencies and cost-saving provisions of the e-commerce statutes in order to convert day-to-day paper operations to an electronic format without losing any legal protections.

Education is the key, and that is why it is critical that public and private enterprises develop collaborative initiatives whereby all in-house stake-holders come to the table to air their concerns when launching new electronic activities. For instance, it is likely that many licenses/permits can be issued electronically instead of in hard-copy, but it is necessary for the attorneys to sign off on the legal aspects of conveyance and the legal strength of the electronic document; tech specialists must design an efficient delivery system with proper record retention, etc.; and policy people must be convinced that the electronic version has the same strength and attributes of hard-copy should it be challenged subsequent to delivery.

Management reaps the benefit of such a collaborative effort as manpower, cost and response times all will be reduced, and so it is critical that the developmental team have management's buy-in on the front side of such an initiative, but all too often such projects are not coordinated properly and eventually die of their own weight before the true benefits are realized. In the end, it is the tax-payer/customer who really benefits anytime cumbersome paper transactions can be converted to electronic as long as both parties to the transaction are protected and agree to the process.

With that as a backdrop, it is important that anyone looking to design new electronic delivery systems be acquainted with e-commerce laws, regulations, e-discovery initiatives and some important recent court rulings in order to be aware of the "hot buttons" and specific requirements that need be addressed.

## ESIGN and UETA

ESIGN, the federal Electronic Signatures in Global and National Commerce Act, and UETA, the state-enacted Uniform Electronic Transactions Act, were drafted with the intent of ensuring that electronic transactions would be afforded the same validity and legality as paper transactions—to accommodate and promote the efficiencies of digital information.

The foundation upon which the two laws are based can be broken down to the following rules:

♦ A record or signature may not be denied legal effect or enforceability solely because it is in electronic form;

♦ A contract may not be denied legal effect or enforceability solely because an electronic record was used in its formation;

♦ If a law requires a record to be in writing, an electronic record satisfies the law; and

♦ If a law requires a signature, an electronic signature satisfies the law.[2]

Those three building blocks are themselves built upon three defined terms: "record, electronic record and electronic signature."

Both UETA and ESIGN define a "record" as information that is inscribed on a tangible medium or that is stored in an electronic or other medium and is retrievable in perceivable form.

An "electronic record" is similarly defined as a record created, generated, sent, communicated, received or stored by electronic means. As a result, any type of document, contract or other record of information could meet the definition of an electronic record if it were created, used or stored in a medium other than paper.

An "electronic signature" is an electronic sound, symbol or process attached to or logically associated with a record and executed or adopted by a person with the intent to sign the record.

Also, the drafters of ESIGN and UETA, in their desire to facilitate the development of technology, were cautious and took an agnostic approach to avoid specific technology requirements for the creation of records, electronic contracts, electronic signatures, etc.[3]

UETA was promulgated in 1999 by the National Conference of Commissioners on Uniform Laws (NCUSL) [see www.nccusl.org for a copy] with 46 states and D.C., Puerto Rico and the Virgin Islands having adopted it in some form. The U.S. Congress became concerned about the slow pace of states adopting UETA, and for some states their substantial changes to UETA, and so it enacted on June 30, 2000, a uniform national standard for the treatment of electronic records and signatures, ESIGN. Note: ESIGN shares many of the same provisions of UETA, but adds special consent requirements for consumer disclosures. There is an exception to ESIGN preemptive authority "only if" a state statute, rule or regulation does not specify procedures that require or accord greater legal status to specific technologies or technical specifications.[4]

While most of the Uniform Commercial Code (UCC) other than Article 2 and 2A is excluded from coverage under both UETA and ESIGN, the UCC Articles governing funds transfers, letters of credit, security interests in personal property and securities all permit the use of electronic records and signatures for most purposes, according to their own terms. Consequently, most types of commercial agreements and related documents now may be delivered and executed electronically.

*Note: The issue of preemption or deferral arises because of the mix of statutory authority one encounters when conducting electronic business in a variety of states—federal law, ESIGN and state law: majority being the Uniform Electronic Transactions Act (UETA) and some states being non-UETA statutes or common law, e.g., N.Y. Electronic Signatures and Records Act (ESRA.) In short, conducting business transactions electronically in many states can raise the question of whether ESIGN preempts or defers to UETA and other state law.*

## Special rules for electronic records (*SPeRS Handbook* 4/15/03 page 3)

While ESIGN and UETA set no special standards for the use of electronic signatures, they do have a number of special rules for electronic records that are intended to substitute for certain types of writings. Those rules include:

♦ If a person is required by law to provide or deliver information in writing to another person, an electronic record only satisfies that requirement if the recipient may keep copy of the record for later reference and review. If the sender deliberately inhibits the recipient's ability to print or store the record, then the record doesn't satisfy the legal requirement.

♦ If a law or regulation requires that a record be retained, an electronic record satisfies that requirement only if it is accurate and remains accessible for later reference. The UETA does not say for how long it must be retained or to whom it must remain accessible. ESIGN provides that the record must be accessible to all people entitled by law to access for the retention period prescribed by law. Neither statute requires that the electronic record necessarily be accessible in a particular place—the parties entitled to access can, by agreement, establish a storage location.

♦ If a particular writing is required by law to be displayed in a particular format, the UETA does not change that requirement. For example, if a law requires a notice to be printed in at least 12-point type and a boldface font, that requirement remains in place under the UETA. If the law requires two elements of a document to be placed in a particular physical relationship to each other or some other part of the document, that requirement is not changed by the UETA. For example, if the law requires a disclosure to be displayed just above a contacting party's signature, that rule must be observed within the electronic record.

♦ If a law expressly requires a writing to be delivered by U.S. mail by hand delivery, the UETA does not change those delivery rules.[5]

Generally speaking, those rules are not variable by agreement under either ESIGN or UETA; however, under UETA if the underlying statute requirement that information be delivered in writing, or by a particular delivery method, may be varied by agreement, then the requirement that an equivalent electronic record be capable of storage, or be delivered by the same method as a writing, may also be waived.[6]

## Digital information—Burden of proof

Permitting electronic records to substitute for writings serves little purpose if the records are not admissible as evidence in the event of a dispute. The rule stated above is simple: A record or signature may not be excluded from evidence solely because it is in electronic form. An electronic record also qualifies as an original, even if that record is not the original form of the document, and satisfies statutory audit and record retention requirements. Beyond that, the ordinary rules of evidence will apply.

With that in mind, it is critical that private and public sector enterprises create and handle their electronic information properly so that there is proper accountability, authenticity is insured and records can be easily retained and retrieved. Federal regulatory requirements to prove certain characteristics of electronic information in order to prove authenticity have arisen in the fields of health care, the financial services sector and in publicly traded companies. Consequently, business organizations must put electronic information policies in place to avoid regulatory non-compliance but, more importantly, to prevent electronic records from becoming compromised or worthless. Everyday electronic communication must be able to stand the test of evidentiary proof along with that of electronic records, transactions, etc., and it is the content not the technology that is critical during a challenge.

## Federal Rules of Civil Procedure

The U.S. Federal Courts in 2006 amended the Federal Rules of Civil Procedure with respect to e-discovery procedures. That action focused attention on the need for enterprises to take a proactive approach in managing their electronically stored information, primarily e-mail, in order to successfully defend against a possible lawsuit. The Civil Procedure amendments were to clarify the following:

♦ ESI, including all e-mail messages and attachments, is discoverable and may be used as evidence in litigation—for or against an organization.

♦ During discovery, business record e-mail and all ESI related to current or potential litigation must be retained, stored and produced in a timely and legally compliant manner.

♦ Stored ESI can be purged if it is not relevant to ongoing litigation.

♦ Once litigation has commenced, back-up tapes cannot be written over, as that would be deemed to be illegal destruction of ESI.

♦ In order to be accepted as evidence, e-mail must be shown to have been recorded, preserved and retrieved in a tamper-proof manner that is trustworthy and does not affect the authenticity of the original e-mail.

While ESI/e-discovery issues have received much more attention in the past year from legal departments, the *Second Annual ESI Trends Report* issued by Kroll Ontrack, world leader in legal technologies found that "…both in the US and UK survey respondents are increasingly looking to IT departments to shoulder some of the ESI burden in policy development and enforcement. These finding reiterate that ESI management is no simple task and a true partnership with IT is required to make one's policy a success."

## Electronic transactions—Value for governmental entities

1. Reduced transaction costs
   – Reduce paper storage costs
   – Reduce processing time and internal mail costs
   – Reduce postage/overnight courier costs

2. Reduce labor/mail room costs

3. Reduced cost to taxpayers and enhanced service satisfaction

4. Increase taxpayer response times

5. Increase accountability and more efficient employee deployment

6. Decrease risk of failing to meet deadlines/response requirements

## Electronic transactions—Attributes

1. Properly managed, e-mail records are admissible in court,

2. With proper protections taken, e-mail record provides legal proof of delivery, content and official time stamps, and

3. Electronic signatures can be as effective as "wet ink" signatures if properly executed.

## Electronic transactions—What is needed for protection and increased accountability

When reviewing software in the market, one should look for a core service that provides the sender with legal proof of delivery, content and official time stamp, including all attachments, where the recipient does not have to take compliant action for the sender to be protected. Additional service features that may be considered include electronic signature, electronic contracting and end-to-end e-mail encryption. For instance, a service could deliver a registered e-mail message with attachments and automatically return verifiable delivery evidence in the form of a registered receipt e-mail containing a digital snapshot of the content (message body and all attachments) and the official time the e-mail was sent and received by each designated recipient. An e-sign-off feature would incorporate a valid electronic signature of the recipient into the process where needed.

As a means of providing accountable electronic communication, consider a technology that: a) does not store information on a central server; b) maintains the integrity of electronic communications and the security of the transmission using cryptography; c) provides the sender proof of delivery to the recipient; and d) provides an encrypted, tamper-proof record of the transaction that may include verifiable proof of both the delivery and acknowledgement or execution of any document.

*Note: RPost Registered E-mail service provider is uniquely positioned to accomplish those tasks and many more.*

## Chapter supplement

## Key court decisions that impact ESI management concerns

1. *Lorraine v. Markel American Insurance Company,* 2007 WL 1300739 (DMd May 4, 2007) by US Magistrate Judge Paul W. Gram. If you are to read only one recent court decision relating to admissibility of e-mails in evidence, etc., you should make it this one. Judge Grimm not only speaks to his instant opinion on the care needed in introducing electronic information into evidence under the Federal Rules of Evidence, but he goes on to create a basic primer dealing with some of the technology and document management issues raised by those requirements, such as hash values and other indicia of authenticity, metadata and collection techniques. He points out that a great deal had been written about rules regarding discovery of ESI, but little had been done to focus attention on "what is required to insure that ESI obtained during discovery is admissible into evidence at trial, or whether it constitutes 'such facts as would be admissible in evidence' for use in summary judgment practice."

Judge Grimm's opinion should be read by those involved in designing and implementing processes for the treatment of ESI in general, e-contracting in particular and overall management systems, with an eye on document creation, storage and retrieval, search capabilities, access rules, reproduction and admissibility. The opinion also points out that while neither ESIGN nor UETA afford greater strength to e-contracts and electronic signatures, all other rules that apply to wet signatures and hard-copy contracts, including rules of evidence, apply equally to e-records and e-contracts.

2. *Long v. Time Insurance Co.,* 572 F. Supp.2d 907, 2008 US Dist., LEXIS 79212. The court held in favor of the insurer on its motion for summary judgment based on the insured's false answer to a medical question on the application. The case speaks to the strength of an electronic signature and should give some comfort to those looking to design e-contracting type solutions or other business processes.

3. *Aguilar v. Immigration & Customs Enforcement Div. of the US Dept. of Homeland Security,* 2008 WL 5062700 (S.D.N.Y. Nov. 21 2008). This U.S. District Court issued a definitive ruling explaining that the U.S. Federal Rules of Civil Procedure require that metadata associated with e-mails and electronic files be preserved, maintained and produced in the course of legal discovery. The case underscores the importance of preserving ESI and its associated metadata in order to avoid significant legal risk for not collecting and maintaining such digital evidence.

4. *EPCO Carbondioxide Products, Inc. v. JP Morgan Chase Bank,* NA, 2005 US Dist. LEXIS 43707 (W.D. La. June 6, 2005), rev'd and remanded 467 F.3d 466 (5th Cir. October 6, 2006). This decision is important as the 5th Circuit noted that UETA "allows an electronic signature to satisfy the signature requirements for most legal documents...(and) applies only to transactions between parties who have 'agreed to conduct transactions by electronic means.'" This is an important decision to review if one is proceeding with an e-contracting system.

5. *Bell v. Hollywood Entm't Corp.,* 2006 Ohio App. LEXIS 3950 (Aug. 3, 2006). Bell sued Hollywood for hostile work environment, sexual harassment and civil battery. In the employment application process, Bell completed her application electronically and in so doing acknowledged an arbitration clause. Because the electronic application process was shown to be handled correctly with the Plaintiff having selected the "yes" box in agreeing to take all disputes to arbitration, the court found that "Federal and Ohio law both authorize the use of electronic signatures and deem such signatures binding."

6. *Stevens v. Publicis,* 854 NYS 2d 690 (App. Div. 2008). The Court denied summary judgment to Stevens who was attempting to have enforced the original terms of his employment agreement, which had been amended by both parties in a series of e-mails containing typed signatures of both parties. The Court held that the typed name of the employing company's CEO at the end of the e-mail and Plaintiff's response, containing his typed name at the end of the e-mal, constituted "signed writings" and satisfied § 13(d) of Plaintiff's employment agreement, which required any modification be signed by both parties.

7. *State of New York v. Patanian*, 2008 NY Misc. LEXIS 2668. Electronically prepared traffic ticket with the police officer's pre-printed signature was deemed valid. The Court referenced ESIGN in finding that the officer's electronic signature had the "same validity and effect as one handwritten."

8. *Poly USA, Inc. v. Trex Co., Inc.*, W.D. Va. No. %:05–CV-0031 (March 1, 2006). This decision clarifies that an e-mail sent by means of an office account does not automatically confer an electronic signature. The District Court found that "the use of a [Defendant's] Trex e-mail account to send an e-mail does not necessarily constitute an electronic signature under 15 U.S.C. § 7006 and, moreover, that Trex did not intend to electronically sign the e-mailed document by sending it from a Trex e-mail account" and, therefore, the document in question was not binding.

9. *JSO Assoc., Inc. V. Price*, 2008 NY Misc. LEXIS 2227 (Nassau Co. 2008). This case involved the question of whether Defendant was liable for a broker's commission to Plaintiff despite the fact that a memorandum included within the e-mail exchange appeared to be unsigned. The Defendant's name appeared in the e-mail address at the top of the e-mail, but the e-mail itself was unsigned. The issue arose as to whether the statute of frauds had been satisfied since that statute required "a writing at the end of the memorandum." The Court pointed out that the law is still evolving as to how the statute of frauds will be satisfied for e-mail, etc., and, therefore, found that it must look for assurance as to "the source of the e-mail and authority of the person who sent it." This decision is quite significant as the Court held that "where there is no question as to the source and authenticity of an e-mail, the e-mail is 'signed' for purposes of the statute of frauds if Defendant's name clearly appears in the e-mail as the sender."

10. *Sims v. Stapleton Realty, Ltd.*, 2007 Wisc. App. LEXIS 741 (August 23, 2007). The Court of Appeals of Wisconsin found that the parties had in fact amended a paper listing contract by e-mail exchange that "constituted a written document under Wisconsin's Uniform Electronic Transactions Act (UETA)," and the e-mail amendments to the original listing contract withstood legal challenge after the fact.

---

## Discussion questions

1. Does your organization spend a lot of money and resources on managing incoming e-mail with spam and phishing filters, etc., but does little to protect outgoing e-mail?
2. Does your organization use e-mail to send important communications, such as regulatory notices, confirmation of change orders, personnel actions, commitments or agreements, but has nothing to provide "legal proof" of these actions should a challenge arise?
3. Does your organization rely upon the traditional methods such as an archive, the "Sent" folder and/or Outlook read receipts to record the sending and receipt of e-mail, without regard to the fact that "legal delivery" under the electronic statutes requires proof that an e-mail made it to the recipient's mail server?

4. Have you ever stopped to wonder why the federal electronic signature and record statute, ESIGN, which was signed into law in 2000, remains somewhat obscure nine years later?

5. With little legal expertise available in the area of electronic law, not to mention common knowledge, do you and your organization appreciate that recent e-discovery and e-admissibility court rulings raise the bar when it comes to placing e-mail system protections in place?

6. Have you seen that attorneys are relying more on tech experts in taking a proactive approach to manage electronically stored information, ESI to successfully defend against a possible lawsuit? Evolving legal and regulatory governance of ESI compound the problem, and e-discovery concerns grow with increasing case law precedent. Have you noticed an increase in significant time, effort and manpower spent in answering questions that stem from the need to manage ESI properly given such changes?

7. As a result of all of these points, have you come to realize that your job responsibilities have expanded such that you now must become acquainted with e-commerce laws, related regulations, e-discovery initiatives and recent court rulings that speak to "hot button" issues and requirements that need to be addressed in overseeing today's electronic delivery systems?

8. To prevent "re-inventing the wheel" in moving more paper transactions to electronic format, are you aware of an invaluable handbook, SPeRS that speaks clearly to specific standards that one must meet in order to comply with ESIGN requirements?

9. Did you know that both legal and tech resource information can be found in SPeRS— Standards and Procedures for Electronic Records and Signatures, a best practices guide assembled by a private industry initiative to fill the regulatory void relative to ESIGN?

10. Did you know that failure to meet the ESIGN standards may impair the enforceability of electronic records? It is critical to understand that permitting electronic records to substitute for paper under the law serves little practical purpose if the records are not admissible as evidence in the event of a legal dispute.

11. Did you stop to consider that it is content, not technology that is critical during a challenge involving electronic records? With that in mind, it is critical that organizations create and handle their electronic information such that there is proper accountability, authenticity is insured, and records are easily retained and retrieved.

12. Did you realize that it is far more expensive to address system shortcomings after a challenge has been filed than to be properly prepared beforehand, which again requires close cooperation with your legal department on an ongoing basis?

**Frank Maguire,** *Vice President for Business Planning and Strategy, is an executive with RPost, the Registered E-Mail company, headquartered in Los Angeles, California. He joined the young company five years ago to open a Washington, D.C., office and to expand its East Coast presence. Frank has had an extended professional career within official Washington, having worked on both the House and Senate sides of Capitol Hill on three separate occasions, the last being with the House Republican Leadership. He served as Senior Deputy Comptroller of the Currency for almost a dozen years, where he moved after having served at the U.S. Department of the Treasury in its Executive offices. Frank also has worked for a trade association and a private consulting firm.*

# REFERENCES

1 **Electronic records and signatures—Challenge and opportunity:** New e-commerce laws make possible the widespread replacement of paper documents with electronic records. They also enable the broad use of electronic signatures. Many businesses have begun converting their operations to avail themselves of the enormous advantages offered by electronic records systems.

While the new e-commerce laws permit the use of electronic records and signatures, they also require that electronic systems and processes meet specific standards for:

♦ Obtaining consent to use electronic records and signatures,
♦ Presentation of information,
♦ Execution of signatures and creation of agreements,
♦ Record retention,
♦ Printing, and
♦ Delivery.

Failure to meet those standards may impair the enforceability of electronic records. As a result, companies are being forced to invest significant time, effort and manpower in answering questions about how to handle the practical, routine aspects of electronic transactions. Much of that time and effort could be avoided if industry-wide standards for those elements of electronic transactions could be established.

To address that problem, industry leaders have undertaken a cross-industry initiative to establish commonly understood "rules of the road" available to all parties seeking to take advantage of the powers conferred by ESIGN and UETA. The product of that initiative is the Standards and Procedures for Electronic Records and Signatures (SPeRS).

2 UETA § 7; ESIGN § 101(a)

3 Prefatory Note UETA 15 U.S.C. § 7004

4 101 (a)(2)(A)(ii) of ESIGN, 15 U.S.C. § 7002 (a)(2)(A)(ii)

5 UETA §§ 8 and 12(a); ESIGN §§ 101(d) and (e)

6 UETA § 8(d)